Political Man
and Social Man

READINGS
IN POLITICAL
PHILOSOPHY

POLITICAL MAN AND SOCIAL MAN

Readings in Political Philosophy

Edited with Introductions by

ROBERT PAUL WOLFF
COLUMBIA UNIVERSITY

 Random House   New York

TO MY

Mother AND Father

CONTENTS

Part Two:
The Individual and Society

Political Man
and Social Man
READINGS
IN POLITICAL
PHILOSOPHY

INTRODUCTION

Political philosophy, as distinguished from the history, sociology, or psychology of politics, consists of two sorts of intellectual activities. The first, which I shall call analytic political philosophy, is the analysis of the concepts which are used by political actors and students of politics. Plato's *Republic,* for example, is an extended analysis of the concept of justice. The dialogue begins with several common definitions of "justice," which Socrates easily shows to be contradictory or confused, and moves on to a systematic theory of human virtue. Analytic political philosophy is not confined to clarifications of isolated concepts, however; it includes also the development of whole systems of concepts and the tracing of the logical relationships among them.

The second type of political philosophy is the statement and defense of the moral truths which ought to govern men in their political behavior: the proper goals of the state, the principles of justice, the rights and duties of the citizen. All this I shall label normative political theory. The *Republic* is a classic example of this genre as well, a fact which calls attention to the close connections between the two branches of political philosophy.

"Conceptual analysis" has about it the sound of an armchair activity, requiring mental agility and logical facility but little in the way of a substantive knowledge of politics. Normative political philosophy, too, seems the sort of pursuit for which one would hardly need preparation in the social sciences. Nevertheless, I wish to maintain that *it is impossible to engage in either sort of political philosophy fruitfully without a constant attention to the insights and data of social psychology, sociology, anthropology, economics, history, and political science.* I have therefore taken the somewhat unusual course of including in this book of readings in political philosophy a number of selections from the works of social scientists such as Emile Durkheim, Erik Erikson, and David Riesman. In the remainder of these introductory pages I shall try to defend this experiment in disciplinary crossbreeding. My arguments may suggest some useful approaches to the readings as well as some questions which are worth considering in their own right.

I.

Man is by nature an active rather than a contemplative creature. He enters the world with needs, drives, desires, and his time is spent in wresting satisfaction from his natural and human environment. His whole life is a striving, a *conatus* as Baruch Spinoza called it. Thought is an instrument employed by men in their striving, and like all instruments it is judged according to its usefulness for the task at hand. Consequently, fruitfulness is a legitimate demand to make of an idea or judgment in addition to truth or consistency. It has frequently been remarked that in the case of most social problems, the difficulty lies not in saying something true, but in saying something relevant.

To deal with the world effectively, man must subdue the chaos of perceptual experience in at least two different ways. He must ignore much of what he perceives, focusing attention on the things which will prove dangerous or useful or satisfying. And he must identify patterns in experience so that he can foresee what is to come and cope with it. Concepts are tools for performing both of these organizing tasks. They select particular aspects of experience, group them together, and thereby enable us to notice them without taking account of the surrounding environment. They also serve as general categories under which we gather similar experiences, so that we may discover repetitions and make predictions. Whether or not a concept is useful depends, obviously, both on the nature of the environment and the direction of our purposes. The concept of a substance with negative weight (phlogiston) is of no use because in fact there are no such substances. There is nothing wrong with the concept, except that it fails to assist us in understanding the phenomenon of combustion. By the same token, if I wish to design and sell women's clothes I will do well to have a wide assortment of color terms at my disposal, for minor differences of hue or brightness will matter considerably to me. On the other hand, if I am simply sorting colored balls for Christmas trees, that spectrum of concepts will be so much excess intellectual baggage. Here it is my purpose, not the world, which determines the usefulness of the concepts.

The role of concepts in helping us to understand the world can be illustrated by the example of two men watching a construction site. To the first, who knows nothing about the building trades, the scene is chaotic in the extreme. Workmen hurry about in all directions, wheeling loads of brick and moving planks. To his untutored eye the least significant person in the area is a motionless man standing before a table on which some papers are laid out. The other spectator is a builder, and to him the scene is perfectly orderly. He can see that the bricklayers are working smoothly, but that a bottleneck is developing in the supply of cement. He knows that the man looking at the papers is in fact directing the entire operation from blueprints and hence is the key figure at the site. The two men perceive roughly the same things, but the concepts which they bring to the occasion enable the second to understand what is happening much better than the first.

But this statement is, strictly speaking, misleading. The builder's conception of the scene is better than the casual onlooker's, *if they both want to know what the workmen are trying to accomplish and how well they are succeeding.* In short, if both men have the same end, then we can judge which one has the superior conceptual tools for achieving it. But the first man might be a painter, estimating the aesthetic potentialities of the scene. In that case, he would look for light, shadow, balance, and color, and the builder's concepts would do him little or no good. Indeed, the builder might actually be hindered in making an artistic judgment, for in order to see the scene as an organized construction site he must suppress his awareness of color and light (which make no difference to the efficiency of the work activity) until he virtually does not see them at all.

Concepts can be judged by the criteria of consistency, truth, or usefulness. (Strictly speaking, judgments are true or false, not concepts, but we may say that a concept is false if it does not accurately represent what it is said—in a judgment—to represent.) The consistency or truth of a concept is independent of our interests or needs, but usefulness is a different matter. Nothing is ever useful *simpliciter;* it is always useful *to someone* or *for something.* Consequently, if we wish to guide the activity of conceptual analysis by the criterion of usefulness, as well as by the logical criteria of consistency and truth, we shall always have to proceed with some purpose in mind for which the concepts are to be used. There is never an answer to the question, "What is *the correct* analysis of a concept?" any more than to the question "What is the best sort of knife?" To either, we can only reply, "For what purposes?"

Consider for example the development of systems for classifying plants. Early botanists fixed upon gross observable features, such as the presence or absence of flowers, size, color, and so forth. Later, the sexual reproduction of plants was discovered, and this fact was used as the basis for a new classification. The second system would usually be said to be better than the first. But better for what? So long as a botanist faithfully attends to the facts of size, color, etc., he is not *wrong* to classify plants in the earlier way. Suppose he has set up four categories: A (large with flowers); B (small with flowers); C (large without flowers); and D (small without flowers). When he says, tulips are A and crocuses are B, he is perfectly correct. His conceptual scheme is clear and consistent, thus meeting the logical criteria. The trouble is that the system is scientifically unfruitful. It does not suggest interesting generalizations or lead to new discoveries. By contrast, a classificatory system which puts tulips and crocuses together as bulb-reproducing perennials opens the way for a fruitful theory of plant reproduction. Similarly, the classification of animals into mammals, etc., is superior to the earlier categories "land-dwelling" and "sea-dwelling" because it brings out the kinship between whales and seals and land mammals.

But I have once more slipped into the mistake which I have been arguing against, for the modern systems of plant and animal classification are only better *for certain purposes.* They might be worse for others. If I am a decorator who works a great deal with flowers, size will be important to me and mode of reproduction irrelevant. It will then be convenient for me to have a system of classification which is based on size.

The history of ideas offers many illustrations of the notion of conceptual usefulness. For example, consider the enormous influence of the German philosopher Hegel throughout the nineteenth century. The early 1800's were a time of rapid political, social, and economic change. The Napoleonic wars, following close upon the dramatic overthrow of the French monarchy, sparked revolts of national independence across the face of Europe. The effects of industrialization were making themselves felt in Western Europe, and populist ideologies flourished as men sought to grapple with the problems of a new age. It was a major task simply to comprehend what was going on, for although Marx was to write that the time had come for men to change the world and not merely understand it, he himself clearly thought that the first could not be done without the second. One obstacle to understanding was the conceptual heritage of the previous ages. By and large, men since the days of the ancient Greeks had identified form and order with the unchanging, chaos or disorder with change. Since understanding was a matter of grasping the form of an event or object, it followed that only the unchanging could truly be understood. Change was merely to be deplored. Even the changes of place of the heavenly bodies were comprehended by reducing them to circular motion, which most closely approximated perfect rest. In the human realm, an unchanging hierarchy of powers and positions was conceived as the most orderly—hence the best—arrangement of society.

When men looked about them in the nineteenth century, they saw virtually nothing but change. Old dynasties were falling, monarchy itself as a form of government was threatened. The settled organization of social classes was being overthrown, the age-old domination of the countryside was challenged by the new industrial cities, religious faith gave way to science and secular ideologies. Those who equated change with disorder were completely unable to get a conceptual grasp on the events around them.

Hegel offered men a new way of thinking about change. His dialectical logic was a conceptual analysis of patterns of change. For him, conflict, growth, decay, even revolution, were orderly stages in a program of development. Instead of relegating social upheaval to the residual category of incomprehensible chaos, Hegel fitted it into a framework of generation and reconciliation of opposites.

As a conceptual system, Hegel's philosophy wasn't more *true* than that of his predecessors. There is, after all, nothing false about calling change chaotic, if "chaos" means "change." But Hegel's philosophy was more *useful* to his contemporaries because it enabled them to understand social phenomena which hitherto had puzzled them. So it was that in art history (Burckhardt), sociology (Durkheim), politics (Marx), and even religion (Feuerbach, Kierkegaard), the most creative continental thinkers took over Hegel's theories and turned them to new uses. Hegel was difficult, it is true, often unclear, anything but a model of conceptual precision. Nevertheless, he helped men to see the world in illuminating ways, thereby performing the primary task of the philosopher.

Analytic political philosophy has just this function. When political men find their environment puzzling, intractable, morally ambiguous, it *may* be that their concepts are inadequate. In that case, philosophers who are trained in the techniques of conceptual clarification can be of great assistance, *if they also have a grasp of the political context within which the conceptual problem has arisen.* For example, students of democratic politics have long assumed that a multi-party system is essential to genuine democracy. The party system, it has been thought, guarantees a legitimate role to opposition elements, thereby protecting the interests and rights of those who are disadvantaged by government action. Recently in the newly established African states, a form of politics has appeared which resembles western democracy in many respects but is built upon a single party, usually the descendant of the independence movement of colonial days. The question arises whether it is legitimate to label such nations "one-party democracies." This is no mere terminological quibble, for behind it lies the real issue whether multi-party politics is necessary to democracy, or whether the party system of western nations is merely one among many ways in which the moral principles of democracy may be realized. The problem is partly empirical, of course, but it requires as well an analysis of the concept of democracy and related concepts. If one has no real understanding of the concrete situation which is creating the conceptual problem—namely western and African politics—then it will be logically impossible to produce a useful analysis save by sheer accident. If you aren't puzzled by a problem, you can't know when you have relieved the puzzlement. There is no such thing as *the* correct analysis of the concept of democracy. The political realm is not made up of distinct, natural, unchanging types which the political philosopher puts on a pin and classifies. For some purposes, the distinction between one-party and multi-party systems may be significant; for other purposes, it may be irrelevant. Independent of some interest, aim, or purpose, there is simply no answer to the disembodied question "Do Nigeria and the United States have the same type of political system?"

Some analytic philosophers have supposed that they could get round the innate relativity of conceptual analysis by basing their arguments on "ordinary language," rather in the way that Plato based his arguments on ideal forms and Aristotle his on essences. The attempt is a mistake, however, for *at best* ordinary language exhibits the (unreflective) conceptual decisions of previous generations of interested parties. Even if the concepts of ordinary thought are perfectly suited to those interests, we will still wish to entertain revised analyses as new problems arise and different interests come to the fore.

It is particularly important not to confuse precision, elegance, and niceness of conceptual distinction—which are marks of an expert philosophical technician—with the relevance and usefulness which are the principal aims of analytic political philosophy. A philosopher who sets out to analyze a concept without some concrete problem in mind will do about as much good as a highly skilled wood carver who idly applies his razor-sharp knives to a side of beef. He may make exquisite incisions and produce perfectly symmetrical cubes, but the net result will be a large pile of stew meat. A butcher, on the other hand, may be nothing like so elegant a workman, but having a well-defined end in cutting the meat, he finishes with a very serviceable pile of steaks, roasts, and joints. Many contemporary philosophers produce technically perfect conceptual stew instead of a useful assortment of rough but relevant clarifications.

The analysis of the concept of political loyalty which I have included in this volume at the end of Part One is an earnest of my belief in this theory of analytic philosophy. In writing it, I was guided not only by a desire to illuminate the loyalty debates of the 1950's, but also by a partisan concern for the coherence and effectiveness of the liberal position. The analysis is not invalidated by my bias, but it is directed by it. Hence, someone concerned with a different aspect of the problem, such as the conflict between religious and political loyalties, should probably find my essay unhelpful. This is as it should be, for one can no more produce a conceptual analysis which is equally useful in all directions than a tool which would serve indifferently for all the tasks of the shop.

In order to avoid misunderstanding, let me add that the analytic political philosopher is by no means limited to conceptual problems that political men or students of politics have actually become aware of. He may play a catalytic role by calling attention to serious confusions which, unnoticed, have undermined political action and discussion. He may also use conceptual analysis as a political tool by forcing men to acknowledge the logical consequences of their professed principles and then either embrace or renounce them. In my analysis of loyalty, for example, I try to show that the modern liberal's penchant for sociological and psychological argument leads straight to such anti-liberal practices as guilt-by-association. My aim, of course, is to force liberals to reconsider their reliance upon sociological evidence in defenses of political liberties. I am counting on them to dislike guilt-by-association more than they like their sociology. Needless to say, they may confound me by cheerfully accepting a practice which they once rejected, but that is one of the dangers of philosophical argument. Some years ago, for example, political scientists began to argue that voter apathy was a source of political stability since a phlegmatic public was unlikely to support extremist demagogues or disturb the public peace with street riots and revolutions. One might have expected liberals to react to the discovery by deciding that political stability was not worth having at the price of a stagnant polity. Instead, they have taken to stating in forthright terms that political apathy is a Good Thing!

II.

Normative political theory can boast as distinguished a lineage as the analytic variety, but it has fallen into disrepute among Anglo-American philosophers of late. This is a reflection of an extreme modesty about all matters of morality which has afflicted philosophers of the analytic school. The general attitude seems to be that it is arrogant and presumptuous for a professor of philosophy to lay down substantive moral principles for general adoption, as though his professional training gave him privileged access to a store of human wisdom. One might have thought that a superbly developed analytical capacity married to wide and systematic knowledge of human affairs—which are the two prerequisites of successful analytic philosophy—would constitute excellent preparation for deliberation on moral questions. But no, the philosopher is merely an Ordinary Man when he lays down his analytical tools and turns to face life.

Each man knows himself best, I suppose, and there is nothing to be gained by thrusting responsibilities upon those who confess themselves unable to meet them. I shall not therefore argue that professors of philosophy are especially qualified to engage in what I have called normative political philosophy. It will be enough simply to characterize the activity and indicate the ways in which it depends upon the social sciences as well as on the techniques of philosophy.

The first question to be answered by any normative political philosophy is whether it itself is an autonomous sphere of human thought or merely a subsidiary branch of moral philosophy. Is there a distinctive political condition with principles and problems of its own, or should one simply apply the general principles of ethics to political situations, taking into account the special circumstances of political institutions? We need what Kant would have called a "deduction" of the concept of normative politics. Philosophers have differed sharply on this issue. Locke, for example, quite clearly believes that there is only one "natural law" of human conduct, applying equally to men in their pre-political "state of nature" and in a legitimately constituted commonwealth. Rousseau, on the other hand, claims that man takes on a new moral condition when he enters political society, and it follows that he is there subject to principles which have no application to a state of nature.

If Locke is correct, then normative political philosophy is essentially casuistry, in the proper sense of the term—i.e., application of general moral principles to particular political situations. If one adopts Rousseau's position, the first task of normative political philosophy becomes the discovery and validation of the highest principles of political behavior. An introduction to a book of readings is hardly the place to discuss this question, but my meaning will perhaps be clearer if I briefly sketch one possible line such an investigation might take.

The political realm is the arena of human affairs in which moral autonomy and legitimate authority meet. Moral autonomy is a necessary condition for politics since without it there is no responsibility, and hence nothing which could be called political action. Authority must be legitimate or it is mere a-political force. Now immediately we encounter an obstacle, for autonomy appears incompatible with authority. If a man is master of his soul and author of the moral injunctions to which he submits, then who can legitimately command him? An autonomous subject seems a contradiction in terms. Either each man is free to dictate the moral law to himself, or some men have the right to rule and others the duty to obey. If we reply that the strong rule the weak, we reduce politics to the level of prudence, each taking what he can and giving what he must.

Democratic theory is an attempt to resolve this conflict. Social contracts, majority rule, responsible ministries, representative parliaments, are all devices for making the authority of the state compatible with the liberty of the individual. A great deal of literature of political philosophy can therefore be placed in the normative category.

Following upon the fundamental question of normative political philosophy are a host of particular questions relating to specific aspects of political life. What are the rights and duties of inherited property? Is there some objective measuring-stick of social needs or ought the priorities of social action to be determined by popular choice? If the latter, what method should be used? Is a rehabilitory penal system compatible with the principle of individual responsibility for one's acts? Has the state the right to demand loyalty from its subjects, or only an outward conformity to law? Is social equality inconsistent with the reward of merit? There is no end to the list, nor can there be, for the emergence of new social institutions and political forms brings in its train new problems for normative political philosophy.

I have argued that useful analytic political philosophy can only be produced by someone who is imbued with the methods, data, and problems of the empirical disciplines relating to the study of politics. The same must be said for normative political philosophy. Insofar as we are concerned only with the application of previously determined moral principles, it is obvious that we need detailed factual information about the cases at hand. Perhaps less obviously, the establishment of the highest normative principles of political philosophy depends equally upon the latest discoveries of the social sciences. This dependence is paradoxical, for it seems to reduce moral principles to the status of tentative hypotheses—what science establishes today it may supersede tomorrow. If normative political philosophy waits upon a Freud or a Keynes, an Erikson or a Weber, how can it confidently make the majestic pronouncements which fill the pages of Plato, Rousseau, and Marx?

The answer is that it both cannot and must! This is the dilemma of all moral philosophy. Kant sought to evade it by eliminating empirical assumptions from his ethical theory; Plato took the other path and laid down psychological theories as eternal truths. Both were wrong. Moral philosophy issues in categorical normative statements based upon merely probable empirical premises. Our ethical beliefs are absolutely binding upon us, but they are always open to criticism and correction. So too with the principles of a normative political philosophy. How can this be so?

Briefly, a moral principle can be analyzed as a compound, asserting that creatures of a specified sort should behave in a certain manner, and that men are creatures of that sort. The first half of the compound bears the normative content of the principle, while the second half is a factual assertion about human nature. The normative part is hypothetical in form (if a being has the specified nature, then it ought to act in such and such a way), and is established by *a priori* argument. The factual part is categorical in form, and is established by empirical evidence. The same analysis can be made of principles concerning political institutions. The factual component may then be the assertion that an actual institution is of a certain sort, or more generally that such an institution is in principle feasible. For example, much social contract theory presupposes the possibility of emigration, just as democratic theory in general assumes the workability of some method of collective social decision.

The peculiarity of all this is that the factual presupposition which I make in asserting a moral principle is not about some natural or social situation but about myself, my own nature. I am in the position of laying down moral principles which depend for their relevance upon my own uncertain knowledge of myself. Every lawgiver must exhibit outwardly an assurance which inwardly he may be far from feeling. It is the paradox of morality that each man bears this ambiguous relationship to himself. In order that moral deliberations have relevance to my situation, I must descend from the safety of hypotheticals and assert that I am such a creature as this or that principle speaks of.

An example may make all this somewhat clearer. The classical liberal theory of Bentham and Smith teaches that man is a rationally self-interested maximizer of subjective value (pleasure) who ought to guide his political efforts by the principle of the greatest happiness for the greatest number. The theory need not assert that men actually are perfectly rational—presumably it asserts the contrary, since it seeks to make them so. But it must assume that the ideal of the rational pleasure-calculator is a goal toward which men can direct themselves. Now this theory treats individuals as isolated centers of consciousness to whom other persons present themselves as external objects. Sympathy, even altruism, is not excluded by such a view, for a man may take pleasure in the happiness of others or feel pain at their sorrow; but the individual is presumed to be psychologically autonomous. One implication is that rational man is simply natural man, undistorted by prejudice or the pressures of public opinion. This picture of the possibilities of human nature is wrong. Social psychology has taught us that the individual personality develops through a process of internalization of social norms and values. Society is not a distorting pressure upon the individual but a creative force. The child who assimilates no particular culture is an animal, not a free man. Indeed, even the term "assimilate" is misleading, for it suggests that the individual ego is already formed prior to the absorption. Actually the coherent ego emerges as an end-product of the enculturation process and can only come into existence by means of it. John Stuart Mill's plea for an end to the pressure of social opinion would, if carried to its limit, result in mentally ill or undeveloped children, not free spirits. By the same token, the constraints of the group upon adults are indispensable conditions of psychological stability. The great aristocratic eccentrics and free-thinkers who led the fight against conformity in the last century were not free in spite of their upbringing but because of it. Man is not naturally a Millian liberal any more than he is "naturally" anything else. The autonomous personality, as David Riesman calls it, must be nurtured, developed, sustained, and protected by social institutions and cultural patterns reaching (as Erik Erikson shows) into the intimate sphere of infant-rearing itself.

If these psychological remarks are correct, then liberal theory is simply irrelevant to human concerns insofar as it posits an isolated center of value-maximization as its subject. Bentham may not be wrong to assert that *such* creatures ought to be utilitarians, but he *is* wrong to assume that his principles apply to men.

The dilemma of the political philosopher should be apparent. Modern social psychology offers a better picture of the human personality than we can find in the pages of Plato or Mill, but the picture is still incomplete, tentative, open to revision. It is absurd to do normative political philosophy on the basis of the psychology of ancient Greece or eighteenth century England, but impossible to wait until the modern sciences of man have said their final word. The only course is to base our moral arguments on the most advanced knowledge available and recognize that each new day may bring discoveries which make our conclusions irrelevant. Note that I say "irrelevant," not "false," for moral philosophy is not composed of factual assertions which can be falsified by empirical evidence. Rather it consists of normative assertions established by *a priori* arguments. What *is* empirically falsifiable is the implicit claim that the moral philosophy applies to men.

Both normative and analytic political philosophy are thus dependent upon the empirical sciences of man, for relevance and significance if not for truth. They are enterprises which can never definitively be completed, for their points of reference shift as political life changes and our knowledge of social man grows.

III.

So much for the ideology of this book of readings. Now let me say a few words about the selections themselves. There are twenty-seven readings in all, of which sixteen come from the works of more-or-less standard authors in the history of political philosophy. Plato is represented twice, the only author to be so. Among the others are familiar stalwarts like Aristotle, Locke, and Hume, together with figures less often encountered in political philosophy, Dostoyevsky and Hooker, for example. Seven readings are drawn from classical and contemporary social science. Great originators like Max Weber and Emile Durkheim are joined by the young contemporary political scientist John Schaar and his colleague at the University of California, Erving Goffman. This group of selections has fewer separate readings, but they are rather longer individually. In addition to the philosophical and social scientific readings, I have included three case studies as material for the section on political loyalty. Two of these—Supreme Court decisions on flag-salute cases—are already familiar to students of political science. The third is a find of which I am rather proud: a series of letters written by a young French lieutenant during a year in prison awaiting trial for refusing to fight against the Algerians. The letters were published in the French journal *Esprit* six years ago and are here translated into English for the first time.

Finally, the only example of contemporary political philosophy included in the book is my piece on the concept of political loyalty. I have not devoted more space to modern philosophical work because the two volumes entitled *Philosophy, Politics, and Society* edited by Peter Laslett and W. G. Runciman have already made a fine selection of papers available. My own essay is included as a concrete example of what I have here called analytic political philosophy, and in that sense is really an extension of these introductory remarks.

There is obviously no pretense at system or completeness in the choice of readings. The social science offerings in particular are included because they are exciting and provocative rather than authoritative. Each reading should raise a host of analytic and substantive issues which can serve as the basis of class discussion or further reading. The organization of the book is suggestive only; many readings can be used profitably in several sections. For example, Erikson's dissection of the personality and appeal of Hitler, in Part Two, can serve as a case study of charismatic authority, discussed by Max Weber in Part One. Equally, one can read the letters of Jean Le Meur for the insight they give into Erving Goffman's analysis of life in total institutions.

PART ONE

The Individual
and the State

POLITICAL AUTHORITY:

ITS SOURCES

AND VARIETIES

The distinguishing mark of politics, as opposed to other spheres of human activity, is a certain form of authority which some men exercise over other men. The locus of political authority is the *state,* and its customary expression is *law.* A study of the problems of political theory begins, therefore, with the nature of political authority and of law, and the nature and functions of the state. Some political theorists attempt to justify law and political authority by appeal to religious or moral principles; others offer merely a factual account of the factors which induce some men to obey other men. Political theorists differ as well over whether the state is a natural human institution serving inherent human needs or an artificial device brought into being to deal with problems of pre-political society. There are four positions which can be taken on these two issues, and each of them has had its defenders in the history of political philosophy. First, the state may be a natural institution, and its authority may be susceptible of a moral justification; Plato, Aristotle, St. Thomas, and others in the natural law tradition have maintained this view. Second, the state may be a natural institution for which no moral justification is possible; the ancient Sophists, Machiavelli and in a certain sense Marx and Engels have all held this. Third, the state may be described as an artificial contrivance brought into being for specific and limited purposes, which are however moral in character—this is the doctrine of John Locke and the generality of social contract theorists. Fourth, the state may be characterized as both artificial and amoral, its authority deriving from force and motives of self-preservation. Thomas Hobbes espouses this view in his *Leviathan*.

Variations and mutations of these four positions have been common in the history of political theory. Marx and Engels, for example, claim that the emergence of the state as a human institution is natural and inevitable at a certain stage in social development, but that its disappearance, or "withering away," in the last communist stage is equally natural and inevitable. They thus appear to imply that political philosophy, as a general theory of the nature and justification of the state, must really consist only of political ideologies of one economic class or another, together with sociological analyses of those ideologies. Max Weber, too, opens up the possibility for a different kind of political philosophy by his empirical analysis of the types of justification which are given for political authority. He shows us that it is rare for obedience to authority to depend purely on coercion, since in most cases the subjects, as well as the rulers, are restrained by a concept of the "legitimacy" of the government. Weber distinguishes sharply between a moral justification of that legitimacy and the empirical fact that men believe in it. He is thus able to deal scientifically with men's value attitudes without engaging in either defense or criticism of them.

The issue of state authority is as old as political history itself. It appears sometimes as a debate over the limits of monarchical power, sometimes as a conflict between secular and religious authorities, more recently as a search for the rationale of popular government. In the present century, the state has grown so great that opposition to its authority seems merely quixotic; the crimes committed in the name of the state, unfortunately, have also been so great that we cannot shun the obligation to examine the grounds of its authority and subject them to a rigorous critique.

The Law of Nature

Richard Hooker, 1554–1600, was an Anglican divine of the Eliza-bethan Age. His great work, Of the Laws of Ecclesiastical Polity, is a vast systematic defense of the theological and political position of the Church of England, set in the Christian tradition of natural law. The book had great influence, on John Locke among others, and remains one of the best-known pieces of theological writing in English. The theory of natural law, which has its roots in the metaphysics of Plato and Aristotle, conceives the universe as inherently purposive. The natural laws which govern the motions of inanimate bodies are thought to have their analogues in the moral laws which govern the behavior of individuals and the laws of society regulating the behavior of governments. All these laws issue from God, who guides the universe according to his divine purpose. St. Thomas Aquinas thought it possible to develop a purposive theory of law and morality without reference to divine revelation. John Austin, in the next selection, expresses a directly opposed view.

* * *

II. All things that are, have some operation not violent or casual. Neither doth any thing ever begin to exercise the same, without some fore-conceived end for which it worketh. And the end which it worketh for is not obtained, unless the work be also fit to obtain it by. For unto every end every operation will not serve. That which doth assign unto each thing the kind, that which doth moderate the force and power, that which doth appoint the form and measure, of working, the same we term a Law. So that no certain end could ever be attained, unless the actions whereby it is attained were regular; that is to say, made suitable, fit and correspondent unto their end, by some canon, rule or law. Which thing doth first take place in the works even of God himself.

[2.] All things therefore do work after a sort according to law:

Reprinted from Richard Hooker, *Of the Laws of Ecclesiastical Policy,* in *Works,* 2 vols. (Oxford, Eng.: Clarendon Press, 1885).

all other things according to a law, whereof some superior, unto whom they are subject, is author; only the works and operations of God have Him both for their worker, and for the law whereby they are wrought. The being of God is a kind of law to his working: for that perfection which God is, giveth perfection to that he doth. Those natural, necessary, and internal operations of God, the Generation of the Son, the Proceeding of the Spirit, are without the compass of my present intent: which is to touch only such operations as have their beginning and being by a voluntary purpose, wherewith God hath eternally decreed when and how they should be. Which eternal decree is that we term an eternal law.

*   *   *

III. I am not ignorant that by "law eternal" the learned for the most part do understand the order, not which God hath eternally purposed himself in all his works to observe, but rather that which with himself he hath set down as expedient to be kept by all his creatures, according to the several condition wherewith he hath endued them. They who thus are accustomed to speak apply the name of Law unto that only rule of working which superior authority imposeth; whereas we somewhat more enlarging the sense thereof term any kind of rule or canon, whereby actions are framed, a law. Now that law which, as it is laid up in the bosom of God, they call *Eternal*, receiveth according unto the different kinds of things which are subject unto it different and sundry kinds of names. That part of it which ordereth natural agents we call usually *Nature's* law; that which Angels do clearly behold and without any swerving observe is a law *Celestial* and heavenly; the law of *Reason*, that which bindeth creatures reasonable in this world, and with which by reason they may most plainly perceive themselves bound; that which bindeth them, and is not known but by special revelation from God, *Divine* law; *Human* law, that which out of the law either of reason or of God men probably gathering to be expedient, they make it a law. All things therefore, which are as they ought to be, are conformed unto *this second law eternal;* and even those things which to this eternal law are not conformable are notwithstanding in some sort ordered by *the first eternal law.* For what good or evil is there under the sun, what action correspondent or repugnant unto the law which God hath imposed upon his creatures, but in or upon it God doth work according to the law which himself hath eternally purposed to keep; that is to say, the *first law eternal*? So that a twofold law eternal being thus made, it is not hard to conceive how they both take place in all things.

* * *

V. God alone excepted, who actually and everlastingly is whatsoever he may be, and which cannot hereafter be that which now he is not; all other things besides are somewhat in possibility, which as yet they are not in act. And for this cause there is in all things an appetite or desire, whereby they incline to something which they may be; and when they are it, they shall be perfecter than now they are. All which perfections are contained under the general name of Goodness. And because there is not in the world any thing whereby another may not some way be made the perfecter, therefore all things that are, are good.

[2.] Again, sith there can be no goodness desired which proceedeth not from God himself, as from the supreme cause of all things; and every effect doth after a sort contain, at leastwise resemble, the cause from which it proceedeth: all things in the world are said in some sort to seek the highest, and to covet more or less the participation of God himself. Yet this doth no where so much appear as it doth in man, because there are so many kinds of perfections which man seeketh. The first degree of goodness is that general perfection which all things do seek, in desiring the continuance of their being. All things therefore coveting as much as may be to be like unto God in being ever, that which cannot hereunto attain personally doth seek to continue itself another way, that is by offspring and propagation. The next degree of goodness is that which each thing coveteth by affecting resemblance with God in the constancy and excellency of those operations which belong unto their kind. The immutability of God they strive unto, by working either always or for the most part after one and the same manner; his absolute exactness they imitate, by tending unto that which is most exquisite in every particular. Hence have risen a number of axioms in philosophy, showing how "the works of nature do always aim at that which cannot be bettered."

* * *

VIII. Wherefore to return to our former intent of discovering the natural way, whereby rules have been found out concerning that goodness wherewith the Will of man ought to be moved in human actions; as every thing naturally and necessarily doth desire the utmost good and greatest perfection whereof Nature hath made it capable, even so man. Our felicity therefore being the object and accomplishment of our desire, we cannot choose but wish and covet it. All particular things which are subject unto action, the Will doth so far forth incline unto, as Reason judgeth them the better for us, and consequently the more available to our bliss. If Reason err, we fall into evil, and are so far forth deprived of the general perfection we seek. Seeing therefore that for the framing of men's actions the knowledge of good from evil is necessary, it only resteth that we search how this may be had. Neither must we suppose that there needeth one rule to know the good and another the evil by. For he that knoweth what is straight doth even thereby discern what is crooked, because the absence of straightness in bodies capable thereof is crookedness. Goodness in actions is like unto straightness; wherefore that which is done well we term *right*. For as the straight way is most acceptable to him that travelleth, because by it he cometh soonest to his journey's end; so in action, that which doth lie the evenest between us and the end we desire must needs be the fittest for our use. Besides which fitness for use, there is also in rectitude, beauty; as contrariwise in obliquity, deformity. And that which is good in the actions of men, doth not only delight as profitable, but as amiable also. In which consideration the Grecians most divinely have given to the active perfection of men a name expressing both beauty and goodness, because goodness in ordinary speech is for the most part applied only to that which is beneficial. But we in the name of goodness do here imply both.

*   *   *

[3.] Signs and tokens to know good by are of sundry kinds; some more certain and some less. The most certain token of evident goodness is, if the general persuasion of all men do so account it. And therefore a common received error is never utterly overthrown, till such time as we go from signs unto causes, and shew some manifest root or fountain thereof common unto all, whereby it may clearly appear how it hath come to pass that so many have been overseen. In which case surmises and slight probabilities will not serve, because the universal consent of men is the perfectest and strongest in this kind, which comprehendeth only the signs and tokens of goodness. Things casual do vary, and that which a man doth but chance to think well of cannot still have the like hap. Wherefore although we know not the cause, yet thus much we may know; that some necessary cause there is, whensoever the judgments of all men generally or for the most part run one and the same way, especially in matters of natural discourse. For of things necessarily and naturally done there is no more affirmed but this, "They keep either always or for the most part one tenure." The general and perpetual voice of men is as the sentence of God himself. For that which all men have at all times learned, Nature herself must needs have taught; and God being the author of Nature, her voice is but his instrument. By her from Him we receive whatsoever in such sort we learn. Infinite duties there are, the goodness whereof is by this rule sufficiently manifested, although we had no other warrant besides to approve them. The Apostle St. Paul having speech concerning the heathen saith of them, "They are a law unto themselves." His meaning is, that by force of the light of Reason, wherewith God illuminateth every one which cometh into the world, men being enabled to know truth from falsehood, and good from evil, do thereby learn in many things what the will of God is; which will himself not revealing by any extraordinary means unto them, but they by natural discourse attaining the knowledge thereof, seem the makers of those Laws which indeed are his, and they but only the finders of them out.

[4.] A law therefore generally taken, is a directive rule unto goodness of operation. The rule of divine operations outward, is the definitive appointment of God's own wisdom set down within himself. The rule of natural agents that work by simple necessity, is the determination of the wisdom of God, known to God himself the principal director of them, but not unto them that are directed to execute the same. The rule of natural agents which work after a sort of their own accord, as the beasts do, is the judgment of common sense or fancy concerning the sensible goodness of those objects wherewith they are moved. The rule of ghostly or immaterial natures, as spirits and angels, is their intuitive intellectual judgment concerning the amiable beauty and high goodness of that object, which with unspeakable joy and delight doth set them on work. The rule of voluntary agents on earth is the sentence that Reason giveth concerning the goodness of those things which they are to do. And the sentences which Reason giveth are some more some less general, before it come to define in particular actions what is good.

[5.] The main principles of Reason are in themselves apparent. For to make nothing evident of itself unto man's understanding were to take away all possibility of knowing any thing. And herein that of Theophrastus is true, "They that seek a reason of all things do utterly overthrow Reason." In every kind of knowledge some such grounds there are, as that being proposed the mind doth presently embrace them as free from all possibility of error, clear and manifest without proof. In which kind axioms or principles more general are such as this, "that the greater good is to be chosen before the less." If therefore it should be demanded what reason there is, why the Will of Man, which doth necessarily shun harm and covet whatsoever is pleasant and sweet, should be commanded to count the pleasures of sin gall, and notwithstanding the bitter accidents wherewith virtuous actions are compassed, yet still to rejoice and delight in them: surely this could never stand with Reason, but that wisdom thus prescribing groundeth her laws upon an infallible rule of comparison; which is, "That small difficulties, when exceeding great good is sure to ensue, and on the other side momentary benefits, when the hurt which they draw after them is unspeakable, are not at all to be respected." This rule is the ground whereupon the wisdom of the Apostle buildeth a law, enjoining patience unto himself; "The present lightness of our affliction worketh unto us even with abundance upon abundance an eternal weight of glory; while we look not on the things which are seen, but on the things which are not seen: for the things which are seen are temporal, but the things which are not seen are eternal": therefore Christianity to be embraced, whatsoever calamities in those times it was accompanied withal. Upon the same ground our Saviour proveth the law most reasonable, that doth forbid those crimes which men for gain's sake fall unto. "For a man to win the world if it be with the loss of his soul, what benefit or good is it?" Axioms less general, yet so manifest that they need no further proof, are such as these, "God to be worshipped"; "parents to be honoured"; "others to be used by us as we ourselves would by them." Such things, as soon as they are alleged, all men acknowledge to be good; they require no proof or further discourse to be assured of their goodness.

Notwithstanding whatsoever such principle there is, it was at the first found out by discourse, and drawn from out of the very bowels of heaven and earth. For we are to note, that things in the world are to us discernible, not only so far forth as serveth for our vital preservation, but further also in a twofold higher respect. For first, if all other uses were utterly taken away, yet the mind of man being by nature speculative and delighted with contemplation in itself, they were to be known even for mere knowledge and understanding's sake. Yea further besides this, the knowledge of every the least thing in the whole world hath in it a second peculiar benefit unto us, inasmuch as it serveth to minister rules, canons, and laws, for men to direct those actions by, which we properly term human. This did the very heathens themselves obscurely insinuate, by making *Themis,* which we call *Jus,* or Right, to be the daughter of heaven and earth.

[6.] We know things either as they are in themselves, or as they are in mutual relation one to another. The knowledge of that which man is in reference unto himself, and other things in relation unto man, I may justly term the mother of all those principles, which are as it were edicts, statutes, and decrees, in that Law of Nature, whereby human actions are framed. First therefore having observed that the best things, where they are not hindered, do still produce the best operations, (for which cause, where many things are to concur unto one effect, the best is in all congruity of reason to guide the residue, that it prevailing most, the work principally done by it may have greatest perfection:) when hereupon we come to observe in ourselves, of what excellency our souls are in comparison of our bodies, and the diviner part in relation unto the baser of our souls; seeing that all these concur in producing human actions, it cannot be well unless the chiefest do command and direct the rest. The soul then ought to conduct the body, and the spirit of our minds the soul. This is therefore the first Law, whereby the highest power of the mind requireth general obedience at the hands of all the rest concurring with it unto action.

*   *   *

X. That which hitherto we have set down is (I hope) sufficient to shew their brutishness, which imagine that religion and virtue are only as men will account of them; that we might

make as much account, if we would, of the contrary, without
any harm unto ourselves, and that in nature they are as indifferent one as the other. We see then how nature itself teacheth
laws and statutes to live by. The laws which have been hitherto
mentioned do bind men absolutely even as they are men, although they have never any settled fellowship, never any solemn
agreement amongst themselves what to do or not to do. But
forasmuch as we are not by ourselves sufficient to furnish ourselves with competent store of things needful for such a life as
our nature doth desire, a life fit for the dignity of man; therefore
to supply those defects and imperfections which are in us living
single and solely by ourselves, we are naturally induced to seek
communion and fellowship with others. This was the cause of
men's uniting themselves at the first in politic Societies, which
societies could not be without Government, nor Government
without a distinct kind of Law from that which hath been already declared. Two foundations there are which bear up public
societies; the one, a natural inclination, whereby all men desire
sociable life and fellowship; the other, an order expressly or
secretly agreed upon touching the manner of their union in
living together. The latter is that which we call the Law of a
Commonweal, the very soul of a politic body, the parts whereof
are by law animated, held together, and set on work in such
actions, as the common good requireth. Laws politic, ordained
for external order and regiment amongst men, are never framed
as they should be, unless presuming the will of man to be inwardly obstinate, rebellious, and averse from all obedience unto
the sacred laws of his nature; in a word, unless presuming man
to be in regard of his depraved mind little better than a wild
beast, they do accordingly provide notwithstanding so to frame
his outward actions, that they be no hindrance unto the common
good for which societies are instituted: unless they do this, they
are not perfect. It resteth therefore that we consider how nature
findeth out such laws of government as serve to direct even
nature depraved to a right end.

[2.] All men desire to lead in this world a happy life. That
life is led most happily, wherein all virtue is exercised without
impediment or let. The Apostle, in exhorting men to contentment
although they have in this world no more than very bare food
and raiment, giveth us thereby to understand that those are even
the lowest of things necessary; that if we should be stripped of

all those things without which we might possibly be, yet these must be left; that destitution in these is such an impediment, as till it be removed suffereth not the mind of man to admit any other care. For this cause, first God assigned Adam maintenance of life, and then appointed him a law to observe. For this cause, after men began to grow to a number, the first thing we read they gave themselves unto was the tilling of the earth and the feeding of cattle. Having by this mean whereon to live, the principal actions of their life afterward are noted by the exercise of their religion. True it is, that the kingdom of God must be the first thing in our purposes and desires. But inasmuch as righteous life presupposeth life; inasmuch as to live virtuously it is impossible except we live; therefore the first impediment, which naturally we endeavour to remove, is penury and want of things without which we cannot live. Unto life many implements are necessary; more, if we seek (as all men naturally do) such a life as hath in it joy, comfort, delight, and pleasure. To this end we see how quickly sundry arts mechanical were found out, in the very prime of the world. As things of greatest necessity are always first provided for, so things of greatest dignity are most accounted of by all such as judge rightly. Although therefore riches be a thing which every man wisheth, yet no man of judgment can esteem it better to be rich, than wise, virtuous, and religious. If we be both or either of these, it is not because we are so born. For into the world we come as empty of the one as of the other, as naked in mind as we are in body. Both which necessities of man had at the first no other helps and supplies than only domestical; such as that which the Prophet implieth, saying, "Can a mother forget her child?" such as that which the Apostle mentioneth, saying, "He that careth not for his own is worse than an infidel"; such as that concerning Abraham, "Abraham will command his sons and his household after him, that they keep the way of the Lord."

[3.] But neither that which we learn of ourselves nor that which others teach us can prevail, where wickedness and malice have taken deep root. If therefore when there was but as yet one only family in the world, no means of instruction human or divine could prevent effusion of blood; how could it be chosen but that when families were multiplied and increased upon earth, after separation each providing for itself, envy, strife, contention and violence must grow amongst them? For hath not Nature

furnished man with wit and valour, as it were with armour, which
may be used as well unto extreme evil as good? Yea, were they
not used by the rest of the world unto evil; unto the contrary
only by Seth, Enoch, and those few the rest in that line? We all
make complaint of the iniquity of our times: not unjustly; for
the days are evil. But compare them with those times wherein
there were no civil societies, with those times wherein there
was as yet no manner of public regiment established, with those
times wherein there were not above eight persons righteous
living upon the face of the earth; and we have surely good
cause to think that God hath blessed us exceedingly, and hath
made us behold most happy days.

[4.] To take away all such mutual grievances, injuries, and
wrongs, there was no way but only by growing unto composition and agreement amongst themselves, by ordaining some kind
of government public, and by yielding themselves subject thereunto; that unto whom they granted authority to rule and govern,
by them the peace, tranquillity, and happy estate of the rest
might be procured. Men always knew that when force and injury was offered they might be defenders of themselves; they
knew that howsoever men may seek their own commodity, yet if
this were done with injury unto others it was not to be suffered,
but by all men and by all good means to be withstood; finally
they knew that no man might in reason take upon him to determine his own right, and according to his own determination
proceed in maintenance thereof, inasmuch as every man is
towards himself and them whom he greatly affecteth partial;
and therefore that strifes and troubles would be endless, except
they gave their common consent all to be ordered by some
whom they should agree upon: without which consent there
were no reason that one man should take upon him to be lord or
judge over another; because, although there be according to the
opinion of some very great and judicious men a kind of natural
right in the noble, wise, and virtuous, to govern them which are
of servile disposition; nevertheless for manifestation of this their
right, and men's more peaceable contentment on both sides, the
assent of them who are to be governed seemeth necessary.

To fathers within their private families Nature hath given a
supreme power; for which cause we see throughout the world
even from the foundation thereof, all men have ever been taken
as lords and lawful kings in their own houses. Howbeit over a

whole grand multitude having no such dependency upon any one, and consisting of so many families as every politic society in the world doth, impossible it is that any should have complete lawful power, but by consent of men, or immediate appointment of God; because not having the natural superiority of fathers, their power must needs be either usurped, and then unlawful; or, if lawful, then either granted or consented unto by them over whom they exercise the same, or else given extraordinarily from God, unto whom all the world is subject. It is no improbable opinion therefore which the arch-philosopher was of, that as the chiefest person in every household was always as it were a king, so when numbers of households joined themselves in civil society together, kings were the first kind of governors amongst them. Which is also (as it seemeth) the reason why the name of *Father* continued still in them, who of fathers were made rulers; as also the ancient custom of governors to do as Melchisedec, and being kings to exercise the office of priests, which fathers did at the first, grew perhaps by the same occasion.

Howbeit not this the only kind of regiment that hath been received in the world. The inconveniences of one kind have caused sundry other to be devised. So that in a word all public regiment of what kind soever seemeth evidently to have risen from deliberate advice, consultation, and composition between men, judging it convenient and behoveful; there being no impossibility in nature considered by itself, but that men might have lived without any public regiment. Howbeit, the corruption of our nature being presupposed, we may not deny but that the Law of Nature doth now require of necessity some kind of regiment, so that to bring things unto the first course they were in, and utterly to take away all kind of public government in the world, were apparently to overturn the whole world.

[5.] The case of man's nature standing therefore as it doth, some kind of regiment the Law of Nature doth require; yet the kinds thereof being many, Nature tieth not to any one, but leaveth the choice as a thing arbitrary. At the first when some certain kind of regiment was once approved, it may be that nothing was then further thought upon for the manner of governing, but all permitted unto their wisdom and discretion which were to rule; till by experience they found this for all parts very inconvenient, so as the thing which they had devised for a remedy did indeed but increase the sore which it should have cured. They saw that to live by one man's will became the cause of all men's misery. This constrained them to come unto laws, wherein all men might see their duties beforehand, and know the penalties of transgressing them. If things be simply good or evil, and withal universally so acknowledged, there needs no new law to be made for such things. The first kind therefore of things appointed by laws human containeth whatsoever being in itself naturally good or evil, is notwithstanding more secret than that it can be discerned by every man's present conceit, without some deeper discourse and judgment. In which discourse because there is difficulty and possibility many ways to err, unless such things were set down by laws, many would be ignorant of their duties which now are not, and many that know what they should do would nevertheless dissemble it, and to excuse themselves pretend ignorance and simplicity, which now they cannot.

[6.] And because the greatest part of men are such as prefer their own private good before all things, even that good which is sensual before whatsoever is most divine; and for that the labour of doing good, together with the pleasure arising from the contrary, doth make men for the most part slower to the one and proner to the other, than that duty prescribed them by law can prevail sufficiently with them: therefore unto laws that men do make for the benefit of men it hath seemed always needful to add rewards, which may more allure unto good than any hardness deterreth from it, and punishments, which may more deter from evil than any sweetness thereto allureth. Wherein as the generality is natural, *virtue rewardable and vice punishable;* so the particular determination of the reward or punishment belongeth unto them by whom laws are made. Theft is naturally punishable, but the kind of punishment is positive, and such lawful as men shall think with discretion convenient by law to appoint.

[7.] In laws, that which is natural bindeth universally, that which is positive not so. To let go those kind of positive laws which men impose upon themselves, as by vow unto God, contract with men, or such like; somewhat it will make unto our purpose, a little more fully to consider what things are incident into the making of the positive laws for the government of them that live united in public society. Laws do not only teach what is good, but they enjoin it, they have in them a certain constraining force. And to constrain men unto any thing inconvenient doth seem unreasonable. Most requisite therefore it is that to devise laws which all men shall be forced to obey none but wise men be admitted. Laws are matters of principal consequence; men of common capacity and but ordinary judgment are not able (for how should they?) to discern what things are fittest for each kind and state of regiment. We cannot be ignorant how much our obedience unto laws dependeth upon this point. Let a man though never so justly oppose himself unto them that are disordered in their ways, and what one amongst them commonly doth not stomach at such contradiction, storm at reproof, and hate such as would reform them? Notwithstanding even they which brook it worst that men should tell them of their duties, when they are told the same by a law, think very well and reasonably of it. For why? They presume that the law doth speak with all indifferency; that the law hath no side-respect to their persons; that the law is as it were an oracle proceeded from wisdom and understanding.

[8.] Howbeit laws do not take their constraining force from the quality of such as devise them, but from that power which doth give them the strength of laws. That which we spake before concerning the power of government must here be applied unto the power of making laws whereby to govern; which power God hath over all: and by the natural law, whereunto he hath made all subject, the lawful power of making laws to command whole politic societies of men belongeth so properly unto the same entire societies, that for any prince or potentate of what kind soever upon earth to exercise the same of himself, and not either by express commission immediately and personally received from God, or else by authority derived at the first from their consent upon whose persons they impose laws, it is no better than mere tyranny.

Laws they are not therefore which public approbation hath not made so. But approbation not only they give who personally declare their assent by voice sign or act, but also when others do it in their names by right originally at the least derived from them. As in parliaments, councils, and the like assemblies, although we be not personally ourselves present, notwithstanding our assent is by reason of others agents there in our behalf. And what we do by others, no reason but that it should stand as our deed, no less effectually to bind us than if ourselves had done it in person. In many things assent is given, they that give it not imagining they do so, because the manner of their assenting is not apparent. As for example, when an absolute monarch commandeth his subjects that which seemeth good in his own discretion, hath not his edict the force of a law whether they approve or dislike it? Again, that which hath been received long sithence and is by custom now established, we keep as a law which we may not transgress; yet what consent was ever thereunto sought or required at our hands?

Of this point therefore we are to note, that sith men naturally have no full and perfect power to command whole politic multitudes of men, therefore utterly without our consent we could in such sort be at no man's commandment living. And to be commanded we do consent, when that society whereof we are part hath at any time before consented, without revoking the same after by the like universal agreement. Wherefore as any man's deed past is good as long as himself continueth; so the act of a public society of men done five hundred years sithence standeth as theirs who presently are of the same societies, because corporations are immortal; we were then alive in our predecessors, and they in their successors do live still. Laws therefore human, of what kind soever, are available by consent.

*   *   *

JOHN AUSTIN

The Nature of Law

◆

John Austin, 1790–1859, is a major figure in the Anglo-American tradition of positivistic political theory. A close friend of Jeremy Bentham, James Mill, and John Stuart Mill, he systematically developed in the field of jurisprudence their doctrine of utilitarianism. The analysis of the concept of law in this selection rests on the sharp separation of factual from normative questions which David Hume had insisted upon. Austin identifies laws with commands, issued by one who has

Reprinted from John Austin, *The Province of Jurisprudence Determined*, Lecture I (London, 1832).

*the power to enforce them. On this view, whether something is a law
is entirely distinct from whether it is a good law. The natural law
tradition, in contrast, treats the two questions as inseparable. The issue
remains a major subject of debate in legal and philosophical circles
today.*

The matter of jurisprudence is positive law: law, simply and
strictly so called: or law set by political superiors to political inferiors. But positive law (or law, simply and strictly so called)
is often confounded with objects to which it is related by *resemblance,* and with objects to which it is related in the way of
analogy: with objects which are *also* signified, *properly* and
improperly, by the large and vague expression *law.* To obviate
the difficulties springing from that confusion, I begin my projected Course with determining the province of jurisprudence,
or with distinguishing the matter of jurisprudence from those
various related objects: trying to define the subject of which I
intend to treat, before I endeavour to analyse its numerous and
complicated parts.

A law, in the most general and comprehensive acceptation in
which the term, in its literal meaning, is employed, may be said
to be a rule laid down for the guidance of an intelligent being
by an intelligent being having power over him. Under this
definition are concluded, and without impropriety, several
species. It is necessary to define accurately the line of demarca-
tion which separates these species from one another, as much
mistiness and intricacy has been infused into the science of
jurisprudence by their being confounded or not clearly distinguished. In the comprehensive sense above indicated, or in
the largest meaning which it has, without extension by metaphor
or analogy, the term *law* embraces the following objects:—Laws
set by God to his human creatures, and laws set by men to men.

The whole or a portion of the laws set by God to men is frequently styled the law of nature, or natural law: being, in truth,
the only natural law of which it is possible to speak without a
metaphor, or without a blending of objects which ought to be
distinguished broadly. But, rejecting the appellation Law of Nature as ambiguous and misleading, I name those laws or rules,
as considered collectively or in a mass, the *Divine law,* or the
law of God.

Laws set by men to men are of two leading or principal

classes: classes which are often blended, although they differ
extremely; and which, for that reason, should be severed precisely, and opposed distinctly and conspicuously.

Of the laws or rules set by men to men, some are established
by *political* superiors, sovereign and subject: by persons exercising supreme and subordinate *government,* in independent
nations, or independent political societies. The aggregate of the
rules thus established, or some aggregate forming a portion of
that aggregate, is the appropriate matter of jurisprudence, general
or particular. To the aggregate of the rules thus established, or
to some aggregate forming a portion of that aggregate, the term
law, as used simply and strictly, is exclusively applied. But, as
contradistinguished to *natural* law, or to the law of *nature* (meaning, by those expressions, the law of God), the aggregate of the
rules, established by political superiors, is frequently styled *positive* law, or law existing *by position.* As contradistinguished to
the rules which I style *positive morality,* and on which I shall
touch immediately, the aggregate of the rules, established by
political superiors, may also be marked commodiously with the
name of *positive law.* For the sake, then, of getting a name brief
and distinctive at once, and agreeable to frequent usage, I style
that aggregate of rules, or any portion of that aggregate, *positive
law:* though rules, which are *not* established by political superiors, are also *positive,* or exist *by position,* if they be rules or
laws, in the proper signification of the term.

Though *some* of the laws or rules, which are set by men to
men, are established by political superiors, *others* are *not* established by political superiors, or are *not* established by political
superiors, in that capacity or character.

Closely analogous to human laws of this second class, are a
set of objects frequently but *improperly* termed *laws,* being
rules set and enforced by *mere opinion,* that is, by the opinions
or sentiments held or felt by an indeterminate body of men in
regard to human conduct. Instances of such a use of the term
law are the expressions—'The law of honour;' 'The law set by
fashion;' and rules of this species constitute much of what is
usually termed 'International law.'

The aggregate of human laws properly so called belonging to
the second of the classes above mentioned, with the aggregate
of objects *improperly* but by *close analogy* termed laws, I place
together in a common class, and denote them by the term *posi-*

tive morality. The name *morality* severs them from *positive law,* while the epithet *positive* disjoins them from the *law of God.* And to the end of obviating confusion, it is necessary or expedient that they *should* be disjoined from the latter by that distinguishing epithet. For the name *morality* (or *morals*), when standing unqualified or alone, denotes indifferently either of the following objects: namely, positive morality *as it is,* or without regard to its merits; and positive morality *as it would be,* if it conformed to the law of God, and were, therefore, deserving of *approbation.*

Besides the various sorts of rules which are included in the literal acceptation of the term law, and those which are by a close and striking analogy, though improperly, termed laws, there are numerous applications of the term law, which rest upon a slender analogy and are merely metaphorical or figurative. Such is the case when we talk of *laws* observed by the lower animals; of *laws* regulating the growth or decay of vegetables; of *laws* determining the movements of inanimate bodies or masses. For where *intelligence* is not, or where it is too bounded to take the name of *reason,* and, therefore, is too bounded to conceive the purpose of a law, there is not the *will* which law can work on, or which duty can incite or restrain. Yet through these misapplications of a *name,* flagrant as the metaphor is, has the field of jurisprudence and morals been deluged with muddy speculation.

Having suggested the *purpose* of my attempt to determine the province of jurisprudence: to distinguish positive law, the appropriate matter of jurisprudence, from the various objects to which it is related by resemblance, and to which it is related, nearly or remotely, by a strong or slender analogy: I shall now state the essentials of *a law* or *rule* (taken with the largest signification which can be given to the term *properly*).

Every *law* or *rule* (taken with the largest signification which can be given to the term *properly*) is a *command.* Or, rather, laws or rules, properly so called, are a *species* of commands.

Now, since the term *command* comprises the term *law,* the first is the simpler as well as the larger of the two. But, simple as it is, it admits of explanation. And, since it is the *key* to the sciences of jurisprudence and morals, its meaning should be analysed with precision.

Accordingly, I shall endeavour, in the first instance, to analyse the meaning of '*command:*' an analysis which I fear, will task the patience of my hearers, but which they will bear with cheerfulness, or, at least, with resignation, if they consider the difficulty of performing it. The elements of a science are precisely the parts of it which are explained least easily. Terms that are the largest, and, therefore, the simplest of a series, are without equivalent expressions into which we can resolve them *concisely*. And when we endeavour to *define* them, or to translate them into terms which we suppose are better understood, we are forced upon awkward and tedious circumlocutions.

If you express or intimate a wish that I shall do or forbear from some act, and if you will visit me with an evil in case I comply not with your wish, the *expression* or *intimation* of your wish is a *command*. A command is distinguished from other significations of desire, not by the style in which the desire is signified, but by the power and the purpose of the party commanding to inflict an evil or pain in case the desire be disregarded. If you cannot or will not harm me in case I comply not with your wish, the expression of your wish is not a command, although you utter your wish in imperative phrase. If you are able and willing to harm me in case I comply not with your wish, the expression of your wish amounts to a command, although you are prompted by a spirit of courtesy to utter it in the shape of a request. 'Preces erant, sed *quibus contradici non posset.*' Such is the language of Tacitus, when speaking of a petition by the soldiery to a son and lieutenant of Vespasian.

A command, then, is a signification of desire. But a command is distinguished from other significations of desire by this peculiarity: that the party to whom it is directed is liable to evil from the other, in case he comply not with the desire.

Being liable to evil from you if I comply not with a wish which you signify, I am *bound* or *obliged* by your command, or I lie under a *duty* to obey it. If, in spite of that evil in prospect, I comply not with the wish which you signify, I am said to disobey your command, or to violate the duty which it imposes.

Command and duty are, therefore, correlative terms: the meaning denoted by each being implied or supposed by the other. Or (changing the expression) wherever a duty lies, a command has been signified; and whenever a command is signified, a duty is imposed.

Concisely expressed, the meaning of the correlative expressions is this. He who will inflict an evil in case his desire be disregarded, utters a command by expressing or intimating his desire: He who is liable to the evil in case he disregard the desire, is bound or obliged by the command.

The evil which will probably be incurred in case a command be disobeyed or (to use an equivalent expression) in case a duty be broken, is frequently called a *sanction,* or an *enforcement of obedience.* Or (varying the phrase) the command or the duty is said to be *sanctioned* or *enforced* by the chance of incurring the evil.

Considered as thus abstracted from the command and the duty which it enforces, the evil to be incurred by disobedience is frequently styled a *punishment.* But, as punishments, strictly so called, are only a *class* of sanctions, the term is too narrow to express the meaning adequately.

I observe that Dr. Paley, in his analysis of the term *obligation,* lays much stress upon the *violence* of the motive to compliance. In so far as I can gather a meaning from his loose and inconsistent statement, his meaning appears to be this: that unless the motive to compliance be *violent* or *intense,* the expression or intimation of a wish is not a *command,* nor does the party to whom it is directed lie under a *duty* to regard it.

If he means, by a *violent* motive, a motive operating with certainty, his proposition is manifestly false. The greater the evil to be incurred in case the wish be disregarded, and the greater the chance of incurring it on that same event, the greater, no doubt, is the *chance* that the wish will *not* be disregarded. But no conceivable motive will *certainly* determine to compliance, or no conceivable motive will render obedience inevitable. If Paley's proposition be true, in the sense which I have now ascribed to it, commands and duties are simply impossible. Or, reducing his proposition to absurdity by a consequence as manifestly false, commands and duties are possible, but are never disobeyed or broken.

If he means by a *violent* motive, an evil which inspires fear, his meaning is simply this: that the party bound by a command is bound by the prospect of an evil. For that which is not feared is not apprehended as an evil: or (changing the shape of the expression) is not an evil in prospect.

The truth is, that the magnitude of the eventual evil, and the magnitude of the chance of incurring it, are foreign to the matter in question. The greater the eventual evil, and the greater the chance of incurring it, the greater is the efficacy of the command, and the greater is the strength of the obligation: Or (substituting expressions exactly equivalent), the greater is the *chance* that the command will be obeyed, and that the duty will not be broken. But where there is the smallest chance of incurring the smallest evil, the expression of a wish amounts to a command, and, therefore, imposes a duty. The sanction, if you will, is feeble or insufficient; but still there *is* a sanction, and, therefore, a duty and a command.

By some celebrated writers (by Locke, Bentham, and, I think, Paley), the term *sanction,* or *enforcement of obedience,* is applied to conditional good as well as to conditional evil: to reward as well as to punishment. But, with all my habitual veneration for the names of Locke and Bentham, I think that this extension of the term is pregnant with confusion and perplexity.

Rewards are, indisputably, *motives* to comply with the wishes of others. But to talk of commands and duties as *sanctioned* or *enforced* by rewards, or to talk of rewards as *obliging* or *constraining* to obedience, is surely a wide departure from the established meaning of the terms.

If *you* expressed a desire that *I* should render a service, and if you proffered a reward as the motive or inducement to render it, *you* would scarcely be said to *command* the service, nor should *I*, in ordinary language, be *obliged* to render it. In ordinary language, *you* would *promise* me a reward, on condition of my rendering the service, whilst *I* might be *incited* or *persuaded* to render it by the hope of obtaining the reward.

Again: If a law hold out a *reward* as an inducement to do some act, an eventual *right* is conferred, and not an *obligation* imposed, upon those who shall act accordingly: The *imperative* part of the law being addressed or directed to the party whom it requires to *render* the reward.

In short, I am determined or inclined to comply with the wish of another, by the fear of disadvantage or evil. I am also determined or inclined to comply with the wish of another, by the hope of advantage or good. But it is only by the chance of incurring *evil,* that I am *bound* or *obliged* to compliance. It is only by conditional *evil,* that duties are *sanctioned* or *enforced.* It is the power and the purpose of inflicting eventual *evil,* and *not* the power and the purpose of imparting eventual *good,* which gives to the expression of a wish the name of a *command.*

If we put *reward* into the import of the term *sanction,* we must engage in a toilsome struggle with the current of ordinary speech; and shall often slide unconsciously, notwithstanding our efforts to the contrary, into the narrower and customary meaning.

It appears, then, from what has been premised, that the ideas or notions comprehended by the term *command* are the following. 1. A wish or desire conceived by a rational being, that another rational being shall do or forbear. 2. An evil to proceed from the former, and to be incurred by the latter, in case the latter comply not with the wish. 3. An expression or intimation of the wish by words or other signs.

It also appears from what has been premised, that *command, duty,* and *sanction* are inseparably connected terms: that each embraces the same ideas as the others, though each denotes those ideas in a peculiar order or series.

'A wish conceived by one, and expressed or intimated to another, with an evil to be inflicted and incurred in case the wish be disregarded,' are signified directly and indirectly by each of the three expressions. Each is the name of the same complex notion.

But when I am talking *directly* of the expression or intimation of the wish, I employ the term *command:* The expression or intimation of the wish being presented *prominently* to my hearer; whilst the evil to be incurred, with the chance of incurring it, are kept (if I may so express myself) in the background of my picture.

When I am talking *directly* of the chance of incurring the evil, or (changing the expression) of the liability or obnoxiousness to the evil, I employ the term *duty,* or the term *obligation:* The liability or obnoxiousness to the evil being put foremost, and the rest of the complex notion being signified implicitly.

When I am talking *immediately* of the evil itself, I employ the term *sanction,* or a term of the like import: The evil to be incurred being signified directly; whilst the obnoxiousness to that evil, with the expression or intimation of the wish, are indicated indirectly or obliquely.

To those who are familiar with the language of logicians (language unrivalled for brevity, distinctness, and precision), I can express my meaning accurately in a breath.—Each of the three terms *signifies* the same notion; but each *denotes* a different part of that notion, and *connotes* the residue.

Commands are of two species. Some are *laws* or *rules*. The others have not acquired an appropriate name, nor does language afford an expression which will mark them briefly and precisely. I must, therefore, note them as well as I can by the ambiguous and inexpressive name of '*occasional* or *particular* commands.'

The term *laws* or *rules* being not unfrequently applied to occasional or particular commands, it is hardly possible to describe a line of separation which shall consist in every respect with established forms of speech. But the distinction between laws and particular commands may, I think, be stated in the following manner.

By every command, the party to whom it is directed is obliged to do or to forbear.

Now where it obliges *generally* to acts or forbearances of a *class*, a command is a law or rule. But where it obliges to a *specific* act or forbearance, or to acts or forbearances which it determines *specifically* or *individually*, a command is occasional or particular. In other words, a class or description of acts is determined by a law or rule, and acts of that class or description are enjoined or forbidden generally. But where a command is occasional or particular, the act or acts, which the command enjoins or forbids, are assigned or determined by their specific or individual natures as well as by the class or description to which they belong.

The statement which I have given in abstract expressions I will now endeavour to illustrate by apt examples.

If you command your servant to go on a given errand, or *not* to leave your house on a given evening, or to rise at such an hour on such a morning, or to rise at that hour during the next week or month, the command is occasional or particular. For the act or acts enjoined or forbidden are specially determined or assigned.

But if you command him *simply* to rise at that hour, or to rise at that hour *always*, or to rise at that hour *till further orders*, it may be said, with propriety, that you lay down a *rule* for the guidance of your servant's conduct. For no specific act is assigned by the command, but the command obliges him generally to acts of a determined class.

If a regiment be ordered to attack or defend a post, or to quell a riot, or to march from their present quarters, the command is occasioned or particular. But an order to exercise daily till further orders shall be given would be called a *general* order, and *might* be called a *rule*.

If Parliament prohibited simply the exportation of corn, either for a given period or indefinitely, it would establish a law or rule: a *kind* or *sort* of acts being determined by the command, and acts of that kind or sort being *generally* forbidden. But an order issued by Parliament to meet an impending scarcity, and stopping the exportation of corn *then shipped and in port,* would not be a law or rule, though issued by the sovereign legislature. The order regarding exclusively a specified quantity of corn, the negative acts or forbearances, enjoined by the command, would be determined specifically or individually by the determinate nature of their subject.

As issued by a sovereign legislature, and as wearing the form of a law, the order which I have now imagined would probably be *called* a law. And hence the difficulty of drawing a distinct boundary between laws and occasional commands.

Again: An act which is not an offense, according to the existing law, moves the sovereign to displeasure: and, though the authors of the act are legally innocent or unoffending, the sovereign commands that they shall be punished. As enjoining a specific punishment in that specific case, and as not enjoining generally acts or forbearances of a class, the order uttered by the sovereign is not a law or rule.

Whether such an order would be *called* a law, seems to depend upon circumstances which are purely immaterial: immaterial, that is, with reference to the present purpose, though material with reference to others. If made by a sovereign assembly deliberately, and with the forms of legislation, it would probably be called a law. If uttered by an absolute monarch, without deliberation or ceremony, it would scarcely be confounded with acts of legislation, and would be styled an arbitrary command. Yet, on either of these suppositions, its nature would be the same. It would not be a law or rule, but an occasional or particular command of the sovereign One or Number.

To conclude with an example which best illustrates the distinction, and which shows the importance of the distinction most conspicuously, *judicial commands* are commonly occasional or particular, although the commands which they are calculated to enforce are commonly laws or rules.

For instance, the lawgiver commands that thieves shall be hanged. A specific theft and a specified thief being given, the judge commands that the thief shall be hanged, agreeably to the command of the lawgiver.

Now the lawgiver determines a class or description of acts; prohibits acts of the class generally and indefinitely; and commands, with the like generality, that punishment shall follow transgression. The command of the lawgiver is, therefore, a law or rule. But the command of the judge is occasional or particular. For he orders a specific punishment, as the consequence of a specific offence.

MAX WEBER

Types of Legitimate Authority

Max Weber, 1846–1920, was a German professor of law, economics, and sociology. Enormously learned, capable both of broad systematic synthesis and of carefully focused analysis, he stands as one of the truly great students of society and social man. In his many works, Weber seeks to exhibit the connections between the formal patterns of behavior which collectively constitute society, and the significance with which men invest those patterns. He deals, in short, with the relations between institutions and values. In the present selection, Weber is trying to account for the fact that voluntary (though perhaps unhappy) compliance with authority is the norm in human society, and either disobedience or coercion the exception. Weber finds a key in the concept of "legitimacy," the belief by both superior and inferior that the superior has a right to issue commands. Weber, like Austin, deliberately sets to one side the question whether the commands are good ones. Unlike Austin, however, he reduces to a secondary role the fear of sanctions as a psychological explanation for obedience.

Reprinted with permission of The Free Press of Glencoe from Max Weber, *Theory of Social and Economic Organization*, translated by A. M. Henderson and T. Parsons (New York: Oxford University Press, 1947). Copyright 1947 by the Oxford University Press, New York, Inc.

I. The Basis of Legitimacy

1: THE DEFINITION, CONDITIONS, AND TYPES OF IMPERATIVE CONTROL

"Imperative co-ordination" was defined above as the probability that certain specific commands (or all commands) from a given source will be obeyed by a given group of persons. It thus does not include every mode of exercising "power" or "influence" over other persons. The motives of obedience to commands in this sense can rest on considerations varying over a wide range from case to case; all the way from simple habituation to the most purely rational calculation of advantage. A criterion of every true relation of imperative control, however, is a certain minimum of voluntary submission; thus an interest (based on ulterior motives or genuine acceptance) in obedience.

Not every case of imperative co-ordination makes use of economic means; *still less* does it always have economic objectives. But normally (not always) the imperative co-ordination of the action of a considerable number of men requires control of a staff of persons. It is necessary, that is, that there should be a relatively high probability that the action of a definite, supposedly reliable group of persons will be primarily oriented to the execution of the supreme authority's general policy and specific commands.

The members of the administrative staff may be bound to obedience to their superior (or superiors) by custom, by affectual ties, by a purely material complex of interests, or by ideal (*wertrational*) motives. *Purely* material interests and calculations of advantage as the basis of solidarity between the chief and his administrative staff result, in this as in other connexions, in a relatively unstable situation. Normally other elements, affectual and ideal, supplement such interests. In certain exceptional, temporary cases the former may be alone decisive. In everyday routine life these relationships, like others, are governed by custom and in addition, material calculation of advantage. But these factors, custom and personal advantage, purely affectual or ideal motives of solidarity, do not, even taken together, form a sufficiently reliable basis for a system of imperative co-ordination. In addition there is normally a further element, the belief in legitimacy.

It is an induction from experience that no system of authority voluntarily limits itself to the appeal to material or affectual or ideal motives as a basis for guaranteeing its continuance. In addition every such system attempts to establish and to cultivate the belief in its "legitimacy." But according to the kind of legitimacy which is claimed, the type of obedience, the kind of administrative staff developed to guarantee it, and the mode of exercising authority, will all differ fundamentally. Equally fundamental is the variation in effect. Hence, it is useful to classify the types of authority according to the kind of claim to legitimacy typically made by each. In doing this it is best to start from modern and therefore more familiar examples.

1. The choice of this rather than some other basis of classification can only be justified by its results. The fact that certain other typical criteria of variation are thereby neglected for the time being and can only be introduced at a later stage is not a decisive difficulty. The "legitimacy" of a system of authority has far more than a merely "ideal" significance, if only because it has very definite relations to the legitimacy of property.

2. Not every "claim" which is protected by custom or by law should be spoken of as involving a relation of authority. Otherwise the worker, in his claim for fulfilment of the wage contract, would be exercising "authority" over his employer because his claim can, on occasion, be enforced by order of a court. Actually his formal status is that of party to a contractual relationship with his employer, in which he has certain "rights" to receive payments. At the same time the concept of a relation of authority naturally does not exclude the possibility that it has originated in a formally free contract. This is true of the authority of the employer over the worker as manifested in the former's rules and instructions regarding the work process; and also of the authority of a feudal lord over a vassal who has freely entered into the relation of fealty. That subjection to military discipline is formally "involuntary" while that to the discipline of the factory is voluntary does not alter the fact that the latter is also a case of subjection to authority. The position of a bureaucratic official is also entered into by contract and can be freely resigned, and even the status of "subject" can often be freely entered into and (in certain circumstances) freely repudiated. Only in the limiting case of the slave is formal subjection to authority absolutely involuntary.

Another case, in some respects related, is that of economic "power" based on monopolistic position; that is, in this case, the possibility of "dictating" the terms of exchange to contractual partners. This will not, taken by itself, be considered to constitute "authority" any more than any other kind of "influence" which is derived from some kind of superiority, as by virtue of erotic attractiveness, skill in sport or in discussion. Even if a big bank is in a position to force other banks into a cartel arrangement, this will not alone be sufficient to justify calling it a relation of imperative co-ordination. But if there is an immediate relation of command and obedience such that the management of the first bank can give orders to the others with the claim that they shall, and the probability that they will, be obeyed purely as such regardless of particular content, and if their carrying out is supervised, it is another matter. Naturally, here as everywhere the transitions are gradual; there are all sorts of intermediate steps between mere indebtedness and debt slavery. Even the position of a "salon" can come very close to the borderline of authoritarian domination and yet not necessarily constitute a system of authority. Sharp differentiation in concrete fact is often impossible, but this makes clarity in the analytical distinctions all the more important.

3. Naturally, the legitimacy of a system of authority may be treated sociologically only as the probability that to a relevant degree the appropriate attitudes will exist, and the corresponding practical conduct ensue. It is by no means true that every case of submissiveness to persons in positions of power is primarily (or even at all) oriented to this belief. Loyalty may be hypocritically simulated by individuals or by whole groups on purely opportunistic grounds, carried out in practice for reasons of material self-interest. Or people may submit from individual weakness and helplessness because there is no acceptable alternative. But these considerations are not decisive for the classification of types of imperative co-ordination. What is important is the fact that in a given case the particular claim to legitimacy is to a significant degree and according to its type treated as "valid"; that this fact confirms the position of the persons claiming authority and that it helps to determine the choice of means of its exercise.

Furthermore a system of imperative co-ordination may—as often occurs in practice—be so completely assured of dominance, on the one hand by the obvious community of interests between the chief and his administrative staff as opposed to the subjects (bodyguards, Pretorians, "red" or "white" guards), on the other hand by the helplessness of the latter, that it can afford to drop even the pretence of a claim to legitimacy. But even then the mode of legitimation of the relation between chief and his staff may vary widely according to the type of basis of the relation of authority between them, and, as will be shown, this variation is highly significant for the structure of imperative co-ordination.

4. "Obedience" will be taken to mean that the action of the person obeying follows in essentials such a course that the content of the command may be taken to have become the basis of action for its own sake. Furthermore, the fact that it is so taken is referable only to the formal obligation, without regard to the actor's own attitude to the value or lack of value of the content of the command as such.

5. Subjectively, the causal sequence may vary, especially as between "submission" and "sympathetic agreement." This distinction is not, however, significant for the present classification of types of authority.

6. The scope of determination of social relationships and cultural phenomena by authority and imperative co-ordination is considerably broader than appears at first sight. For instance, the authority exercised in the school has much to do with the determination of the forms of speech and of written language which are regarded as orthodox. The official languages of autonomous political units, hence of their ruling groups, have often become in this sense orthodox forms of speech and writing and have even led to the formation of separate "nations" (for instance, the separation of Holland from Germany). The authority of parents and of the school, however, extends far beyond the determination of such cultural patterns which are perhaps only apparently formal, to the formation of the character of the young, and hence of human beings generally.

7. The fact that the chief and his administrative staff often appear formally as servants or agents of those they rule, naturally does nothing whatever to disprove the authoritarian character of the relationship. There will be occasion later to speak of the substantive features of so-called "democracy." But a certain minimum of assured power to issue commands, thus of "authority," must be provided for in nearly every conceivable case.

2: THE THREE PURE TYPES OF LEGITIMATE AUTHORITY

There are three pure types of legitimate authority. The validity of their claims to legitimacy may be based on:

1. Rational grounds—resting on a belief in the "legality" of patterns of normative rules and the right of those elevated to authority under such rules to issue commands (legal authority);

2. Traditional grounds—resting on an established belief in the sanctity of immemorial traditions and the legitimacy of the status of those exercising authority under them (traditional authority); or finally,

3. Charismatic grounds—resting on devotion to the specific and exceptional sanctity, heroism or exemplary character of an individual person, and of the normative patterns or order revealed or ordained by him (charismatic authority).

In the case of legal authority, obedience is owed to the legally established impersonal order. It extends to the persons exercising the authority of office under it only by virtue of the formal legality of their commands and only within the scope of authority of the office. In the case of traditional authority, obedience is owed to the *person* of the chief who occupies the traditionally sanctioned position of authority and who is (within its sphere) bound by tradition. But here the obligation of obedience is not based on the impersonal order, but is a matter of personal loyalty within the area of accustomed obligations. In the case of charismatic authority, it is the charismatically qualified leader as such who is obeyed by virtue of personal trust in him and his revelation, his heroism or his exemplary qualities so far as they fall within the scope of the individual's belief in his charisma.

1. The usefulness of the above classification can only be judged by its results in promoting systematic analysis. The concept of "charisma" ("the gift of grace") is taken from the vocabulary of early Christianity. For the Christian religious organization Rudolf Sohm, in his *Kirchenrecht,* was the first to clarify the substance of the concept, even though he did not use the same terminology. Others (for instance, Hollin, *Enthusiasmus und Bussgewalt*) have clarified certain important consequences of it. It is thus nothing new.

2. The fact that none of these three ideal types, the elucidation of which will occupy the following pages, is usually to be found in historical cases in "pure" form, is naturally not a valid objec-

tion to attempting their conceptual formulation in the sharpest possible form. In this respect the present case is no different from many others. Later on (§ 11 ff.) the transformation of pure charisma by the process of routinization will be discussed and thereby the relevance of the concept to the understanding of empirical systems of authority considerably increased. But even so it may be said of every empirically historical phenomenon of authority that it is not likely to be "as an open book." Analysis in terms of sociological types has, after all, as compared with purely empirical historical investigation, certain advantages which should not be minimized. That is, it can in the particular case of a concrete form of authority determine what conforms to or approximates such types as "charisma," "hereditary charisma" (§ 10, 11), "the charisma of office," "patriarchy" (§ 7), "bureaucracy" (§ 4), the authority of status groups, and in doing so it can work with relatively unambiguous concepts. But the idea that the whole of concrete historical reality can be exhausted in the conceptual scheme about to be developed is as far from the author's thoughts as anything could be.

II. Legal Authority with a Bureaucratic Administrative Staff *

3: LEGAL AUTHORITY: THE PURE TYPE WITH EMPLOYMENT OF A BUREAUCRATIC ADMINISTRATIVE STAFF

The effectiveness of legal authority rests on the acceptance of the validity of the following mutually inter-dependent ideas.

1. That any given legal norm may be established by agreement or by imposition, on grounds of expediency or rational values or both, with a claim to obedience at least on the part of the members of the corporate group. This is, however, usually extended to include all persons within the sphere of authority or of power in question—which in the case of territorial bodies is the territorial area—who stand in certain social relationships or carry out forms of social action which in the order governing the corporate group have been declared to be relevant.

2. That every body of law consists essentially in a consistent

---

* The specifically modern type of administration has intentionally been taken as a point of departure in order to make it possible later to contrast the others with it.

system of abstract rules which have normally been intentionally established. Furthermore, administration of law is held to consist in the application of these rules to particular cases; the administrative process in the rational pursuit of the interests which are specified in the order governing the corporate group within the limits laid down by legal precepts and following principles which are capable of generalized formulation and are approved in the order governing the group, or at least not disapproved in it.

3. That thus the typical person in authority occupies an "office." In the action associated with his status, including the commands he issues to others, he is subject to an impersonal order to which his actions are oriented. This is true not only for persons exercising legal authority who are in the usual sense "officials," but, for instance, for the elected president of a state.

4. That the person who obeys authority does so, as it is usually stated, only in his capacity as a "member" of the corporate group and what he obeys is only "the law." He may in this connexion be the member of an association, of a territorial commune, of a church, or a citizen of a state.

5. In conformity with point 3, it is held that the members of the corporate group, in so far as they obey a person in authority, do not owe this obedience to him as an individual, but to the impersonal order. Hence, it follows that there is an obligation to obedience only within the sphere of the rationally delimited authority which, in terms of the order, has been conferred upon him.

The following may thus be said to be the fundamental categories of rational legal authority:—

(1) A continuous organization of official functions bound by rules.

(2) A specified sphere of competence. This involves: (a) A sphere of obligations to perform functions which has been marked off as part of a systematic division of labour. (b) The provision of the incumbent with the necessary authority to carry out these functions. (c) That the necessary means of compulsion are clearly defined and their use is subject to definite conditions. A unit exercising authority which is organized in this way will be called an "administrative organ."

There are administrative organs in this sense in large-scale private organizations, in parties and armies, as well as in the state and the church. An elected president, a cabinet of ministers, or a body of elected representatives also in this sense constitute administrative organs. This is not, however, the place to discuss these concepts. Not every administrative organ is provided with compulsory powers. But this distinction is not important for present purposes.

(3) The organization of offices follows the principle of hierachy; that is, each lower office is under the control and supervision of a higher one. There is a right of appeal and of statement of grievances from the lower to the higher. Hierarchies differ in respect to whether and in what cases complaints can lead to a ruling from an authority at various points higher in the scale, and as to whether changes are imposed from higher up or the responsibility for such changes is left to the lower office, the conduct of which was the subject of complaint.

(4) The rules which regulate the conduct of an office may be technical rules or norms.* In both cases, if their application is to be fully rational, specialized training is necessary. It is thus normally true that only a person who has demonstrated an adequate technical training is qualified to be a member of the administrative staff of such an organized group, and hence only such persons are eligible for appointment to official positions. The administrative staff of a rational corporate group thus typically consists of "officials," whether the organization be devoted to political, religious, economic—in particular, capitalistic —or other ends.

(5) In the rational type it is a matter of principle that the members of the administrative staff should be completely separated from ownership of the means of production or administration. Officials, employees, and workers attached to the administrative staff do not themselves own the non-human means of production and administration. These are rather provided for their use in kind or in money, and the official is obligated to render an accounting of their use. There exists, furthermore, in principle complete separation of the property belonging to the

---

* Weber does not explain this distinction. By a "technical rule" he probably means a prescribed course of action which is dictated primarily on grounds touching efficiency of the performance of the immediate functions, while by "norms" he probably means rules which limit conduct on grounds other than those of efficiency. Of course, in one sense all rules are norms in that they are prescriptions for conduct, conformity with which is problematical.—Trans.

organization, which is controlled within the sphere of office, and the personal property of the official, which is available for his own private uses. There is a corresponding separation of the place in which official functions are carried out, the "office" in the sense of premises, from living quarters.

(6) In the rational type case, there is also a complete absence of appropriation of his official position by the incumbent. Where "rights" to an office exist, as in the case of judges, and recently of an increasing proportion of officials and even of workers, they do not normally serve the purpose of appropriation by the official, but of securing the purely objective and independent character of the conduct of the office so that it is oriented only to the relevant norms.

(7) Administrative acts, decisions, and rules are formulated and recorded in writing, even in cases where oral discussion is the rule or is even mandatory. This applies at least to preliminary discussions and proposals, to final decisions, and to all sorts of orders and rules. The combination of written documents and a continuous organization of official functions constitutes the "office" * which is the central focus of all types of modern corporate action.

(8) Legal authority can be exercised in a wide variety of different forms which will be distinguished and discussed later. The following analysis will be deliberately confined for the most part to the aspect of imperative co-ordination in the structure of the administrative staff. It will consist in an analysis in terms of ideal types of officialdom or "bureaucracy."

In the above outline no mention has been made of the kind of supreme head appropriate to a system of legal authority. This is a consequence of certain considerations which can only be made entirely understandable at a later stage in the analysis. There are very important types of rational imperative co-ordination which,

---

* *Bureau.* It has seemed necessary to use the English word "office" in three different meanings, which are distinguished in Weber's discussion by at least two terms. The first is *Amt,* which means "office" in the sense of the institutionally defined status of a person. The second is the "work premises" as in the expression "he spent the afternoon in his office." For this Weber uses *Bureau* as also for the third meaning which he has just defined, the "organized work process of a group." In this last sense an office is a particular type of "organization," or *Betrieb* in Weber's sense. This use is established in English in such expressions as "the District Attorney's Office has such and such functions." Which of the three meanings is involved in a given case will generally be clear from the context.—Trans.

with respect to the ultimate source of authority, belong to other categories. This is true of the hereditary charismatic type, as illustrated by hereditary monarchy and of the pure charismatic type of a president chosen by plebiscite. Other cases involve rational elements at important points, but are made up of a combination of bureaucratic and charismatic components, as is true of the cabinet form of government. Still others are subject to the authority of the chief of other corporate groups, whether their character be charismatic or bureaucratic; thus the formal head of a government department under a parliamentary regime may be a minister who occupies his position because of his authority in a party. The type of rational, legal administrative staff is capable of application in all kinds of situations and contexts. It is the most important mechanism for the administration of everyday profane affairs. For in that sphere, the exercise of authority and, more broadly, imperative co-ordination, consists precisely in administration.

*   *   *

5: THE MONOCRATIC TYPE OF BUREAUCRATIC ADMINISTRATION

Experience tends universally to show that the purely bureaucratic type of administrative organization—that is, the monocratic variety of bureaucracy—is, from a purely technical point of view, capable of attaining the highest degree of efficiency and is in this sense formally the most rational known means of carrying out imperative control over human beings. It is superior to any other form in precision, in stability, in the stringency of its discipline, and in its reliability. It thus makes possible a particularly high degree of calculability of results for the heads of the organization and for those acting in relation to it. It is finally superior both in intensive efficiency and in the scope of its operations, and is formally capable of application to all kinds of administrative tasks.

The development of the modern form of the organization of corporate groups in all fields is nothing less than identical with the development and continual spread of bureaucratic administration. This is true of church and state, of armies, political parties, economic enterprises, organizations to promote all kinds of causes, private associations, clubs, and many others. Its development is, to take the most striking case, the most crucial phenomenon of the modern Western state. However many forms there may be which do not appear to fit this pattern, such as collegial representative bodies, parliamentary committees, soviets, honorary officers, lay judges, and what not, and however much people may complain about the "evils of bureaucracy," it would be sheer illusion to think for a moment that continuous administrative work can be carried out in any field except by means of officials working in offices. The whole pattern of everyday life is cut to fit this framework. For bureaucratic administration is, other things being equal, always, from a formal, technical point of view, the most rational type. For the needs of mass administration to-day, it is completely indispensable. The choice is only that between bureaucracy and dilletantism in the field of administration.

The primary source of the superiority of bureaucratic administration lies in the role of technical knowledge which, through the development of modern technology and business methods in the production of goods, has become completely indispensable. In this respect, it makes no difference whether the economic system is organized on a capitalistic or a socialistic basis. Indeed, if in the latter case a comparable level of technical efficiency were to be achieved, it would mean a tremendous increase in the importance of specialized bureaucracy.

When those subject to bureaucratic control seek to escape the influence of the existing bureaucratic apparatus, this is normally possible only by creating an organization of their own which is equally subject to the process of bureaucratization. Similarly the existing bureaucratic apparatus is driven to continue functioning by the most powerful interests which are material and objective, but also ideal in character. Without it, a society like our own—with a separation of officials, employees, and workers from ownership of the means of administration, dependent on discipline and on technical training—could no longer function. The only exception would be those groups, such as the peasantry, who are still in possession of their own means of subsistence. Even in case of revolution by force or of occupation by an enemy, the bureaucratic machinery will normally continue to function just as it has for the previous legal government.

The question is always who controls the existing bureaucratic machinery. And such control is possible only in a very limited degree to persons who are not technical specialists. Generally speaking, the trained permanent official is more likely to get his way in the long run than his nominal superior, the Cabinet minister, who is not a specialist.

Though by no means alone, the capitalistic system has undeniably played a major role in the development of bureaucracy. Indeed, without it capitalistic production could not continue and any rational type of socialism would have simply to take it over and increase its importance. Its development, largely under capitalistic auspices, has created an urgent need for stable, strict, intensive, and calculable administration. It is this need which gives bureaucracy a crucial role in our society as the central element in any kind of large-scale administration. Only by reversion in every field—political, religious, economic, etc.—to small-scale organization would it be possible to any considerable extent to escape its influence. On the one hand, capitalism in its modern stages of development strongly tends to foster the development of bureaucracy, though both capitalism and bureaucracy have arisen from many different historical sources. Conversely, capitalism is the most rational economic basis for bureaucratic administration and enables it to develop in the most rational form, especially because, from a fiscal point of view, it supplies the necessary money resources.

Along with these fiscal conditions of efficient bureaucratic administration, there are certain extremely important conditions in the fields of communication and transportation. The precision of its functioning requires the services of the railway, the telegraph, and the telephone, and becomes increasingly dependent on them. A socialistic form of organization would not alter this fact. It would be a question whether in a socialistic system it would be possible to provide conditions for carrying out as stringent bureaucratic organization as has been possible in a capitalistic order. For socialism would, in fact, require a still higher degree of formal bureaucratization than capitalism. If this should prove not to be possible, it would demonstrate the existence of another of those fundamental elements of irrationality in social systems— a conflict between formal and substantive rationality of the sort which sociology so often encounters.

Bureaucratic administration means fundamentally the exercise of control on the basis of knowledge. This is the feature of it which makes it specifically rational. This consists on the one hand in technical knowledge which, by itself, is sufficient to ensure it a position of extraordinary power. But in addition to this, bureaucratic organizations, or the holders of power who make use of them, have the tendency to increase their power still further by the knowledge growing out of experience in the service. For they acquire through the conduct of office a special knowledge of facts and have available a store of documentary material peculiar to themselves. While not peculiar to bureaucratic organizations, the concept of "official secrets" is certainly typical of them. It stands in relation to technical knowledge in somewhat the same position as commercial secrets do to technological training. It is a product of the striving for power.

Bureaucracy is superior in knowledge, including both technical knowledge and knowledge of the concrete fact within its own sphere of interest, which is usually confined to the interests of a private business—a capitalistic enterprise. The capitalistic entrepreneur is, in our society, the only type who has been able to maintain at least relative immunity from subjection to the control of rational bureaucratic knowledge. All the rest of the population have tended to be organized in large-scale corporate groups which are inevitably subject to bureaucratic control. This is as inevitable as the dominance of precision machinery in the mass production of goods.

The following are the principal more general social consequences of bureaucratic control:—

(1) The tendency to "levelling" in the interest of the broadest possible basis of recruitment in terms of technical competence.

(2) The tendency to plutocracy growing out of the interest in the greatest possible length of technical training. To-day this often lasts up to the age of thirty.

(3) The dominance of a spirit of formalistic impersonality, "*Sine ira et studio*," without hatred or passion, and hence without affection or enthusiasm. The dominant norms are concepts of straightforward duty without regard to personal considerations. Everyone is subject to formal equality of treatment; that is, everyone in the same empirical situation. This is the spirit in which the ideal official conducts his office.

The development of bureaucracy greatly favours the levelling of social classes and this can be shown historically to be the normal tendency. Conversely, every process of social levelling creates a favourable situation for the development of bureaucracy; for it tends to eliminate class privileges, which include the appropriation of means of administration and the appropriation of authority as well as the occupation of offices on an honarary basis or as an avocation by virtue of wealth. This combination everywhere inevitably foreshadows the development of mass democracy, which will be discussed in another connexion.

The "spirit" of rational bureaucracy has normally the following general characteristics:

(1) Formalism, which is promoted by all the interests which are concerned with the security of their own personal situation, whatever this may consist in. Otherwise the door would be open to arbitrariness and hence formalism is the line of least resistance.

(2) There is another tendency, which is apparently in contradiction to the above, a contradiction which is in part genuine. It is the tendency of officials to treat their official function from what is substantively a utilitarian point of view in the interest of the welfare of those under their authority. But this utilitarian tendency is generally expressed in the enactment of corresponding regulatory measures which themselves have a formal character and tend to be treated in a formalistic spirit. This tendency to substantive rationality is supported by all those subject to authority who are not included in the class mentioned above as interested in the security of advantages already controlled. The problems which open up at this point belong in the theory of "democracy."

III. Traditional Authority

6: TRADITIONAL AUTHORITY

A system of imperative co-ordination will be called "traditional" if legitimacy is claimed for it and believed in on the basis of the sanctity of the order and the attendant powers of control as they have been handed down from the past, "have always existed." The person or persons exercising authority are designated according to traditionally transmitted rules. The object of obedience is the personal authority of the individual which he enjoys by virtue of his traditional status. The organized group exercising authority is, in the simplest case, primarily based on relations of personal loyalty, cultivated through a common process of education. The person exercising authority is not a "superior," but a personal "chief."

His administrative staff does not consist primarily of officials, but of personal retainers. Those subject to authority are not "members" of an association, but are either his traditional "comrades" or his "subjects." What determines the relations of the administrative staff to the chief is not the impersonal obligation of office, but personal loyalty to the chief.

Obedience is not owed to enacted rules, but to the person who occupies a position of authority by tradition or who has been chosen for such a position on a traditional basis. His commands are legitimized in one of two ways: (a) Partly in terms of traditions which themselves directly determine the content of the command and the objects and extent of authority. In so far as this is true, to overstep the traditional limitations would endanger his traditional status by undermining acceptance of his legitimacy. (b) In part, it is a matter of the chief's free personal decision, in that tradition leaves a certain sphere open for this. This sphere of traditional prerogative rests primarily on the fact that the obligations of obedience on the basis of personal loyalty are essentially unlimited.* There is thus a double sphere: on the one hand, of action which is bound to specific tradition; on the other hand, of that which is free of any specific rules.

In the latter sphere, the chief is free to confer "grace" on the basis of his personal pleasure or displeasure, his personal likes and dislikes, quite arbitrarily, particularly in return for gifts which often become a source of regular income. So far as his action follows principles at all, these are principles of substantive ethical common sense, of justice, or of utilitarian expediency. They are not, however, as in the case of legal authority, formal principles. The exercise of authority is normally oriented to the question of what the chief and his administrative staff will normally permit, in view of the traditional obedience of the subjects and what will or will not arouse their resistance. When resistance occurs, it is directed against the person of the chief or of a member of his staff. The accusation is that he has failed to observe the traditional limits of his authority. Opposition is not directed against the system as such.

It is impossible in the pure type of traditional authority for

* This does not seem to be a very happy formulation of the essential point. It is not necessary that the authority of a person in such a position, such as the head of a household, should be unlimited. It is rather that its extent is unspecified. It is generally limited by higher obligations, but the burden of proof rests upon the person on whom an obligation is laid that there is such a conflicting higher obligation.—Trans.

law or administrative rules to be deliberately created by legislation. What is actually new is thus claimed to have always been in force but only recently to have become known through the wisdom of the promulgator. The only documents which can play a part in the orientation of legal administration are the documents of tradition; namely, precedents.

*   *   *

IV. Charismatic Authority

10: THE PRINCIPAL CHARACTERISTICS OF CHARISMATIC AUTHORITY AND ITS RELATION TO FORMS OF COMMUNAL ORGANIZATION

The term "charisma" will be applied to a certain quality of an individual personality by virtue of which he is set apart from ordinary men and treated as endowed with supernatural, superhuman, or at least specifically exceptional powers or qualities. These are such as are not accessible to the ordinary person, but are regarded as of divine origin or as exemplary, and on the basis of them the individual concerned is treated as a leader. In primitive circumstances this peculiar kind of deference is paid to prophets, to people with a reputation for therapeutic or legal wisdom, to leaders in the hunt, and heroes in war. It is very often thought of as resting on magical powers. How the quality in question would be ultimately judged from any ethical, aesthetic, or other such point of view is naturally entirely indifferent for purposes of definition. What is alone important is how the individual is actually regarded by those subject to charismatic authority, by his "followers" or "disciples."

For present purposes it will be necessary to treat a variety of different types as being endowed with charisma in this sense. It includes the state of a "berserker" whose spells of maniac passion have, apparently wrongly, sometimes been attributed to the use of drugs. In Medieval Byzantium a group of people endowed with this type of charismatic war-like passion were maintained as a kind of weapon. It includes the "shaman," the kind of magician who in the pure type is subject to epileptoid seizures as a means of falling into trances. Another type is that of Joseph Smith, the founder of Mormonism, who, however, cannot be classified in this way with absolute certainty since there is a possibility that he was a very sophisticated type of deliberate swindler. Finally it includes the type of intellectual, such as Kurt

Eisner,* who is carried away with his own demagogic success. Sociological analysis, which must abstain from value judgments, will treat all these on the same level as the men who, according to conventional judgments, are the "greatest" heroes, prophets, and saviours.

1. It is recognition on the part of those subject to authority which is decisive for the validity of charisma. This is freely given and guaranteed by what is held to be a "sign" or proof, originally always a miracle, and consists in devotion to the corresponding revelation, hero worship, or absolute trust in the leader. But where charisma is genuine, it is not this which is the basis of the claim to legitimacy. This basis lies rather in the conception that it is the *duty* of those who have been called to a charismatic mission to recognize its quality and to act accordingly. Psychologically this "recognition" is a matter of complete personal devotion to the possessor of the quality, arising out of enthusiasm, or of despair and hope.

No prophet has ever regarded his quality as dependent on the attitudes of the masses toward him. No elective king or military leader has ever treated those who have resisted him or tried to ignore him otherwise than as delinquent in duty. Failure to take part in a military expedition under such leader, even though recruitment is formally voluntary, has universally been met with disdain.

2. If proof of his charismatic qualification fails him for long, the leader endowed with charisma tends to think his god or his magical or heroic powers have deserted him. If he is for long unsuccessful, above all if his leadership fails to benefit his followers, it is likely that his charismatic authority will disappear. This is the genuine charismatic meaning of the "gift of grace."

Even the old Germanic kings were sometimes rejected with scorn. Similar phenomena are very common among so-called "primitive" peoples. In China the charismatic quality of the monarch, which was transmitted unchanged by heredity, was upheld so rigidly that any misfortune whatever, not only defeats in war, but drought, floods, or astronomical phenomena which were considered unlucky, forced him to do public penance and might even force his abdication. If such things occurred, it was a sign that he did not possess the requisite charismatic virtue, he was thus not a legitimate "Son of Heaven."

* The leader of the communistic experiment in Bavaria in 1919.—Trans.

3. The corporate group which is subject to charismatic authority is based on an emotional form of communal relationship. The administrative staff of a charismatic leader does not consist of "officials"; at least its members are not technically trained. It is not chosen on the basis of social privilege nor from the point of view of domestic or personal dependency. It is rather chosen in terms of the charismatic qualities of its members. The prophet has his disciples; the war lord his selected henchmen; the leader, generally, his followers. There is no such thing as "appointment" or "dismissal," no career, no promotion. There is only a "call" at the instance of the leader on the basis of the charismatic qualification of those he summons. There is no hierarchy; the leader merely intervenes in general or in individual cases when he considers the members of his staff inadequate to a task with which they have been entrusted. There is no such thing as a definite sphere of authority and of competence, and no appropriation of official powers on the basis of social privileges. There may, however, be territorial or functional limits to charismatic powers and to the individual's "mission." There is no such thing as a salary or a benefice. Disciples or followers tend to live primarily in a communistic relationship with their leader on means which have been provided by voluntary gift. There are no established administrative organs. In their place are agents who have been provided with charismatic authority by their chief or who possess charisma of their own. There is no system of formal rules, of abstract legal principles, and hence no process of judicial decision oriented to them. But equally there is no legal wisdom oriented to judicial precedent. Formally concrete judgments are newly created from case to case and are originally regarded as divine judgments and revelations. From a substantive point of view, every charismatic authority would have to subscribe to the proposition, "It is written . . . , but I say unto you. . ." The genuine prophet, like the genuine military leader and every true leader in this sense, preaches, creates, or demands *new* obligations. In the pure type of charisma, these are imposed on the authority of revolution by oracles, or of the leader's own will, and are recognized by the members of the religious, military, or party group, because they come from such a source. Recognition is a duty. When such an authority comes into conflict with the competing authority of another who also claims charismatic sanction, the only recourse is to some kind of a contest, by magical

means or even an actual physical battle of the leaders. In principle, only one side can be in the right in such a conflict; the other must be guilty of a wrong which has to be expiated.

Charismatic authority is thus specifically outside the realm of everyday routine and the profane sphere. In this respect, it is sharply opposed both to rational, and particularly bureaucratic, authority, and to traditional authority, whether in its patriarchal, patrimonial, or any other form. Both rational and traditional authority are specifically forms of everyday routine control of action; while the charismatic type is the direct antithesis of this. Bureaucratic authority is specifically rational in the sense of being bound to intellectually analysable rules; while charismatic authority is specifically irrational in the sense of being foreign to all rules. Traditional authority is bound to the precedents handed down from the past and to this extent is also oriented to rules. Within the sphere of its claims, charismatic authority repudiates the past, and is in this sense a specifically revolutionary force. It recognizes no appropriation of positions of power by virtue of the possession of property, either on the part of a chief or of socially privileged groups. The only basis of legitimacy for it is personal charisma, so long as it is proved; that is, as long as it receives recognition and is able to satisfy the followers or disciples. But this lasts only so long as the belief in its charismatic inspiration remains.

The above is scarcely in need of further discussion. What has been said applies to the position of authority of such elected monarchs as Napoleon, with his use of the plebiscite. It applies to the "rule of genius," which has elevated people of humble origin to thrones and high military commands, just as much as it applies to religious prophets or war heroes.

4. Pure charisma is specifically foreign to economic considerations. Whenever it appears, it constitutes a "call" in the most emphatic sense of the word, a "mission" or a "spiritual duty." In the pure type, it disdains and repudiates economic exploitation of the gifts of grace as a source of income, though, to be sure, this often remains more an ideal than a fact. It is not that charisma always means the renunciation of property or even of acquisition, as under certain circumstances prophets and their disciples do. The heroic warrior and his followers actively seek "booty"; the elective ruler or the charismatic party leader requires the material means of power. The former in addition requires a

brilliant display of his authority to bolster his prestige. What is despised, so long as the genuinely charismatic type is adhered to, is traditional or rational everyday economizing, the attainment of a regular income by continuous economic activity devoted to this end. Support by gifts, sometimes on a grand scale involving foundations, even by bribery and grand-scale honoraria, or by begging, constitute the strictly voluntary type of support. On the other hand, "booty," or coercion, whether by force or by other means, is the other typical form of charismatic provision for needs. From the point of view of rational economic activity, charisma is a typical anti-economic force. It repudiates any sort of involvement in the everyday routine world. It can only tolerate, with an attitude of complete emotional indifference, irregular, unsystematic, acquisitive acts. In that it relieves the recipient of economic concerns, dependence on property income can be the economic basis of a charismatic mode of life for some groups; but that is not usually acceptable for the normal charismatic "revolutionary."

The fact that incumbency of church office has been forbidden to the Jesuits is a rationalized application of this principle of discipleship. The fact that all the "virtuosi" of asceticism, the mendicant orders, and fighters for a faith belong in this category, is quite clear. Almost all prophets have been supported by voluntary gifts. The well-known saying of St. Paul, "If a man does not work, neither shall he eat," was directed against the swarm of charismatic missionaries. It obviously has nothing to do with a positive valuation of economic activity for its own sake, but only lays it down as a duty of each individual somehow to provide for his own support. This because he realized that the purely charismatic parable of the lilies of the field was not capable of literal application, but at best "taking no thought for the morrow" could be hoped for. On the other hand, in such a case as primarily an artistic type of charismatic discipleship, it is conceivable that insulation from economic struggle should mean limitation of those who were really eligible to the "economically independent"; that is, to persons living on income from property. This has been true of the circle of Stefan George, at least in its primary intentions.

5. In traditionally stereotyped periods, charisma is the greatest revolutionary force. The equally revolutionary force of "reason" works from without by altering the situations of action, and

hence its problems finally in this way changing men's attitudes toward them; or it intellectualizes the individual. Charisma, on the other hand, may involve a subjective or internal reorientation born out of suffering, conflicts, or enthusiasm. It may then result in a radical alteration of the central system of attitudes and directions of action with a completely new orientation of all attitudes toward the different problems and structures of the "world." In prerationalistic periods, tradition and charisma between them have almost exhausted the whole of the orientation of action.

*   *   *

JOHN LOCKE

The Origins and Purposes of Political Societies

John Locke, 1632–1702, the most influential English thinker before Hume, is known today principally for two works, the long Essay Concerning Human Understanding, *and the relatively brief* Second Treatise Concerning Civil Government, *from which this selection is taken. The two treatises on civil government, published after the Glorious Revolution of 1688 but probably written some years earlier, contain an extended attack on the theory of the divine right of kings as expounded by Sir Robert Filmer, and a systematic account of the social contract theory which Locke wished to put in its place. Locke follows the ancient custom of tracing civil government back to a supposed beginning in pre-political society—the so-called state of nature—but his argument makes it clear that he is interested in the moral justification of political authority rather than its natural history. Note the very clear connection which Locke establishes between the ends, or purposes, of government, and the extent of its authority. The ruler may exercise only those rights which the citizens have given up, and then only for the express purposes which led them originally to conclude the social contract.*

Reprinted from John Locke, *Second Treatise on Civil Government,* 1689.

Of the Beginning of Political Societies

Men being, as has been said, by nature all free, equal, and independent, no one can be put out of this estate, and subjected to the political power of another, without his own consent, which is done by agreeing with other men to join and unite into a community for their comfortable, safe, and peaceable living one amongst another, in a secure enjoyment of their properties, and a greater security against any that are not of it. This any number of men may do, because it injures not the freedom of the rest; they are left as they were in the liberty of the state of nature. When any number of men have so consented to make one community or government, they are thereby presently incorporated, and make one body politic, wherein the majority have a right to act and conclude the rest.

For when any number of men have, by the consent of every individual, made a community, they have thereby made that community one body, with a power to act as one body, which is only by the will and determination of the majority. For that which acts any community being only the consent of the individuals of it, and it being one body must move one way, it is necessary the body should move that way whither the greater force carries it, which is the consent of the majority; or else it is impossible it should act or continue one body, one community, which the consent of every individual that united into it agreed that it should; and so every one is bound by that consent to be concluded by the majority. And therefore we see that in assemblies empowered to act by positive laws, where no number is set by that positive law which empowers them, the act of the majority passes for the act of the whole, and of course determines, as having by the law of nature and reason the power of the whole.

And thus every man, by consenting with others to make one body politic under one government, puts himself under an obligation to every one of that society, to submit to the determination of the majority, and to be concluded by it; or else this original compact, whereby he with others incorporates into one society, would signify nothing, and be no compact, if he be left free and under no other ties than he was in before in the state of nature. For what appearance would there be of any compact? What new engagement if he were no farther tied by any decrees of the society, than he himself thought fit, and did actually consent to? This would be still as great a liberty as he himself had before his compact, or any one else in the state of nature hath, who may submit himself and consent to any acts of it if he thinks fit.

For if the consent of the majority shall not in reason be received as the act of the whole and conclude every individual, nothing but the consent of every individual can make anything to be the act of the whole which considering the infirmities of health and avocations of business, which in a number, though much less than that of a commonwealth, will necessarily keep many away from the public assembly, and the variety of opinions, and contrariety of interest, which unavoidably happen in all collections of men, 'tis next to impossible ever to be had. And therefore if the coming into society be upon such terms it will be only like Cato's coming into the theatre, *tantum ut exiret*. Such a constitution as this would make the mighty leviathan of a shorter duration than the feeblest creatures, and not let it outlast the day it was born in; which cannot be supposed till we can think that rational creatures should desire and constitute societies only to be dissolved. For where the majority cannot conclude the rest, there they cannot act as one body, and consequently will be immediately dissolved again.

Whosoever therefore out of a state of nature unite into a community must be understood to give up all the power necessary to the ends for which they unite into society, to the majority of the community, unless they expressly agree in any number greater than the majority. And this is done by barely agreeing to unite into one political society, which is all the compact that is, or needs be, between the individuals that enter into or make up a commonwealth. And thus that which begins and actually constitutes any political society is nothing but the consent of any number of freemen capable of a majority to unite and incorporate into such a society. And this is that, and that only, which did or could give beginning to any lawful government in the world.

To this I find two objections made.

First: That there are no instances to be found in story of a company of men independent, and equal one amongst another, that met together and in this way began and set up a government.

Secondly: 'Tis impossible of right that men should do so, because all men being born under government, they are to submit to that, and are not at liberty to begin a new one.

To the first there is this to answer—That it is not at all to be wondered that history gives us but a very little account of men that lived together in the state of nature. The inconveniences of that condition, and the love and want of society, no sooner brought any number of them together, but they presently united and incorporated if they designed to continue together. And if we may not suppose men ever to have been in the state of nature, because we hear not much of them in such a state, we may as well suppose the armies of Salmanasser of Xerxes were never children, because we hear little of them till they were men, and embodied in armies. Government is everywhere antecedent to records, and letters seldom come in amongst a people, till a long continuation of civil society has, by other more necessary arts, provided for their safety, ease, and plenty. And then they begin to look after the history of their founders, and search into their original, when they have outlived the memory of it. For 'tis with commonwealths as with particular persons, they are commonly ignorant of their own birth and infancies. And if they know anything of their original, they are beholden for it to the accidental record that others have kept of it. And those that we have of the beginning of any politics in the world, excepting that of the Jews, where God Himself immediately interposed, and which favours not at all paternal dominion, are all either plain instances of such a beginning as I have mentioned, or at least have manifest footsteps of it.

He must show a strange inclination to deny evident matter of fact when it agrees not with his hypothesis, who will not allow that the beginning of Rome and Venice were by the uniting together of several men free and independent one of another, amongst whom there was no natural superiority or subjection. And if Josephus Acosta's word may be taken, he tells us that in many parts of America there was no government at all. "There are great and apparent conjectures," says he, "that these men," speaking of those of Peru, "for a long time had neither kings nor commonwealths, but lived in troops, as they do this day in Florida, the Cheriquanas, those of Brazil, and many other nations, which have no certain kings, but as occasion is offered in peace or war, they choose their captains as they please" (1.

i., c. 25). If it be said that every man there was born subject to his father, or the head of his family, that the subjection due from a child to a father took not away his freedom of uniting into what political society he thought fit, has been already proved. But be that as it will, these men, it is evident, were actually free; and whatever superiority some politicians now would place in any of them, they sometimes claimed it not; but by consent were all equal, till by the same consent they set rulers over themselves. So that their politic societies all began from a voluntary union, and the mutual agreement of men freely acting in the choice of their governors and forms of government.

And I hope those who went away from Sparta with Palantus, mentioned by Justin, 1. iii, c. 4, will be allowed to have been freemen, independent one of another, and to have set up a government over themselves, by their own consent. Thus I have given several examples out of history of people free and in the state of nature that, being met together, incorporated and began a commonwealth. And if the want of such instances be an argument to prove that government were not nor could not be so begun, I suppose the contenders to paternal empire were better let it alone than urge it against natural liberty. For if they can give so many instances, out of history, of governments begun upon paternal right, I think (though at best an argument from what has been, to what should of right be, has no great force) one might, without any great danger, yield them the cause. But if I might advise them in the case, they would do well not to search too much into the original of governments as they have begun *de facto*, lest they should find at the foundation of most of them something very little favourable to the design they promote and such a power as they contend for.

But to conclude, reason being plain on our side, that men are naturally free, and the examples of history showing that the governments of the world, that were begun in peace, had their beginning laid on that foundation, and were made by the consent of the people, there can be little room for doubt, either where the right is, or what has been the opinion or practice of mankind, about the first erecting of governments.

I will not deny, that if we look back as far as history will direct us, towards the original of commonwealths, we shall generally find them under the government and administration of one man. And I am also apt to believe that where a family were

numerous enough to subsist by itself, and continued entire together, without mixing with others, as it often happens where
there is much land and few people, the government commonly
began in the father. For the father having, by the law of nature,
the same power with every man else to punish as he thought fit
any offences against that law, might thereby punish his transgressing children, even when they were men, and out of their
pupilage; and they were very likely to submit to his punishment,
and all join with him against the offender, in their turns, giving
him thereby power to execute his sentence against any transgression, and so in effect make him the lawmaker and governor
over all that remained in conjunction with his family. He was
fittest to be trusted; paternal affection secured their property
and interest under his care; and the custom of obeying him in
their childhood made it easier to submit to him rather than to
any other. If therefore they must have one to rule them, as government is hardly to be avoided amongst men that live together,
who so likely to be the man as he that was their common father;
unless negligence, cruelty, or any other defect of mind or body
made him unfit for it? But when either the father died, and left
his next heir, for want of age, wisdom, courage, or any other
qualities, less fit for rule, or where several families met and consented to continue together, there it is not to be doubted but
they used their natural freedom to set up him whom they judged
the ablest and most likely to rule well over them. Conformable
hereunto we find the people of America who (living out of the
reach of the conquering swords and spreading domination of the
two great empires of Peru and Mexico) enjoyed their own natural freedom, though, *cœteris paribus*, they commonly prefer the
heir of their deceased king; yet if they find him any way weak
or incapable they pass him by and set up the stoutest and
bravest man for their ruler.

Thus, though looking back as far as records give us any account of peopling the world, and the history of nations, we commonly find the government to be in one hand; yet it destroys not
that which I affirm, viz.: that the beginning of politic society
depends upon the consent of the individuals to join into, and
make one society; who when they are thus incorporated, might
set up what form of government they thought fit. But this having
given occasion to men to mistake, and think that by nature government was monarchical, and belonged to the father, it may not

be amiss here to consider why people in the beginning generally pitched upon this form, which, though perhaps the father's preeminence might in the first institution of some commonwealths give a rise to, and place in the beginning, the power in one hand; yet it is plain that the reason that continued the form of government in a single person was not any regard or respect to paternal authority, since all petty monarchies, that is, almost all monarchies, near their original, have been commonly—at least upon occasion—elective.

First then, in the beginning of things, the father's government of the childhood of those sprung from him having accustomed them to the rule of one man, and taught them that where it was exercised with care and skill, with affection and love to those under it, it was sufficient to procure and preserve men all the political happiness they sought for in society. It was no wonder that they should pitch upon and naturally run into that form of government, which from their infancy they had been all accustomed to, and which, by experience, they had found both easy and safe. To which, if we add, that monarchy being simple and most obvious to men whom neither experience had instructed in forms of government, nor the ambition or insolence of empire had taught to beware of the encroachments of prerogative, or the inconveniences of absolute power, which monarchy in succession was apt to lay claim to, and bring upon them; it was not at all strange that they should not much trouble themselves to think of methods of restraining any exorbitances of those to whom they had given the authority over them, and of balancing the power of government, by placing several parts of it in different hands. They had neither felt the oppression of tyrannical dominion, nor did the fashion of the age, nor their possessions or way of living (which afforded little matter for covetousness or ambition), give them any reason to apprehend or provide against it; and therefore it is no wonder they put themselves into such a frame of government as was not only, as I said, most obvious and simple, but also best suited to their present state and condition, which stood more in need of defence against foreign invasions and injuries than of multiplicity of laws, where there was but very little property; and wanted not variety of rulers and abundance of officers to direct and look after their execution, where there were but few trespasses and few offenders. Since, then, those who liked one another so well as to join into society, cannot but be supposed to have some acquaintance and friendship together, and some trust one in another, they could not but have greater apprehensions of others than of one another; and therefore their first care and thought cannot but be supposed to be how to secure themselves against foreign force. It was natural for them to put themselves under a frame of government which might best serve that end; and choose the wisest and bravest man to conduct them in their wars, and lead them out against their enemies, and in this chiefly be their ruler.

Thus we see that the kings of the Indians in America—which is still a pattern of the first ages in Asia and Europe whilst the inhabitants were too few for the country, and want of people and money gave men no temptation to enlarge their possessions of land, or contest for wider extent of ground—are little more than generals of their armies; and though they command absolutely in war, yet at home and in time of peace they exercise very little dominion, and have but a very moderate sovereignty; the resolutions of peace and war being ordinarily either in the people or in a council. Though the war itself, which admits not of plurality of governors, naturally devolves the command into the king's sole authority.

And thus in Israel itself, the chief business of their judges and first kings seems to have been to be captains of war, and leaders of their armies; which (besides what is signified by going out and in before the people, which was, to march forth to war, and home again in the heads of their forces) appears plainly in the story of Jephtha. The Ammonites making war upon Israel, the Gileadites in fear send to Jephtha, a bastard of their family whom they had cast off, and article with him, if he will assist them against the Ammonites, to make him their ruler; which they do in these words: "And the people made him head and captain over them" (Judges, xi. 11), which was, as it seems, all one as to be judge. "And he judged Israel" (Judges, xii. 7), that is, was their captain-general, six years. So when Jotham upbraids the Shechemites with the obligation they had to Gideon, who had been their judge and ruler, he tells them "He fought for you, and adventured his life for, and delivered you out of the hands of Midian" (Judges, ix. 17). Nothing mentioned of him but what he did as a general; and indeed that is all is found in his history, or in any of the rest of the judges. And Abimelech particularly is called king, though at most he was but their general.

And when, being weary of the ill-conduct of Samuel's sons, the Children of Israel desired a king "like all the nations, to judge them and to go out before them, and to fight their battles" (1 Samuel, viii. 20), God, granting their desire, says to Samuel: "I will send thee a man, and thou shalt anoint him to be captain over my people Israel, that he may save my people out of the hands of the Philistines" (ix. 16). As if the only business of a king had been to lead out their armies, and fight in their defence; and accordingly at his inauguration pouring a vial of oil upon him, declares to Saul that "the Lord had anointed him to be captain over his inheritance" (x. 1). And, therefore, those who, after Saul's being solemnly chosen and saluted king by the tribes at Mizpah, were unwilling to have him their king, make no other objection but this: "How shall this man save us?" (verse 27) as if they should have said, "This man is unfit to be our king, not having skill and conduct enough in war to be able to defend us." And when God resolved to transfer the government to David, it is in these words: "But now thy kingdom shall not continue. The Lord hath sought him a man after his own heart, and the Lord hath commanded him to be captain over his people" (xiii. 4), as if the whole kingly authority were nothing else but to be their general; and, therefore, the tribes who had stuck to Saul's family, and opposed David's reign, when they came to Hebron with terms of submission to him, they tell him, amongst other arguments, they had to submit to him as to their king, that he was, in effect, their king in Saul's time, and therefore, they had no reason but to receive him as their king now. "Also," say they, "in time past, when Saul was king over us, thou wast he that leddest out and broughtest in Israel, and the Lord said unto thee, 'Thou shalt feed my people Israel, and thou shalt be a captain over Israel.'"

Thus, whether a family by degrees grew up into a commonwealth, and the fatherly authority being continued on to the elder son, every one in his turn growing up under it, tacitly submitted to it; and the easiness and equality of it not offending any one, every one acquiesced, till time seemed to have confirmed it, and settled a right of succession by prescription; or whether several families, or the descendants of several families, whom chance, neighbourhood, or business brought together, uniting into a society, the need of a general, whose conduct might defend them against their enemies in war, and the great confidence the innocency and sincerity of that poor but virtuous age (such as are almost all those which began governments that ever come to last in the world) gave men one of another, made the first beginners of commonwealth generally put the rule into one man's hand, without any other express limitation or restraint, but what the nature of the thing and the end of government required. It was given them for the public good and safety, and to those ends, in the infancies of commonwealths, they commonly used it. And unless they had done so, young societies could not have subsisted. Without such nursing fathers, without this care of the governors, all governments would have sunk under the weakness and infirmities of their infancy, the prince and people had soon perished together.

But the golden age (though before vain ambition, and *amor sceleratus habendi,* evil concupiscence had corrupted men's minds into a mistake of true power and honour) had more virtue, and consequently better governors, as well as less vicious subjects; and there was then no stretching prerogative, on the one side, to oppress the people, nor consequently, on the other, any dispute about privilege, to lessen or restrain the power of the magistrate, and so no context betwixt rulers and people about governors or government.* Yet, when ambition and luxury in future ages would retain and increase the power, without doing the business for which it was given, and, aided by flattery, taught princes to have distinct and separate interests from their people, men found it necessary to examine more carefully the original and rights of government, and to find out ways to restrain the exorbitances, and prevent the abuses of that power which, they having entrusted in another's hands only for their own good, they found was made use of to hurt them.

Thus we may see how probable it is that people that were naturally free, and by their own consent either submitted to the government of their father, or united together out of dif-

* "At the first, when some certain kind of regimen was once approved, it may be that nothing was then further thought upon for the manner of governing, but all permitted unto their wisdom and discretion, which were to rule till, by experience, they found this for all parts very inconvenient, so as the thing which they had devised for a remedy did indeed but increase the sore which it should have cured. They saw that to live by one man's will became the cause of all men's misery. This constrained them to come unto laws wherein all men might see their duty beforehand, and know the penalties of transgressing them."—Hooker (Eccl. Pol., lib. i., sec. 10).

ferent families to make a government, should generally put the
rule into one man's hands, and choose to be under the conduct
of a single person, without so much as by express conditions
limiting or regulating his power, which they thought safe enough
in his honesty and prudence, though they never dreamt of monarchy being *pure divino*, which we never heard of among mankind till it was revealed to us by the divinity of this last age, nor
ever allowed paternal power to have a right to dominion, or to be
the foundation of all government. And thus much may suffice to
show that, as far as we have any light from history, we have
reason to conclude that all peaceful beginnings of government
have been laid in the consent of the people. I say peaceful, because I shall have occasion in another place to speak of conquest, which some esteem a way of beginning of governments.

The other objection I find urged against the beginning of
polities in the way I have mentioned is this, viz.:—

That all men being born under government, some or other, it
is impossible any of them should ever be free and at liberty to
unite together and begin a new one, or ever be able to erect
a lawful government.

If this argument be good, I ask, how came so many lawful
monarchies into the world? For if anybody, upon this supposi-
tion, can show me any one man, in any age of the world, free to
begin a lawful monarchy, I will be bound to show him ten other
free men at liberty at the same time to unite and begin a new
government under a regal, or any other form, it being demon-
stration that if any one, born under the dominion of another,
may be so free as to have a right to command others in a new
and distinct empire, every one that is born under the dominion
of another may be so free too, and may become a ruler or subject of a distinct separate government. And so by this their own
principle either all men, however born, are free, or else there is
but one lawful prince, one lawful government in the world. And
then they have nothing to do but barely to show us which that
is; which, when they have done, I doubt not but all mankind
will easily agree to pay obedience to him.

Though it be a sufficient answer to their objection to show that
it involves them in the same difficulties that it doth those they
use it against, yet I shall endeavour to discover the weakness of
this argument a little farther.

"All men," say they, "are born under government, and therefore they cannot be at liberty to begin a new one. Every one is born a subject to his father, or his prince, and is therefore under the perpetual tie of subjection and allegiance." It is plain mankind never owned nor considered any such natural subjection that they were born in, to one or to the other that tied them without their own consents, to a subjection to them and their heirs.

For there are no examples so frequent in history, both sacred and profane, as those of men withdrawing themselves and their obedience from the jurisdiction they were born under, and the family or community they were bred up in, and setting up new governments in other places; from whence sprang all that number of petty commonwealths in the beginning of ages, and which always multiplied, as long as there was room enough, till the stronger or more fortunate swallowed the weaker; and those great ones again breaking to pieces, dissolved into lesser dominions, all which are so many testimonies against paternal sovereignty, and plainly prove that it was not the natural right of the father descending to his heirs that made government in the beginning, since it was impossible upon that ground there should have been so many little kingdoms, but only one universal monarchy if men had not been at liberty to separate themselves from their families and their government, be it what it will, that was set up in it, and go and make distinct commonwealths and other governments as they thought fit.

This has been the practice of the world from its first beginning to this day; nor is it now any more hindrance to the freedom of mankind that they are born under constituted and ancient polities that have established laws and set forms of government, than if they were born in the woods amongst the unconfined inhabitants that run loose in them. For those who would persuade us that by being born under any government we are naturally subjects to it, and have no more any title or pretence to the freedom of the state of Nature, have no other reason (barring that of paternal power, which we have already answered) to produce for it, but only because our fathers or progenitors passed away their natural liberty, and thereby bound up themselves and their posterity to a perpetual subjection to the government which they themselves submitted to. It is true that whatever engagements or promises any one made for himself, he is under the obligation of them, but cannot by any compact whatsoever bind his children or posterity. For his son when a man being altogether as free as his father, any act of the father can no more give away the liberty of the son than it can of anybody else. He may indeed annex such conditions to the land he enjoyed as a subject of any commonwealth as may oblige his son to be of that community, if he will enjoy those possessions which were his father's, because that estate being his father's property he may dispose or settle it as he pleases.

And this has generally given the occasion to the mistake in this matter, because commonwealths not permitting any part of their dominions to be dismembered, nor to be enjoyed by any but those of their community, the son cannot ordinarily enjoy the possessions of his father but under the same terms his father did: by becoming a member of the society; whereby he puts himself presently under the government he finds there established as much as any other subject of that commonwealth. And thus the consent of freemen, born under government, which only makes them members of it, being given separately in their turns, as each comes to be of age, and not in a multitude together. People take no notice of it, and thinking it not done at all, or not necessary, conclude they are naturally subjects as they are men.

But it is plain governments themselves understand it otherwise; they claim no power over the son, because of that they had over the father; nor look on children as being their subjects by their father's being so. If a subject of England have a child by an English woman in France, whose subject is he? Not the King of England's, for he must have leave to be admitted to the privileges of it; nor the King of France's, for how then has his father a liberty to bring him away and breed him as he pleases? And whoever was judged as a traitor or deserter, if he left or warred against a country, for being barely born in it of parents that were aliens there? It is plain then by the practice of governments themselves, as well as by the law of right reason, that a child is born a subject of no country or government. He is under his father's tuition and authority till he comes to age of discretion, and then he is a freeman, at liberty what government he will put himself under, what body politic he will unite himself to. For if an Englishman's son, born in France, be at liberty, and may do so, it is evident there is no tie upon him by his father's being a subject of that kingdom; nor is he bound up by any compact of his ancestors. And why then hath not his son by the same reason, the same liberty, though he be born anywhere else? Since the power that a father hath naturally over his children is the same wherever they be born, and the ties of natural obligations are not bounded by the positive limits of kingdoms and commonwealths.

Every man being, as has been shown, naturally free, and nothing being able to put him into subjection to any earthly power but only his own consent, it is to be considered what shall be understood to be sufficient declaration of a man's consent to make him subject to the laws of any government. There is a common distinction of an express and a tacit consent, which will concern our present case. Nobody doubts but an express consent of any man entering into any society makes him a perfect member of that society, a subject of that government. The difficulty is, what ought to be looked upon as a tacit consent, and how far it binds, *i.e.*, how far any one shall be looked on to have consented, and thereby submitted to any government, where he has made no expressions of it at all. And to this I say that every man that hath any possession or enjoyment of any part of the dominions of any government doth thereby give his tacit consent, and is as far forth obliged to obedience to the laws of that government during such enjoyment as any one under it; whether this his possession be of land to him and his heirs for ever, or a lodging only for a week; or whether it be barely travelling freely on the highway; and in effect it reaches as far as the very being of any one within the territories of that government.

To understand this the better, it is fit to consider that every man when he at first incorporates himself into any commonwealth, he, by his uniting himself thereunto, annexes also, and submits to the community those possessions which he has or shall acquire that do not already belong to any other government; for it would be a direct contradiction for any one to enter into society with others for the securing and regulating of property, and yet to suppose his land, whose property is to be regulated by the laws of the society, should be exempt from the jurisdiction of that government to which he himself, and the property of the land, is a subject. By the same act, therefore, whereby any one unites his person, which was before free, to any commonwealth, by the same he unites his possessions, which was before free, to it also; and they become, both of them, person and possession, subject to the government and dominion of that commonwealth as long as it hath a being. Whoever therefore from thenceforth by inheritance, purchases, permission, or otherwise, enjoys any part of the land so annexed to, and under the government of that commonwealth, must take it with the condition it is under, that is, of submitting to the government of the commonwealth under whose jurisdiction it is as far forth as any subject of it.

But since the government has a direct jurisdiction only over the land, and reaches the possessor of it (before he has actually incorporated himself in the society), only as he dwells upon, and enjoys that: the obligation any one is under, by virtue of such enjoyment, to submit to the government, begins and ends with the enjoyment; so that whenever the owner, who has given nothing but such a tacit consent to the government, will by donation, sale, or otherwise, quit the said possession, he is at liberty to go and incorporate himself into any other commonwealth, or to agree with others to begin a new one (*in vacuis locis*) in any part of the world they can find free and unpossessed. Whereas he that has once by actual agreement and of any express declaration given his consent to be of any commonweal is perpetually and indispensably obliged to be and remain unalterably a subject to it, and can never be again in the liberty of the state of nature; unless, by any calamity, the government he was under comes to be dissolved, or else by some public acts cuts him off from being any longer a member of it.

But submitting to the laws of any country, living quietly and enjoying privileges and protection under them makes not a man a member of that society. This is only a local protection and homage due to and from all those who, not being in the state of war, come within the territories belonging to any government to all parts whereof the force of its law extends. But this no more makes a man a member of that society a perpetual subject of that commonwealth, than it would make a man a subject to another in whose family he found it convenient to abide for some time; though whilst he continued in it he were obliged to comply with the laws, and submit to the government he found there. And thus we see, that foreigners by living all their lives under another government, and enjoying the privileges and protection of it, though they are bound even in conscience to submit to its administration as far forth as any denizen, yet do not thereby come to be subjects or members of that commonwealth. Nothing can make any man so, but his actually entering into it by positive engagement, and express promise and compact. This is that, which I think, concerning the beginning of political societies, and that consent which makes any one a member of any commonwealth.

Of the Ends of Political Society and Government

If man in the state of nature be so free, as has been said, if he be absolute lord of his own person and possessions, equal to the greatest, and subject to nobody, why will he part with his freedom, this empire, and subject himself to the dominion and control of any other power? To which, it is obvious to answer, that though in the state of nature he hath such a right, yet the enjoyment of it is very uncertain, and constantly exposed to the invasions of others. For all being kings as much as he, every man his equal, and the greater part no strict observers of equity and justice, the enjoyment of the property he has in this state is very unsafe, very unsecure. This makes him willing to quit this condition, which, however free, is full of fears and continual dangers; and it is not without reason that he seeks out and is willing to join in society with others, who are already united, or have a mind to unite, for the mutual preservation of their lives, liberties, and estates, which I call by the general name, property.

The great and chief end, therefore, of men's uniting into commonwealths, and putting themselves under government, is the preservation of their property; to which in the state of nature there are many things wanting.

First, There wants an established, settled, known law, received and allowed by common consent to be the standard of right and wrong, and the common measure to decide all controversies between them. For though the law of nature be plain and intelligible to all rational creatures; yet men, being biased by their interest, as well as ignorant for want of study of it, are not apt to allow of it as a law binding to them in the application of it to their particular cases.

Secondly, In the state of nature there wants a known and indifferent judge, with authority to determine all differences according to the established law. For every one in that state, being both judge and executioner of the law of nature, men being partial to themselves, passion and revenge is very apt to carry them too far, and with too much heat in their own cases, as well as negligence and unconcernedness, to make them too remiss in other men's.

Thirdly, In the state of nature there often wants power to back and support the sentence when right, and to give it due execution. They who by any injustice offend will seldom fail, where they are able by force to make good their injustice; such resistance many times makes the punishment dangerous, and frequently destructive to those who attempt it.

Thus mankind, notwithstanding all the privileges of the state of nature, being but in an ill condition, while they remain in it, are quickly driven into society. Hence it comes to pass that we seldom find any number of men live any time together in this state. The inconveniences that they are therein exposed to by the irregular and uncertain exercise of the power every man has of punishing the transgressions of others, make them take sanctuary under the established laws of government, and therein seek the preservation of their property. It is this makes them so willingly give up every one his single power of punishing, to be exercised by such alone, as shall be appointed to it amongst them; and by such rules as the community, or those authorised by them to that purpose, shall agree on. And in this we have the original right and rise of both the legislative and executive power, as well as of the governments and societies themselves.

For in the state of nature, to omit the liberty he has of innocent delights, a man has two powers.

The first is to do whatsoever he thinks fit for the preservation of himself, and others within the permission of the law of nature, by which law, common to them all, he and all the rest of mankind are of one community, make up one society, distinct from all other creatures. And were it not for the corruption and viciousness of degenerate men there would be no need of any other, no necessity that men should separate from this great and natural community, and associate into lesser combinations.

The other power a man has in the state of nature is the power to punish the crimes committed against that law. Both these he gives up when he joins in a private, if I may so call it, or particular political society, and incorporates into any commonwealth separate from the rest of mankind.

The first power, viz., of doing whatsoever he thought fit for the preservation of himself and the rest of mankind, he gives up to be regulated by laws made by the society, so far forth as the preservation of himself and the rest of that society shall require; which laws of the society in many things confine the liberty he had by the law of nature.

Secondly, The power of punishing he wholly gives up, and engages his natural force (which he might before employ in the execution of the law of nature, by his own single authority as he thought fit), to assist the executive power of the society, as the law thereof shall require. For being now in a new state, wherein he is to enjoy many conveniences, from the labour, assistance, and society of others in the same community, as well as protection from its whole strength; he has to part also with as much of his natural liberty, in providing for himself, as the good, prosperity and safety of the society shall require; which is not only necessary but just, since the other members of the society do the like.

But though men when they enter into society give up the equality, liberty and executive power they had in the state of nature into the hands of the society, to be so far disposed of by the legislative as the good of the society shall require; yet it being only with an intention in every one the better to preserve himself, his liberty and property (for no rational creature can be supposed to change his condition with an intention to be worse), the power of the society, or legislative constituted by them, can never be supposed to extend farther than the common good, but is obliged to secure every one's property by providing against those three defects above mentioned that made the state of nature so unsafe and uneasy. And so whoever has the legislative or supreme power of any commonwealth is bound to govern by established standing laws, promulgated and known to the people, and not by extemporary decrees; by indifferent and upright judges, who are to decide controversies by those laws; and to employ the force of the community at home only in the execution of such laws, or abroad, to prevent or redress foreign injuries, and secure the community from inroads and invasion. And all this to be directed to no other end but the peace, safety, and public good of the people.

Of the Original Contract

David Hume, 1711–1776, is today considered the most important philosopher of the tradition known as British empiricism, but in his own time he was famous principally for a history of England and several volumes of essays on literary, philosophical, and political subjects. Hume's criticisms of the social contract theory leave him open to the charge of ignoratio elenchi, *or missing the point, for while he argues at length that few if any governments are in fact founded upon a contract, Locke and others are maintaining that governments ought so to be based. The issue is joined in the latter part of the essay, where Hume presents a philosophical attack on the moral foundations of contract theory. Despite its historical implausibility, the theory of an original contract has held the attention of political philosophers for nearly 2500 years. It is only one of many examples of the influence of legal concepts—here the contract—on political theory.*

As no party, in the present age, can well support itself, without a philosophical or speculative system of principles, annexed to its political or practical one; we accordingly find, that each of the factions, into which this nation is divided, has reared up a fabric of the former kind, in order to protect and cover that scheme of actions, which it pursues. The people being commonly very rude builders, especially in this speculative way and more especially still, when actuated by party-zeal; it is natural to imagine, that their workmanship must be a little unshapely, and discover evident marks of that violence and hurry, in which it was raised. The one party, by tracing up government to the Deity, endeavour to render it so sacred and so inviolate, that it must be little less than sacrilege, however tyrannical it may become, to touch or invade it, in the smallest article. The other party, by founding government altogether on the consent of the People, suppose that there is a kind of *original contract*, by which they have, for certain purposes, voluntarily

Reprinted from David Hume, *Essays and Treatises on Several Subjects,* 2 vols. (Dublin, 1779).

entrusted him. These are the speculative principles of the two parties; and these too are the practical consequences deduced from them.

I shall venture to affirm, *That both these* systems *of speculative principles are just; though not in the sense, intended by the parties:* And, *That both the* schemes *of practical consequences are prudent; tho' not in the extremes, to which each party in opposition to the other, has commonly endeavoured to carry them.*

That the Deity is the ultimate author of all government, will never be denied by any, who admit a general providence, and allow, that all events in the universe are conducted by an uniform plan, and directed to wise purposes. As it is impossible for the human race to subsist, at least in any comfortable or secure state, without the protection of government; this institution must certainly have been intended by that beneficent Being, who means the good of all his creatures: And as it has universally, in fact, taken place, in all countries, and all ages; we may conclude, with still greater certainty, that it was intended by that omniscient Being, who can never be deceived by any event or operation. But since he gave rise to it, not by any particular or miraculous interposition, but by his concealed and universal efficacy; a sovereign cannot, properly speaking, be called his vicegerent, in any other sense than every power or force, being derived from him, may be said to act by his commission. Whatever actually happens is comprehended in the general plan or intention of providence; nor has the greatest and most lawful prince any more reason, upon that account, to plead a peculiar sacredness or inviolable authority, than an inferior magistrate, or even an usurper, or even a robber and a pirate. The same divine superintendent, who, for wise purposes, invested a Titus, or a Trajan with authority did also, for purposes, no doubt equally wise, though unknown, bestow power on a Borgia or an Angria. The same causes which gave rise to the sovereign power in every state established likewise every petty jurisdiction in it, and every limited authority. A constable, therefore, no less than a king, acts by a divine commission, and possesses an indefeasible right.

When we consider how nearly equal all men are in their bodily force, and even in their mental powers and faculties, till cultivated by education; we must necessarily allow, that nothing but their own consent could, at first, associate them together, and subject them to any authority. The people, if we trace government to its first origin in the woods and deserts, are the source of all power and jurisdiction, and voluntarily, for the sake of peace and order, abandoned their native liberty, and received laws from their equal and companion. The conditions, upon which they were willing to submit, were either expressed, or were so clear and obvious, that it might well be esteemed superfluous to express them. If this, then, be meant by the *original contract*, it cannot be denied, that all government is, at first, founded on a contract, and that the most ancient rude combinations of mankind were formed chiefly by that principle. In vain we are asked in what records this charter of our liberties is registered. It was not written on parchment, nor yet on leaves or barks of trees. It preceded the use of writing and all the other civilized arts of life. But we trace it plainly in the nature of man, and in the equality, or something approaching equality, which we find in all the individuals of that species. The force, which now prevails, and which is founded on fleets and armies, is plainly political, and derived from authority, the effect of established government. A man's natural force consists only in the vigour of his limbs, and the firmness of his courage; which could never subject multitudes to the command of one. Nothing but their own consent, and their sense of the advantages resulting from peace and order, could have had that influence.

Yet even this consent was long very imperfect, and could not be the basis of a regular administration. The chieftain, who had probably acquired his influence during the continuance of war, ruled more by persuasion than command; and till he could employ force to reduce the refractory and disobedient, the society could scarcely be said to have attained a state of civil government. No compact or agreement, it is evident, was expressly formed for general submission; an idea far beyond the comprehension of savages: Each exertion of authority in the chieftain must have been particular, and called forth by the present exigencies of the case: The sensible utility, resulting from his interposition, made these exertions become daily more frequent; and their frequency gradually produced an habitual, and, if you please to call it so, a voluntary, and therefore precarious, acquiescence in the people.

But philosophers, who have embraced a party (if that be not

a contradiction in terms) are not contented with these concessions. They assert, not only that government in its earliest infancy arose from consent or rather the voluntary acquiescence
of the people; but also, that, even at present, when it has attained its full maturity, it rests on no other foundation. They
affirm, that all men are still born equal, and owe allegiance to no
prince or government, unless bound by the obligation and
sanction of a *promise*. And as no man, without some equivalent,
would forego the advantages of his native liberty, and subject
himself to the will of another; this promise is always understood
to be conditional, and imposes on him no obligation, unless he
meet with justice and protection from his sovereign. These advantages the sovereign promises him in return; and if he fail
in the execution, he has broken, on his part, the articles of engagement, and has thereby freed his subject from all obligations
to allegiance. Such, according to these philosophers, is the
foundation of authority in every government; and such the right
of resistance, possessed by every subject.

But would these reasoners look abroad into the world, they
would meet with nothing that, in the least, corresponds to their
ideas, or can warrant so refined and philosophical a system. On
the contrary, we find, every where, princes, who claim their subjects as their property, and assert their independent right of
sovereignty from conquest or succession. We find also, every
where, subjects who acknowledge this right in their prince, and
suppose themselves born under obligations of obedience to a
certain sovereign, as much as under the ties of reverence and
duty to certain parents. These connections are always conceived
to be equally independent of our consent, in Persia and China;
in France and Spain; and even in Holland and England, wherever the doctrines above-mentioned have not been carefully inculcated. Obedience or subjection becomes so familiar, that most
men never make any enquiry about the principle of gravity, resistance, or the most universal laws of nature. Or if curiosity
ever move them; as soon as they learn, that they themselves and
their ancestors have, for several ages, or from time immemorial,
been subject to such a form of government or such a family;
they immediately acquiesce, and acknowledge their obligation
to allegiance. Were you to preach, in most parts of the world,
that political connections are founded altogether on voluntary consent or a mutual promise, the magistrates would soon

imprison you, as seditious, for loosening the ties of obedience; if your friends did not before shut you up as delirious for advancing such absurdities. It is strange, that an act of the mind, which every individual is supposed to have formed, and after he came to the use of reason too, otherwise it could have no authority; that this act, I say, should be so much unknown to all of them, that, over the face of the whole earth, there scarcely remain any traces or memory of it.

But the contract, on which government is founded, is said to be the *original contract;* and consequently may be supposed too old to fall under the knowledge of the present generation. If the agreement, by which savage men first associated and conjoined their force, be here meant, this is acknowledged to be real; but being so ancient, and being obliterated by a thousand changes of government and princes, it cannot now be supposed to retain any authority. If we would say any thing to the purpose, we must assert, that every particular government, which is lawful, and which imposes any duty of allegiance on the subject, was, at first, founded on consent and a voluntary compact. But besides that this supposes the consent of the fathers to bind the children even to the most remote generations, (which republican writers will never allow) besides this, I say, it is not justified by history or experience, in any age or country of the world.

Almost all the governments, which exist at present, or of which there remains any record in story, have been founded originally, either on usurpation or conquest, or both, without any pretence of a fair consent, or voluntary subjection of the people. When an artful and bold man is placed at the head of an army or faction, it is often easy for him, by employing, sometimes violence, sometimes false pretences, to establish his dominion over a people a hundred times more numerous than his partisans. He allows no such open communication, that his enemies can know, with certainty, their number or force. He gives them no leisure to assemble together in a body to oppose him. Even all those, who are the instruments of his usurpation, may wish his fall; but their ignorance of each other's intention keeps them in awe, and is the sole cause of his security. By such arts as these, many governments have been established; and this is all the *original contract*, which they have to boast of.

The face of the earth is continually changing, by the encrease of small kingdoms into great empires, by the dissolution of great empires into smaller kingdoms, by the planting of colonies, by the migration of tribes. Is there any thing discoverable in all these events, but force and violence? Where is the mutual agreement or voluntary association so much talked of?

Even the smoothest way, by which a nation may receive a foreign master, by marriage or a will, is not extremely honourable for the people; but supposes them to be disposed of, like a dowry or a legacy, according to the pleasure or interest of their rulers.

But where no force interposes, and election takes place; what is this election so highly vaunted? It is either the combination of a few great men, who decide for the whole, and will allow of no opposition: or it is the fury of a multitude, that follow a seditious ringleader, who is not known, perhaps, to a dozen among them, and who owes his advancement merely to his own impudence, or to the momentary caprice of his fellows.

Are these disorderly elections, which are rare too, of such mighty authority, as to be the only lawful foundation of all government and allegiance?

In reality, there is not a more terrible event, than a total dissolution of government, which gives liberty to the multitude, and makes the determination or choice of a new establishment depend upon a number, which nearly approaches to that of the body of the people: For it never comes entirely to the whole body of them. Every wise man, then, wishes to see, at the head of a powerful and obedient army, a general, who may speedily seize the prize, and give to the people a master, which they are so unfit to choose for themselves. So little correspondent is fact and reality to those philosophical notions.

Let not the establishment at the *Revolution* deceive us, or make us so much in love with a philosophical origin to government, as to imagine all others monstrous and irregular. Even that event was far from corresponding to these refined ideas. It was only the succession, and that only in the regal part of the government, which was then changed; and it was only the majority of seven hundred, who determined that change for near ten millions. I doubt not, indeed, but the bulk of those ten millions acquiesced willingly in the determination. But was the matter left, in the least, to their choice? Was it not justly supposed to be, from that moment, decided, and every man punished, who refused to submit to the new sovereign? How otherwise could the matter have ever been brought to any issue or conclusion?

The republic of Athens was, I believe, the most extensive democracy, that we read of in history; yet if we make the requisite allowances for the women, the slaves, and the strangers, we shall find, that that establishment was not, at first, made, nor any law ever voted, by a tenth part of those who were bound to pay obedience to it. Not to mention the islands and foreign dominions, which the Athenians claimed as theirs by right of conquest. And it is well known, that popular assemblies in that city were always full of licence and disorder, notwithstanding the institutions and laws by which they were checked. How much more disorderly must they prove, where they form not the established constitution, but meet tumultuously on the dissolution of the ancient government, in order to give rise to a new one? How chimerical must it be to talk of a choice in such circumstances?

The Achæans enjoyed the freest and most perfect democracy of all antiquity; yet they employed force to oblige some cities to enter into their league, as we learn from Polybius.

Henry the IVth and Henry VIIth of England, have really no title to the throne but a parliamentary election; yet they never would acknowledge it, lest they should thereby weaken their authority. Strange, if the only real foundation of all authority be consent and promise!

It is in vain to say, that all governments are or should be, at first, founded on popular consent, as much as the necessity of human affairs will admit. This favours entirely my pretension. I maintain, that human affairs will never admit of this consent; seldom of the appearance of it. But that conquest or usurpation, that is, in plain terms, force, by dissolving the ancient governments, is the origin of almost all the new ones, which were ever established in the world. And that in the few cases, where consent may seem to have taken place, it was commonly so irregular, so confined, or so much intermixed either with fraud or violence, that it cannot have any great authority.

My intention here is not to exclude the consent of the people from being one just foundation of government where it has place. It is surely the best and most sacred of any. I only pretend, that it has very seldom had place in any degree, and never almost in its full extent. And that therefore some other foundation of government must also be admitted.

Were all men possessed of so inflexible a regard to justice, that, of themselves, they would totally abstain from the properties of others; they had for ever remained in a state of absolute liberty, without subjection to any magistrate or political society. But this is a state of perfection, of which human nature is justly deemed incapable. Again; were all men possessed of so perfect an understanding, as always to know their own interests, no form of government had ever been submitted to, but what was established on consent, and was fully canvassed by every member of the society. But this state of perfection is likewise much superior to human nature. Reason, history, and experience show us, that all political societies have had an origin much less accurate and regular; and were one to choose a period of time, when the people's consent was the least regarded in public transactions, it would be precisely on the establishment of a new government. In a settled constitution, their inclinations are often consulted; but during the fury of revolutions, conquests, and public convulsions, military force or political craft usually decides the controversy.

When a new government is established, by whatever means, the people are commonly dissatisfied with it, and pay obedience more from fear and necessity, than from any idea of allegiance or of moral obligation. The prince is watchful and jealous, and must carefully guard against every beginning or appearance of insurrection. Time, by degrees, removes all these difficulties, and accustoms the nation to regard, as their lawful or native princes, that family, which, at first, they considered as usurpers or foreign conquerors. In order to found this opinion, they have no recourse to any notion of voluntary consent or promise, which, they know, never was, in this case, either expected or demanded. The original establishment was formed by violence, and submitted to from necessity. The subsequent administration is also supported by power, and acquiesced in by the people, not as a matter of choice, but of obligation. They imagine not, that their consent gives their prince a title; but they willingly consent, because they think, that from long possession, he has acquired a title, independent of their choice or inclination.

Should it be said, that, by living under the dominion of a

prince, which one might leave, every individual has given a *tacit* consent to his authority, and promised him obedience; it may be answered, that such an implied consent can only have place, where a man imagines, that the matter depends on his choice. But where he thinks (as all mankind do who are born under established governments) that by his birth he owes allegiance to a certain prince or certain form of government; it would be absurd to infer a consent or choice, which he expressly, in this case, renounces and disclaims.

Can we seriously say, that a poor peasant or artizan has a free choice to leave his country, when he knows no foreign language or manners, and lives from day to day, by the small wages which he acquires? We may as well assert, that a man, by remaining in a vessel freely consents to the dominion of the master; though he was carried on board while asleep, and must leap into the ocean, and perish, the moment he leaves her.

What if the prince forbid his subjects to quit his dominions; as in Tiberius's time, it was regarded as a crime in a Roman knight that he had attempted to fly to the Parthians, in order to escape the tyranny of that emperor? Or as the ancient Muscovites prohibited all travelling under pain of death? And did a prince observe, that many of his subjects were seized with the frenzy of migrating to foreign countries, he would doubtless, with great reason and justice, restrain them in order to prevent the depopulation of his own kingdom. Would he forfeit the allegiance of all his subjects, by so wise and reasonable a law? Yet the freedom of their choice is surely, in that case, ravished from them.

A company of men, who should leave their native country, in order to people some uninhabited region, might dream of recovering their native freedom; but they would soon find, that their prince still laid claim to them, and called them his subjects, even in their new settlement. And in this he would but act conformably to the common ideas of mankind.

The truest *tacit* consent of this kind, that is ever observed, is when a foreigner settles in any country, and is beforehand acquainted with the prince, and government, and laws, to which he must submit. Yet is his allegiance, though more voluntary, much less expected or depended on, than that of a natural born subject. On the contrary, his native prince still asserts a claim to him. And if he punish not the renegade, when he seizes him in war with his new prince's commission; this clemency is not founded on the municipal law, which in all countries condemns the prisoner; but on the consent of princes who have agreed to this indulgence, in order to prevent reprisals.

Did one generation of men go off the stage at once, and another succeed, as is the case with silk-worms and butterflies, the new race, if they had sense enough to choose their government, which surely is never the case with men, might voluntarily, and by general consent, establish their own form of civil polity, without any regard to the laws or precedents, which prevailed among their ancestors. But as human society is in perpetual flux, one man every hour going out of the world, another coming into it, it is necessary, in order to preserve stability in government, that the new brood should conform themselves to the established constitution, and nearly follow the path which their fathers, treading in the footsteps of theirs, had marked out to them. Some innovations must necessarily have place in every human institution, and it is happy where the enlightened genius of the age give these a direction to the side of reason, liberty, and justice: but violent innovations no individual is entitled to make; they are even dangerous to be attempted by the legislature, more ill than good is ever to be expected from them; and if history affords examples to the contrary, they are not to be drawn into precedent, and are only to be regarded as proofs, that the science of politics affords few rules, which will not admit of some exception, and which may not sometimes be controlled by fortune and accident. The violent innovations in the reign of Henry VIII proceeded from an imperious monarch, seconded by the appearance of legislative authority. Those in the reign of Charles I were derived from faction and fanaticism; and both of them have proved happy in the issue. But even the former were long the source of many disorders, and still more dangers; and if the measures of allegiance were to be taken from the latter, a total anarchy must have place in human society, and a final period at once be put to every government.

Suppose that an usurper, after having banished his lawful prince and royal family, should establish his dominion for ten or a dozen years in any country, and should preserve so exact a discipline in his troops, and so regular a disposition in his garrisons, that no insurrection had ever been raised, or even murmur heard, against his administration. Can it be asserted, that the people, who in their hearts abhor his treason, have tacitly consented to his authority, and promised him allegiance, merely because, from necessity, they live under his dominion? Suppose again their native prince restored, by means of an army, which he levies in foreign countries. They receive him with joy and exultation, and show plainly with what reluctance they had submitted to any other yoke. I may now ask, upon what foundation the prince's title stands? Not on popular consent surely; for though the people willingly acquiesce in his authority, they never imagine, that their consent made him sovereign. They consent because they apprehend him to be already, by birth, their lawful sovereign. And as to that tacit consent, which may now be inferred from their living under his dominion, this is no more than what they formerly gave to the tyrant and usurper.

When we assert, that all lawful government arises from the consent of the people, we certainly do them a great deal more honour than they deserve, or even expect and desire from us. After the Roman dominions became too unwieldy for the republic to govern them, the people, over the whole known world, were extremely grateful to Augustus for that authority, which, by violence, he had established over them; and they showed an equal disposition to submit to the successor, whom he left them, by his last will and testament. It was afterwards their misfortune, that there never was, in one family, any long regular succession; but that their line of princes was continually broken, either by private assassinations or public rebellions. The *prætorian* bands, on the failure of every family, set up one emperor; the legions in the East a second; those in Germany, perhaps, a third: And the sword alone could decide the controversy. The condition of the people, in that mighty monarchy, was to be lamented, not because the choice of the emperor was never left to them; for that was impracticable, but because they never fell under any succession of masters, who might regularly follow each other. As to the violence and wars and bloodshed, occasioned by every new settlement; these were not blameable, because they were inevitable.

The house of Lancaster ruled in this island about sixty years; yet the partisans of the white rose seemed daily to multiply in England. The present establishment has taken place during a still longer period. Have all views of right in another family been utterly extinguished; even though scarce any man now alive had arrived at years of discretion, when it was expelled, or could have consented to its dominion, or have promised it allegiance? A sufficient indication surely of the general sentiment of mankind on this head. For we blame not the partisans of the abdicated family, merely on account of the long time, during which they have preserved their imaginary loyalty. We blame them for adhering to a family, which, we affirm, has been justly expelled, and which, from the moment the new settlement took place, had forfeited all title to authority.

But would we have a more regular, at least a more philosophical, refutation of this principle of an original contract or popular consent; perhaps, the following observations may suffice.

All *moral* duties may be divided into two kinds. The *first* are those, to which men are impelled by a natural instinct or immediate propensity, which operates on them, independent of all ideas of obligation, and of all views, either to public or private utility. Of this nature are, love of children, gratitude to benefactors, pity to the unfortunate. When we reflect on the advantage, which results to society from such humane instincts, we pay them the just tribute of moral approbation and esteem; but the person, actuated by them, feels their power and influence, antecedent to any such reflection.

The *second* kind of moral duties are such as are not supported by any original instinct of nature, but are performed entirely from a sense of obligation, when we consider the necessities of human society, and the impossibility of supporting it, if these duties were neglected. It is thus *justice* or a regard to the property of others, *fidelity* or the observance of promises, become obligatory, and acquire an authority over mankind. For as it is evident, that every man loves himself better than any other person, he is naturally impelled to extend his acquisitions as much as possible; and nothing can restrain him in this propensity, but reflection and experience, by which he learns the pernicious effects of that licence, and the total dissolution of society which must ensue from it. His original inclination, therefore, or instinct, is here checked and restrained by a subsequent judgment or observation.

The case is precisely the same with the political or civil duty of *allegiance,* as with the natural duties of justice and fidelity. Our primary instincts lead us, either to indulge ourselves in unlimited freedom, or to seek dominion over others. And it is reflection only, which engages us to sacrifice such strong passions to the interests of peace and public order. A small degree of experience and observation suffices to teach us, that society cannot possibly be maintained without the authority of magistrates, and that this authority must soon fall into contempt, where exact obedience is not paid to it. The observation of these general and obvious interests is the source of all allegiance, and of that moral obligation, which we attribute to it.

What necessity, therefore, is there to found the duty of *allegiance* or obedience to magistrates on that of *fidelity* or a regard to promises, and to suppose, that it is the consent of each individual, which subjects him to government; when it appears, that both allegiance and fidelity stand precisely on the same foundation, and are both submitted to by mankind, on account of the apparent interests and necessities of human society? We are bound to obey our sovereign, it is said; because we have given a tacit promise to that purpose. But why are we bound to observe our promise? It must here be asserted, that the commerce and intercourse of mankind, which are of such mighty advantage, can have no security where men may pay no regard to their engagements. In like manner, may it be said, that men could not live at all in society, at least in a civilized society, without laws and magistrates and judges, to prevent the encroachments of the strong upon the weak, of the violent upon the just and equitable. The obligation to allegiance being of little force and authority with the obligation to fidelity, we gain nothing by resolving the one into the other. The general interests or necessities of society are sufficient to establish both.

If the reason be asked of that obedience, which we are bound to pay to government, I readily answer, *because society could not otherwise subsist:* And this answer is clear and intelligible to all mankind. Your answer is, *because we should keep our word.* But besides, that no body, till trained in a philosophical system, can either comprehend or relish this answer: Besides this, I say, you find yourself embarrassed, when it is asked, *why we are bound to keep our word?* Nor can you give any answer, but what would, immediately, without any circuit, have accounted for our obligation to allegiance.

But *to whom is allegiance due? And who is our lawful sovereign?* This question is often the most difficult of any, and liable to infinite discussions. When people are so happy, that they can answer, *Our present sovereign, who inherits, in a direct line, from ancestors, that have governed us for many ages;* this answer admits of no reply; even though historians, in tracing up to the remotest antiquity, the origin of that royal family, may find, as commonly happens, that its first authority was derived from usurpation and violence. It is confessed, that private justice, or the abstinence from the properties of others, is a most cardinal virtue. Yet reason tells us that there is no durable objects, such as lands or houses, when carefully examined in passing from hand to hand, but must, in some period, have been founded on fraud and injustice. The necessities of human society, neither in private nor public life, will allow of such an accurate enquiry; and there is no virtue or moral duty, but what may, with facility, be refined away, if we indulge a false philosophy, in sifting and scrutinizing it, by every captious rule of logic, in every light or position, in which it may be placed.

The questions with regard to private property have filled infinite volumes of law and philosophy, if in both we add the commentators to the original text; and in the end, we may safely pronounce, that many of the rules, there established, are uncertain, ambiguous, and arbitrary. The like opinion may be formed with regard to the succession and rights of princes and forms of government. Several cases, no doubt, occur, especially in the infancy of any constitution, which admit of no determination from the laws of justice and equity; and our historian Rapin pretends, that the controversy between Edward the Third and Philip de Valois was of this nature, and could be decided only by an appeal to heaven, that is by war and violence.

Who shall tell me, whether Germanicus or Drusus ought to have succeeded to Tiberius, had he died, while they were both alive, without naming any of them for his successor? Ought the right of adoption to be received as equivalent to that of blood, in a nation, where it had the same effect in private families, and already, in two instances, taken place in the public? Ought Germanicus to be esteemed the elder son because he was born before Drusus; or the younger, because he was adopted after the birth of his brother? Ought the right of the elder to be regarded in a nation, where he had no advantage in the succession of private families? Ought the Roman empire at that time to be deemed hereditary, because of two examples; or ought it, even so early, to be regarded as belonging to the stronger or to the present possessor, as being founded on so recent an usurpation?

Commodus mounted the throne after a pretty long succession of excellent emperors, who had acquired their title, not by birth, or public election, but by the fictitious rite of adoption. That bloody debauchee being murdered by a conspiracy suddenly formed between his wench and her gallant, who happened at that time to be *Prætorian Præfect;* these immediately deliberated about choosing a master to human kind, to speak in the style of those ages; and they cast their eyes on Pertinax. Before the tyrant's death was known, the *Præfect* went secretly to that senator, who, on the appearance of the soldiers, imagined that his execution had been ordered by Commodus. He was immediately saluted emperor by the officer and his attendants; cheerfully proclaimed by the populace; unwillingly submitted to by the guards; formally recognized by the senate; and passively received by the provinces and armies of the empire.

The discontent of the *Prætorian* bands broke out in a sudden sedition, which occasioned the murder of that excellent prince; and the world being now without a master and without government, the guards thought proper to set the empire formally to sale. Julian, the purchaser, was proclaimed by the soldiers, recognized by the senate, and submitted to by the people; and must also have been submitted to by the provinces, had not the envy of the legions begotten opposition and resistance. Pescennius Niger in Syria elected himself emperor, gained the tumultuary consent of his army, and was attended with the secret good-will of the senate and people of Rome. Albinus in Britain found an equal right to set up his claim; but Severus, who governed Pannonia, prevailed in the end above both of them. That able politician and warrior finding his own birth and dignity too much inferior to the imperial crown, professed, at first, an intention only of revenging the death of Pertinax. He marched as general into Italy; defeated Julian; and without our being able to fix any precise commencement even of the soldiers' consent, he was from necessity acknowledged emperor by the senate and people; and fully established his violent authority by subduing Niger and Albinus.

Inter hæc Gordianus Cæsar (says Capitolinus, speaking of

another period) *sublatus a militibus.* Imperator *est appelatus, quia non erat alius in præsenti.* It is to be remarked, that Gordian was a boy of fourteen years of age.

Frequent instances of a like nature occur in the history of the emperors; in that of Alexander's successors; and of many other countries. Nor can anything be more unhappy than a despotic government of this kind; where the succession is disjointed and irregular, and must be determined, on every vacancy, by force or election. In a free government, the matter is often unavoidable, and is also much less dangerous. The interests of liberty may there frequently lead the people in their own defence, to alter the succession of the crown. And the constitution, being compounded of parts, may still maintain a sufficient stability, by resting on the aristocratical or democratical members, though the monarchical be altered, from time to time, in order to accommodate it to the former.

In an absolute government, when there is no legal prince, who has a title to that throne, it may safely be determined to belong to the first occupant. Instances of this kind are but too frequent, especially in the eastern monarchies. When any race of princes expires, the will or destination of the last sovereign will be regarded as a title. Thus the edict of Lewis the XIVth, who called the bastard princes to the succession in case of the failure of all the legitimate princes, would, in such an event, have some authority. Thus the will of Charles the Second disposed of the whole Spanish monarchy. The cession of the ancient proprietor, especially when joined to conquest, is likewise deemed a good title. The general obligation, which binds us to government, is the interest and necessities of society; and this obligation is very strong. The determination of it to this or that particular prince or form of government is frequently more uncertain and dubious. Present possession has considerable authority in these cases, and greater than in private property; because of the disorders which attend all revolutions and changes of government.

We shall only observe, before we conclude, that, though an appeal to general opinion may justly, in the speculative sciences of metaphysics, natural philosophy, or astronomy, be deemed unfair and inconclusive, yet in all questions with regard to morals, as well as criticism, there is really no other standard, by which any controversy can ever be decided. And nothing is a clearer proof, that a theory of this kind is erroneous, than to find, that it leads to paradoxes, repugnant to the common sentiments of mankind, and to the practice and opinion of all nations and all ages. The doctrine, which founds all lawful government on an *original contract,* or consent of the people, is plainly of this kind; nor has the most noted of its partisans, in prosecution of it, scrupled to affirm, *that absolute monarchy is inconsistent with civil society, and so can be no form of civil government at all;* and *that the supreme power in a state cannot take from any man, by taxes and impositions, any part of his property, without his own consent or that of his representatives.* What authority any moral reasoning can have, which leads into opinions so wide of the general practice of mankind, in every place but this single kingdom, it is easy to determine.

The only passage I meet with in antiquity, where the obligation of obedience to government is ascribed to a promise, is in Plato's *Crito:* where Socrates refuses to escape from prison, because he had tacitly promised to obey the laws. Thus he builds a *tory* consequence of passive obedience, on a *whig* foundation of the original contract.

New discoveries are not to be expected in these matters. If scarce any man, till very lately, ever imagined that government was founded on compact, it is certain, that it cannot, in general, have any such foundation.

The crime of rebellion among the ancients was commonly expressed by the terms νεωτερίζειν, *novas res moliri.*

FRIEDRICH ENGELS

The Origin of the State

———————————————————————◆

Friedrich Engels, 1820–1895, was the life-long partner of Karl Marx in the creation and elaboration of the theory known variously as dialectical materialism, historical materialism, or simply communism. In the

Reprinted by permission of the publishers from Friedrich Engels, *The Origin of the Family, Private Property, and the State* (New York: International Publishers Co., Inc., 1942).

informal division of intellectual labor between Engels and Marx, it usually fell to Engels to apply Marx's central insights to new or peripheral fields of knowledge. Here we find him making use of a recently published anthropological study by Lewis Morgan as a peg on which to hang a Marxian theory of the state. Engels aligns himself with the dominant tradition of political theory in asserting that the state, as a human institution, has an historical beginning; but he breaks with the tradition in claiming that the state will disappear in the not too distant future. Students who are curious to see the varied uses to which great minds can put the same materials should read Sigmund Freud's essay Totem and Taboo, *which is based on the same book by Morgan.*

*   *   *

The three main forms in which the state arises on the ruins of the gentile constitution have been examined in detail above. Athens provides the purest, classic form; here the state springs directly and mainly out of the class oppositions which develop within gentile society itself. In Rome, gentile society becomes a closed aristocracy in the midst of the numerous *plebs* who stand outside it, and have duties but no rights; the victory of *plebs* breaks up the old constitution based on kinship, and erects on its ruins the state, into which both the gentile aristocracy and the *plebs* are soon completely absorbed. Lastly, in the case of the German conquerors of the Roman Empire, the state springs directly out of the conquest of large foreign territories, which the gentile constitution provides no means of governing. But because this conquest involves neither a serious struggle with the original population nor a more advanced division of labor; because conquerors and conquered are almost on the same level of economic development, and the economic basis of society remains therefore as before—for these reasons the gentile constitution is able to survive for many centuries in the altered, territorial form of the mark constitution and even for a time to rejuvenate itself in a feebler shape in the later noble and patrician families, and indeed in peasant families, as in Ditmarschen.*

The state is therefore by no means a power imposed on society from without; just as little is it "the reality of the moral idea,"

---

* The first historian who had at any rate an approximate conception of the nature of the gens was Niebuhr, and for this he had to thank his acquaintance with the Ditmarschen families, though he was overhasty in transferring their characteristics to the gens.

"the image and the reality of reason," as Hegel maintains. Rather, it is a product of society at a particular stage of development; it is the admission that this society has involved itself in insoluble self-contradiction and is cleft into irreconcilable antagonisms which it is powerless to exorcise. But in order that these antagonisms, classes with conflicting economic interests, shall not consume themselves and society in fruitless struggle, a power, apparently standing above society, has becomes necessary to moderate the conflict and keep it within the bounds of "order"; and this power, arisen out of society, but placing itself above it and increasingly alienating itself from it, is the state.

In contrast to the old gentile organization, the state is distinguished firstly by the grouping of its members *on a territorial basis.* The old gentile bodies, formed and held together by ties of blood, had, as we have seen, become inadequate largely because they presupposed that the gentile members were bound to one particular locality, whereas this had long ago ceased to be the case. The territory was still there, but the people had become mobile. The territorial division was therefore taken as the starting point and the system introduced by which citizens exercised their public rights and duties where they took up residence, without regard to gens or tribe. This organization of the citizens of the state according to domicile is common to all states. To us, therefore, this organization seems natural; but, as we have seen, hard and protracted struggles were necessary before it was able in Athens and Rome to displace the old organization founded on kinship.

The second distinguishing characteristic is the institution of a *public force* which is no longer immediately identical with the people's own organization of themselves as an armed power. This special public force is needed because a self-acting armed organization of the people has become impossible since their cleavage into classes. The slaves also belong to the population: as against the 365,000 slaves, the 90,000 Athenian citizens constitute only a privileged class. The people's army of the Athenian democracy confronted the slaves as an aristocratic public force, and kept them in check; but to keep the citizens in check as well, a police-force was needed, as described above. This public force exists in every state; it consists not merely of armed men, but also of material appendages, prisons and coercive institutions of all kinds, of which gentile society knew nothing. It may be very insignificant, practically negligible, in societies with still undeveloped class antagonisms and living in remote areas, as at times and in places in the United States of America. But it becomes stronger in proportion as the class antagonisms within the state become sharper and as adjoining states grow larger and more populous. It is enough to look at Europe today, where class struggle and rivalry in conquest have brought the public power to a pitch that it threatens to devour the whole of society and even the state itself.

In order to maintain this public power, contributions from the state citizens are necessary—*taxes*. These were completely unknown to gentile society. We know more than enough about them today. With advancing civilization, even taxes are not sufficient; the state draws drafts on the future, contracts loans, *state debts*. Our old Europe can tell a tale about these, too.

In possession of the public power and the right of taxation, the officials now present themselves as organs of society standing *above* society. The free, willing respect accorded to the organs of the gentile constitution is not enough for them, even if they could have it. Representatives of a power which estranges them from society, they have to be given prestige by means of special decrees, which invest them with a peculiar sanctity and inviolability. The lowest police officer of the civilized state has more "authority" than all the organs of gentile society put together; but the mightiest prince and the greatest statesman or general of civilization might envy the humblest of the gentile chiefs the unforced and unquestioned respect accorded to him. For the one stands in the midst of society; the other is forced to pose as something outside and above it.

As the state arose from the need to keep class antagonisms in check, but also arose in the thick of the fight between the classes, it is normally the state of the most powerful, economically ruling class, which by its means becomes also the politically ruling class, and so acquires new means of holding down and exploiting the oppressed class. The ancient state was, above all, the state of the slave-owners for holding down the slaves, just as the feudal state was the organ of the nobility for holding down the peasant serfs and bondsmen, and the modern representative state is the instrument for exploiting wage-labor by capital. Exceptional periods, however, occur when the warring classes are so nearly equal in forces that the state power, as apparent mediator, acquires for the moment a certain independence in relation to both. This applies to the absolute monarchy of the seventeenth and eighteenth centuries, which balances the nobility and the bourgeoisie against one another; and to the Bonapartism of the First and particularly of the Second French Empire, which played off the proletariat against the bourgeoisie and the bourgeoisie against the proletariat. The latest achievement in this line, in which ruler and ruled look equally comic, is the new German Empire of the Bismarckian nation; here the capitalists and the workers are balanced against one another and both of them fleeced for the benefit of the decayed Prussian cabbage junkers.

Further, in most historical states the rights conceded to citizens are graded on a property basis, whereby it is directly admitted that the state is an organization for the protection of the possessing class against the non-possessing class. This is already the case in the Athenian and Roman property classes. Similarly in the medieval feudal state, in which the extent of political power was determined by the extent of land-ownership. Similarly, also, in the electoral qualifications in modern parliamentary states. This political recognition of property differences is, however, by no means essential. On the contrary, it marks a low stage in the development of the state. The highest form of the state, the democratic republic, which in our modern social conditions becomes more and more an unavoidable necessity and is the form of state in which alone the last decisive battle between proletariat and bourgeoisie can be fought out— the democratic republic no longer officially recognizes differences of property. Wealth here employs its power indirectly, but all the more surely. It does this in two ways: by plain corruption of officials, of which America is the classic example, and by an alliance between the government and the stock exchange, which is effected all the more easily the higher the state debt mounts and the more the joint-stock companies concentrate in their hands not only transport but also production itself, and themselves have their own center in the stock exchange. In addition to America, the latest French republic illustrates this strikingly, and honest little Switzerland has also given a creditable performance in this field. But that a democratic republic is not essential to this brotherly bond between government and stock exchange is proved not only by England, but also by the new

German Empire, where it is difficult to say who scored most by the introduction of universal suffrage, Bismarck or the Bleich-röder bank. And lastly the possessing class rules directly by means of universal suffrage. As long as the oppressed class—in our case, therefore, the proletariat—is not yet ripe for its self-liberation, so long will it, in its majority, recognize the existing order of society as the only possible one and remain politically the tail of the capitalist class, its extreme left wing. But in the measure in which it matures towards its self-emancipation, in the same measure it constitutes itself as its own party and votes for its own representatives, not those of the capitalists. Universal suffrage is thus the gauge of the maturity of the working class. It cannot and never will be anything more in the modern state; but that is enough. On the day when the thermometer of universal suffrage shows boiling-point among the workers, they as well as the capitalists will know where they stand.

The state, therefore, has not existed from all eternity. There have been societies which have managed without it, which had no notion of the state or state power. At a definite stage of economic development, which necessarily involved the cleavage of society into classes, the state became a necessity because of this cleavage. We are now rapidly approaching a stage in the development of production at which the existence of these classes has not only ceased to be a necessity, but becomes a positive hindrance to production. They will fall as inevitably as they once arose. The state inevitably falls with them. The society which organizes production anew on the basis of free and equal association of the producers will put the whole state machinery where it will then belong—into the museum of antiquities, next to the spinning wheel and the bronze ax.

*   *   *

The State and Revolution

V. I. Lenin, 1870–1924, was one of those rare individuals who both make history and write about it. He was the leader of the Bolshevik party before and after the October Revolution of 1917 in Russia, and to this day is its only major theorist. His principal contributions to Marxist doctrine were a theory of imperialism, which Lenin claimed would be a characteristic phenomenon of the late stages of capitalism, and his partly practical, partly theoretical account of the role of the party as the vanguard of the proletarian revolution. In the present passage, which takes the form of a commentary upon some of Engels' writings, Lenin seeks to combat the moderating, gradualist leanings of certain factions of the anti-czarist forces in Russia. Purely as a matter of textual exegesis, Lenin is clearly correct in his interpretation of Engels. The same issue, whether violent revolution is the only way to overcome capitalism, divides the Russians and Chinese Communists today, with the Chinese taking a Leninist position.

The Withering Away of the State and Revolution by Force

Engels' words regarding the "withering away" of the State enjoy such a popularity, are so often quoted, and reveal so clearly the essence of the common adulteration of Marxism in an opportunist sense that we must examine them in detail. Let us give the whole argument from which they are taken.

The proletariat takes control of the State authority and, first of all, converts the means of production into State property. But by this very act it destroys itself, as a proletariat, destroying at the same time all class differences and class antagonisms, and with this, also, the State. Past and present Society, which moved amidst class antagonisms, had to have the State, that is, an organization of the exploiting class for the support of its external conditions of production, therefore, in

Reprinted from V. I. Lenin, *The State and Revolution* (New York: Vanguard Press, 1929).

particular, for the forcible retention of the exploited class in such conditions of oppression (such as slavery, serfdom, wage-labor), as are determined by the given methods of production. The State was the official representative of the whole of Society, its embodiment in a visible corporation; but it was only in so far as it was the State of that class which, in the given epoch, alone represented the whole of society. In ancient times it was the State of the slave-owners— the only citizens of the State; in the middle ages it was the State of the feudal nobility; in our own times it is the State of the capitalists. When, ultimately, the State really becomes the representative of the whole of society, it will make itself superfluous. From the time when, together with class domination and the struggle for individual existence, resulting from the present anarchy in production, those conflicts and excesses which arise from this struggle will all disappear —from that time there will, therefore, be no need for the State. The first act of the State, in which it really acts as the representative of the whole of Society, namely, the assumption of control over the means of production on behalf of society, is also its last independent act as a State. The interference of the authority of the State with social relations will then become superfluous in one field after another, and finally will cease of itself. The authority of the Government over persons will be replaced by the administration of things and the direction of the processes of production. The State will not be "abolished"; it will wither away. It is from this point of view that we must appraise the phrase, "a free popular State"—a phrase which, for a time, had a right to be employed as a purely propaganda slogan, but which in the long run is scientifically untenable. It is also from this point of view that we must appraise the demand of the so-called anarchists that the State "should be abolished overnight." [1]

Without fear of committing an error, it can be said that the only point in this argument by Engels so singularly rich in ideas, which has become an integral part of Socialist thought among modern Socialist parties has been that, according to Marx, the State "withers away" in contradiction to the Anarchist teaching of the "abolition" of the State. To emasculate Marxism in such a manner is simply to reduce it to opportunism, for such an "interpretation" only leaves the semi-articulate conception of a slow, even, continuous change, free from leaps and storms, free from revolution. The current popular conception, if one may say so, of the "withering away" of the State undoubtedly means a quenching, if not negation, of revolution. Yet, such an "interpretation" is a most vulgar distortion of Marxism, advantageous only to the capitalist classes and based theoretically on the neglect of the most important conditions and considerations pointed out in the very passage summarizing Engels' ideas, which we have just quoted in full.

In the first place, at the very outset of his argument, Engels says that in assuming State power, the proletariat "by that very act destroys the State as such." It is not the custom to reflect on what this really means. Generally, it is either ignored altogether or it is considered as a piece of "Hegelian weakness" on Engels' part. As a matter of fact, however, these words express succinctly the experience of one of the greatest proletarian revolutions—the Paris Commune of 1871, of which we shall speak in greater detail in its own place. In reality, Engels speaks here of the *destruction* of the capitalist State by the proletarian revolution, while the words about its withering away refer to the remains of a *proletarian* State *after* the Socialist revolution. The capitalist State does not wither away, according to Engels, but is *destroyed* by the proletariat in the course of the revolution. Only the proletarian State or semi-State withers away after the revolution.

Second, the State is a "particular power of suppression." This splendid and extremely profound definition of Engels is given by him here with complete lucidity. It follows therefrom that the "particular power of suppression" of the proletariat by the capitalist class of the millions of workers by a handful of rich, must be replaced by a "particular power of suppression" of the capitalist class by the proletariat (the dictatorship of the proletariat). It is just this that constitutes the destruction of the State as such. It is just this that constitutes the "act" of taking possession of the means of production on behalf of Society. And it is obvious that such a substitution of one (capitalist) "particular power" by another (proletarian) "particular power" could in no way take place in the form of a "withering away."

Third, in using the term, "withering away," Engels refers quite clearly and definitely to the period *after* "the taking over of the means of production by the State on behalf of the whole of society," that is, after the Socialist Revolution. We all know that the proletarian form of the "State" is then an absolutely complete democracy. But it never enters the head of any of the opportunists who shamelessly distort Marx that Engels deals here with the withering away of the democracy. At first sight this seems very strange. But it will only be unintelligible to one who has not reflected on the fact that democracy is also a State and that, consequently, democracy will also disappear when the State disappears. Only a revolution can "destroy" the capitalist State. The State in general, that is, most complete democracy, can only wither away.

Fourth, having formulated his famous proposition that "the State withers away," Engels at once explains concretely that this proposition is directed equally against the opportunists and the anarchists. In doing this, however, Engels draws, in the first place, that deduction from his proposition, which is directed against the opportunists.

One can wager that out of every ten thousand persons who have read or heard of the "withering away" of the State, 9,990 do not know at all, or do not remember that Engels did not direct his conclusions from this proposition against the anarchists alone. And out of the remaining ten, nine do not know the meaning of a "free popular State" nor the reason why an attack on this watchword contains an attack on the opportunists. This is how history is written! This is how a great revolutionary doctrine is imperceptibly adulterated and adapted to current philistinism! The reference to the anarchists has been repeated thousands of times, has been vulgarized in the crudest fashion possible until it has acquired the strength of a prejudice, whereas the reference to the opportunists has been hushed up and "forgotten."

"A free popular State" was the demand and current watchword in the program of the German Social-Democrats of the 'seventies. There is no political substance in this watchword other than a pompous middle class circumlocution of the idea of democracy. In so far as it pointed in "lawful" manner at a democratic republic, Engels was prepared "for a time" to justify it from a propaganda point of view. But this watchword was really opportunist, for it not only took an exaggerated view of the attractiveness of bourgeois democracy, but also implied a lack of understanding of the Socialist criticism of the State in general. We are in favor of a democratic republic as the best form of the State for the proletariat under capitalism, but we have no right to forget that wage slavery is the lot of the people even in the most democratic middle class republic. Furthermore, every State is a "particular power of suppression" of the oppressed class. Consequently, no State is either "free" or "popular." Marx and Engels explained this repeatedly to their party comrades in the 'seventies.

Fifth, in the same work of Engels, from which everyone remembers his argument on "withering away" of the State, there is also a disquisition on the nature of a violent revolution; and the historical appreciation of its role becomes, with Engels, a veritable panegyric of a revolution by force. This, of course, no one remembers. To talk or even to think of the importance of this idea, is not considered respectable by our modern Socialist parties, and in the daily propaganda and agitation among the masses it plays no part whatever. Yet it is indissolubly bound up with the "withering away" of the State in one harmonious whole. Here is Engels' argument:

That force also plays another part in history (other than that of a perpetuation of evil), namely a *revolutionary* part; that, as Marx says, it is the midwife of every old society when it is pregnant with a new one; that force is the instrument and the means by which social movements hack their way through and break up the dead and fossilized political forms—of all this not a word by Herr Dühring. Duly, with sighs and groans, does he admit the possibility that for the overthrow of the system of exploitation force may, perhaps, be necessary, but most unfortunate if you please, because all use of force, forsooth, demoralizes its user! And this is said in face of the great moral and intellectual advance which has been the result of every victorious revolution! And this is said in Germany where a violent collision—which might perhaps be forced on the people—should have, at the very least, this advantage that it would destroy the spirit of subservience which has been permeating the national mind ever since the degradation and humiliation of the Thirty Years' War. And this turbid, flabby, impotent, parson's mode of thinking dares offer itself for acceptance to the most revolutionary party history has ever known! [2]

How can this eulogy of a revolution by force, which Engels used to propound to the German Social-Democrats between 1878–94, that is, up to the very day of his death, be reconciled with the theory of the "withering away" of the State, and combined into one doctrine? Usually the two views are combined by a process of eclecticism, by an unprincipled, sophistic, arbitrary selection sometimes of passages here and there (to oblige the powers that be)—and in ninety-nine cases out of a hundred (if not more often), it is the idea of the withering away of the

State that is specially emphasized. Dialectics is replaced by eclectics—this is the most usual, the most widespread method used in the official Social-Democratic literature of our day in respect of Marxist teachings. Such a substitution is, of course, not new; one can see it even in the history of classic Greek philosophy. In the process of camouflaging Marxism as opportunism, the substitution of eclecticism for dialectics is the best method of deceiving the masses. It gives an illustory satisfaction. It seems to take into account all sides of the process, all the tendencies of development, all the contradictory factors and so forth, whereas, in reality, it offers no consistent revolutionary view of the process of social development at all.

We have already said above and shall show more fully at a later stage that the teaching of Marx and Engels regarding the inevitability of a violent revolution refers to the capitalist State. It cannot be replaced by the proletarian State (the dictatorship of the proletariat) through mere "withering away," but, in accordance with the general rule, can only be brought about by a violent revolution. The hymn of praise sung in its honour by Engels and fully corresponding to the repeated declarations of Marx (see the concluding passages of the "Poverty of Philosophy" and the "Communist Manifesto," with its proud and open declaration of the inevitability of a violent revolution; also Marx's "Criticism of the Gotha Programme of 1875," in which, thirty years after, he mercilessly castigates its opportunist character)—this praise is by no means a mere "impulse," a mere declamation, or a mere polemical sally. The necessity of systematically fostering among the masses this and only this point of view about violent revolution lies at the root of the whole of Marx's and Engels' teaching, and it is just the neglect of such propaganda and agitation both by the present predominant social-chauvinists and the Kautskian schools that brings their betrayal of it into prominent relief.

The substitution of a proletarian for the capitalist State is impossible without a violent revolution, while the abolition of the proletarian State, that is, of all States, is only possible through "withering away."

Marx and Engels gave a full and concrete illustration of these views in their study of each revolutionary situation separately, by an analysis of the lessons of the experience of each individual revolution. To this, undoubtedly the most important part of their work, we shall now pass.

Notes

1. Herr Eugen Dühring, *Umwälzung der Wissenschaft*, 3rd German Edition, pp. 302–303.
2. *Ibid.*, p. 193.

Suggestions for Further Reading

(Books marked with * are available in paperback editions.)

The debate between the positivist and natural law traditions has been carried on in contemporary literature on jurisprudence, notably in the interchange between Lon Fuller and H. L. A. Hart, in the *Harvard Law Review* for 1958. Hans Kelsen, in his *General Theory of Law and the State* (New York, 1961), takes a position like Austin's while A. P. D'Entrèves, in *Natural Law* (New York, 1951), argues the opposing view. D'Entrèves' *The Medieval Contribution to Political Thought* (London, 1939) is an excellent guide to the fundamental doctrines of St. Thomas Aquinas.

Max Weber's manifold theoretical writings on social institutions can all be read with profit on the subjects of law and authority. In particular, the student can consult *Max Weber on Law in Economy and Society* (Cambridge, Mass., 1954), a translation of certain portions of his great *Wirtschaft und Gesellschaft*, and *From Max Weber: Essays in Sociology* (New York, 1958). Reinhardt Bendix's *Max Weber: An Intellectual Portrait* (New York, 1960) * is a competent survey of Weber's thought, with emphasis on the empirical writings.

Among contemporary discussions on the problem of political authority, Yves Simon, *A General Theory of Authority* (Notre Dame, 1962), presents the Catholic position. Bertrand de Jouvenel's *Power: The Natural History of Its Growth* (London, 1952) is a subtle treatment of the subject from a conservative viewpoint; Bertrand Russell's *Authority and the Individual* (Boston, 1960) * offers a rather different perspective. Difficult but suggestive is "What Is Authority?" in Hannah Arendt's book of essays, *Between Past and Future* (New York, 1961).*

Peter Laslett's edition of Locke's *Second Treatise* is the best critical edition (Cambridge, Eng., 1960). Hume's general views on politics can be found in a number of his essays, and many of the relevant writings have been gathered together in *Hume's Moral and Political Philosophy* (New York, 1948),* edited by Henry David Aiken. Needless to say, the student interested in the problem of the social contract should read Hobbes' *Leviathan* and Rousseau's *Social Contract*. In addition, a very useful secondary work is J. W. Gough, *The Social Contract: A Critical Study of Its Development* (New York, 1957).

The Marxist theory of the state must be gleaned from a number of the writings of Marx and Engels, as there is no convenient exposition of it in their works. Marx's *Critique of the Gotha Program* contains the famous description of the withering away of the state, and *The Communist Manifesto* is of course the *locus classicus* for the doctrine of the revolution of the proletariat. For a general biographical survey, Isaiah Berlin's *Karl Marx* (New York, 1961) * is useful, and G. D. H. Cole, in *What Marx Really Meant* (New York, 1934), tries to make the doctrine more meaningful for mid-twentieth century readers. Sidney Hook's *Towards the Understanding of Karl Marx* (London, 1933) is a philosophical approach to Marxist thought, while *Karl Marx's Interpretation of History* (Cambridge, 1948) by M. M. Bober, is a more scholarly treatment of the general theory.

THE LIMITS OF
POLITICAL AUTHORITY

The duty to obey is the converse of the right to command. In this section, therefore, we take a look at some of the literature on the problem of political loyalty. Since ancient times, the most mysterious and awesome rituals of society have been reserved for the adoration of the state. Disloyalty to clan, tribe, or nation has been punished more severely than even murder. No problem has vexed political philosophers more than the apparently irreconcilable conflict between the authority of the ruler and the rights of the individual. All gradations of opinion have found expression from the theory of the divine and absolute right of kings, popular in the sixteenth and seventeenth centuries, to the anarchism of Mikhail Bakunin in the nineteenth century. The selections in this section are designed to give some indication of the variety and complexity of the problems arising out of the question of loyalty.

We begin with Plato's *Crito*, in which Socrates defends his decision to accept death at the hands of the Athenian state. In the "dialogue with the Laws," Socrates argues both that he owes a filial obligation to his motherland, and—what is very different indeed—that he has made a contractual agreement with the state which he now has a duty to fulfill. Henry David Thoreau, in his moving essay "Civil Disobedience," defends the liberty of individual conscience against the claims of a distant and impersonal government. Thoreau's insistence upon the responsibility of the individual for the consequences of his acts is appealing, but it reflects at times an unrealistic nostalgia for an earlier, pre-industrial America where men could see the connections between their personal acts and the general march of events. Plato and Thoreau take the nature of loyalty as understood, and disagree only on the extent of the individual's obligation to the state. John Schaar, on the other hand, focuses on loyalty itself as the object of his study and argues that loyalty to men and institutions is an essential factor in the formation of the human personality. If Schaar is correct, no sane man can ask *whether* he should be loyal, but only to what or to whom.

With the next selections, we take up several actual cases in which the authority of the state clashes with the liberty of individual conscience. The two flag-salute opinions handed down by the Supreme Court involve familiar issues of constitutional law and civil liberties. More dramatic and less well-known to American readers will be the case of a young French intellectual, Jean Le Meur, who went to jail rather than take part in the brutal Algerian war. Le Meur is a left-wing Catholic, a type common in Continental Europe but relatively rare in the United States where orthodox religion of every sort is usually associated with conservative politics.

The last piece was written especially for this volume. I have tried to make it a concrete example of the kind of political philosophy for which I plead in the Introduction. The argument is purely analytical; it aims at clarifying concepts rather than describing political phenomena or supporting a moral principle. All the same, it is guided throughout by a concern for the kinds of practical issues which Le Meur and the Supreme Court cases raise. I have also tried in my analysis to take account of the results of political scientists like Schaar. Even if I have succeeded in untangling the many conceptual strands woven together in the idea of loyalty, I will, of course, not have resolved the problem itself. To do that, it would still be necessary to show how the liberty of individual conscience could be made compatible with the legitimate authority of the state.

Crito

◆————————————————————————————————

Plato, 427–347 B.C. *has recorded the last days of his teacher, Socrates, in a series of four dialogues, of which the Crito is the third. Socrates had been tried and found guilty of impiety and corrupting the youth of Athens. Condemned to death, he awaited the return of the sacred ship from Delos so that the sentence could be carried out. Crito, a wealthy disciple of Socrates, seeks in this dialogue to persuade him to escape from prison, as he apparently could have done, and flee from Athens. Socrates explains to Crito why he must stay in Athens and submit to a punishment which he knows to be unjust. In the argument which Socrates imagines the Laws of Athens to offer against his flight, we find both an early version of the social contract theory, and an appeal to the natural obligation which the citizen owes to the land of his birth.*

PERSONS OF THE DIALOGUE

SOCRATES.   CRITO.

SCENE:—*The Prison of Socrates.*

Socrates. Why have you come at this hour, Crito? it must be quite early?

Crito. Yes, certainly.

Soc. What is the exact time?

Cr. The dawn is breaking.

Soc. I wonder that the keeper of the prison would let you in.

Cr. He knows me, because I often come, Socrates; moreover, I have done him a kindness.

Soc. And are you only just come?

Cr. No, I came some time ago.

Soc. Then why did you sit and say nothing, instead of awakening me at once?

Cr. Why, indeed, Socrates, I myself would rather not have all

Reprinted from Plato, *Dialogues*, 4 vols., translated by B. Jowett, *Crito*, Vol. I.

this sleeplessness and sorrow. But I have been wondering at your peaceful slumbers, and that was the reason why I did not awaken you, because I wanted you to be out of pain. I have always thought you happy in the calmness of your temperament; but never did I see the like of the easy, cheerful way in which you bear this calamity.

Soc. Why, Crito, when a man has reached my age he ought not to be repining at the prospect of death.

Cr. And yet other old men find themselves in similar misfortunes, and age does not prevent them from repining.

Soc. That may be. But you have not told me why you come at this early hour.

Cr. I come to bring you a message which is sad and painful; not, as I believe, to yourself, but to all of us who are your friends, and saddest of all to me.

Soc. What! I suppose that the ship has come from Delos, on the arrival of which I am to die?

Cr. No, the ship has not actually arrived, but she will probably be here to-day, as persons who have come from Sunium tell me that they left her there; and therefore to-morrow, Socrates, will be the last day of your life.

Soc. Very well, Crito; if such is the will of God, I am willing; but my belief is that there will be a delay of a day.

Cr. Why do you say this?

Soc. I will tell you. I am to die on the day after the arrival of the ship?

Cr. Yes; that is what the authorities say.

Soc. But I do not think that the ship will be here until to-morrow; this I gather from a vision which I had last night, or rather only just now, when you fortunately allowed me to sleep.

Cr. And what was the nature of the vision?

Soc. There came to me the likeness of a woman, fair and comely, clothed in white raiment, who called to me and said: O Socrates,

"The third day hence to Phthia shalt thou go."

Cr. What a singular dream, Socrates!

Soc. There can be no doubt about the meaning, Crito, I think.

Cr. Yes; the meaning is only too clear. But, Oh! my beloved Socrates, let me entreat you once more to take my advice and escape. For if you die I shall not only lose a friend who can never be replaced, but there is another evil: people who do not know you and me will believe that I might have saved you if I had been willing to give money, but that I did not care. Now, can there be a worse disgrace than this—that I should be thought to value money more than the life of a friend? For the many will not be persuaded that I wanted you to escape, and that you refused.

Soc. But why, my dear Crito, should we care about the opinion of the many? Good men, and they are the only persons who are worth considering, will think of these things truly as they happened.

Cr. But do you see, Socrates, that the opinion of the many must be regarded, as is evident in your own case, because they can do the very greatest evil to any one who has lost their good opinion.

Soc. I only wish, Crito, that they could; for then they could also do the greatest good, and that would be well. But the truth is, that they can do neither good nor evil: they cannot make a man wise or make him foolish; and whatever they do is the result of chance.

Cr. Well, I will not dispute about that; but please to tell me, Socrates, whether you are not acting out of regard to me and your other friends: are you not afraid that if you escape hence we may get into trouble with the informers for having stolen you away, and lose either the whole or a great part of our property; or that even a worse evil may happen to us? Now, if this is your fear, be at ease; for in order to save you, we ought surely to run this, or even a greater risk; be persuaded, then, and do as I say.

Soc. Yes, Crito, that is one fear which you mention, but by no means the only one.

Cr. Fear not. There are persons who at no great cost are willing to save you and bring you out of prison; and as for the informers, you may observe that they are far from being exorbitant in their demands; a little money will satisfy them. My means, which, as I am sure, are ample, are at your service, and if you have a scruple about spending all mine, here are strangers who will give you the use of theirs; and one of them, Simmias the Theban, has brought a sum of money for this very purpose; and Cebes and many others are willing to spend their money too. I say therefore, do not on that account hesitate about making your escape, and do not say, as you did in the court, that you will have a difficulty in knowing what to do with yourself if you escape. For men will love you in other places to which you may go, and not in Athens only; there are friends of mine in Thessaly, if you like to go to them, who will value and protect you, and no Thessalian will give you any trouble. Nor can I think that you are justified, Socrates, in betraying your own life when you might be saved; this is playing into the hands of your enemies and destroyers; and moreover I should say that you were betraying your children; for you might bring them up and educate them; instead of which you go away and leave them, and they will have to take their chance; and if they do not meet with the usual fate of orphans, there will be small thanks to you. No man should bring children into the world who is unwilling to persevere to the end in their nurture and education. But you are choosing the easier part, as I think, not the better and manlier, which would rather have become one who professes virtue in all his actions, like yourself. And indeed, I am ashamed not only of you, but of us who are your friends, when I reflect that this entire business of yours will be attributed to our want of courage. The trial need never have come on, or might have been brought to another issue; and the end of all, which is the crowning absurdity, will seem to have been permitted by us, through cowardice and baseness, who might have saved you, as you might have saved yourself, if we had been good for anything (for there was no difficulty in escaping); and we did not see how disgraceful, Socrates, and also miserable all this will be to us as well as to you. Make your mind up then, or rather have your mind already made up, for the time of deliberation is over, and there is only one thing to be done, which must be done, if at all, this very night, and which any delay will render all but impossible; I beseech you therefore, Socrates, to be persuaded by me, and to do as I say.

Soc. Dear Crito, your zeal is invaluable, if a right one; but if wrong, the greater the zeal the greater the evil; and therefore we ought to consider whether these things shall be done or not. For I am and always have been one of those natures who must be guided by reason, whatever the reason may be which upon reflection appears to me to be the best; and now that this fortune has come upon me, I cannot put away the reasons which I have before given: the principles which I have hitherto honoured and revered I still honour, and unless we can find other and better principles on the instant, I am certain not to agree with you; no, not even if the power of the multitude could inflict many more imprisonments, confiscations, deaths, frightening us like children with hobgoblin terrors. But what will be the fairest way of considering the question? Shall I return to your old argument about the opinions of men? some of which are to be regarded, and others, as we were saying, are not to be regarded. Now were we right in maintaining this before I was condemned? And has the argument which was once good now proved to be talk for the sake of talking;—in fact an amusement only, and altogether vanity? That is what I want to consider with your help, Crito:—whether, under my present circumstances, the argument appears to be in any way different or not; and is to be allowed by me or disallowed. That argument, which, as I believe, is maintained by many who assume to be authorities, was to the effect, as I was saying, that the opinions of some men are to be regarded, and of other men not to be regarded. Now you, Crito, are a disinterested person who are not going to die to-morrow—at least, there is no human probability of this, and you are therefore not liable to be deceived by the circumstances in which you are placed. Tell me then, whether I am right in saying that some opinions, and the opinions of some men only, are to be valued, and other opinions, and the opinions of other men, are not to be valued. I ask you whether I was right in maintaining this?

Cr. Certainly.

Soc. The good are to be regarded, and not the bad?

Cr. Yes.

Soc. And the opinions of the wise are good, and the opinions of the unwise are evil?

Cr. Certainly.

Soc. And what was said about another matter? Was the disciple in gymnastics supposed to attend to the praise and blame and opinion of every man, or of one man only—his physician or trainer, whoever that was?

Cr. Of one man only.

Soc. And he ought to fear the censure and welcome the praise of that one only, and not of the many?

Cr. That is clear.

Soc. And he ought to live and train, and eat and drink in the way which seems good to his single master who has understanding, rather than according to the opinion of all other men put together?

Cr. True.

Soc. And if he disobeys and disregards the opinion and approval of the one, and regards the opinion of the many who have no understanding, will he not suffer evil?

Cr. Certainly he will.

Soc. And what will the evil be, whither tending and what affecting, in the disobedient person?

Cr. Clearly, affecting the body; that is what is destroyed by the evil.

Soc. Very good; and is not this true, Crito, of other things which we need not separately enumerate? In the matter of just and unjust, fair and foul, good and evil, which are the subjects of our present consultation, ought we to follow the opinion of the many and to fear them; or the opinion of the one man who has understanding, and whom we ought to fear and reverence more than all the rest of the world: and whom deserting we shall destroy and injure that principle in us which may be assumed to be improved by justice and deteriorated by injustice;—is there not such a principle?

Cr. Certainly there is, Socrates.

Soc. Take a parallel instance:—if, acting under the advice of men who have no understanding, we destroy that which is improvable by health and deteriorated by disease—when that has been destroyed, I say, would life be worth having? And that is—the body?

Cr. Yes.

Soc. Could we live, having an evil and corrupted body?

Cr. Certainly not.

Soc. And will life be worth having, if that higher part of man be depraved, which is improved by justice and deteriorated by injustice? Do we suppose that principle, whatever it may be in man, which has to do with justice and injustice, to be inferior to the body?

Cr. Certainly not.

Soc. More honoured, then?

Cr. Far more honoured.

Soc. Then, my friend, we must not regard what the many say of us: but what he, the one man who has understanding of just and unjust, will say, and what the truth will say. And therefore you begin in error when you suggest that we should regard the opinion of the many about just and unjust, good and evil, honourable and dishonourable.—Well, some one will say, "but the many can kill us."

Cr. Yes, Socrates; that will clearly be the answer.

Soc. That is true: but still I find with surprise that the old argument is, as I conceive, unshaken as ever. And I should like to know whether I may say the same of another proposition— that not life, but a good life, is to be chiefly valued?

Cr. Yes, that also remains.

Soc. And a good life is equivalent to a just and honorable one —that holds also?

Cr. Yes, that holds.

Soc. From these premisses I proceed to argue the question whether I ought or ought not to try and escape without the consent of the Athenians: and if I am clearly right in escaping, then I will make the attempt; but if not, I will abstain. The other considerations which you mention, of money and loss of character and the duty of educating children, are, as I fear, only the doctrines of the multitude, who would be as ready to call people to life, if they were able, as they are to put them to death—and with as little reason. But now, since the argument has thus far prevailed, the only question which remains to be considered is, whether we shall do rightly either in escaping or in suffering others to aid in our escape and paying them in money and thanks, or whether we shall not do rightly; and if the latter, then death or any other calamity which may ensue on my remaining here must not be allowed to enter into the calculation.

Cr. I think that you are right, Socrates; how then shall we proceed?

Soc. Let us consider the matter together, and do you either refute me if you can, and I will be convinced; or else cease, my dear friend, from repeating to me that I ought to escape against the wishes of the Athenians: for I am extremely desirous to be persuaded by you, but not against my own better judgment. And now please to consider my first position, and do your best to answer me.

Cr. I will do my best.

Soc. Are we to say that we are never intentionally to do wrong, or that in one way we ought and in another way we ought not to do wrong, or is doing wrong always evil and dishonourable, as I was just now saying, and as has been already acknowledged by us? Are all our former admissions which were made within a few days to be thrown away? And have we, at our age, been earnestly discoursing with one another all our life long only to discover that we are no better than children? Or are we to rest assured, in spite of the opinion of the many, and in spite of consequences whether better or worse, of the truth of what was then said, that injustice is always an evil and dishonour to him who acts unjustly? Shall we affirm that?

Cr. Yes.

Soc. Then we must do no wrong?

Cr. Certainly not.

Soc. Nor when injured injure in return, as the many imagine; for we must injure no one at all?

Cr. Clearly not.

Soc. Again, Crito, may we do evil?

Cr. Surely not, Socrates.

Soc. And what of doing evil in return for evil, which is the morality of the many—is that just or not?

Cr. Not just.

Soc. For doing evil to another is the same as injuring him?

Cr. Very true.

Soc. Then we ought not to retaliate or render evil for evil to any one, whatever evil we may have suffered from him. But I would have you consider, Crito, whether you really mean what you are saying. For this opinion has never been held, and never will be held, by any considerable number of persons; and those who are agreed and those who are not agreed upon this point have no common ground, and can only despise one another when they see how widely they differ. Tell me, then, whether you agree with and assent to my first principle, that neither injury nor retaliation nor warding off evil by evil is ever right. And shall that be the premiss of our argument? Or do you decline and dissent from this? For this has been of old and is still my opinion; but, if you are of another opinion, let me hear what you have to say. If, however, you remain of the same mind as formerly, I will proceed to the next step.

Cr. You may proceed, for I have not changed my mind.

Soc. Then I will proceed to the next step, which may be put in the form of a question:—Ought a man to do what he admits to be right, or ought he to betray the right?

Cr. He ought to do what he thinks right.

Soc. But if this is true, what is the application? In leaving the prison against the will of the Athenians, do I wrong any? or rather do I not wrong those whom I ought least to wrong? Do I not desert the principles which were acknowledged by us to be just? What do you say?

Cr. I cannot tell, Socrates; for I do not know.

Soc. Then consider the matter in this way:—Imagine that I am about to play truant (you may call the proceeding by any name which you like), and the laws and the government come and interrogate me: "Tell us, Socrates," they say, "what are you about? are you going by an act of yours to overturn us—the laws and the whole state, as far as in you lies? Do you imagine that a state can subsist and not be overthrown, in which the decisions of law have no power, but are set aside and overthrown by individuals?" What will be our answer, Crito, to these and the like words? Any one, and especially a clever rhetorician, will have a good deal to urge about the evil of setting aside the law which requires a sentence to be carried out; and we might reply, "Yes; but the state has injured us and given an unjust sentence." Suppose I say that?

Cr. Very good, Socrates.

Soc. "And was that our agreement with you?" the law would say, "or were you to abide by the sentence of the state?" And if I were to express astonishment at their saying this, the law would probably add: "Answer, Socrates, instead of opening your eyes: you are in the habit of asking and answering questions. Tell us what complaint you have to make against us which justifies you in attempting to destroy us and the state? In the first place did we not bring you into existence? Your father married your mother by our aid and begat you. Say whether you have any objection to urge against those of us who regulate marriage?" None, I should reply. "Or against those of us who regulate the system of nurture and education of children in which you were trained? Were not the laws, who have the charge of this, right in commanding your father to train you in music and gymnastic?" Right, I should reply. "Well then, since you were brought into the world and nurtured and educated by us, can you deny in the first place that you are our child and slave, as your fathers were before you? And if this is true you are not on equal terms with us; nor can you think that you have a right to do to us what we are doing to you. Would you have any right to strike or revile or do any other evil to a father or to your master, if you had one, when you have been struck or reviled by him, or received some other evil at his hands?— you would not say this? And because we think right to destroy you, do you think that you have any right to destroy us in return, and your country as far as in you lies? And will you, O professor of true virtue, say that you are justified in this? Has a philosopher like you failed to discover that our country is more to be valued and higher and holier far than mother or father or any ancestor, and more to be regarded in the eyes of the gods and of men of understanding? also to be soothed, and gently and reverently entreated when angry, even more than a father, and if not persuaded, obeyed? And when we are punished by her, whether with imprisonment or stripes, the punishment is to be endured in silence; and if she lead us to wounds or death in battle, thither we follow as is right; neither may any one yield or retreat or leave his rank, but whether in battle or in a court of law, or in any other place, he must do what his city and his country order him; or he must change their view of what is just: and if he may do no violence to his father or mother, much less may he do violence to his country." What answer shall we make to this, Crito? Do the laws speak truly, or do they not?

Cr. I think that they do.

Soc. Then the laws will say: "Consider, Socrates, if this is true, that in your present attempt you are going to do us wrong. For, after having brought you into the world, and nurtured and educated you, and given you and every other citizen a share in every good that we had to give, we further proclaim and give the right to every Athenian, that if he does not like us when he has come of age and has seen the ways of the city, and made our acquaintance, he may go where he pleases and take his goods with him; and none of us laws will forbid him or interfere with him. Any of you who does not like us and the city, and who wants to go to a colony or to any other city, may go where he likes, and take his goods with him. But he who has experience of the manner in which we order justice and administer the state, and still remains, has entered into an implied contract that he will do as we command him. And he who disobeys us is, as we maintain, thrice wrong; first, because in disobeying us he is disobeying his parents; secondly, because

we are the authors of his education; thirdly, because he has
made an agreement with us that he will duly obey our commands; and he neither obeys them nor convinces us that our
commands are wrong; and we do not rudely impose them, but
give him the alternative of obeying or convincing us;—that is
what we offer, and he does neither. These are the sort of accusa-
tions to which, as we were saying, you, Socrates, will be exposed
if you accomplish your intentions; you, above all other Athenians." Suppose I ask, why is this? they will justly retort upon
me that I above all other men have acknowledged the agreement. "There is clear proof," they will say, "Socrates, that we
and the city were not displeasing to you. Of all Athenians you
have been the most constant resident in the city, which, as you
never leave, you may be supposed to love. For you never went
out of the city either to see the games, except once when you
went to the Isthmus, or to any other place unless when you were
on military service; nor did you travel as other men do. Nor had
you any curiosity to know other states or their laws: your affec-
tions did not go beyond us and our state; we were your special
favourites, and you acquiesced in our government of you; and
this is the state in which you begat your children, which is a
proof of your satisfaction. Moreover, you might, if you had
liked, have fixed the penalty at banishment in the course of the
trial—the state which refuses to let you go now would have
let you go then. But you pretended that you preferred death
to exile, and that you were not grieved at death. And now you
have forgotten these fine sentiments, and pay no respect to us
the laws, of whom you are the destroyer; and are doing what
only a miserable slave would do, running away and turning
your back upon the compacts and agreements which you made
as a citizen. And first of all answer this very question: Are we
right in saying that you agreed to be governed according to
us in deed, and not in word only? Is that true or not?" How
shall we answer that, Crito? Must we not agree?

Cr. There is no help, Socrates.

Soc. Then will they not say: "You, Socrates, are breaking the
covenants and agreements which you made with us at your
leisure, not in any haste or under any compulsion or deception,
but having had seventy years to think of them, during which
time you were at liberty to leave the city, if we were not to
your mind, or if our covenants appeared to you to be unfair.

You had your choice, and might have gone either to Lacedae-
mon or Crete, which you often praise for their good government,
or to some other Hellenic or foreign state. Whereas you, above
all other Athenians, seemed to be so fond of the state, or, in
other words, of us her laws (for who would like a state that has
no laws), that you never stirred out of her; the halt, the blind,
the maimed were not more stationary in her than you were. And
now you run away and forsake your agreements. Not so,
Socrates, if you will take our advice; do not make yourself
ridiculous by escaping out of the city.

"For just consider, if you transgress and err in this sort of
way, what good will you do either to yourself or to your friends?
That your friends will be driven into exile and deprived of
citizenship, or will lose their property, is tolerably certain; and
you yourself, if you fly to one of the neighbouring cities, as, for
example, Thebes or Megara, both of which are well-governed
cities, will come to them as an enemy, Socrates, and their government will be against you, and all patriotic citizens will cast
an evil eye upon you as a subverter of the laws, and you will
confirm in the minds of the judges the justice of their own
condemnation of you. For he who is a corruptor of the laws
is more than likely to be corruptor of the young and foolish
portion of mankind. Will you then flee from well-ordered cities
and virtuous men? and is existence worth having on these terms?
Or will you go to them without shame, and talk to them,
Socrates? And what will you say to them? What you say here
about virtue and justice and institutions and laws being the
best things among men. Would that be decent of you? Surely
not. But if you go away from well-governed states to Crito's
friends in Thessaly, where there is great disorder and licence,
they will be charmed to have the tale of your escape from
prison, set off with ludicrous particulars of the manner in which
you were wrapped in a goatskin or some other disguise, and
metamorphosed as the fashion of runaways is—that is very likely;
but will there be no one to remind you that in your old age
you violated the most sacred laws from a miserable desire of a
little more life. Perhaps not, if you keep them in a good temper;
but if they are out of temper you will hear many degrading
things; you will live, but how?—as the flatterer of all men, and
the servant of all men; and doing what?—eating and drinking in
Thessaly, having gone abroad in order that you may get a din-

ner. And where will be your fine sentiments about justice and virtue then? Say that you wish to live for the sake of your children, that you may bring them up and educate them—will you take them into Thessaly and deprive them of Athenian citizenship? Is that the benefit which you would confer upon them? Or are you under the impression that they will be better cared for and educated here if you are still alive, although absent from them; for that your friends will take care of them? Do you fancy that if you are an inhabitant of Thessaly they will take care of them, and if you are an inhabitant of the other world they will not take care of them? Nay; but if they who call themselves friends are truly friends, they surely will.

"Listen, then, Socrates, to us who have brought you up. Think not of life and children first, and of justice afterwards, but of justice first, that you may be justified before the princes of the world below. For neither will you nor any that belong to you be happier or holier or juster in this life, or happier in another, if you do as Crito bids. Now you depart in innocence, a sufferer and not a doer of evil; a victim, not of the laws, but of men. But if you go forth, returning evil for evil, and injury for injury, breaking the covenants and agreements which you have made with us, and wronging those whom you ought least to wrong, that is to say, yourself, your friends, your country, and us, we shall be angry with you while you live, and our brethren, the laws in the world below, will receive you as an enemy; for they will know that you have done your best to destroy us. Listen, then, to us and not to Crito."

This is the voice which I seem to hear murmuring in my ears, like the sound of the flute in the ears of the mystic; that voice, I say, is humming in my ears, and prevents me from hearing any other. And I know that anything more which you may say will be vain. Yet speak, if you have anything to say.

Cr. I have nothing to say, Socrates.

Soc. Then let me follow the intimations of the will of God.

Civil Disobedience

Henry David Thoreau, 1817–1862, is best known for Walden, *a diary of a year spent in the woods near Concord, Massachusetts. Thoreau, like his close friend Ralph Waldo Emerson, belonged to the transcendentalist tradition in American letters which was influenced by German and English idealist philosophy of the nineteenth century. Thoreau's account in this essay of his stay in jail for refusing to pay taxes grows into a full-scale defense of the liberty and responsibility of individual conscience. A direct line joins Thoreau to the conscientious objectors and civil rights demonstrators of this century. It is striking to contrast this essay with the letters of Jean Le Meur. The reasons for their decisions are quite similar despite the extreme dissimilarity of their situations.*

I heartily accept the motto,—"That government is best which governs least;" and I should like to see it acted up to more rapidly and systematically. Carried out, it finally amounts to this, which also I believe,—"That government is best which governs not at all;" and when men are prepared for it, that will be the kind of government which they will have. Government is at best but an expedient; but most governments are usually, and all governments are sometimes, inexpedient. The objections which have been brought against a standing army, and they are many and weighty, and deserve to prevail, may also at last be brought against a standing government. The standing army is only an arm of the standing government. The government itself, which is only the mode which the people have chosen to execute their will, is equally liable to be abused and perverted before the people can act through it. Witness the present Mexican war, the work of comparatively a few individuals using the standing government as their tool; for, in the outset, the people would not have consented to this measure.

This American government,—what is it but a tradition, though

From Henry David Thoreau, *Civil Disobedience*, 1849.

a recent one, endeavoring to transmit itself unimpaired to posterity, but each instant losing some of its integrity? It has not the vitality and force of a single living man; for a single man can bend it to his will. It is a sort of wooden gun to the people themselves. But it is not the less necessary for this; for the people must have some complicated machinery or other, and hear its din, to satisfy that idea of government which they have. Governments show thus how successfully men can be imposed on, even impose on themselves, for their own advantage. It is excellent, we must all allow. Yet this government never of itself furthered any enterprise, but by the alacrity with which it got out of its way. *It* does not keep the country free. *It* does not settle the West. *It* does not educate. The character inherent in the American people has done all that has been accomplished; and it would have done somewhat more, if the government had not sometimes got in its way. For government is an expedient by which men would fain succeed in letting one another alone; and, as has been said, when it is most expedient, the governed are most let alone by it. Trade and commerce, if they were not made of India-rubber, would never manage to bounce over the obstacles which legislators are continually putting in their way; and, if one were to judge these men wholly by the effects of their actions and not partly by their intentions, they would deserve to be classed and punished with those mischievous persons who put obstructions on the railroads.

But, to speak practically and as a citizen, unlike those who call themselves no-government men, I ask for, not at once no government, but *at once* a better government. Let every man make known what kind of government would command his respect, and that will be one step toward obtaining it.

After all, the practical reason why, when the power is once in the hands of the people, a majority are permitted, and for a long period continue, to rule is not because they are most likely to be in the right, nor because this seems fairest to the minority, but because they are physically the strongest. But a government in which the majority rule in all cases cannot be based on justice, even as far as men understand it. Can there not be a government in which majorities do not virtually decide right and wrong, but conscience?—in which majorities decide only those questions to which the rule of expediency is applicable? Must the citizen ever for a moment, or in the least degree, resign his conscience to the legislator? Why has every man a conscience, then? I think that we should be men first, and subjects afterward. It is not desirable to cultivate a respect for the law, so much as for the right. The only obligation which I have a right to assume is to do at any time what I think right. It is truly enough said, that a corporation has no conscience; but a corporation of conscientious men is a corporation *with* a conscience. Law never made men a whit more just; and, by means of their respect for it, even the well-disposed are daily made the agents of injustice. A common and natural result of an undue respect for law is, that you may see a file of soldiers, colonel, captain, corporal, privates, powder-monkeys, and all, marching in admirable order over hill and dale to the wars, against their wills, ay, against their common sense and consciences, which makes it very steep marching indeed, and produces a palpitation of the heart. They have no doubt that it is a damnable business in which they are concerned; they are all peaceably inclined. Now, what are they? Men at all? or small movable forts and magazines, at the service of some unscrupulous man in power? Visit the Navy-Yard, and behold a marine, such a man as an American government can make, or such as it can make a man with its black arts,—a mere shadow and reminiscence of humanity, a man laid out alive and standing, and already, as one may say, buried under arms with funeral accompaniments, though it may be,—

> "Not a drum was heard, not a funeral note,
>   As his corse to the rampart we hurried;
> Not a soldier discharged his farewell shot
>   O'er the grave where our hero we buried."

The mass of men serve the state thus, not as men mainly, but as machines, with their bodies. They are the standing army, and the militia, jailors, constables, posse comitatus, etc. In most cases there is no free exercise whatever of the judgment or of the moral sense; but they put themselves on a level with wood and earth and stones; and wooden men can perhaps be manufactured that will serve the purpose as well. Such command no more respect than men of straw or a lump of dirt. They have the same sort of worth only as horses and dogs. Yet such as these even are commonly esteemed good citizens. Others—as most legislators, politicians, lawyers, ministers, and office-holders—serve the state chiefly with their heads; and, as they rarely make any moral distinctions, they are as likely to serve the Devil, without *intending*

it, as God. A very few, as heroes, patriots, martyrs, reformers in
the great sense, and *men*, serve the state with their consciences
also, and so necessarily resist it for the most part; and they are
commonly treated as enemies by it. A wise man will only be useful as a man, and will not submit to be "clay," and "stop a hole to
keep the wind away," but leave that office to his dust at least:—

> "I am too high-born to be propertied,
> To be a secondary at control,
> Or useful serving-man and instrument
> To any sovereign state throughout the world."

He who gives himself entirely to his fellow-men appears to
them useless and selfish; but he who gives himself partially to
them is pronounced a benefactor and philanthropist.

How does it become a man to behave toward this American
government to-day? I answer, that he cannot without disgrace be
associated with it. I cannot for an instant recognize that political
organization as *my* government which is the *slave's* government
also.

All men recognize the right of revolution; that is, the right to
refuse allegiance to, and to resist, the government, when its tyranny or its inefficiency are great and unendurable. But almost all
say that such is not the case now. But such was the case, they
think, in the Revolution of '75. If one were to tell me that this
was a bad government because it taxed certain foreign commodities brought to its ports, it is most probable that I should not
make an ado about it, for I can do without them. All machines
have their friction; and possibly this does enough good to coun-
terbalance the evil. At any rate, it is a great evil to make a stir
about it. But when the friction comes to have its machine, and
oppression and robbery are organized, I say, let us not have such
a machine any longer. In other words, when a sixth of the population of a nation which has undertaken to be the refuge of liberty are slaves, and a whole country is unjustly overrun and conquered by a foreign army, and subjected to military law, I think
that it is not too soon for honest men to rebel and revolutionize.
What makes this duty the more urgent is the fact that the country so overrun is not our own, but ours is the invading army.

Paley, a common authority with many on moral questions, in
his chapter on the "Duty of Submission to Civil Government,"
resolves all civil obligation into expediency; and he proceeds to

say, "that so long as the interest of the whole society requires it, that is, so long as the established government cannot be resisted or changed without public inconveniency, it is the will of God that the established government be obeyed, and no longer. . . . This principle being admitted, the justice of every particular case of resistance is reduced to a computation of the quantity of the danger and grievance on the one side, and of the probability and expense of redressing it on the other." Of this, he says, every man shall judge for himself. But Paley appears never to have contemplated those cases to which the rule of expediency does not apply, in which a people, as well as an individual, must do justice, cost what it may. If I have unjustly wrested a plank from a drowning man, I must restore it to him though I drown myself. This, according to Paley, would be inconvenient. But he that would save his life, in such a case, shall lose it. This people must cease to hold slaves, and to make war on Mexico, though it cost them their existence as a people.

In their practice, nations agree with Paley; but does any one think that Massachuetts does exactly what is right at the present crisis?

"A drab of state, a cloth-o'-silver slut,
    To have her train borne up, and her soul trail in the dirt."

Practically speaking, the opponents to a reform in Massachusetts are not a hundred thousand politicians at the South, but a hundred thousand merchants and farmers here, who are more interested in commerce and agriculture than they are in humanity, and are not prepared to do justice to the slave and to Mexico, *cost what it may.* I quarrel not with far-off foes, but with those who, near at home, coöperate with, and do the bidding of, those far away, and without whom the latter would be harmless. We are accustomed to say, that the mass of men are unprepared; but improvement is slow, because the few are not materially wiser or better than the many. It is not so important that many should be as good as you, as that there be some absolute goodness somewhere; for that will leaven the whole lump. There are thousands who are *in opinion* opposed to slavery and to the war, who yet in effect do nothing to put an end to them; who, esteeming themselves children of Washington and Franklin, sit down with their hands in their pockets, and say that they know not what to do, and do nothing; who even postpone the question of freedom to the question of free-trade, and quietly read the prices-current along with the latest advices from Mexico, after dinner, and, it may be, fall asleep over them both. What is the price-current of an honest man and patriot to-day? They hesitate, and they regret, and sometimes they petition; but they do nothing in earnest and with effect. They will wait, well disposed, for others to remedy the evil, that they may no longer have it to regret. At most, they give only a cheap vote, and a feeble countenance and God-speed, to the right, as it goes by them. There are nine hundred and ninety-nine patrons of virtue to one virtuous man. But it is easier to deal with the real possessor of a thing than with the temporary guardian of it.

All voting is a sort of gaming, like checkers or backgammon, with a slight moral tinge to it, a playing with right and wrong, with moral questions; and betting naturally accompanies it. The character of the voters is not staked. I cast my vote, perchance, as I think right; but I am not vitally concerned that that right should prevail. I am willing to leave it to the majority. Its obligation, therefore, never exceeds that of expediency. Even voting *for the right* is *doing* nothing for it. It is only expressing to men feebly your desire that it should prevail. A wise man will not leave the right to the mercy of chance, nor wish it to prevail through the power of the majority. There is but little virtue in the action of masses of men. When the majority shall at length vote for the abolition of slavery, it will be because they are indifferent to slavery, or because there is but little slavery left to be abolished by their vote. *They* will then be the only slaves. Only *his* vote can hasten the abolition of slavery who asserts his own freedom by his vote.

I hear of a convention to be held at Baltimore, or elsewhere, for the selection of a candidate for the Presidency, made up chiefly of editors, and men who are politicians by profession; but I think, what is it to any independent, intelligent, and respectable man what decision they may come to? Shall we not have the advantage of his wisdom and honesty, nevertheless? Can we not count upon some independent votes? Are there not many individuals in the country who do not attend conventions? But no: I find that the respectable man, so called, has immediately drifted from his position, and despairs of his country, when his country has more reason to despair of him. He forthwith adopts one of the candidates thus selected as the only *available* one, thus proving that he is himself *available* for any purposes of the demagogue. His vote is of no more worth than that of any unprincipled foreigner or hireling native, who may have been bought. O for a man who is a *man*, and, as my neighbor says, has a bone in his back which you cannot pass your hand through! Our statistics are at fault: the population has been returned too large. How many *men* are there to a square thousand miles in this country? Hardly one. Does not America offer any inducement for men to settle here? The American has dwindled into an Odd Fellow, —one who may be known by the development of his organ of gregariousness, and a manifest lack of intellect and cheerful self-reliance; whose first and chief concern, on coming into the world, is to see that the Almhouses are in good repair; and, before yet he has lawfully donned the virile garb, to collect a fund for the support of the widows and orphans that may be; who, in short, ventures to live only by the aid of the Mutual Insurance company, which has promised to bury him decently.

It is not a man's duty, as a matter of course, to devote himself to the eradication of any, even the most enormous wrong; he may still properly have other concerns to engage him; but it is his duty, at least, to wish his hands of it, and, if he gives it no thought longer, not to give it practically his support. If I devote myself to other pursuits and contemplations, I must first see, at least, that I do not pursue them sitting upon another man's shoulders. I must get off him first, that he may pursue his contemplations too. See what gross inconsistency is tolerated. I have heard some of my townsmen say, "I should like to have them order me out to help put down an insurrection of the slaves, or to march to Mexico;—see if I would go;" and yet these very men have each, directly by their allegiance, and so indirectly, at least, by their money, furnished a substitute. The soldier is applauded who refuses to serve in an unjust war by those who do not refuse to sustain the unjust government which makes the war; is applauded by those whose own act and authority he disregards and sets at naught; as if the state were penitent to that degree that it hired one to scourge it while it sinned, but not to that degree that it left off sinning for a moment. Thus, under the name of Order and Civil Government, we are all made at last to pay homage to and support our own meanness. After the first blush of sin comes its indifference; and from immoral it becomes, as it were, *unmoral*, and not quite unnecessary to that life which we have made.

The broadest and most prevalent error requires the most disinterested virtue to sustain it. The slight reproach to which the virtue of patriotism is commonly liable, the noble are most likely to incur. Those who, while they disapprove of the character and measures of a government, yield to it their allegiance and support are undoubtedly its most conscientious supporters, and so frequently the most serious obstacles to reform. Some are petitioning the state to dissolve the Union, to disregard the requisitions of the President. Why do they not dissolve it themselves,—the union between themselves and the state,—and refuse to pay their quota into its treasury? Do not they stand in the same relation to the state that the state does to the Union? And have not the same reasons prevented the state from resisting the Union which have prevented them from resisting the state?

How can a man be satisfied to entertain an opinion merely, and enjoy *it?* Is there any enjoyment in it, if his opinion is that he is aggrieved? If you are cheated out of a single dollar by your neighbor, you do not rest satisfied with knowing that you are cheated, or with saying that you are cheated, or even with petitioning him to pay you your due; but you take effectual steps at once to obtain the full amount, and see that you are never cheated again. Action from principle, the perception and the performance of right, changes things and relations; it is essentially revolutionary, and does not consist wholly with anything which was. It not only divides states and churches, it divides families; ay, it divides the *individual,* separating the diabolical in him from the divine.

Unjust laws exist: shall we be content to obey them, or shall we endeavor to amend them, and obey them until we have succeeded, or shall we transgress them at once? Men generally, under such a government as this, think that they ought to wait until they have persuaded the majority to alter them. They think that, if they should resist, the remedy would be worse than the evil. But it is the fault of the government itself that the remedy *is* worse than the evil. *It* makes it worse. Why is it not more apt to anticipate and provide for reform? Why does it not cherish its wise minority? Why does it cry and resist before it is hurt? Why does it not encourage its citizens to be on the alert to point out its faults and *do* better than it would have them? Why does it always crucify Christ, and excommunicate Copernicus and Luther, and pronounce Washington and Franklin rebels?

One would think, that a deliberate and practical denial of its authority was the only offense never contemplated by government; else, why has it not assigned its definite, its suitable and proportionate penalty? If a man who has no property refuses but once to earn nine shillings for the state, he is put in prison for a period unlimited by any law that I know, and determined only by the discretion of those who placed him there; but if he should steal ninety times nine shillings from the state, he is soon permitted to go at large again.

If the injustice is part of the necessary friction of the machine of government, let it go, let it go: perchance it will wear smooth, —certainly the machine will wear out. If the injustice has a spring, or a pulley, or a rope, or a crank, exclusively for itself, then perhaps you may consider whether the remedy will not be worse than the evil; but if it is of such a nature that it requires you to be the agent of injustice to another, then, I say, break the law. Let your life be a counter friction to stop the machine. What I have to do is to see, at any rate, that I do not lend myself to the wrong which I condemn.

As for adopting the ways which the state has provided for remedying the evil, I know not of such ways. They take too much time, and a man's life will be gone. I have other affairs to attend to. I came into this world, not chiefly to make this a good place to live in, but to live in it, be it good or bad. A man has not everything to do, but something; and because he cannot do *everything*, it is not necessary that he should do *something* wrong. It is not my business to be petitioning the Governor or the Legislature any more than it is theirs to petition me; and if they should not hear my petition, what should I do then? But in this case the state has provided no way: its very Constitution is the evil. This may seem to be harsh and stubborn and unconciliatory; but it is to treat with the utmost kindness and consideration the only spirit that can appreciate or deserves it. So is all change for the better, like birth and death, which convulse the body.

I do not hesitate to say, that those who call themselves Abolitionists should at once effectually withdraw their support, both in person and property, from the government of Massachusetts and not wait till they constitute a majority of one, before they suffer the right to prevail through them. I think that it is enough if they have God on their side, without waiting for that other one. Moreover, any man more right than his neighbors constitutes a majority of one already.

I meet this American government, or its representative, the state government, directly, and face to face, once a year—no more—in the person of its tax-gatherer; this is the only mode in which a man situated as I am necessarily meets it; and it then says distinctly, Recognize me; and the simplest, most effectual, and, in the present posture of affairs, the indispensablest mode of treating with it on this head, of expressing your little satisfaction with and love for it, is to deny it then. My civil neighbor, the tax-gatherer, is the very man I have to deal with,—for it is, after all, with men and not with parchment that I quarrel,—and he has voluntarily chosen to be an agent of the government. How shall he ever know well what he is and does as an officer of the government, or as a man, until he is obliged to consider whether he shall treat me, his neighbor, for whom he has respect, as a neighbor and well-disposed man, or as a maniac and disturber of the peace, and see if he can get over this obstruction to his neighborliness without a ruder and more impetuous thought or speech corresponding with his action. I know this well, that if one thousand, if one hundred, if ten men whom I could name,—if ten *honest* men only,—ay, if *one* HONEST man, in this State of Massachusetts, *ceasing to hold slaves,* were actually to withdraw from this copartnership, and be locked up in the county jail therefor, it would be the abolition of slavery in America. For it matters not how small the beginning may seem to be: what is once well done is done forever. But we love better to talk about it: that we say is our mission. Reform keeps many scores of newspapers in its service, but not one man. If my esteemed neighbor, the State's ambassador, who will devote his days to the settlement of the question of human rights in the Council Chamber, instead of being threatened with the prisons of Carolina, were to sit down the prisoner of Massachusetts, that State which is so anxious to foist the sin of slavery upon her sister,—though at present she can discover only an act of inhospitality to be the ground of a quarrel with her,—the Legislature would not wholly waive the subject the following winter.

Under a government which imprisons any unjustly, the true place for a just man is also a prison. The proper place to-day, the only place which Massachusetts has provided for her freer and less desponding spirits, is in her prisons, to be put out and locked

out of the State by her own act, as they have already put themselves out by their principles. It is there that the fugitive slave,
and the Mexican prisoner on parole, and the Indian come to
plead the wrongs of his race should find them; on that separate,
but more free and honorable ground, where the State places
those who are not *with* her, but *against* her,—the only house in
a slave State in which a free man can abide with honor. If any
think that their influence would be lost there, and their voices no
longer afflict the ear of the State, that they would not be as an
enemy within its walls, they do not know by how much truth is
stronger than error, nor how much more eloquently and effectively he can combat injustice who has experienced a little in his
own person. Cast your whole vote, not a strip of paper merely,
but your whole influence. A minority is powerless while it conforms to the majority; it is not even a minority then; but it is ir-
resistible when it clogs by its whole weight. If the alternative is
to keep all just men in prison, or give up war and slavery, the
State will not hesitate which to choose. If a thousand men were
not to pay their tax-bills this year, that would not be a violent
and bloody measure, as it would be to pay them, and enable the
State to commit violence and shed innocent blood. This is, in
fact, the definition of a peaceable revolution, if any such is possible. If the tax-gatherer, or any other public officer, asks me, as
one has done, "But what shall I do?" my answer is, "If you really
wish to do anything, resign your office." When the subject has
refused allegiance, and the officer has resigned his office, then the
revolution is accomplished. But even suppose blood should flow.
Is there not a sort of blood shed when the conscience is
wounded? Through this wound a man's real manhood and immortality flow out, and he bleeds to an everlasting death. I see
this blood flowing now.

I have contemplated the imprisonment of the offender, rather
than the seizure of his goods,—though both will serve the same
purpose,—because they who assert the purest right, and consequently are most dangerous to a corrupt State, commonly have
not spent much time in accumulating property. To such the State
renders comparatively small service, and a slight tax is wont to
appear exorbitant, particularly if they are obliged to earn it by
special labor with their hands. If there were one who lived
wholly without the use of money, the State itself would hesitate
to demand it of him. But the rich man—not to make any invidi-

ous comparison—is always sold to the institution which makes him rich. Absolutely speaking, the more money, the less virtue; for money comes between a man and his objects, and obtains them for him; and it was certainly no great virtue to obtain it. It puts to rest many questions which he would otherwise be taxed to answer; while the only new question which it puts is the hard but superfluous one, how to spend it. Thus his moral ground is taken from under his feet. The opportunities of living are diminished in proportion as what are called the "means" are increased. The best thing a man can do for his culture when he is rich is to endeavor to carry out those schemes which he entertained when he was poor. Christ answered the Herodians according to their condition. "Show me the tribute-money," said he;—and one took a penny out of his pocket;—if you use money which has the image of Cæsar on it and which he has made current and valuable, that is, *if you are men of the State,* and gladly enjoy the advantages of Cæsar's government, then pay him back some of his own when he demands it: "Render therefore to Cæsar that which is Cæsar's, and to God those things which are God's,"—leaving them no wiser than before as to which was which; for they did not wish to know.

When I converse with the freest of my neighbors, I perceive that, whatever they may say about the magnitude and seriousness of the question, and their regard for the public tranquillity, the long and the short of the matter is, that they cannot spare the protection of the existing government, and they dread the consequences to their property and families of disobedience to it. For my own part, I should not like to think that I ever rely on the protection of the State. But, if I deny the authority of the State when it presents its tax-bill, it will soon take and waste all my property, and so harass me and my children without end. This is hard. This makes it impossible for a man to live honestly, and at the same time comfortably, in outward respects. It will not be worth the while to accumulate property; that would be sure to go again. You must hire or squat somewhere, and raise but a small crop, and eat that soon. You must live within yourself, and depend upon yourself always tucked up and ready for a start, and not have many affairs. A man may grow rich in Turkey even, if he will be in all respects a good subject of the Turkish government. Confucius said: "If a state is governed by the principles of reason, poverty and misery are subjects of shame; if a state is not governed by the principles of reason, riches and honors are the subjects of shame." No: until I want the protection of Massachusetts to be extended to me in some distant Southern port, where my liberty is endangered, or until I am bent solely on building up an estate at home by peaceful enterprise, I can afford to refuse allegiance to Massachusetts, and her right to my property and life. It costs me less in every sense to incur the penalty of disobedience to the State than it would to obey. I should feel as if I were worth less in that case.

Some years ago, the State met me in behalf of the Church, and commanded me to pay a certain sum toward the support of a clergyman whose preaching my father attended, but never I myself. "Pay," it said, "or be locked up in the jail." I declined to pay, But, unfortunately, another man saw fit to pay it. I did not see why the schoolmaster should be taxed to support the priest, and not the priest the schoolmaster; for I was not the State's schoolmaster, but I supported myself by voluntary subscription. I did not see why the lyceum should not present its tax-bill, and have the State to back its demand, as well as the Church. However, at the request of the selectmen, I condescended to make some such statement as this in writing:—"Know all men by these presents, that I, Henry Thoreau, do not wish to be regarded as a member of any incorporated society which I have not joined." This I gave to the town clerk; and he has it. The State, having thus learned that I did not wish to be regarded as a member of that church, has never made a like demand on me since; though it said that it must adhere to its original presumption that time. If I had known how to name them, I should then have signed off in detail from all the societies which I never signed on to; but I did not know where to find a complete list.

I have paid no poll-tax for six years. I was put into a jail once on this account, for one night; and, as I stood considering the walls of solid stone, two or three feet thick, the door of wood and iron, a foot thick, and the iron grating which strained the light, I could not help being struck with the foolishness of that institution which treated me as if I were mere flesh and blood and bones, to be locked up. I wondered that it should have concluded at length that this was the best use it could put me to, and had never thought to avail itself of my services in some way. I saw that, if there was a wall of stone between me and my townsmen, there was a still more difficult one to climb or break through before they could get to be as free as I was. I did not for a moment feel confined, and the walls seemed a great waste of stone and mortar. I felt as if I alone of all my townsmen had paid my tax. They plainly did not know how to treat me, but behaved like persons who are underbred. In every threat and in every compliment there was a blunder; for they thought that my chief desire was to stand the other side of that stone wall. I could not but smile to see how industriously they locked the door on my meditations, which followed them out again without let or hindrance, and *they* were really all that was dangerous. As they could not reach me, they had resolved to punish my body; just as boys, if they cannot come at some person against whom they have a spite, will abuse his dog. I saw that the State was half-witted, that it was timid as a lone woman with her silver spoons, and that it did not know its friends from its foes, and I lost all my remaining respect for it, and pitied it.

Thus the State never intentionally confronts a man's sense, intellectual or moral, but only his body, his senses. It is not armed with superior wit or honesty, but with superior physical strength. I was not born to be forced. I will breath after my own fashion. Let us see who is the strongest. What force has a multitude? They only can force me who obey a higher law than I. They force me to become like themselves. I do not hear of *men* being *forced* to live this way or that by masses of men. What sort of life were that to live? When I meet a government which says to me, "Your money or your life," why should I be in haste to give it my money? It may be in a great strait, and not know what to do: I cannot help that. It must help itself; do as I do. It is not worth the while to snivel about it. I am not responsible for the successful working of the machinery of society. I am not the son of the engineer. I perceive that, when an acorn and a chestnut fall side by side, the one does not remain inert to make way for the other, but both obey their own laws, and spring and grow and flourish as best they can, till one, perchance, overshadows and destroys the other. If a plant cannot live according to its nature, it dies; and so a man.

The night in prison was novel and interesting enough. The prisoners in their shirt-sleeves were enjoying a chat and the evening air in the doorway, when I entered. But the jailer said, "Come, boys, it is time to lock up;" and so they dispersed, and I heard the sound of their steps returning into the hollow apartments. My room-mate was introduced to me by the jailer as "a first-rate fellow and a clever man." When the door was locked, he showed me where to hang my hat, and how he managed matters there. The rooms were white-washed once a month; and this one, at least, was the whitest, most simply furnished, and probably the neatest apartment in the town. He naturally wanted to know where I came from, and what brought me there; and, when I had told him, I asked him in my turn how he came there, presuming him to be an honest man, of course; and, as the world goes, I believe he was. "Why," said he, "they accuse me of burning a barn; but I never did it." As near as I could discover, he had probably gone to bed in a barn when drunk, and smoked his pipe there; and so a barn was burnt. He had the reputation of being a clever man, had been there some three months waiting for his trial to come on, and would have to wait as much longer; but he was quite domesticated and contented, since he got his board for nothing, and thought that he was well treated.

He occupied one window, and I the other; and I saw that if one stayed there long, his principal business would be to look out the window. I had soon read all the tracts that were left there, and examined where former prisoners had broken out, and where a grate had been sawed off, and heard the history of the various occupants of that room; for I found that even here there was a history and a gossip which never circulated beyond the walls of the jail. Probably this is the only house in the town where verses are composed, which are afterward printed in a circular form, but not published. I was shown quite a long list of verses which were composed by some young men who had been detected in an attempt to escape, who avenged themselves by singing them.

I pumped my fellow-prisoner as dry as I could, for fear I should never see him again; but at length he showed me which was my bed, and left me to blow out the lamp.

It was like travelling into a far country, such as I had never expected to behold, to lie there for one night. It seemed to me that I never had heard the town-clock strike before, nor the evening sounds of the village; for we slept with the windows open, which were inside the grating. It was to see my native village in the light of the Middle Ages, and our Concord was turned into a Rhine stream, and visions of knights and castles passed before me. They were the voices of old burghers that I heard in the streets. I was an involuntary spectator and auditor of whatever

was done and said in the kitchen of the adjacent village-inn,—
a wholly new and rare experience to me. It was a closer view of
my native town. I was fairly inside of it. I never had seen its
institutions before. This is one of its peculiar institutions; for it is
a shire town. I began to comprehend what its inhabitants were
about.

In the morning, our breakfasts were put through the hole in
the door, in small oblong-square tin pans, made to fit, and holding a pint of chocolate, with brown bread, and an iron spoon.
When they called for the vessels again, I was green enough to return what bread I had left; but my comrade seized it, and said
that I should lay that up for lunch or dinner. Soon after he was
let out to work at haying in a neighboring field, whither he went
every day, and would not be back till noon; so he bade me good-
day, saying that he doubted if he should see me again.

When I came out of prison,—for some one interfered, and
paid that tax,—I did not perceive that great changes had taken
place on the common, such as he observed who went in a youth
and emerged a tottering and gray-headed man; and yet a change
had to my eyes come over the scene,—the town, and State, and
country,—greater than any that mere time could effect. I saw
yet more distinctly the State in which I lived. I saw to what
extent the people among whom I lived could be trusted as good
neighbors and friends; that their friendship was for summer
weather only; that they did not greatly propose to do right; that
they were a distinct race from me by their prejudices and super-
stitions, as the Chinamen and Malays are; that in their sacrifices
to humanity they ran no risks, not even to their property; that
after all they were not so noble but they treated the thief as he
had treated them, and hoped, by a certain outward observance
and a few prayers, and by walking in a particular straight though
useless path from time to time, to save their souls. This may be to
judge my neighbors harshly; for I believe that many of them are
not aware that they have such an institution as the jail in their
village.

It was formerly the custom in our village, when a poor debtor
came out of jail, for his acquaintances to salute him, looking
through their fingers, which were crossed to represent the grating of a jail window, "How do ye do?" My neighbors did not
thus salute me, but first looked at me, and then at one another,
as if I had returned from a long journey. I was put into jail as

I was going to the shoemaker's to get a shoe which was mended. When I was let out the next morning, I proceeded to finish my errand, and, having put on my mended shoe, joined a huckleberry party, who were impatient to put themselves under my conduct; and in half an hour,—for the horse was soon tackled,— was in the midst of a huckleberry field, on one of our highest hills, two miles off, and then the State was nowhere to be seen.

This is the whole history of "My Prisons."

I have never declined paying the highway tax, because I am as desirous of being a good neighbor as I am of being a bad subject; and as for supporting schools, I am doing my part to educate my fellow-countrymen now. It is for no particular item in the tax-bill that I refuse to pay it. I simply wish to refuse allegiance to the State, to withdraw and stand aloof from it effectually. I do not care to trace the course of my dollar, if I could, till it buys a man or a musket to shoot with,—the dollar is innocent,—but I am concerned to trace the effects of my allegiance. In fact, I quietly declare war with the State, after my fashion, though I will still make what use and get what advantage of her I can, as is usual in such cases.

If others pay the tax which is demanded of me, from a sympathy with the State, they do but what they have already done in their own case, or rather they abet injustice to a greater extent than the State requires. If they pay the tax from a mistaken interest in the individual taxed, to save his property, or prevent his going to jail, it is because they have not considered wisely how far they let their private feelings interfere with the public good.

This, then, is my position at present. But one cannot be too much on his guard in such a case, lest his action be biased by obstinacy or an undue regard for the opinions of men. Let him see that he does only what belongs to himself and to the hour.

I think sometimes, Why, this people mean well, they are only ignorant; they would do better if they knew how: why give your neighbors this pain to treat you as they are not inclined to? But I think again, This is no reason why I should do as they do, or permit others to suffer much greater pain of a different kind. Again, I sometimes say to myself, When many millions of men, without heat, without ill will, without personal feeling of any kind, demand of you a few shillings only, without the possibility, such is their constitution, of retracting or altering their present demand,

and without the possibility, on your side, of appeal to any other millions, why expose yourself to this overwhelming brute force? You do not resist cold and hunger, the winds and the waves, thus obstinately; you quietly submit to a thousand similar necessities. You do not put your head into the fire. But just in proportion as I regard this as not wholly a brute force, but partly a human force, and consider that I have relations to those millions as to so many millions of men, and not of mere brute or inanimate things, I see that appeal is possible, first and instantaneously, from them to the Maker of them, and, secondly, from them to themselves. But if I put my head deliberately into the fire, there is no appeal to fire or to the Maker of fire, and I have only myself to blame. If I could convince myself that I have any right to be satisfied with men as they are, and to treat them accordingly, and not according, in some respects, to my requisitions and expectations of what they and I ought to be, then, like a good Mussulman and fatalist, I should endeavor to be satisfied with things as they are, and say it is the will of God. And, above all, there is this difference between resisting this and a purely brute or natural force, that I can resist this with some effect; but I cannot expect, like Orpheus, to change the nature of the rocks and trees and beasts.

I do not wish to quarrel with any man or nation. I do not wish to split hairs, to make fine distinctions, or set myself up as better than my neighbors. I seek rather, I may say, even an excuse for conforming to the laws of the land. I am but too ready to conform to them. Indeed, I have reason to suspect myself on this head; and each year, as the tax-gatherer comes round, I find myself disposed to review the acts and position of the general and State governments, and the spirit of the people, to discover a pretext for conformity.

> "We must affect our country as our parents,
>   And if at any time we alienate
>   Our love or industry from doing it honor,
>   We must respect effects and teach the soul
>   Matter of conscience and religion,
>   And not desire of rule or benefit."

I believe that the State will soon be able to take all my work of this sort out of my hands, and then I shall be no better a patriot than my fellow-countrymen. Seen from a lower point of view, the Constitution, with all its faults, is very good; the law and the courts are very respectable; even this State and this American government are, in many respects, very admirable, and rare things, to be thankful for, such as a great many have described them; but seen from a point of view a little higher, they are what I have described them; seen from a higher still, and the highest, who shall say what they are, or that they are worth looking at or thinking of at all?

However, the government does not concern me much, and I shall bestow the fewest possible thoughts on it. It is not many moments that I live under a government, even in this world. If a man is thought-free, fancy-free, imagination-free, that which *is not* never for a long time appearing *to be* to him, unwise rulers or reformers cannot fatally interrupt him.

I know that most men think differently from myself; but those whose lives are by profession devoted to the study of these or kindred subjects content me as little as any. Statesmen and legislators, standing so completely within the institution, never distinctly and nakedly behold it. They speak of moving society, but have no resting-place without it. They may be men of a certain experience and discrimination, and have no doubt invented ingenious and even useful systems, for which we sincerely thank them; but all their wit and usefulness lie within certain not very wide limits. They are wont to forget that the world is not governed by policy and expediency. Webster never goes behind government, and so cannot speak with authority about it. His words are wisdom to those legislators who contemplate no essential reform in the existing government; but for thinkers, and those who legislate for all time, he never once glances at the subject. I know of those whose serene and wise speculations on this theme would soon reveal the limits of his mind's range and hospitality. Yet, compared with the cheap professions of most reformers, and the still cheaper wisdom and eloquence of politicians in general, his are almost the only sensible and valuable words, and we thank Heaven for him. Comparatively, he is always strong, original, and, above all, practical. Still, his quality is not wisdom, but prudence. The lawyer's truth is not Truth, but consistency or a consistent expediency. Truth is always in harmony with herself, and is not concerned chiefly to reveal the justice that may consist with wrong-doing. He well deserves to be called, as he has been called, the Defender of the Constitution. There are really no blows to be given by him but defensive ones. He is not a leader, but a follower. His leaders are the men of '87. "I have never made an effort," he says, "and never propose to make an effort; I have never countenanced an effort, and never mean to countenance an effort, to disturb the arrangement as originally made, by which the various States came into the Union." Still thinking of the sanction which the Constitution gives to slavery, he says, "Because it was a part of the original compact,—let it stand." Notwithstanding his special acuteness and ability, he is unable to take a fact out of its merely political relations, and behold it as it lies absolutely to be disposed of by the intellect,—what, for instance, it behooves a man to do here in America to-day with regard to slavery,—but ventures, or is driven, to make some such desperate answer as the following, while professing to speak absolutely, and as a private man,— from which what new and singular code of social duties might be inferred? "The manner," says he, "in which the governments of those States where slavery exists are to regulate it is for their own consideration, under their responsibility to their constituents, to the general laws of propriety, humanity, and justice, and to God. Associations formed elsewhere, springing from a feeling of humanity, or other cause, have nothing whatever to do with it. They have never received any encouragement from me, and they never will."*

They who know of no purer sources of truth, who have traced up its stream no higher, stand, and wisely stand, by the Bible and the Constitution, and drink at it there with reverence and humility; but they who behold where it comes trickling into this lake or that pool, gird up their loins once more, and continue their pilgrimage toward its fountainhead.

No man with a genius for legislation has appeared in America. They are rare in the history of the world. There are orators, politicians, and eloquent men, by the thousand; but the speaker has not yet opened his mouth to speak who is capable of settling the much-vexed questions of the day. We love eloquence for its own sake, and not for any truth which it may utter, or any heroism it may inspire. Our legislators have not yet learned the comparative value of free-trade and of freedom, of union, and of rectitude, to a nation. They have no genius or talent for comparatively humble questions of taxation and finance, commerce and manufactures and agriculture. If we were left solely to the wordy wit of

---

* These extracts have been inserted since the lecture was read.

legislators in Congress for our guidance, uncorrected by the seasonable experience and the effectual complaints of the people, America would not long retain her rank among the nations. For eighteen hundred years, though perchance I have no right to say it, the New Testament has been written; yet where is the legislator who has wisdom and practical talent enough to avail himself of the light which it sheds on the science of legislation?

The authority of government, even such as I am willing to submit to,—for I will cheerfully obey those who know and can do better than I, and in many things even those who neither know nor can do so well,—is still an impure one: to be strictly just, it must have the sanction and consent of the governed. It can have no pure right over my person and property but what I concede to it. The progress from an absolute to a limited monarchy, from a limited monarchy to a democracy, is a progress toward a true respect for the individual. Even the Chinese philosopher was wise enough to regard the individual as the basis of the empire. Is a democracy, such as we know it, the last improvement possible in government? Is it not possible to take a step further towards recognizing and organizing the rights of man? There will never be a really free and enlightened State until the State comes to recognize the individual as a higher and independent power, from which all its own power and authority are derived, and treats him accordingly. I please myself with imagining a State at last which can afford to be just to all men, and to treat the individual with respect as a neighbor; which even would not think it inconsistent with its own repose if a few were to live aloof from it, not meddling with it, nor embraced by it, who fulfilled all the duties of neighbors and fellow-men. A State which bore this kind of fruit, and suffered it to drop off as fast as it ripened, would prepare the way for a still more perfect and glorious State, which also I have imagined, but not yet anywhere seen.

The Psychology of Loyalty

———————————————————————◆

*John Schaar, 1928– , is Associate Professor of Political Science at
the University of California, Berkeley.* *His essay,* Loyalty in America,
*from which this selection is taken, clarifies the confused subject of
political loyalty by drawing on contemporary materials from social
psychology and sociology. Schaar, like Emile Durkheim, considers
group solidarity natural and good, and sees the social bonds as non-
rational, although not therefore contrary to reason. Note particularly
that Schaar's description of the formation of loyalty implies that
loyalties are* essential *components of human personality, for every
person who grows to maturity identifies with some group or other,
and internalizes its values as his own.*

A First View of Loyalty

Out of their centuries-old tradition, political philosophers have
distilled a peculiar vocabulary. "State," "sovereignty," "obligation," "freedom," "right," and a host of others, are terms of special significance to them. They are the political philosopher's
"careful words," as Perry calls them, words he ponders deeply,
and does not use lightly.[1] This vocabulary demarcates the political philosopher's intellectual world and distinguishes his discourse from that of other writers. Since the present essay is, after
all, addressed to specialists, the specialist may properly ask
where "loyalty" belongs in his list of "careful words."

LOYALTY IN THE VOCABULARY OF POLITICAL SCIENCE

Loyalty occupies the ground between patriotism and obligation.
It is something less than the uncritical adulation and defense of
one's own land which is the essence of patriotism. It is something
more than the formal duty to obey law which is the meaning of
obligation. Loyalty is more rational and less comprehensive in

Reprinted by permission of the publishers from John Schaar, *Loyalty in
America* (Berkeley: University of California Press, 1957).

its objects than patriotism, less rational and more comprehensive than obligation.

Patriotism appears to be the inevitable companion of the development of solidarity sentiments in human groups. "Communities of all types," writes William Aylott Orton, "as they become organized and self-conscious, have a tendency also to become closed. The 'I belong' tends increasingly to imply 'you don't.' Consciousness of kind becomes increasingly consciousness of difference. And consciousness of difference tends . . . to be translated in terms of superior and inferior." [2] It is this sense of superiority in difference that most closely expresses the essence of patriotic feeling and action. Each community feels itself unique and inherently above the other communities in its environment —there are always "Greeks" and "Barbarians." These feelings may be expressed in the tolerant paternalism of Pericles' Funeral Oration which pictured Athens as the school of Greece, in the missionary ardor of the medieval Church for the conversion of the infidel, in Hitler's rabidly nationalistic tirades, in the historical mission and elite qualities conferred upon the proletariat by Marx, or in various other forms. They need rest on no objective basis to be vehement in expression—who can prove the Germans better than the Jews? Patriotic sentiment, the special political name for this sense of superiority in difference, rests more on emotion than on reason, and comprehends many facets of the life and culture of a group.

The question of obligation is the question of why political authority should be obeyed. T. H. Green, at the outset of his study of political obligation, defines the scope of his subject as including ". . . the obligation of the subject towards the sovereign, the obligation of the citizen towards the state, and the obligation of individuals to each other as enforced by a political superior." [3] Men have not been content to rest obedience merely on the given fact that the only life we know is life lived in society and thus under the restraints of authority and law. It is not enough to obey out of habit or custom; obedience must have moral grounds as well. Brute obedience must be transmuted into moral obligation. Inquiries into the grounds and limits of obligation are, in this respect, the political analogue of Milton's effort to "justify the ways of God to man." Such inquiries direct their appeal as much to the mind as to the heart and often rest on close argument and reasoning. Moreover, obligation is usually

limited in its objects to political authority as expressed in validly
enacted laws and does not enclose the broad and shifting objects
of patriotism.

Loyalty, then, lies between the two, partakes partially of each,
yet differs from both. But to insert loyalty at its proper place
in the vocabulary of political science is not to go far toward
understanding all that the word implies. Although it makes communication easier, strict adherence to traditional categories may
also imprison the mind within a cell which excludes much of the
realm of reality. Emancipation from accepted forms is often the
first step toward knowledge. No discussion of loyalty can dwell
long on the heights of political speculation without falling victim
to the vertigo that comes from abandoning the concrete for the
abstract. The empirical phenomena collected under the rubric
"loyalty" are, in the first place, data of psychology and sociology,
and must be examined as such before analysis can proceed to
other aspects.

LOYALTY AS AN ATTITUDE

Josiah Royce, who perhaps had a sharper perception of the meaning of loyalty than most moral philosophers, defined it as ". . . *the
willing and practical and thorough-going devotion of a person
to a cause.*" [4] Each descriptive carries a special cargo of meaning:
loyalty must be freely given; must manifest itself in action; and
is intense in emotional tone. Each also raises a number of questions which this section will try to answer.

Another writer points out additional factors which cast Royce's
conception into fuller and more precise form and bring to view
other aspects of loyalty:

Man in society finds himself the focal point of innumerable loyalties.
. . . Each one of these represents some special aspect of his nature
which seeks outlet in association with others of similar interest. A
loyalty, then, would appear to be the identification of one's own interest with that of a group. It implies the associated necessity of
furthering both the larger purpose which the group fosters and the
integral unity of the individual himself with the group and the group
purpose.[5]

These two definitions direct attention to a number of related
problems important in the psychology of loyalty. Each insists
that loyalty has at least two dimensions, internal or personal, and

external or social. This means that loyalty is a relation between subject and object and is manifested both in internal mental states and in external behavior. It means also that loyalty has consequences for both individual and society. Both definitions view the relation of loyalty as similar to the process which the psychologist calls identification. Royce draws attention to the affective tone of loyalty whereas Bloch reminds that loyalty serves the interests of individual and group. Bloch pictures man-in-society as the focal point of innumerable loyalties and points out that each loyalty serves a particular aspect of one's nature This suggests the possibility of conflicts among loyalties together with changes in the content of individual loyalties. It is these psychological problems of loyalty—its formation, growth, tone, functions, and conflicts—that will concern us here. Although it is true that loyalty also has moral dimensions, they are best left for later treatment. We can plead for clarity on the facts before plunging into the values.

But before plunging anywhere, one caution. The difficulties in presenting the psychology of loyalty are not so much substantive as procedural. They inhere in the tools of inquiry, not in the subject itself. We must deal here not with linear cause and effect but with relations of mutual dependence. Yet our language, and thereby our "natural" patterns of thought, is a language of cause and effect.* We must treat of multiple variables ever changing in quantity and relation one to the other, but the logic of our grammar treats of fixed states and distinct entities. There is here a practical difficulty which cannot be solved with entire satisfac-

* Compare with this the following: "The common inherited scheme of conception which is all around us, and comes to us as naturally and un-objectionally as our native air, is none the less imposed upon us, and limits our intellectual movements in countless ways—all the more surely and irresistibly because, being inherent in the very language we must use to express the simplest meaning, it is adopted and assimilated before we can so much as begin to think for ourselves at all." F. M. Cornford, *From Religion to Philosophy: A Study in the Origins of Western Speculation* (London: Edward Arnold, 1912), p. 45, as quoted in C. K. Ogden and I. A. Richards, *The Meaning of Meaning: A Study of the Influence of Language upon Thought and of the Science of Symbolism* (10th ed.; London: Routledge and Kegan Paul, 1952), pp. 25–26. Also, "A Cause indeed, in the sense of something which forces another something called an effect to occur, is so obvious a phantom that it has been rejected even by metaphysicians. The current scientific account, on the other hand, which reduces causation to correlation, is awkward for purposes of exposition, since in the absence of a 'conjugating' vocabulary constant periphrasis is unavoidable." (P. 55).

tion. For at the very outset of inquiry we must break into the circle of loyalty at some point and push onward from there, knowing even as we do so that a circle is without beginning, end, or direction.

It can be said, as a first approximation, that the psychology of loyalty is a branch of the psychology of attitude and identification. This proposition affords the amateur in psychology a measure of security, since both attitudes and identification have been studied extensively by the psychologists and there is general agreement on their nature.[6]

Granted the assertion that loyalty is but a special type of attitude, it is possible to derive a typology of loyalty by reference to the psychology of attitude. After this typology is firmly in mind, the different task of studying the formation and growth of loyalty can be undertaken. The attempt here is to describe the general structure of loyalty rather than to analyze the detailed properties of loyal word or deed. To this end, it is suggested that loyalty has five major characteristics.[7]

1. *Loyalty implies a subject-object relationship and the content of loyalty, which changes with that relationship, can be highly various.* Loyalty is always the loyalty of some person for or toward something else. That "something else"—the object of loyalty —can be another person, a group, a cause, an ideal, an institution, and so forth. The content of a loyalty is established by the subject-object relationship and varies with it. Thus, for example, Protestant and Catholic may worship the same God in principle but display their worship in quite different ways inasmuch as the religious practices of each are prescribed by different religious institutions to which they are loyal. Or, by way of further illustration, the content of loyalty may be described as political or religious according as it runs to the institutions of government or of God.

2. *Loyalties vary in intensity of emotional tone.* This proposition asserts that loyalty may be manifested in diverse ways and degrees. Loyalty in its richest expression is the passionate devotion of an individual to a cause combined with zealous exertions to advance its projected aims. In its more meager manifestations it may be an almost habitual, barely conscious, and diffuse sense of sharing in a common purpose. Within this range, intensity of loyalty will vary.

This idea contains further implications. First, it suggests that loyalties might be measured along a scale ranging from fanaticism at the one pole to resigned acceptance at the other. The behavioral components useful in measuring the tone of a given loyalty might include, for example, the degree of participation and absorption of a person in his object of loyalty, and the sacrifice he will endure for it. It suggests, secondly, that the strength of loyalty has considerable impact on behavior. Loyalties are programs of action and the strengths of a man's loyalties must be known before permitting him to undertake certain tasks. As Sidney Hook warns, it would be unwise to staff an institution for the aged and infirm with doctors who believe wholly that the old should not continue the burdens of this life. Nor will a society that cares for its own well-being fill positions of trust with agents dedicated to its destruction.[8]

3. *Loyalties differ in specificity and particularity.* Loyalties develop as by-products of experience and thought. As a result, the extent and diversity of stimuli to which a loyalty is related will vary in accordance with the situation in which the loyalty originated and with the kind of cognitive connections established between the loyalty and the immediate stimulus situation. If the original matrix from which a loyalty emerged is capable of partial representation in other situations, then the loyalty may be evoked in these other contexts. The relation between the generative matrix and the specificity of a loyalty is direct: as the matrix tends toward formlessness, the loyalty becomes less specific; conversely, as the matrix increases in precision of structure, the loyalty increases in specificity. The less specific a loyalty, the more easily it is transferred to a greater number of situations.

Although some few loyalties may be evoked only in face of the situation in which they originated, it is more usual that an established loyalty will be related to objects not directly present and influential in its original crystallization. An original loyalty of a particular son for a particular father may be evoked in an altered form when that son enters other situations where authority is exercised over him by persons of greater age and higher status. Many loyalties are operative in a wide variety of situations because the stimulus field in which the loyalty originally grew was itself extensive and diffuse and therefore capable of representation or reproduction in many other contexts.

Particularity refers to the degree of relatedness one loyalty has with others. The more particular a loyalty is, the less connection it has with other loyalties. The relevant consideration is whether a loyalty stands sharply alone or as part of a larger constellation of attitudes. Thus, my loyalty to political authority may stand quite apart from my loyalty to family but closely connected with my loyalties to political party or religious society.

4. *Loyalties differ in precision and endurance.* Some loyalties are tightly structured, clearly formulated, and highly articulate; others are amorphous and flowing, vague, nearly inarticulate. Some loyalties have but a short life while others endure through long time, ending only when he who holds them ends. There is no clear relation between these two qualities, for even the deepest and most enduring loyalties may not be highly articulate and organized. Conversely, it often happens that the explicit profession of a systematic and idealized loyalty is but the mask of one more deeply concealed and profoundly rooted in the most fundamental attitudes of one's character.

It is a material point that the clearest fact about a loyalty is its persistence through time. Our loyalties are not easily escaped, for they are rooted in our deepest sentiments and needs. Man in his pride may admire his intellect as an engine of limitless liberating power, but he must recognize still that his very thought modes and life habits can never shake the bonds of existing loyalties and the attitudes implicit in them. Even though he in his freedom revolt, the bounds of that revolt are circumscribed by past loyalties and attitudes. Still, loyalties do change. Even our dearest convictions are not spared the awful necessity of adapting to novel circumstances. From this it can be seen that the processes of loyalty formation and alteration are central to the process of social change itself. Although the point will be elaborated later, it should be noted here that the complexity and instability characteristic of modern political institutions are basic to an understanding of contemporary issues of loyalty.

5. *Loyalties vary in importance.* This proposition requires little embellishment. The point is simply that from the standpoint of their impact on political behavior all loyalties are not of equal importance. In addition, the same loyalty may acquire different weights in accordance with the person holding it as well as with the situation in which it receives expression.

FORMATION AND MODIFICATION OF LOYALTY

Freud remarks somewhere in his writings that from his earliest history man has been "forced into coöperation" with his fellows.

This, although it savors of a paradox similar to Jean Jacques's famous attempt to force men into freedom, is perhaps as good a place as any to open a discussion of the formation and modification of loyalty. For the sentiment of loyalty, although it emerges from a social matrix and binds men together in adherence to prescribed ideals and patterns of action, also affords bountiful opportunities for free choice and responsible action. Loyalty is Janus-faced. In this duality some of the deepest problems of human conduct and social organization find their roots.

No matter where we look, nor how far back in time we go, man is never seen alone but always is found in association with others of his kind. It is unnecessary to posit any "gregarious instinct" to explain this phenomenon when other more easily verified hypotheses will do as well. Indeed, little would be lost by foregoing attempts to explain the origins of group living and holding with Dewey that "associated activity needs no explanation; things are made that way." [9] Men have always combined in social units because it was necessary and, if we can infer from our own lives, because it was pleasant. Necessary because "there must be," on the authority of Aristotle, "a union of those who cannot exist without each other; namely, of male and female, that the race may continue. . . ." Necessary, secondly, because the lone individual lacks adequate defenses against the hazards of nature and the aggressions of other men. Association is pleasant in that it seems good and satisfying to live in communion with others. It was Aristotle, again, who said that the solitary is either a god or a beast. Furthermore, in this calculus of pleasure one should not forget that the human sexual drive, being continuous rather than intermittent in its demand for expression, also urges toward permanent association. Association, then, can be accepted as a datum of fact without probing further into its causes.

Loyalty in its primordial forms grows from association. It is a felt sentiment of attachment to something outside the self, usually other persons or an ideal. Only at later and higher levels does it acquire more complex and rational layers of meaning. The sentiment grows naturally, that is, it flows effortlessly from the basic and repeated interactions one has with his fellows. At the earliest stage this growth is largely unconscious; there is little or no awareness that it is occurring and there are few or no agencies with the specific social function of instilling loyalty. The individual wears his loyalties comfortably and becomes intensely aware of them only when social changes push them to the forefront of consciousness.*

It is not enough to gloss over this subject with the declaration that loyalty emerges from a social matrix. The subject deserves more care than that. In the following pages an attempt will be made to delineate at least the outlines of these processes of growth and change. The discussion rests on the previously stated premise that, considered psychologically, loyalty is but a particular type of attitude. The analytic problem, therefore, becomes one of applying existing knowledge concerning the nature of attitudes to the immediate problem.†

It is clear, first of all, that one's beliefs and attitudes are in great measure shaped by the culture in which he lives. This proposition is supported by both empirical studies and basic psychological theory. Many correlational studies have been made between attitudes and such cultural components as family background, education, religion, socioeconomic status, and so forth. A few such studies might be cited.[10] (1) P. F. Lazarsfeld, B. Berelson, and H. Gaudet have shown that if a person's economic status, place of residence, and religious affiliation are known, a reasonably reliable index of his "political predisposition" can be constructed. (2) T. M. Newcomb and G. Svehla showed that there are high positive correlations between parents and children in their attitudes about internationalism.[11] (3) A 1936 study by E. L. Horowitz on the formation of attitudes toward the Negro

---

* Writing of primitive society, one anthropologist states: "Until the rise of civilization, mankind lived in communities so small that every adult could, and no doubt did, know everybody else." Under such conditions, men are held in community by strong bonds of status, kinship, and shared attitudes concerning the moral ends of life. Thus: "We may say that the members of the precivilized community had a strong sense of group solidarity." Robert Redfield, *The Primitive World and Its Transformations* (Ithaca: Cornell University Press, 1953), pp. 7, 8.

† The analysis here would not placate the professional conscience of the psychologist. A fully satisfactory treatment would begin with a study of motivation, perception, and learning, move on to examine the structural properties of social-psychological fields, and only then consider the final problem of how norms and sentiments emerge from social interaction. Such a comprehensive presentation is beyond the scope of this study. The analysis here deals mainly with the final level and neglects the prior levels, even while confessing that to do so is without any justification other than convenience. One wishes he might remedy these omissions by performing the legislator's adroit trick of "incorporation by reference" and merely cite the rich psychological literature available.

concluded that ". . . attitudes toward Negroes are now chiefly determined not by contact with Negroes, but by contact with the prevalent attitude toward Negroes." [12] Horowitz applied a series of attitude tests to children and adolescents from various groups —e.g., rural and urban Southern white children, white children in New York City, and New York children of Communist parents. It is not the point of least interest in his study that he discovered that only the children of Communist parents were innocent of anti-Negro prejudice.

The point is upheld also by certain theoretical considerations. One's needs, perceptions, and tensions are affected by the stimulus patterns he confronts. The cultural environment is a main stimulus source for the individual. Since no social environment is composed of factors selected in a purely random fashion (i.e., there is a *pattern* of culture), it follows that each society presents its members with stimulus *patterns* which encourage the emergence of only certain kinds of needs, emotions, goals, and attitudes. Therefore, variations among social patterns will be reflected in differences in the beliefs and attitudes held by individuals in those societies.

The idea hardly requires emphasis for it is a germinal doctrine of much modern social science. It does require modification. Sociologists and educators, particularly, have accented cultural influences in explaining individual beliefs and attitudes. Indeed, there is a school of thought in modern sociology, marching under the banner of "cultural determinism," which holds that individual character is entirely the creature of culture. Here, perhaps, the doctrine runs too far and is vulnerable to criticism:

Modern sociology has an inherent disposition to regard the human individual as a mere by-product of social or cultural forces, a mere overlapping point of innumerable groups; and so to deny him any significance or efficacy in his own right. A large body of fact supports this view: the sort of fact that the methods of sociology are adapted to discover.[13]

That is the crucial point—"the sort of fact that the methods of sociology are adapted to discover." The result of such methods is to reduce the individual to the pallid existence of an epiphenomenon. When viewed in historical perspective, this phenomenon is recognized as an exact analogue of the "reductive fallacy" so widespread in nineteenth-century social thought. Someone has called the nineteenth the "nothing but" century, for social theory then was often an effort to reduce social problems to a single simple base. Marx explained that all social change was basically nothing but economic change. Likewise, Spencer demonstrated that society was nothing but the struggle for existence and the survival of the fittest. Now, in our own more enlightened day, we learn that human character is nothing but the product of cultural forces.* Yet, the individual resists this aggression and pleads for salvation from the forces of culture. And surely he is right: exposure to a regular and patterned range of stimulations does not, in and of itself, issue in uniform beliefs and attitudes among those exposed. There are still individual differences.

Beliefs and attitudes develop selectively. The process of perception itself is selective. No person perceives and registers everything in the external environment. This selectivity is systematic. As Krech and Crutchfield state, ". . . the objects that are accentuated are usually those objects which serve some immediate purpose of the perceiving individual." [14] The success of "projective techniques" in diagnosing personality corroborates this notion. The technique itself depends upon the fact that responses to stimuli reflect personal needs and demands. Since one's beliefs and attitudes must be built on his perceptions, it is apparent that attitudes and beliefs too will vary with individual needs and demands. Therefore, attitudes will not reflect with perfect fidelity the "real" stimulus conditions presented by cultural patterns. Beliefs and attitudes are formed selectively, are intimately related to individual needs, and are not a simple "carry-over" from cultural patterns.

Furthermore, the very heterogeneity of cultural influences to which one is exposed will make for large individual variations in held attitudes. Culture is not an assembly line which turns out identical human products as Ford produces automobiles. No culture is a single, homogeneous pattern. The cultural influences

* In Tolstoy's monumental *War and Peace* there appears a passage keenly appreciative of the durability and strength of this urge to reduce complex situations to single causes. He writes: "The combination of causes of phenomena is beyond the grasp of the human intellect. But the impulse to seek causes is innate in the soul of man. And the human intellect, with no inkling of the immense variety and complexity of circumstances conditioning a phenomenon, any one of which may be separately conceived of as the cause of it, snatches at the first and most easily understood approximation, and says here is the cause." (Modern Library ed.; New York: Random House, n.d.), p. 918.

to which one is exposed are diverse and not infrequently contradictory. Thus, even if beliefs and attitudes mirrored objective stimulations, there would still be great individual differences within the same culture. What is true of individuals here is equally true of subgroups within the same social system.

The tenable conclusion is that beliefs and attitudes are products of complex interactions between cultural and functional determinants. Functional determinants include such things as an individual's needs, emotions, and specific personality traits. Under cultural factors are bunched such items as family and educational background, socio-economic status, and religious affiliation. One selects from the stimulations presented by culture those that have most relevance for himself. Both types of factors must be included in any analysis of attitude formation.

Over and above the functional meanings that particular attitudes and beliefs may have for particular individuals, there are general needs which beliefs and attitudes fulfill for human personality as such. First of all, they impart structure and continuity to existence. Human existence without enduring beliefs is inconceivable. Without lasting belief structures, each experience would be novel and the individual would be a "new" person in each situation. Second, there is a very important cluster of attitudes that define the individual to himself, telling him who he is and how he is related to others. These are the "ego-attitudes" which Sherif and Cantril explain as follows:

In brief, the ego consists of many attitudes which from infancy on are related to the "I," "me," "mine" experiences. These attitudes, which may be designated as ego-attitudes, are constituent components of the ego. Apart from the constellation of these ego-attitudes, there is no such entity as the ego. . . . They are attitudes that define and qualify an individual's relative standing to other persons or to institutions in some more or less lasting way. They are attitudes that determine the more or less enduring character of one's personal identity with the values or norms incorporated in him.[15]

Third, beliefs and attitudes aid in the human search for meaning. The modern psychologist's concept of man as a striver for meaning echoes Aristotle's classic definition of man as the rational animal. There is in human nature an insistent urge to understand, to find meaning and significance in the events of life. Man does not accept events as just so many unrelated phenomena; he builds of them not a catalog, but a story, with a plot and a moral. Man is not only a thinking but a believing creature. This search for beliefs which can impart meaning to life may be explicit and systematic, as in the search of the philosopher for "fundamentals"; or it may be only the inchoate wonderings we all engage in when faced with the unfamiliar.

Before moving on to other subjects, it is necessary to treat, however briefly, the problem of change in attitudes. It has been mentioned previously that this problem is inseparably bound to the whole process of social change. Anything learned about the former problem, therefore, should indicate some of the workings of the latter.

It is a part of everyday knowledge that beliefs and attitudes tenaciously resist change. So important is this phenomenon that it should be examined in some detail. The subject can be approached by specifying the major factors that account for the resistance of attitudes to change.

1) One has a "vested interest" in his attitudes and beliefs. It was noted above that attitudes and beliefs provide a structure of meaning for the self in its journey through the world of experience. When the structure is shaken, personal insecurity often results; therefore, one relinquishes established attitudes with reluctance.

2) Beliefs and attitudes influence perception.[16] New facts hostile to one's beliefs may not even be perceived. If perception is impaired in this way, reorganization of beliefs will not automatically occur with changes in the real environment. Each of us views the world through a special pair of glasses and what we "see" is tinted by our beliefs and attitudes. If the attitudes are of great functional significance, they can even occlude factors in the external environment. Or, if contradictory data are perceived, they will be interpreted in such a way as to produce the slightest possible impact on existing belief and attitude configurations.

3) Finally, beliefs and attitudes tend to persist if they receive social support. It was pointed out earlier that beliefs and attitudes are affected by cultural patterns. This correlation operates so as to offer social support to one's attitudes if they are consonant with the group mores. Attitudes and beliefs thus often function to meet the needs of social acceptance and approval. When attitudes receive social approval, it is exceedingly difficult to force changes in them. Sometimes it can be done only by the substitution of a different approval group.[17]

Although the foregoing pages have been framed in the language of the general psychology of attitudes, their bearing on the topic of loyalty is easily determined. One's loyalties emerge from the dynamic interaction of cultural and functional determinants. We can therefore expect the members of a social unit to share a common cluster of loyalties. But this does not mean uniformity. Cultural diversity, plus special functional determinants, produces individual variations. A man's loyalties perform for him the supremely important tasks of providing self-definition and interpreting experience. Shared loyalties facilitate communication among members of a social group and provide the cement of unity. Once formed, loyalties are not easily changed, not only because they receive social support but also because individuals build up vested interests in them, and because established loyalties predispose those who hold them to perceive their environment selectively. These are the basic principles of the psychology of loyalty; with them in mind, we can advance to a broader frame of analysis.

GEMEINSCHAFT AND GESELLSCHAFT LOYALTIES

Ferdinand Tönnies contributed to modern sociology a pair of concepts which can further an understanding of loyalty in larger contexts than those considered thus far.[18] Tönnies began with the proposition that social relationships are products of human will. He moved on to divide social structures into two major categories dependent upon the type of will and the quality of the inner relationships that compose them. A group can be created (i.e., willed into being) for limited and definite ends and without regard for sentimental values in the relations among members. Then the structure created is a Gesellschaft and the type of willing operative is *Kurwille*—the rational will which distinguishes between ends and means and is based upon expedient calculations of interest. On the other hand, there may be willed into being a group felt to be valuable in and of itself and in which inner relationships are charged with sentimental values. In this instance, the structure created is a Gemeinschaft, and the type of willing operative is *Wesenwille*—the emotional will which springs from temperament and looks not solely toward expedient calculations of interest but toward relationships with moral and sentimental values.[19]

Although some have not been so cautious, Tönnies himself was careful to explain that the two categories are "pure concepts" or abstractions; they are not found *as such* in reality. They are useful abbreviations for phenomena which, in varying proportions, appear in social entities. For example, the observer should not label the family or the tribe a Gemeinschaft, and the trading company a Gesellschaft, but should ascertain to what extent the family under particular conditions (e.g., the middle-class urban family) partakes more of the Gemeinschaft type than it does under other (e.g., rural) conditions.

Corresponding to these type divisions of social structures, there are divisions of loyalty. Different social entities vary as to the types of loyalty dominant in them. To some groups, the individual's loyalty runs only so far as interest dictates. But to others his loyalty transcends personal interest and takes on complex overlays of sentiment. The social units to which strongest loyalty is given are of the Gemeinschaft type. The particular entities of Gemeinschaft character vary in time and place but are most frequently family, clan or tribe, religious body, and nation. These units usually include ". . . solidarity sentiments making it a magical, sacred, or moral obligation of the members to give such sentiments priority over all considerations of expediency." [20] Thus, many legends are woven around those who have sacrificed even the precious gift of life itself for family or religion. Organizations of the Gesellschaft type do not arouse this kind of loyalty; few indeed are the martyrs for the limited liability corporation. Individuals, then, may be attached to institutions or causes in two general ways which are dependent upon the nature of the object of loyalty itself.

It is obvious that in the modern nation-state loyalty is largely of the Gemeinschaft character. The nation-state can usually muster more of the loyalties and energies of its members than any other social structure. But, as is well known, this was not always so. In Western Europe, for example, religious institutions commanded more loyalty than their secular counterparts for a great many centuries. The Gemeinschaft loyalty of the national community is inherently aggressive and exclusive; it is the modern manifestation of that sense of in-group versus out-group that has always been part of the meaning of loyalty.

Another modern social structure which tends increasingly toward the creation of Gemeinschaft loyalty is the political party. This is most evident in certain of the totalitarian parties and movements, such as the Russian Communist party or the former German National Socialist movement, but is not restricted to them. Certain continental Social Democratic parties, as in Germany and Austria, have displayed the same tendencies. The modern party tries to attract loyalties of this sort by fostering *Weltanschauung* ideologies, by extensive propaganda campaigns, by programs of cadre training, and other like techniques. The party strives to become for its membership the object of supreme loyalty and the fountainhead of all other loyalties. In National Socialist Germany and Communist Russia the parties attained this tremendous goal. The whole society became, as it were, a magnified version of the patriarchal family, with all loyalties ultimately directed to, and all power and prestige flowing from, one leader at the apex of a monolithic and elitist party structure.

One further cognate point should be made before leaving this subject. Just as different types of social entities elicit different types of loyalty, so do different social circumstances condition the strength with which loyalties are expressed. It appears that the strength of the members' loyalty to an organization varies directly with the felt needs of the group.[21]

Within limits which cannot be fixed with precision, but which are undoubtedly broad, this holds true regardless of whether loyalty aids or injures a member's private interests. For many millions of men loyalty to nation offers no obvious and immediate benefits. Frequently, such loyalties are actually destructive of personal interest, as when the youth is asked to give his life in war. Yet our loyalties are often most strongly expressed when the entities to which they are given are threatened. During times of peace, national loyalties may seem to weaken and dissolve under the corrosive effects of individualism, sectionalism, or class conflict. But—let the nation be threatened with foreign attack; particularisms diminish and the populace rises to new heights of effort and sacrifice in a massive display of common loyalty. Observing this phenomenon, some moral philosophers have concluded that war is the noblest endeavor of nations. Herein too lies the wisdom of that notorious political maxim which holds that the final solution for internal crisis is foreign adventure. This same phenomenon explains the secret of the spectacular success of the demagogue's cry for sacrifice in time of real or contrived danger. The point should be made also that in a period like the present, when each nation conceives itself to be living in a world fraught with perils and threats, we should not expect a reduction in the temperature of national sentiment. It is during such times that the cry for loyalty swells, and those who look hopefully toward the creation of the grand and spacious world community must either alter these perilous conditions or resign themselves to a lengthy residence in the cramped quarters of the nation-state.

By now the outlines of the processes of loyalty formation, expression, and change should be fairly clear. The word itself has many shades of meaning, and the phenomena it signifies are not simple. But loyalty is not a supernatural manifestation; it is only complex and entangled. What is called loyalty is really a kind of norm containing the properties ascribed to it by Royce and Bloch, and resting upon the familiar processes of attitude formation and change. The roots of loyalty are to be found in social interaction. Expressed briefly, shared activities evoke shared sentiments of sympathy. As the group lives together as a social unit, members experience mutual debts of gratitude, mutual likes and dislikes, and shared interests which bind them together. This culminates in the simply stated and profoundly felt emotion of owing much to each other and to the group as a whole. Who can forget Socrates' sublime statement of his duty to remain and accept death rather than flee the community which had given him life and being? "Well then," he represents the Laws as asking, "since you were brought into the world and nurtured and educated by us, can you deny in the first place that you are our child and slave . . . ? Has a philosopher like you failed to discover that our country is more to be valued and higher and holier far than mother or father or any ancestor, and more to be regarded in the eyes of gods and of men of understanding?" [22]

One's earliest and strongest loyalties are formed in his childhood primary groups. In these groups too are generated many of the broadest general attitude complexes carried throughout life. Our loyalties are first attached to objects within immediate experience, later radiating outward to enclose more distant objects as experience and knowledge expand. But there are always objects outside the circle of loyalty. *Our* language, *our* customs, *our* beliefs, *our* gods, *our* leaders evoke loyalty from the individual and distinguish him and his group from outsiders. Those outside the group are strangers to whom no loyalty or obligations are owing. Since there is always present a powerful current of feeling which binds the group together against an outside world which—because unknown—is nearly always suspected of hostile designs, it is an easy matter to channel the group into aggressive or defensive measures against the strangers. It is no mere etymological accident that *hospes* (stranger) and *hostis* (enemy) share the same root. As Ranyard West put it, "Human loyalty and human strife came to this world together. . . . And no economic or political organizations of history have checked man's passionate devotion to his 'ain folk'—his little group." [23] Loyalty has an inherent propensity toward exclusionism and aggressiveness.*

Even at the most primitive level loyalty can be a very strong emotion quite capable of overriding the so-called selfish motives. Loyalty is felt to impose obligations which must be fulfilled if one is to please others and be judged worthy in their eyes. There are few explicit and formal sanctions against breach of loyalty; the controls are, as it were, worked into the very fabric of the group life. A breach of loyalty is a disruption of the usual pattern of life, a dissonance in the collective harmony. When such a dissonance sounds in the life of the small group there is an automatic retuning to restore the original harmony.† These restorative forces can range from simple disapproval and admonition to that most terrible of all punishments—ostracism. He who suffers this affliction is cast beyond the pale of society; he is Homer's "tribeless, lawless, hearthless one," and his path there-

---

* A fascinating sidelight on this point is provided by the etymology of the word "rival." Its Latin root, *rivalis*, meant an associate or companion, and *rivales* signified two neighboring communities. Shakespeare too used it to mean colleague or companion. Thus:

> Well, good-night.
> If you do meet Horatio and Marcellus,
> The rivals of my watch, bid them make haste.
> —*Hamlet*, Act I, Scene I

Today, of course, a rival is a competitor or opponent. We tend to think of two communities or groups in close proximity as not only neighbors in the sense of being friends, but also as competitors.

† Redfield, *op. cit.*, p. 14, writes: "In the most primitive societies of living men . . . the controls of action are informal; they rest on the traditional obligations of largely inherited status, and are expressed in talk and gesture and in the patterns of reciprocal action. Political institutions are few and simple, or even entirely absent. . . . People do the kind of things they do, not because somebody just thought up that kind of thing, or because somebody ordered them to do so, but because it seems to the people to flow from the very necessity of existence that they do that kind of thing."

after must move in those dark and shaded regions outside the friendly fires of clan and kin. Human societies have always saved their harshest punishments for betrayal and disloyalty, for these crimes turn the knife in the vitals of the social organism. Rebecca West, in richly metaphorical language, plumbs the depth of this feeling when she describes betrayal as ". . . that sin which is the dark travesty of legitimate hatred because it is felt for kindred, just as incest is the dark travesty of legitimate love." In another place she writes of treachery as ". . . the betrayal of familiars to strangers, of those who are near to those who are far, of those to whom one is bound by real interest to those who, being foreign, will treat one as a foreigner and maybe, in the end, turn against one." [24] For the sin of disloyalty, then, harsh penance is exacted.

Political Loyalty

To see loyalty as a general phenomenon in human intercourse is a first step toward the fuller view of political loyalty which is the object of this essay. It affords a broader view of the terrain without which lesser features cannot be seen in their proper places and relations. With that first step, the perspective shifts from the general to the partial, from the larger to the smaller, narrowing down to focus on loyalty in its specifically political forms.

LOYALTY AND COMMUNITY

In the vocabulary of political science loyalty resides between patriotism and obligation. Political loyalty is a devoted attachment to the political ideals and institutions established in a community. In most of its manifestations political loyalty is a complex mixture of tradition and sentiment, choice and reason. Most of our loyalties are acquired in the course of social conditioning and are integrated into the character structure without conscious thought. We know, for example, that the largest portion of adherents to the Republican party derive their allegiance originally from tradition and justify their continued support by a process which the psychologist would coldly label "rationalization." On the other hand, some loyalties are products of choice, choice which may be based on rational calculations of interest or on emotional considerations. Such a chosen loyalty is illustrated by the conversion of the nonbeliever to religious faith, and by the choice, in contemporary America, of membership in the Communist party. But most loyalties are compound rather than simple and the broadest generalization possible, as will be elaborated later, is that different polities prefer one over another of the components.

Since political loyalty is a devoted attachment to the established political institutions of a community, it is itself a foremost component of community. Through political institutions, policies and ends binding on the whole social order are prescribed.[25] Therefore, popular attachment to these institutions, together with agreement upon the ideals they embody, forms one of the essential elements of group unity. It is loyalty that defines the community and preserves its integrity in the face of changing conditions. Shared loyalty to political ideas and institutions gives to members of a group that faith and confidence in their fellows which lubricates social relations and makes consensus in other projects possible. Shared loyalties are the basis of a man's faith in his fellows and, as Barth writes, "When men lose faith in one another, they lose the substance of what constitutes a community among them." [26]

These ideas, of course, are merely embroideries on the standard argument that "agreement upon the fundamentals" is a precondition of successful community. Lord Balfour has given the proposition its classic political rendering. Referring to the British system, Balfour wrote:

Our alternating Cabinets, though belonging to different Parties, have never differed about the fundamentals of society. And it is evident that our whole political machinery presupposes a people so fundamentally at one that they can safely afford to bicker; and so sure of their own moderation that they are not dangerously disturbed by the never-ending din of political conflict.[27]

He who seeks empirical confirmation on a grand scale of the disastrous effects an absence of shared loyalties can produce in other areas of social life need only consult the history of post-Revolutionary France.

Loyalty, then, is a great good from the standpoint of community. It is equally a good from the standpoint of the individual as it gives him an ease of communication with his fellows and a set of goals which help impart purpose to his life. Through loyalty one becomes related to something outside of and larger than himself. And, through this connection, life acquires meaning and direction. Royce announces this theme early and returns to it repeatedly in his treatise on loyalty.

> Loyalty, again, tends to unify life, to give it centre, fixity, stability.
>
> Now, a loyal man is one who has found, and who sees . . . some social cause . . . so rich, so well knit, and, to him, so fascinating, and withal so kindly in its appeal to his natural self-will, that he says to his cause: "Thy will is mine and mine is thine. In thee I do not lose but find myself, living intensely in proportion as I live for thee."
>
> Wherever loyalty is, there is selfhood, personality, individual purpose embodied in a life.
>
> Disloyalty is moral suicide.[28]

Loyalty is a good for the individual in the additional sense that through it he learns to orient his life toward the achievement of ideal projects. By a process similar to Stendahl's notion of crystallization, loyalty formation always includes the idealization of the object of loyal attachment. The object of loyalty is seen as beautiful and noble beyond all others and as offering great promise for the future good of its adherents. From the viewpoint of the loyal individual this holds true regardless of how the object of loyalty may appear to the external observer. Shaw's cynical definition of love as an exaggeration of the differences that distinguish one woman from another may seem cold truth to the cold man, but the lover knows otherwise. So too is it with the man of loyalty and his cause.

This point should not be passed over casually. The psychology of loyalty, it was explained in the previous chapter, is related to the psychology of identification. And the impulse to identify with a person, a cause, an ideal, possesses nearly everyone at one or another time, with greater or lesser intensity. Given the inherent tendency for loyalty to include idealization of its objects, it is clear that identification with objects of loyalty raises the spiritual tone of life. In serving the idealized objects of loyalty with which we identify ourselves, our lives are made richer, more radiant, more altruistic. We demand much from ourselves, and are satisfied only when we give greatly of what we have. Life and thought are elevated above the lowlands of an existence where we use but a small portion of our capacities to the pinnacle where potency is greater, the inner life more vital.

In summary, loyalty is a good-in-itself for both individual and society. It is the cement that binds men together in harmonious union. It is through shared loyalties that man can break through the shell isolating him from his fellows, enabling him to become a vital part of the ongoing collective process. Through this sharing he becomes part of the organic social being and works for its ends while striving for his own. Violence is done neither to individual nor to social ends; shared loyalties make them identical. It is not rhetoric to say that loyalty is the great design by which anarchy becomes order and isolation communion. Through loyalty, in the words of St. Paul, "We are members one of another."

*   *   *

Notes

1. Ralph Barton Perry, *Realms of Value: A Critique of Human Civilization* (Cambridge: Harvard University Press, 1954), p. 1.
2. William Aylott Orton, *The Liberal Tradition: A Study of the Social and Spiritual Conditions of Freedom* (New Haven: Yale University Press, 1945), p. 19.
3. Thomas Hill Green, *Lectures on the Principles of Political Obligation*, introduction by A. D. Lindsay (London: Longmans, Green, 1950), p. 29.
4. Josiah Royce, *The Philosophy of Loyalty* (New York: Macmillan, 1908), pp. 16–17.
5. Herbert Aaron Bloch, *The Concept of Our Changing Loyalties* (New York: Columbia University Press, 1934), p. 36.
6. Some social psychologists even assert that the study of attitudes is the core of their science. A recent text devotes large sections to the principles governing the formation and operation of beliefs and attitudes. David Krech and Richard S. Crutchfield, *Theory and Problems of Social Psychology* (New York: McGraw-Hill, 1948). Another remarks that "during the past two decades the problem of attitudes has become central in social psychology." Muzafer Sherif and Hadley Cantril, *The Psychology of Ego-Involvements* (New York: John Wiley and Sons, 1947), p. 9.
7. The following works have been used extensively throughout the subsequent discussion: (1) Krech and Crutchfield, *op. cit.*, pp. 158–165; (2) Sherif and Cantril, *op. cit.*, pp. 17–27; (3) E. Nelson, "Attitudes: Their Nature and Development," I, *Journal of General Psychology*, XXI (Oct., 1939), 367–399; (4) A. Strauss, "The Concept of Attitude in Social Psychology," *Journal of Psychology*, XIX (April, 1945), 329–339.
8. Sidney Hook, *Heresy, Yes—Conspiracy, No* (New York: John Day, 1953), p. 74.
9. John Dewey, *The Public and Its Problems* (New York: Henry Holt, 1927), p. 151.
10. P. F. Lazarsfeld, B. Berelson, and H. Gaudet, *The People's Choice:*

How the Voter Makes Up His Mind in a Presidential Campaign (New York: Duell, Sloan and Pearce, 1944).

11. T. M. Newcomb and G. Svehla, "Intra-Family Relationships in Attitude," *Sociometry*, I (July–Oct., 1937), 180–205.

12. E. L. Horowitz, "The Development of Attitude Toward the Negro," *Archives of Psychology*, no. 194 (Jan., 1936).

13. Orton, *op. cit.*, p. 190.

14. Krech and Crutchfield, *op. cit.*, pp. 87–88.

15. Sherif and Cantril, *op. cit.*, p. 4.

16. Gustav Icheiser has done some excellent work on this problem of the selectivity of perception and its social consequences. See *Misunderstandings in Human Relations* (Chicago: University of Chicago Press, 1949); "Misunderstandings in International Relations," *American Sociological Review*, XVI (June, 1951), 311–316.

17. Among many excellent studies on modification of attitudes, a few might be cited to illustrate their tenacity and resistance to change: (1) A. M. Rose, *Studies in Reduction of Prejudice* (Chicago: American Council on Race Relations, 1947); (2) F. T. Smith, *An Experiment in Modifying Attitudes Toward the Negro* (New York: Columbia University Press, 1943); (3) Harold H. Kelley and Edmund H. Volkart, "The Resistance to Change of Group-Anchored Attitudes," *American Sociological Review*, XVII (Aug., 1952), 453–465.

18. Tönnies' principal work was *Gemeinschaft und Gesellschaft*, 1887; it was translated by Charles P. Loomis under the title *Fundamental Concepts of Sociology: Gemeinschaft and Gesellschaft* (New York: American Book Co., 1940). A brief exposition of his ideas may be found in Rudolf Heberle's chapter entitled "The Sociological System of Ferdinand Tönnies: Community and Society," in Harry Elmer Barnes, ed., *An Introduction to the History of Sociology* (Chicago: University of Chicago Press, 1948), pp. 227–248. The following presentation is drawn from Heberle.

19. The distinction is similar to that employed by the political analyst in the concepts of mechanistic and organic political associations. See esp. T. D. Weldon, *States and Morals: A Study in Political Conflicts* (New York: McGraw-Hill, 1947).

20. Hans Gerth and C. Wright Mills, *Character and Social Structure* (New York: Harcourt, Brace, 1953), p. 174.

21. The point was suggested by J. T. MacCurdy, *The Structure of Morale* (Cambridge: Cambridge University Press, 1943), pp. 77–81.

22. Plato, *The Dialogues of Plato*, trans. by Jowett (Amer. ed.; New York: Random House, 1937), I, 434–435.

23. Ranyard West, *Conscience and Society: A Study of the Psychological Prerequisites of Law and Order* (2d ed.; London: Methuen, 1950), p. 215.

24. Rebecca West, *The Meaning of Treason* (2d ed.; London: Reprint Society Ltd., 1952), pp. 3, 248.

25. David Easton, *The Political System: An Inquiry into the State of Political Science* (New York: Knopf, 1953), pp. 125 ff.

26. Alan Barth, *The Loyalty of Free Men*, foreword by Zechariah Chafee, Jr. (New York: Viking, 1951), p. 6.

27. Walter Bagehot, *The English Constitution*, introduction by Lord Balfour (World Classics ed.; London: Oxford University Press, 1928), p. xxiv.

28. Royce, *op. cit.*, pp. 22, 43, 171, 225.

The Flag-Salute Cases

---◆

The two "opinions of the court" presented here record the decision of the United States Supreme Court first to uphold and then to overrule local statutes requiring the flag-salute and pledge of allegiance in public schools. The legal issue is the constitutionality of certain laws, not their wisdom or justice. Both Justice Frankfurter and Justice Jackson, however, discuss at length the underlying social issues. Of particular interest is the conflict between their conceptions of the nature of loyalty, and their consequent estimates of the role of the flag-salute. Frankfurter views loyalty as an emotional identification with the nation, fostered and sustained by "symbols." Jackson, in direct contrast, treats loyalty as a conscious rational commitment for which flags and oaths are merely "shortcuts" of expression. Here, as in the case of civil rights, negligent liability, and many other issues before the Court, legal questions of constitutionality can only be decided on the basis of assumptions which are made about psychology, economics, or sociology.

JUSTICE FRANKFURTER

Minersville District v. Gobitis

A grave responsibility confronts this Court whenever in course of litigation it must reconcile the conflicting claims of liberty and authority. But when the liberty invoked is liberty of conscience, and the authority is authority to safeguard the nation's fellowship, judicial conscience is put to its severest test. Of such a nature is the present controversy.

Lillian Gobitis, aged twelve, and her brother William, aged ten, were expelled from the public schools of Minersville, Pennsylvania, for refusing to salute the national flag as part of a daily school exercise. The local Board of Education required both

Reprinted from *Opinion of the Court* in *Minersville School District v. Gobitis*, 310 U. S. 586, June 3, 1940.

teachers and pupils to participate in this ceremony. The ceremony is a familiar one. The right hand is placed on the breast and the following pledge recited in unison: "I pledge allegiance to the flag, and to the Republic for which it stands; one nation indivisible, with liberty and justice for all." While the words are spoken, teachers and pupils extend their right hands in salute to the flag. The Gobitis family are affiliated with "Jehovah's Witnesses," for whom the Bible as the Word of God is the supreme authority. The children had been brought up conscientiously to believe that such a gesture of respect for the flag was forbidden by command of Scripture.[1]

The Gobitis children were of an age for which Pennsylvania makes school attendance compulsory. Thus they were denied a free education, and their parents had to put them into private schools. To be relieved of the financial burden thereby entailed, their father, on behalf of the children and in his own behalf, brought this suit. He sought to enjoin the authorities from continuing to exact participation in the flag-salute ceremony as a condition of his children's attendance at the Minersville school. After trial of the issues, Judge Maris gave relief in the District Court, 24 F. Supp. 271, on the basis of a thoughtful opinion at a preliminary stage of the litigation, 21 F. Supp. 581; his decree was affirmed by the Circuit Court of Appeals, 108 F. 2d 683. Since this decision ran counter to several *per curiam* dispositions of this Court,[2] we granted *certiorari* to give the matter full reconsideration. 309 U. S. 645. By their able submissions, the Committee on the Bill of Rights of the American Bar Association and the American Civil Liberties Union, as friends of the Court, have helped us to our conclusion.

We must decide whether the requirement of participation in such a ceremony, exacted from a child who refuses upon sincere religious grounds, infringes without due process of law the liberty guaranteed by the Fourteenth Amendment.

Centuries of strife over the erection of particular dogmas as exclusive or all-comprehending faiths led to the inclusion of a guarantee for religious freedom in the Bill of Rights. The First Amendment, and the Fourteenth through its absorption of the First, sought to guard against repetition of those bitter religious struggles by prohibiting the establishment of a state religion and by securing to every sect the free exercise of its faith. So pervasive is the acceptance of this precious right that its scope is brought into question, as here, only when the conscience of individuals collides with the felt necessities of society.

Certainly the affirmative pursuit of one's convictions about the ultimate mystery of the universe and man's relation to it is placed beyond the reach of law. Government may not interfere with organized or individual expression of belief or disbelief. Propagation of belief—or even of disbelief—in the supernatural is protected, whether in church or chapel, mosque or synagogue, tabernacle or meeting-house. Likewise the Constitution assures generous immunity to the individual from imposition of penalties for offending, in the course of his own religious activities, the religious views of others, be they a minority or those who are dominant in government. *Cantwell* v. *Connecticut, ante,* p. 296.

But the manifold character of man's relations may bring his conception of religious duty into conflict with the secular interests of his fellow-men. When does the constitutional guarantee compel exemption from doing what society thinks necessary for the promotion of some great common end, or from a penalty for conduct which appears dangerous to the general good? To state the problem is to recall the truth that no single principle can answer all of life's complexities. The right to freedom of religious belief, however dissident and however obnoxious to the cherished beliefs of others—even of a majority—is itself the denial of an absolute. But to affirm that the freedom to follow conscience has itself no limits in the life of a society would deny that very plurality of principles which, as a matter of history, underlies protection of religious toleration. Compare Mr. Justice Holmes in *Hudson Water Co.* v. *McCarter,* 209 U. S. 349, 355. Our present task, then, as so often the case with courts, is to reconcile two rights in order to prevent either from destroying the other. But, because in safeguarding conscience we are dealing with interests so subtle and so dear, every possible leeway should be given to the claims of religious faith.

In the judicial enforcement of religious freedom we are concerned with a historic concept. See Mr. Justice Cardozo in *Hamilton* v. *Regents,* 293 U. S. at 265. The religious liberty which the Constitution protects has never excluded legislation of general scope not directed against doctrinal loyalties of particular sects. Judicial nullification of legislation cannot be justified by attributing to the framers of the Bill of Rights views for which there is no historic warrant. Conscientious scruples have not, in the course of the long struggle for religious toleration, relieved the individual from obedience to a general law not aimed at the promotion or restriction of religious beliefs.[3] The mere possession of religious convictions which contradict the relevant concerns of a political society does not relieve the citizen from the discharge of political responsibilities. The necessity for this adjustment has again and again been recognized. In a number of situations the exertion of political authority has been sustained, while basic considerations of religious freedom have been left inviolate. *Reynolds* v. *United States*, 98 U. S. 145; *Davis* v. *Beason*, 133 U. S. 333; *Selective Draft Law Cases*, 245 U. S. 366; *Hamilton* v. *Regents*, 293 U. S. 245. In all these cases the general laws in question, upheld in their application to those who refused obedience from religious conviction, were manifestations of specific powers of government deemed by the legislature essential to secure and maintain that orderly, tranquil, and free society without which religious toleration itself is unattainable. Nor does the freedom of speech assured by Due Process move in a more absolute circle of immunity than that enjoyed by religious freedom. Even if it were assumed that freedom of speech goes beyond the historic concept of full opportunity to utter and to disseminate views, however heretical or offensive to dominant opinion, and includes freedom from conveying what may be deemed an implied but rejected affirmation, the question remains whether school children, like the Gobitis children, must be excused from conduct required of all the other children in the promotion of national cohesion. We are dealing with an interest inferior to none in the hierarchy of legal values. National unity is the basis of national security. To deny the legislature the right to select appropriate means for its attainment presents a totally different order of problem from that of the propriety of subordinating the possible ugliness of littered streets to the free expression of opinion through distribution of handbills. Compare *Schneider* v. *State*, 308 U. S. 147.

Situations like the present are phases of the profoundest problem confronting a democracy—the problem which Lincoln cast in memorable dilemma: "Must a government of necessity be too *strong* for the liberties of its people, or too *weak* to maintain its own existence?" No mere textual reading or logical talisman can solve the dilemma. And when the issue demands judicial determination, it is not the personal notion of judges of what wise adjustment requires which must prevail.

Unlike the instances we have cited, the case before us is not concerned with an exertion of legislative power for the promotion of some specific need or interest of secular society—the protection of the family, the promotion of health, the common defense, the raising of public revenues to defray the cost of government. But all these specific activities of government presuppose the existence of an organized political society. The ultimate foundation of a free society is the binding tie of cohesive sentiment. Such a sentiment is fostered by all those agencies of the mind and spirit which may serve to gather up the traditions of a people, transmit them from generation to generation, and thereby create that continuity of a treasured common life which constitutes a civilization. "We live by symbols." The flag is the symbol of our national unity, transcending all internal differences, however large, within the framework of the Constitution. This Court has had occasion to say that ". . . the flag is the symbol of the Nation's power, the emblem of freedom in its truest, best sense. . . . it signifies government resting on the consent of the governed; liberty regulated by law; the protection of the weak against the strong; security against the exercise of arbitrary power; and absolute safety for free institutions against foreign agression." *Halter* v. *Nebraska,* 205 U. S. 34, 43. And see *United States* v. *Gettysburg Electric Ry. Co.,* 160 U. S. 668.[4]

The case before us must be viewed as though the legislature of Pennsylvania had itself formally directed the flag-salute for the children of Minersville; had made no exemption for children whose parents were possessed of conscientious scruples like those of the Gobitis family; and had indicated its belief in the desirable ends to be secured by having its public school children share a common experience at those periods of development when their minds are supposedly receptive to its assimilation, by an exercise appropriate in time and place and setting, and one designed to evoke in them appreciation of the nation's hopes and dreams, its sufferings and sacrifices. The precise issue, then, for us to decide is whether the legislatures of the various states and the authorities in a thousand counties and school districts of this country are barred from determining the appropriateness of various means to evoke that unifying sentiment without which there can ultimately be no liberties, civil or religious.[5] To stigmatize legislative judgment in providing for this universal gesture of respect

for the symbol of our national life in the setting of the common
school as a lawless inroad on that freedom of conscience which
the Constitution protects, would amount to no less than the pro-
nouncement of pedagogical and psychological dogma in a field
where courts possess no marked and certainly no controlling
competence. The influences which help toward a common feeling
for the common country are manifold. Some may seem harsh and
others no doubt are foolish. Surely, however, the end is legitimate. And the effective means for its attainment are still so uncertain and so unauthenticated by science as to preclude us from
putting the widely prevalent belief in flag-saluting beyond the
pale of legislative power. It mocks reason and denies our whole
history to find in the allowance of a requirement to salute our
flag on fitting occasions the seeds of sanction for obeisance to
a leader.

The wisdom of training children in patriotic impulses by those
compulsions which necessarily pervade so much of the educational process is not for our independent judgment. Even were we
convinced of the folly of such a measure, such belief would be
no proof of its unconstitutionality. For ourselves, we might be
tempted to say that the deepest patriotism is best engendered by
giving unfettered scope to the most crochety beliefs. Perhaps it
is best, even from the standpoint of those interests which or-
dinances like the one under review seek to promote, to give
to the least popular sect leave from conformities like those here
in issue. But the courtroom is not the arena for debating issues
of educational policy. It is not our province to choose among
competing considerations in the subtle process of securing effective loyalty to the traditional ideals of democracy, while respecting at the same time individual idiosyncrasies among a people
so diversified in racial origins and religious allegiances. So to hold
would in effect make us the school board for the country. That
authority has not been given to this Court, nor should we assume it.

We are dealing here with the formative period in the development of citizenship. Great diversity of psychological and ethical
opinion exists among us concerning the best way to train children
for their place in society. Because of these differences and because of reluctance to permit a single, iron-cast system of education to be imposed upon a nation compounded of so many
strains, we have held that, even though public education is one
of our most cherished democratic institutions, the Bill of Rights

bars a state from compelling all children to attend the public schools. *Pierce* v. *Society of Sisters*, 268 U. S. 510. But it is a very different thing for this Court to exercise censorship over the conviction of legislatures that a particular program or exercise will best promote in the minds of children who attend the common schools an attachment to the institutions of their country.

What the school authorities are really asserting is the right to awaken in the child's mind considerations as to the significance of the flag contrary to those implanted by the parent. In such an attempt the state is normally at a disadvantage in competing with the parent's authority, so long—and this is the vital aspect of religious toleration—as parents are unmolested in their right to counteract by their own persuasiveness the wisdom and rightness of those loyalties which the state's educational system is seeking to promote. Except where the transgression of constitutional liberty is too plain for argument, personal freedom is best maintained—so long as the remedial channels of the democratic process remain open and unobstructed [6]—when it is ingrained in a people's habits and not enforced against popular policy by the coercion of adjudicated law. That the flag-salute is an allowable portion of a school program for those who do not invoke conscientious scruples is surely not debatable. But for us to insist that, though the ceremony may be required, exceptional immunity must be given to dissidents, is to maintain that there is no basis for a legislative judgment that such an exemption might intoduce elements of difficulty into the school discipline, might cast doubts in the minds of the other children which would themselves weaken the effect of the exercise.

The preciousness of the family relation, the authority and independence which give dignity to parenthood, indeed the enjoyment of all freedom, presuppose the kind of ordered society which is summarized by our flag. A society which is dedicated to the preservation of these ultimate values of civilization may in self-protection utilize the educational process for inculcating those almost unconscious feelings which bind men together in a comprehending loyalty, whatever may be their lesser differences and difficulties. That is to say, the process may be utilized so long as men's right to believe as they please, to win others to their way of belief, and their right to assemble in their chosen places of worship for the devotional ceremonies of their faith, are all fully respected.

Judicial review, itself a limitation on popular government, is a fundamental part of our constitutional scheme. But to the legislature no less than to courts is committed the guardianship of deeply-cherished liberties. See *Missouri, K. & T. Ry. Co.* v. *May*, 194 U. S. 267, 270. Where all the effective means of inducing political changes are left free from interference, education in the abandonment of foolish legislation is itself a training in liberty. To fight out the wise use of legislative authority in the forum of public opinion and before legislative assemblies rather than to transfer such a contest to the judicial arena, serves to vindicate the self-confidence of a free people.[7]

Reversed.

Notes

1. Reliance is especially placed on the following verses from Chapter 20 of Exodus:
   "3. Thou shalt have no other gods before me.
   "4. Thou shalt not make unto thee any graven image, or any likeness of any thing that is in heaven above, or that is in the earth beneath, or that is in the water under the earth:
   "5. Thou shalt not bow down thyself to them, nor serve them: . . ."

2. *Leoles* v. *Landers*, 302 U. S. 656; *Hering* v. *State Board of Education*, 303 U. S. 624; *Gabrielli* v. *Knickerbocker*, 306 U. S. 621; *Johnson* v. *Deerfield*, 306 U. S. 621; 307 U. S. 650. Compare *New York* v. *Sandstrom*, 279 N. Y. 523; 18 N. E. 2d 840; *Nicholls* v. *Mayor and School Committee of Lynn*, 7 N. E. 2d 577 (Mass.).

3. Compare II Writings of Thomas Jefferson (Ford ed.) p. 102; 3 Letters and Other Writings of James Madison, pp. 274, 307–308; 1 Rhode Island Colonial Records, pp. 378–80; 2 *Id;* pp. 5–6; Wiener, Roger Williams' Contribution to Modern Thought, 28 Rhode Island Historical Society Collections, No. 1; Ernst, The Political Thought of Roger Williams, chap. VII; W. K. Jordan, The Development of Religious Toleration in England, *passim*. See *Commonwealth* v. *Herr*, 229 Pa. 132; 78 A. 68.

4. For the origin and history of the American flag, see 8 Journals of the Continental Congress, p. 464; 22 *Id.*, pp. 338–40; Annals of Congress, 15th Cong., 1st Sess., Vol. 1, pp. 566 *et seq.; Id.*, Vol. 2, pp. 1458 *et seq.*

5. Compare Balfour, Introduction to Bagehot's English Constitution, p. XXII; Santayana, Character and Opinion in the United States, pp. 110–11.

6. In cases like *Fiske* v. *Kansas*, 274 U. S. 380; *De Jonge* v. *Oregon*, 299 U. S. 353; *Lovell* v. *Griffin*, 303 U. S. 444; *Hague* v. *C. I. O.*, 307 U. S. 496, and *Schneider* v. *State*, 308 U. S. 147, the Court was concerned with restrictions cutting off appropriate means through which, in a free society, the processes of popular rule may effectively function.

7. It is to be noted that the Congress has not entered the field of legislation here under consideration.

JUSTICE JACKSON

Board of Education v. Barnette

Following the decision by this Court on June 3, 1940, in *Minersville School District* v. *Gobitis*, 310 U. S. 586, the West Virginia legislature amended its statutes to require all schools therein to conduct courses of instruction in history, civics, and in the Constitutions of the United States and of the State "for the purpose of teaching, fostering and perpetuating the ideals, principles and spirit of Americanism, and increasing the knowledge of the organization and machinery of the government." Appellant Board of Education was directed, with advice of the State Superintendent of Schools, to "prescribe the courses of study covering these subjects" for public schools. The Act made it the duty of private, parochial and denominational schools to prescribe courses of study "similar to those required for the public schools." [1]

The Board of Education on January 9, 1942, adopted a resolution containing recitals taken largely from the Court's *Gobitis* opinion and ordering that the salute to the flag become "a regular part of the program of activities in the public schools," that all teachers and pupils "shall be required to participate in the salute honoring the Nation represented by the Flag; provided, however, that refusal to salute the Flag be regarded as an act of insubordination, and shall be dealt with accordingly." [2]

The resolution originally required the "commonly accepted salute to the Flag" which it defined. Objections to the salute as "being too much like Hitler's" were raised by the Parent and Teachers Association, the Boy and Girl Scouts, the Red Cross, and the Federation of Women's Clubs. [3] Some modification appears to have been made in deference to these objections, but no concession was made to Jehovah's Witnesses. [4] What is now required is the "stiff-arm" salute, the saluter to keep the right hand raised with palm turned up while the following is repeated: "I pledge allegiance to the Flag of the United States

Reprinted from *Opinion of the Court* in *West Virginia State Board of Education et al.* v. *Barnette et al.*, 319 U. S. 624, June 14, 1943.

of America and to the Republic for which it stands; one Nation, indivisible, with liberty and justice for all."

Failure to conform is "insubordination" dealt with by expulsion. Readmission is denied by statute until compliance. Meanwhile the expelled child is "unlawfully absent" [5] and may be proceeded against as a delinquent.[6] His parents or guardians are liable to prosecution,[7] and if convicted are subject to fine not exceeding $50 and jail term not exceeding thirty days.[8]

Appellees, citizens of the United States and of West Virginia, brought suit in the United States District Court for themselves and others similarly situated asking its injunction to restrain enforcement of these laws and regulations against Jehovah's Witnesses. The Witnesses are an unincorporated body teaching that the obligation imposed by law of God is superior to that of laws enacted by temporal government. Their religious beliefs include a literal version of Exodus, Chapter 20, verses 4 and 5, which says: "Thou shalt not make unto thee any graven image, or any likeness of anything that is in heaven above, or that is in the earth beneath, or that is in the water under the earth; thou shalt not bow down thyself to them nor serve them." They consider that the flag is an "image" within this command. For this reason they refuse to salute it.

Children of this faith have been expelled from school and are threatened with exclusion for no other cause. Officials threaten to send them to reformatories maintained for criminally inclined juveniles. Parents of such children have been prosecuted and are threatened with prosecutions for causing delinquency.

The Board of Education moved to dismiss the complaint setting forth these facts and alleging that the law and regulations are an unconstitutional denial of religious freedom, and of freedom of speech, and are invalid under the "due process" and "equal protection" clauses of the Fourteenth Amendment to the Federal Constitution. The cause was submitted on the pleadings to a District Court of three judges. It restrained enforcement as to the plaintiffs and those of that class. The Board of Education brought the case here by direct appeal.[9]

This case calls upon us to reconsider a precedent decision as the Court throughout its history often has been required to do.[10] Before turning to the *Gobitis* case, however, it is desirable to notice certain characteristics by which this controversy is distinguished.

The freedom asserted by these appellees does not bring them into collision with rights asserted by any other individual. It is such conflicts which most frequently require intervention of the State to determine where the rights of one end and those of another begin. But the refusal of these persons to participate in the ceremony does not interfere with or deny rights of others to do so. Nor is there any question in this case that their behavior is peaceable and orderly. The sole conflict is between authority and rights of the individual. The State asserts power to condition access to public education on making a prescribed sign and profession and at the same time to coerce attendance by punishing both parent and child. The latter stand on a right of self-determination in matters that touch individual opinion and personal attitude.

As the present CHIEF JUSTICE said in dissent in the *Gobitis* case, the State may "require teaching by instruction and study of all in our history and in the structure and organization of our government, including the guaranties of civil liberty, which tend to inspire patriotism and love of country." 310 U. S. at 604. Here, however, we are dealing with a compulsion of students to declare a belief. They are not merely made acquainted with the flag salute so that they may be informed as to what it is or even what it means. The issue here is whether this slow and easily neglected [11] route to aroused loyalties constitutionally may be short-cut by substituting a compulsory salute and slogan.[12] This issue is not prejudiced by the Court's previous holding that where a State, without compelling attendance, extends college facilities to pupils who voluntarily enroll, it may prescribe military training as part of the course without offense to the Constitution. It was held that those who take advantage of its opportunities may not on ground of conscience refuse compliance with such conditions. *Hamilton* v. *Regents,* 293 U. S. 245. In the present case attendance is not optional. That case is also to be distinguished from the present one because, independently of college privileges or requirements, the State has power to raise militia and impose the duties of service therein upon its citizens.

There is no doubt that, in connection with the pledges, the flag salute is a form of utterance. Symbolism is a primitive but effective way of communicating ideas. The use of an emblem or flag to symbolize some system, idea, institution, or personality, is a short cut from mind to mind. Causes and nations, political parties, lodges and ecclesiastical groups seek to knit the loyalty of their followings to a flag or banner, a color or design. The State announces rank, function, and authority through crowns and maces, uniforms and black robes; the church speaks through the Cross, the Crucifix, the altar and shrine, and clerical raiment. Symbols of State often convey political ideas just as religious symbols come to convey theological ones. Associated with many of these symbols are appropriate gestures of acceptance or respect: a salute, a bowed or bared head, a bended knee. A person gets from a symbol the meaning he puts into it, and what is one man's comfort and inspiration is another's jest and scorn.

Over a decade ago Chief Justice Hughes led this Court in holding that the display of a red flag as a symbol of opposition by peaceful and legal means to organized government was protected by the free speech guaranties of the Constitution. *Stromberg* v. *California,* 283 U. S. 359. Here it is the State that employs a flag as a symbol of adherence to government as presently organized. It requires the individual to communicate by word and sign his acceptance of the political ideas it thus bespeaks. Objection to this form of communication when coerced is an old one, well known to the framers of the Bill of Rights.[13]

It is also to be noted that the compulsory flag salute and pledge requires affirmation of a belief and an attitude of mind. It is not clear whether the regulation contemplates that pupils forego any contrary convictions of their own and become unwilling converts to the prescribed ceremony or whether it will be acceptable if they simulate assent by words without belief and by a gesture barren of meaning. It is now a commonplace that censorship or suppression of expression of opinion is tolerated by our Constitution only when the expression presents a clear and present danger of action of a kind the State is empowered to prevent and punish. It would seem that involuntary affirmation could be commanded only on even more immediate and urgent grounds than silence. But here the power of compulsion is invoked without any allegation that remaining passive during a flag salute ritual creates a clear and present danger that would justify an effort even to muffle expression. To sustain the compulsory flag salute we are required to say that a Bill of Rights which guards the individual's right to speak his own mind, left it open to public authorities to compel him to utter what is not in his mind.

Whether the First Amendment to the Constitution will permit officials to order observance of ritual of this nature does not depend upon whether as a voluntary exercise we would think it to be good, bad or merely innocuous. Any credo of nationalism is likely to include what some disapprove or to omit what others think essential, and to give off different overtones as it takes on different accents or interpretations.[14] If official power exists to coerce acceptance of any patriotic creed, what it shall contain cannot be decided by courts, but must be largely discretionary with the ordaining authority, whose power to prescribe would no doubt include power to amend. Hence validity of the asserted power to force an American citizen publicly to profess any statement of belief or to engage in any ceremony of assent to one, presents questions of power that must be considered independently of any idea we may have as to the utility of the ceremony in question.

Nor does the issue as we see it turn on one's possession of particular religious views or the sincerity with which they are held. While religion supplies appellees' motive for enduring the discomforts of making the issue in this case, many citizens who do not share these religious views hold such a compulsory rite to infringe constitutional liberty of the individual.[15] It is not necessary to inquire whether non-conformist beliefs will exempt from the duty to salute unless we first find power to make the salute a legal duty.

The *Gobitis* decision, however, *assumed,* as did the argument in that case and in this, that power exists in the State to impose the flag salute discipline upon school children in general. The Court only examined and rejected a claim based on religious beliefs of immunity from an unquestioned general rule.[16] The question which underlies the flag salute controversy is whether such a ceremony so touching matters of opinion and political attitude may be imposed upon the individual by official authority under powers committed to any political organization under our Constitution. We examine rather than assume existence of this power and, against this broader definition of issues in this case, reëxamine specific grounds assigned for the *Gobitis* decision.

1. It was said that the flag-salute controversy confronted the Court with "the problem which Lincoln cast in memorable dilemma: 'Must a government of necessity be too *strong* for the liberties of its people, or too *weak* to maintain its own exist-

ence?'" and that the answer must be in favor of strength. *Minersville School District* v. *Gobitis, supra,* at 596.

We think these issues may be examined free of pressure or restraint growing out of such considerations.

It may be doubted whether Mr. Lincoln would have thought that the strength of government to maintain itself would be impressively vindicated by our confirming power of the State to expel a handful of children from school. Such oversimplification, so handy in political debate, often lacks the precision necessary to postulates of judicial reasoning. If validly applied to this problem, the utterance cited would resolve every issue of power in favor of those in authority and would require us to override every liberty thought to weaken or delay execution of their policies.

Government of limited power need not be anemic government. Assurance that rights are secure tends to diminish fear and jealousy of strong government, and by making us feel safe to live under it makes for its better support. Without promise of a limiting Bill of Rights it is doubtful if our Constitution could have mustered enough strength to enable its ratification. To enforce those rights today is not to choose weak government over strong government. It is only to adhere as a means of strength to individual freedom of mind in preference to officially disciplined uniformity for which history indicates a disappointing and disastrous end.

The subject now before us exemplifies this principle. Free public education, if faithful to the ideal of secular instruction and political neutrality, will not be partisan or enemy of any class, creed, party, or faction. If it is to impose any ideological discipline, however, each party or denomination must seek to control, or failing that, to weaken the influence of the educational system. Observance of the limitations of the Constitution will not weaken government in the field appropriate for its exercise.

2. It was also considered in the *Gobitis* case that functions of educational officers in States, counties and school districts were such that to interfere with their authority "would in effect make us the school board for the country." *Id.* at 598.

The Fourteenth Amendment, as now applied to the States, protects the citizen against the State itself and all of its creatures—Boards of Education not excepted. These have, of course, important, delicate, and highly discretionary functions, but none that they may not perform within the limits of the Bill of Rights. That they are educating the young for citizenship is reason for scrupulous protection of Constitutional freedoms of the individual, if we are not to strangle the free mind at its source and teach youth to discount important principles of our government as mere platitudes.

Such Boards are numerous and their territorial jurisdiction often small. But small and local authority may feel less sense of responsibility to the Constitution, and agencies of publicity may be less vigilant in calling it to account. The action of Congress in making flag observance voluntary [17] and respecting the conscience of the objector in a matter so vital as raising the Army [18] contrasts sharply with these local regulations in matters relatively trivial to the welfare of the nation. There are village tyrants as well as village Hampdens, but none who acts under color of law is beyond reach of the Constitution.

3. The *Gobitis* opinion reasoned that this is a field "where courts possess no marked and certainly no controlling competence," that it is committed to the legislatures as well as the courts to guard cherished liberties and that it is constitutionally appropriate to "fight out the wise use of legislative authority in the forum of public opinion and before legislative assemblies rather than to transfer such a contest to the judicial arena," since all the "effective means of inducing political changes are left free." *Id.* at 597–598, 600.

The very purpose of a Bill of Rights was to withdraw certain subjects from the vicissitudes of political controversy, to place them beyond the reach of majorities and officials and to establish them as legal principles to be applied by the courts. One's right to life, liberty, and property, to free speech, a free press, freedom of worship and assembly, and other fundamental rights may not be submitted to vote; they depend on the outcome of no elections.

In weighing arguments of the parties it is important to distinguish between the due process clause of the Fourteenth Amendment as an instrument for transmitting the principles of the First Amendment and those cases in which it is applied for its own sake. The test of legislation which collides with the Fourteenth Amendment, because it also collides with the principles of the First, is much more definite than the test when only the Fourteenth is involved. Much of the vagueness of the due process clause disappears when the specific prohibitions of the First become its standard. The right of a State to regulate, for example, a public utility may well include, so far as the due process test is concerned, power to impose all of the restrictions which a legislature may have a "rational basis" for adopting. But freedoms of speech and of press, of assembly, and of worship may not be infringed on such slender grounds. They are susceptible of restriction only to prevent grave and immediate danger to interests which the State may lawfully protect. It is important to note that while it is the Fourteenth Amendment which bears directly upon the State it is the more specific limiting principles of the First Amendment that finally govern this case.

Nor does our duty to apply the Bill of Rights to assertions of official authority depend upon our possession of marked competence in the field where the invasion of rights occurs. True, the task of translating the majestic generalities of the Bill of Rights, conceived as part of the pattern of liberal government in the eighteenth century, into concrete restraints on officials dealing with the problems of the twentieth century, is one to disturb self-confidence. These principles grew in soil which also produced a philosophy that the individual was the center of society, that his liberty was attainable through mere absence of governmental restraints, and that government should be entrusted with few controls and only the mildest supervision over men's affairs. We must transplant these rights to a soil in which the *laissez-faire* concept or principle of non-interference has withered at least as to economic affairs, and social advancements are increasingly sought through closer integration of society and through expanded and strengthened governmental controls. These changed conditions often deprive precedents of reliability and cast us more than we would choose upon our own judgment. But we act in these matters not by authority of our competence but by force of our commissions. We cannot, because of modest estimates of our competence in such specialties as public education, withhold the judgment that history authenticates as the function of this Court when liberty is infringed.

4. Lastly, and this is the very heart of the *Gobitis* opinion, it reasons that "National unity is the basis of national security," that the authorities have "the right to select appropriate means for its attainment," and hence reaches the conclusion that such compulsory measures toward "national unity" are constitutional.

Id. at 595. Upon the verity of this assumption depends our answer in this case.

National unity as an end which officials may foster by persuasion and example is not in question. The problem is whether under our Constitution compulsion as here employed is a permissible means for its achievement.

Struggles to coerce uniformity of sentiment in support of some end thought essential to their time and country have been waged by many good as well as by evil men. Nationalism is a relatively recent phenomenon but at other times and places the ends have been racial or territorial security, support of a dynasty or regime, and particular plans for saving souls. As first and moderate methods to attain unity have failed, those bent on its accomplishment must resort to an ever-increasing severity. As governmental pressure toward unity becomes greater, so strife becomes more bitter as to whose unity it shall be. Probably no deeper division of our people could proceed from any provocation than from finding it necessary to choose what doctrine and whose program public educational officials shall compel youth to unite in embracing. Ultimate futility of such attempts to compel coherence is the lesson of every such effort from the Roman drive to stamp out Christianity as a disturber of its pagan unity, the Inquisition, as a means to religious and dynastic unity, the Siberian exiles as a means to Russian unity, down to the fast failing efforts of our present totalitarian enemies. Those who begin coercive elimination of dissent soon find themselves exterminating dissenters. Compulsory unification of opinion achieves only the unanimity of the graveyard.

It seems trite but necessary to say that the First Amendment to our Constitution was designed to avoid these ends by avoiding these beginnings. There is no mysticism in the American concept of the State or of the nature or origin of its authority. We set up government by consent of the governed, and the Bill of Rights denies those in power any legal opportunity to coerce that consent. Authority here is to be controlled by public opinion, not public opinion by authority.

The case is made difficult not because the principles of its decision are obscure but because the flag involved is our own. Nevertheless, we apply the limitations of the Constitution with no fear that freedom to be intellectually and spiritually diverse or even contrary will disintegrate the social organization. To believe that patriotism will not flourish if patriotic ceremonies are voluntary and spontaneous instead of a compulsory routine is to make an unflattering estimate of the appeal of our institutions to free minds. We can have intellectual individualism and the rich cultural diversities that we owe to exceptional minds only at the price of occasional eccentricity and abnormal attitudes. When they are so harmless to others or to the State as those we deal with here, the price is not too great. But freedom to differ is not limited to things that do not matter much. That would be a mere shadow of freedom. The test of its substance is the right to differ as to things that touch the heart of the existing order.

If there is any fixed star in our constitutional constellation, it is that no official, high or petty, can prescribe what shall be orthodox in politics, nationalism, religion, or other matters of opinion or force citizens to confess by word or act their faith therein. If there are any circumstances which permit an exception, they do not now occur to us.[19]

We think the action of the local authorities in compelling the flag salute and pledge transcends constitutional limitations on their power and invades the sphere of intellect and spirit which it is the purpose of the First Amendment to our Constitution to reserve from all official control.

The decision of this Court in *Minersville School District* v. *Gobitis* and the holdings of those few *per curiam* decisions which preceded and foreshadowed it are overruled, and the judgment enjoining enforcement of the West Virginia Regulation is

Affirmed.

Notes

1. § 1734, West Virginia Code (1941 Supp.):
   "In all public, private, parochial and denominational schools located within this state there shall be given regular courses of instruction in history of the United States, in civics, and in the constitutions of the United States and of the State of West Virginia, for the purpose of teaching, fostering and perpetuating the ideals, principles and spirit of Americanism, and increasing the knowledge of the organization and machinery of the government of the United States and of the State of West Virginia. The state board of education shall, with the advice of the state superintendent of schools, prescribe the courses of study covering these subjects for the public elementary and grammar schools,

public high schools and state normal schools. It shall be the duty of the officials or boards having authority over the respective private, parochial and denominational schools to prescribe courses of study for the schools under their control and supervision similar to those required for the public schools."

2. The text is as follows:

"WHEREAS, The West Virginia State Board of Education holds in highest regard those rights and privileges guaranteed by the Bill of Rights in the Constitution of the United States of America and in the Constitution of West Virginia, specifically, the first amendment to the Constitution of the United States as restated in the fourteenth amendment to the same document and in the guarantee of religious freedom in Article III of the Constitution of this State, and

"WHEREAS, The West Virginia State Board of Education honors the broad principle that one's convictions about the ultimate mystery of the universe and man's relation to it is placed beyond the reach of law; that the propagation of belief is protected whether in church or chapel, mosque or synagogue, tabernacle or meeting house; that the Constitutions of the United States and of the State of West Virginia assure generous immunity to the individual from imposition of penalty for offending, in the course of his own religious activities, the religious views of others, be they a minority or those who are dominant in the government, but

"WHEREAS, The West Virginia State Board of Education recognizes that the manifold character of man's relations may bring his conceptions of religious duty into conflict with the secular interests of his fellowman; that conscientious scruples have not in the course of the long struggle for religious toleration relieved the individual from obedience to the general law not aimed at the promotion or restriction of the religious beliefs; that the mere possession of convictions which contradict the relevant concerns of political society does not relieve the citizen from the discharge of political responsibility, and

"WHEREAS, The West Virginia State Board of Education holds that national unity is the basis of national security; that the flag of our Nation is the symbol of our National Unity transcending all internal differences, however large within the framework of the Constitution; that the Flag is the symbol of the Nation's power; that emblem of freedom in its truest, best sense; that it signifies government resting on the consent of the governed, liberty regulated by law, protection of the weak against the strong, security against the exercise of arbitrary power, and absolute safety for free institutions against foreign aggression, and

"WHEREAS, The West Virginia State Board of Education maintains that the public school, established by the legislature of the State of West Virginia under the authority of the Constitution of the State of West Virginia and supported by taxes imposed by legally constituted measures, are dealing with the formative period in the development in citizenship that the Flag is an allowable portion of the program of schools thus publicly supported.

"Therefore, be it RESOLVED, That the West Virginia Board of Education does hereby recognize and order that the commonly accepted salute to the Flag of the United States—the right hand is placed upon the breast and the following pledge repeated in unison: 'I pledge allegiance to the Flag of the United States of America and to the Republic for which it stands; one Nation, indivisible, with liberty and justice for all'—now becomes a regular part of the program of activities in the public schools, supported in whole or in part by public funds, and that all teachers as defined by law in West Virginia and pupils in such schools shall be required to participate in the salute, honoring the Nation represented by the Flag; provided, however, that refusal to salute the Flag be regarded as an act of insubordination, and shall be dealt with accordingly."

3. The National Headquarters of the United States Flag Association takes the position that the extension of the right arm in this salute to the flag is not the Nazi-Fascist salute, "although quite similar to it. In the Pledge to the Flag the right arm is extended and raised, palm UPWARD, whereas the Nazis extend the arm practically *straight to the front* (the finger tips being about even with the eyes), *palm* DOWNWARD, and the Fascists do the same except they raise the arm slightly higher." James A. Moss, The Flag of the United States: Its History and Symbolism (1914) 108.

4. They have offered in lieu of participating in the flag salute ceremony "periodically and publicly" to give the following pledge:
   "I have pledged my unqualified allegiance and devotion to Jehovah, the Almighty God, and to His Kingdom, for which Jesus commands all Christians to pray.
   "I respect the flag of the United States and acknowledge it as a symbol of freedom and justice to all.
   "I pledge allegiance and obedience to all the laws of the United States that are consistent with God's law, as set forth in the Bible."

5. § 1851 (1), West Virginia Code (1941 Supp.):
   "If a child be dismissed, suspended, or expelled from school because of refusal of such child to meet the legal and lawful requirements of the school and the established regulations of the county and/or state board of education, further admission of the child to school shall be refused until such requirements and regulations be complied with. Any such child shall be treated as being unlawfully absent from school during the time he refuses to comply with such requirements and regulations, and any person having legal or actual control of such child shall be liable to prosecution under the provisions of this article for the absence of such child from school."

6. § 4904 (4), West Virginia Code (1941 Supp.).

7. See Note 5, *supra.*

8. §§ 1847, 1851, West Virginia Code (1941 Supp.).

9. § 266 of the Judicial Code, 28 U. S. C. § 380.

10. See authorities cited in *Helvering* v. *Griffiths*, 318 U. S. 371, 401, note 52.

11. See the nation-wide survey of the study of American history conducted by the New York Times, the results of which are published in the issue of June 21, 1942, and are there summarized on p. 1, col. 1, as follows:
    "82 per cent of the institutions of higher learning in the United States do not require the study of United States history for the undergraduate degree. Eighteen per cent of the colleges and universities require such history courses before a degree is awarded. It was found that many students complete their four years in college without taking any history courses dealing with this country.
    "Seventy-two per cent of the colleges and universities do not require United States history for admission, while 28 per cent require it. As a result, the survey revealed, many students go through high school,

college and then to the professional or graduate institution without
having explored courses in the history of their country.

Less than 10 per cent of the total undergraduate body was enrolled
in United States history classes during the Spring semester just ended.
Only 8 per cent of the freshman class took courses in United States
history, although 30 per cent was enrolled in European or world
history courses."

12. The Resolution of the Board of Education did not adopt the flag
salute because it was claimed to have educational value. It seems to
have been concerned with promotion of national unity (see footnote
2), which justification is considered later in this opinion. No information
as to its educational aspect is called to our attention except Olander,
Children's Knowledge of the Flag Salute, 35 Journal of Educational Research 300, 305, which sets forth a study of the ability of a large and
representative number of children to remember and state the meaning
of the flag salute which they recited each day in school. His conclusion was that it revealed "a rather pathetic picture of our attempts
to teach children not only the words but the meaning of our Flag
Salute."

13. Early Christians were frequently persecuted for their refusal to participate in ceremonies before the statue of the emperor or other symbol
of imperial authority. The story of William Tell's sentence to shoot an
apple off his son's head for refusal to salute a bailiff's hat is an ancient
one. 21 Encyclopedia Britannica (14th ed.) 911–912. The Quakers,
William Penn included, suffered punishment rather than uncover their
heads in deference to any civil authority. Braithwaite, The Beginnings
of Quakerism (1912) 200, 229–230, 232–233, 447, 451; Fox, Quakers
Courageous (1941) 113.

14. For example: Use of "Republic," if rendered to distinguish our government from a "democracy," or the words "one Nation," if intended
to distinguish it from a "federation," open up old and bitter controversies in our political history; "liberty and justice for all," if it must
be accepted as descriptive of the present order rather than an ideal,
might to some seem an overstatement.

15. Cushman, Constitutional Law in 1939–40, 35 American Political
Science Review 250, 271, observes: "All of the eloquence by which the
majority extol the ceremony of flag saluting as a free expression of
patriotism turns sour when used to describe the brutal compulsion
which requires a sensitive and conscientious child to stultify himself
in public." For further criticism of the opinion in the *Gobitis* case by
persons who do not share the faith of the Witnesses see: Powell,
Conscience and the Constitution, in Democracy and National Unity
(University of Chicago Press, 1941) 1; Wilkinson, Some Aspects of the
Constitutional Guarantees of Civil Liberty, 11 Fordham Law Review
50; Fennell, The "Reconstructed Court" and Religious Freedom: The
Gobitis Case in Retrospect, 19 New York University Law Quarterly
Review 31; Green, Liberty under the Fourteenth Amendment, 27 Wash-
ington University Law Quarterly 497; 9 International Juridical Associa-
tion Bulletin 1; 39 Michigan Law Review 149; 15 St. John's Law
Review 95.

16. The opinion says "That the flag-salute is an allowable portion of a
school program *for those who do not invoke conscientious scruples* is
surely not debatable. But for us to insist that, *though the ceremony
may be required, exceptional immunity must be given to dissidents*, is
to maintain that there is no basis for a legislative judgment that such

an exemption might introduce elements of difficulty into the school
discipline, might cast doubts in the minds of the other children which
would themselves weaken the effect of the exercise." (Italics ours.) 310
U. S. at 599–600. And elsewhere the question under consideration was
stated, "When does the constitutional guarantee *compel exemption*
from doing what society thinks necessary for the promotion of some
great common end, or from a penalty for conduct which appears
dangerous to the general good?" (Italics ours.) *Id.* at 593. And again,
". . . whether school children, like the Gobitis children, must be
excused from conduct required of all the other children in the promotion of national cohesion. . . ." (Italics ours.) *Id.* at 595.
17. Section 7 of House Joint Resolution 359, approved December 22, 1942,
56 Stat. 1074, 36 U. S. C. (1942 Supp.) § 172, prescribes no penalties
for nonconformity but provides:
"That the pledge of allegiance to the flag, 'I pledge allegiance to the
flag of the United States of America and to the Republic for which it
stands, one Nation indivisible, with liberty and justice for all,' be
rendered by standing with the right hand over the heart. However,
civilians will always show full respect to the flag when the pledge is
given by merely standing at attention, men removing the head-
dress . . .''
18. § 5 (a) of the Selective Training and Service Act of 1940, 50 U. S.
C. (App). § 307 (g).
19. The Nation may raise armies and compel citizens to give military
service. *Selective Draft Law Cases*, 245 U. S. 366. It follows, of course,
that those subject to military discipline are under many duties and
may not claim many freedoms that we hold inviolable as to those in
civilian life.

JEAN LE MEUR

The Story of a Responsible Act

———————————————————————➤

*Jean Le Meur, 1932–   , was a young lieutenant in the French army
when by an act of conscience he chose to go to prison rather than
participate in the war against the Algerian rebels. His reasons for this
refusal and the story of what happened to him during the next thirteen months are told in a series of letters to his family, his friends,
and his lawyer. Le Meur's vigorous defense of the responsibility of
individual conscience gains stature from his willingness to act out the
consequences of his principles. The story is brought up to date in
the following statement, translated from a letter written in August,
1964, by M. Paul Thibaud, Editor-in-chief of Esprit: "Jean Le Meur*

Reprinted by permission from *Esprit* (December, 1959), pp. 680–708.
Translation by Mr. Samuel I. Stone, Lecturer in French, Boston University.
Several letters have been omitted from the translation.

was condemned for refusal to obey [military orders] to two years in prison, which were served. He left prison in September, 1960. At that time he was reincorporated into a unit of the army in Algeria and assigned to non-military work. After much hesitation, he decided that it was not useful to renew his refusal to bear arms, given the progressive orientation of the French government's Algerian policy in the direction of negotiation. Upon completion of his military obligation he was named a professor in France. Since the opening of the school year in Autumn, 1962, he has been a professor in Algeria (at the Lycée St. Augustin de Bône), in the ranks of the Cooperation [the French aid program to Algeria]."

Letter from Jean Le Meur to the Staff of "Esprit" (July, 1958)

Jean Le Meur, 26, the son of Catholic Breton parents, a professor of literature and politically, a defeatist intellectual. I attended Officers' Training School at Cherchell where I was graduated as a Second Lieutenant (122nd in a class of 400) on June 15, 1958. At the end of the course, we were offered various garrisons in which to serve and also fifty places in the Department of Algerian Affairs. Colonel Marey, the School Commandant, warmly encouraged his charges to choose the exalting mission of peacemaker. I could have chosen an Instruction Center in France or Germany and just seen what happened. Out of atavism, masochism, candor, idealism, because I felt bound up with and responsible for Algeria, I chose the General Service (youth camps, youth education centers) swearing to myself to retain my freedom of action, to submit in no way whatsoever to the Algérie Française, to the politics of the Committees of Public Safety, and with the secret hope, how clairvoyant! thus to escape from the control of the military. Back from leave, ready for a probationary period as "young builders" of the new and French Algeria, we are told the good news: First, building, of course; but it is necessary, however, at the very first, to take command of a platoon for three or six months. After which you will still be needed; if there are any of you "left." From a military point of view this requirement was legitimate: reserve officers can be asked without any abuse of power to have actually commanded a platoon. What was less justifiable was the subterfuge used by our chiefs (to get us to do what they wanted), by Salan, I believe, which was catching us like birds in a trap.*

As for me, this put me on the spot. I finally had to resolve a problem which until then I had relegated to the wings of mental restrictions. "Could I with a clear conscience, without contradiction, wage war on the fellaghas?" To put the question this way was to answer it and yet it was not so easy. The fact is that one hesitates to confront the imposing machine, to sacrifice comfort, pay, and even military life with its adventures and friendships, and its experience. Nevertheless, I succeeded in being logical and I sent in my resignation. Here is about the way it went:

Cherchell, July 6, 1958

The Secretary (of National Defense)

Dear Sir,

I have the honor to inform you of my deliberate refusal to serve in Algeria in the cadre of operations for the maintenance of order. Consequently, I beg you to be so kind as to accept my resignation from the rank of Second Lieutenant, and I am at your disposition for whatever sanctions are incurred by my lack of discipline.

By accepting the command of a platoon, I would be contributing to the repression of a revolt whose grounds are only too apparent to me, to the overthrow of rebels whose cause I cannot in clear conscience condemn.

Colonel Marey, the Commandant of the Cherchell Military School, has disavowed me without equivocation and has rebuked me strongly for having lacked honesty and courage in evading this problem for so long. I recognize the fact that before accepting the title of officer, I should have gauged more carefully the duties incumbent upon it.

Despite my insubordination, I beg you to accept, Mr. Secretary, the expression of my respectful deference, and to believe in my complete devotion to the service of France.

*   *   *

I had written at first a prolix and impudent letter in which I tried the case of French policy and pointed up a few of its contradictions. Colonel Marey persuaded me to be more diplomatic. Moreover, he was very understanding. I also saw in him a kind

---

* Naturally, the only places remaining were in Algeria; Souk-Ahras, Djidjelli, Laverdure . . .

of chaplain-general of the Algerian troops: a sanctimonious paternalism, a "national" optimism in the *Catholique France* style and then: "These problems are beyond us. It is so complicated!, etc. . . ."

These are circumstances where one finds oneself relatively alone. Moreover, confidences of this type are explosive. One hesitates.

I do not know what repercussions my decision may have had at Cherchell. People hardly ever dropped in on me again once it was known. Nor did I receive any real approbation. A handful of my comrades told me that basically everyone thought "a bit" like me. I also believe that this silence, this distance, was due to a feeling of uneasiness.

I have few illusions about the political efficacy of my gesture. The army which had been well indoctrinated, has settled down in the subversive war, a permanent war as each of us knew. It is playing its all in Algeria. It believes in the metaphysical value of the 13th of May. The officers of lower rank, the non-commissioned officers, and the enlisted men see the military situation with a more lucid eye, "kid" when one talks of pacification, but are resigned to war: "What else is there to do?"

Cherchell, July 8, 1958

Only the chaplain here, more than others, is aware of the realities of this war and the mental confusion of the soldiers in Algeria, of their moral misery; he does not share the official optimism, can talk to me without making me more tired, perhaps because he placed the discussion on its real level. Not that he shares my political "extremism" but one might say that the simple honesty of his consideration reaches the same conclusions as the information I trust. And yet, I believe that the soldiers do not tell everything. That in order to go and find the chaplain one must already have a willingness to be frank which is likely to disappear after certain actions. I believe that the colonels can keep their consciences clear, for the same language is not spoken in front of them. During the one-week trial period that we had to undergo, there were with us about thirty Second Lieutenants who were back from the Bled and who spoke most naturally about tortures, executions of prisoners. This war instills in those who wage it only contempt and hatred for the nigger, and also for the Pieds Noirs, besides. . . .

Kheirane, August 29, 1958

Dear Parents,

I should like to reply to father's objections, which are indeed forceful, because I am particularly anxious to justify myself in your eyes and I keenly hope to be supported without any reticence by our household. The traditional moral position of the Church, as F.X.H. wrote me, acknowledges that a man's moral responsibility is not entirely involved in the activities imposed upon him by the laws of society.

This is true in the case of excusing the participation by Christians in undertakings that are sometimes blameworthy. But can one say that a German at the end of the war, having bcome fully aware of what Naziism implied and actually accomplished, was truly bound by obedience to the laws of his nation? I think, on the contrary, that he is morally obligated to refuse. I am not making an absolute parallel. I hope, without being sure of it yet, that the Algerian War is less serious. But I believe it to be fundamentally bad. If casuists authorize me, out of national solidarity, to help in perpetrating a crime, the casuists are wrong. In an ambiguous situation, one may reserve judgment, keep the benefit of the doubt. Here, as far as I am concerned, there is no possible doubt. I must grasp the possibility to refuse which is left to me. For an ordinary soldier, the situation is not so different, even though it may be more difficult to disengage oneself. For a long time the Church has sought to reassure the conscience of its faithful who are engaged in difficult situations by saying to them: "Don't bang your head against a stone wall. You are not responsible. Your leaders are the ones who make the decisions!" This amounts to saying: "On certain occasions, you are automatons, irresponsible beings." But such statements are the limit of absurdity. In reality, man is always responsible. He cannot unload his responsibility on some one else. It is the doer who in the last recourse makes the decision. This is an extreme position, but sometimes one is backed into it. It is surely an attitude of refusal that in certain respects is essentially negative. It breaks one's solidarity with his community. It cuts oneself off from certain testimonials. But, on the other hand, it also affirms the permanency of moral responsibility, the need of inner coherence, solidarity with other disinherited peoples, the possibility of an ulterior dialogue.

I took part in a one-week operation between Seiar, Guentis,

and Taberdga. Three or four battalions. We caught a gang which left behind a score of victims, two machine-guns, an F.M., some rifles and P.M.'s. On the radio system, the commanding officer of one unit could be heard saying and repeating: "I want no prisoners." So they were tossed from the top of the cliff into the depths of the Wadi below. Without batting an eyelash, they mentioned the prisoners that were being kept "for information." This means just what it says. One sees villages completely destroyed. The inhabitants are "regrouped." What is the difference between this and deportation? I had a run-in with a Lieutenant because in the face of these facts I mentioned "the army of civilization." I am more or less suspect here, but it manifests itself only rarely. The commanding officer is a gentleman. I am just an irritating case and incidents can arise for a yes or a no. For the time being, my life is not unpleasant. I get along well with my boys who are fine and whom I shall regret leaving. I am getting a suntan and eating well. No complaints can be made against the officers. I was paid (about 55,000 francs a month). I am rich and nothing would stop me from fighting this war if I did not have to lie to myself constantly.

Seiar, August 22, 1958

Quiet period in an operation. Some young boys offer me some figs. I give them a pack of cigarettes. Our conversation is limited by my crass ignorance of Arabic. I have learned nothing since I have been here. Numerous experiences indicate, however, that contact would be easy, and there is much to learn from them, even if it were only their way of living. A very handsome young boy, with a head like Nefertiti, the head of certain Arabs of Delacroix. Turned-up eyebrows, green eyes, full lips. Here are some kids, a little boy, a little girl, of ravishing beauty. The little girl, café-au-lait, graceful and delicate. One ought to please and play with them. It's very easy to do.

Kheirane, August 29, 1958

When I informed "my soldiers" that these people live on the equivalent of 30,000 francs a year, that they get along on hard-tack during the *crapahut* (guerrilla campaign) and save their rations for their families, relations improved a little and their instinctive or acquired racism melted away to some extent. But their everyday life is not of a nature to give the recruits the desire to know and understand. Actually, a military post is an isolated cell. Contact with the populations is only very sparse.

Kheirane (South of Khentchela), September 1

Two weeks ago I stirred things up again by telling them that it was really impossible for my attitude to change. In a couple of weeks this business will reach its dénouement. I must tell you that a month ago I received the answer to my letter of resignation. They refused to accept my resignation, they asked me to carry out my duties as an officer, and advised my battalion leader to be vigilant. They had me read article 205 of the Military Code which provides prison and detention for those who . . .

I was rather lucky here to fall in with an understanding battalion leader who toned down my intransigence, getting it to become adjusted to the slowness of procedure. Moreover, he put me in command of a section of half-tracks used solely on protective missions. This gives me a very fragile moral alibi, for it is a form of participation in the war that is just as real as commanding an attack section. But it is a solution to cover the waiting period.

The 1/94 R.I. in which I am is an ordinary infantry unit. A month ago a severe ambush took about ten victims from one of our companies. Our regiment has been in the Nementchas for two years. The state of mind of the people, the officers, indeed, even the enlisted men, is extremely disturbing in the extent of stultification of moral sense that it reveals. It seems that all who are thrown into this war reach the point of justifying systematic violence without any restraint. They strive to explain to me the usefulness of torture "in certain cases." They tell me that seeing our pals slaughtered causes many "illusions" to disappear. They justify the massacre of prisoners. Racism, contempt, incomprehension, most often. I have not yet heard a single supporter of this war speak, as I have, in behalf of the respect for the human person. Must I profess my political radicalism in order to remain still faithful to these old-hat ideas? Sometimes the allusions get under my skin, but as a general rule, I am supported, and my life here is not unpleasant. The officers eat well, drink cool. The climate is beginning to cool off in comparison with the tropical temperatures that overwhelmed us last month and made the nights too hot for sleep. I get along well with the section I command and our sorties do not bother me if I disregard their significance. Besides, the half-track people have an advantage over the others, for they do not hunt guerrillas. They are satisfied to ramble about in the dust of the overheated roads, they always have enough water and even during operations sometimes spend whole days keeping completely quiet under canvas. Moreover, I admire the moral resistance of the soldiers living in conditions that officers cannot imagine. Fatigue duty, guard duty, eating ordinary food, living in overcrowded and poorly laid-out digs, being bawled out right and left for trifles, getting one or two thousand francs per month, celebrating the regiment's party without a single drink at hand, as a result of delayed convoy (one week late).

Besides, the psychological operation hardly produces any proselytism. It is too afraid of being snubbed. There seems to have been established a modus vivendi. "Since it is regulations, we accept the fact that we must do this work. But don't come and stuff our heads and get us to say that we find the greatest satisfaction in it." The rank and file, therefore, are left to themselves, often caught up by the atmosphere of violence that every war secretes, and sometimes want to strike anyway, when given the slip by an unseizable enemy. Neither their political awareness nor their moral conscience enlightens them very much in this universe of contradictions. This contact with the young men of France shows the rarity of political maturity among them and what an immense amount of work still lies before us.

Kheirane, September 1st

Even if one is given a back seat, if one is in an office, or in transportation or supply, one is a cog in the repression machine, bound up with the whole organism—and responsible. What I believe I have precisely discovered is the permanence of individual responsibility in a system that claims improperly to have abolished it. Definitely, whatever the circumstances, it is the doer who makes the final decision.

Khentchela, September 17, 1958

Philippe,

*   *   *

Last night at ten o'clock I heard screams in a nearby hut. I went out to see for myself. It was what you think. An "interrogation" in the next room. A dozen gendarmes were watching the spectacle from the outside. I do not know what method they were using. I think it was electricity. I stayed outside perhaps ten seconds and upon leaving I expressed my disgust. That brought jeers from the gendarmes and a threatening reprimand from a Lieutenant. The session lasted more than an hour. Until then, I knew that this existed. Now I know how those scary lugubrious screams that terminate in a childlike sob can reverberate within me. I am still haunted by a feeling of anguish and despair. The torturers look just like us and are often well bred. They are sorry about "the sad necessities of the war that has been imposed on us." Man's need for self-preservation, and then, these individuals probably have numerous crimes on their conscience. I am reproached for playing the Communist game through stubborn fuzzy thinking. The torture room was right next to the street: on the other side were some Mussulman dwellings. Those groans could be clearly heard fifty meters away. By protesting, I was playing the Communist game . . .

Don't do your service right away, if you can. I think that in khaki you are bound and gagged more than anywhere else and that the solution will come from the civilians. As far away as it may be. And it is dangerous here to say that there are some things that just are not done. In the end just reading military regulations will become a subversive act. I still feel the effects of yesterday's terrible revelation. And, nonetheless, there are worse things, very likely, if I may believe G., for example, and others. But French public opinion, even the opinion of the left, condemns all of this only half-heartedly. Whereas, in fact, this should rob us of our sleep. How afraid I am, my little friend. Yet I believe that my protest, though isolated and fugitive, will not be sterile, that it can germinate. But it is so faint a hope. And then, the mobile gendarmes, they are professionals of the rack.

*   *   *

I write poorly and without sequence. I dream about having a chat and frivolous thoughts. Péguy is of great help to me, and the Psalms. Prayer, so easily neglected when all goes well, becomes the only recourse. There also springs up the desire for perfection.

Yesterday, too, I had the distressing feeling that in this tragic hour my friendships will never succeed in dissipating a compact solitude. We shall need each other.

Khentchela, Friday, September 19, 1958

* * *

I have left Kheirane, my battalion, and my section and I have
been here for two weeks under the guard of the mobile gendarmes who will conduct me to my new destination, according to
the directions of the military court. I made my goodbyes, joy-
lessly, no doubt with little regret from the officers who saw in me
—not without reason—a black sheep. But I loved the boys who
were under me and I would have had no fears about living
among them. And then, I did not detest the military life, the
sun and the mountain. If only there were no war . . . if only there
were not this war! I am still not quite anti-national-military-
service. I would fight a war against the Nazis without any displeasure. But with them, no.

* * *

A torturer is not a sinister brute. He is a man like others. He may
be a good husband, a good family man. He may be of the left,
politically. I heard one who was shocked at the Arabs' brutality
toward their animals. "One of them," he told me, "would constantly prick his donkey with his goad in exactly the same spot
in his rump. From which a wound was developed. What would
he say if the same thing were done to them? I bawled out a few
of them."

What an appalling aberration! A perversion that few soldiers
in Algeria escape. A climate of universal hatred, of racism, of
brutal chauvinism: one Frenchman is worth 100 niggers. Included therein are Communists, Mendésists, professors, deputies,
journalists. Hatred of intellectuals and denial of intelligence. A
very disturbing balance sheet.

* * *

Don't talk too much about my courage. The toughest thing was
to come to a decision a month and a half ago. For the time
being, its consequences are benign. Now I am the plaything
of procedure. But I was so compromised by my ideas, they had
so much on me that I had to follow the rules. The difficult thing
is not to take refuge in the "negativity" that isolation encourages
and also in a spectacular refusal.

Dear little V.,

*   *   *

After all, we still are lucky to have a fine profession * and while earning our daily bread, we can help free men grow up, give them respect for man and a sense of honor. What a privilege and what power! When I think that some seminarians turned on the switches and some professors and doctors, too, I cannot restrain a feeling of hopeless indignation. How deep the corruption must be! Our role will be to restore tirelessly the health of this plague-ridden France. When I think of it, I am filled with tender feelings for the literary studies I scorned, the amusements of mandarins who make music while, on their doorstep, children are dying of starvation. It is something deeper, and spiritual nourishment must be distributed, intellectual honesty taught.

You are impatient with the lack of logic in people. It is a reaction that I well know, opportunities to experience it are not lacking. But I am a little afraid that you may become a prisoner of your anger and made sterile by it. A strong effort must be brought forth (I am beginning to give advice), we must repress our irritation as much as possible and meditate on the art of persuasion. We shall have difficulty in convincing people. When one presents his reasoning in logical form, people think that a trap is being laid, and they turn up their noses when one proves to them with a and b that they are wrong. We must find a new technique, humbler and friendlier, become more preoccupied with advancing the truth than being right. I am saying this in too pretentious a way: I have often done a disservice to what I believed to be true because I would rather win a joust, triumph over an adversary, than to turn on the light.

Little S. has found an elegant solution for all our ills but, my poor V., you have been bitten too hard by your love of justice and your hatred of injustice for it to suit you. There are no two ways about it: it's do or die. We must simply be on our guard against chimerical hopes and do the same work over again with obstinacy, for the sake of our grandnephews. And then, what do you expect, you are not the kind of person who finds pleasure in organized amusement. No working man would ever think of playing cards when there is still work to be done.

*   *   *

*That of Professor—Ed.

I am still with the gendarmes. I have learned that I was indicted for disobedience and "participation in an attempt to demoralize the army." I am curious to see how they will judge it. Now and then, I do not feel reassured at finding myself tossed like fodder into the enormous machine. Like notes falling due in a more or less short time, other vexations, other rancors will sooner or later strike the army, and the desire to make someone pay for them. For the time being, I am waiting for "justice" to be done. After that it will be your turn, your turn to play.

I think that France is closer to totalitarianism than people imagine. Everybody accepts the abuse of authority, once it is done by the authority. The mystification of military discipline must be exposed, too. Authority does not exist in this area, its only basis is the imprescriptible loyalty by its trustees to values that are beyond their comprehension. If I salute a torturer, if I obey a hangman, I am ratifying torture and assassination. These views will probably be shocking, which only shows to what degree we are corrupted.

I would like to talk about something else and I dream about being finally able to think about something else. But everything that is done here is done in the name of the French people, and children are tortured: In other words, I torture, you torture children. Pardon me, my little friend.

So the days pass with great enough austerity, in the sole company of the books that I leaf through absent-mindedly, tiring quickly and carried away again by my dreams. Mail call renews my waiting, often in vain, with a proud bitterness by way of revenge. Do tell the others that this is not the time to let me down, that it is a question of charity: that once I am convicted I may not even be able to write them and I shall need their letters all the more. For some time to come I am getting myself settled into mendicity. Where would I find my strength and my joy if not among the others? What would I be, moreover, without all of you?

*   *   *

You will please pray a little for your little peasant who is afraid of all this, who would like to have cares of his own size and to live nicely in his everyday clothes.

Taberdga, October 11, 1958

They are taking me here this morning. It is not gay. They wake me at five o'clock: "They are coming to get you in ten minutes."

I get into the Commandant's jeep; we exchange a few anodyne words during the fifty-kilometer trip. They let me out and go off, ignoring me like a traitor. What else am I really? A dimwit who gives himself the luxury of making a case out of what so many well-bred people admit, what is taken for granted by others, poses no problem at all to them, standing out like a plug nickel. This is what is most difficult: being cut off from the fraternity, being locked up in a monologue, being incomprehensible.

When I see these troops of young Frenchmen facing fatigue, cold, death, in daily heroism that is a dead end and without a soul, for the sake of an unjust cause, it distresses me greatly.

What wild extravagance in the unreal!

Taberdga, October 11, 1958

Dear little one,
Today I am permeated to the point of desolation with the sadness of my adventure. To have skirted this morning this community which is mine and which considers me a traitor, a poltroon, a four-flushing chatterbox; also, to be an isolated prisoner, without a chain-companion, thrown like an intruder in the midst of men juridically free who are just so many jailers (I am not talking about their feelings but about objective reality). All this makes a little peasant not very gay and rather discomforted who needs all of his friends in order to be able to take the blow.

* * *

I am happy to read that you are happy. It gives me a change from my little headaches and it proves to me that there is no Utopia and that one can dream about it without going too far. It has been many years that I have not missed a Breton summer and I have in view, behind me, a picture of the coast of Plouha, beautiful and wild, quite near Ploubazlanec where my heart often takes a spin as I ride my beautiful black and flame-colored bike. These are terrible years that are going to break up our youth, cast us into the age of manhood and entice us into long separations. Military service is striking the three knocks. Let us move on to the next act. (Take a little look at the metaphor!)

* * *

Taberdga, October 31, 1958

Dear Papa,
I have not yet replied directly to the two letters I received from you in which you informed me about your reservations concern-

ing my disobedience. I am now engaged in an adventure whose outcome remains hazardous but whose reasons only grow deeper roots without ever being shaken. I have, then, no regrets; quite the contrary, if it were to be done over again, I would still do it. I am not saying this to you out of Breton stubbornness but because I believe it very deeply. You say that a soldier is covered by the authority of his superiors, that he is not directly responsible. That is true when the particulars of the general policy escape the agent. The fact remains, nonetheless, that he is participating in a fixed policy, good or bad.

Through a series of divine favors and good luck from which I profited, and for which I shall never thank you and Mama enough, I have the privilege of being able to examine and judge what I am asked to do, and by a still more precious inheritance, I have the will not to betray what I believe to be just and true. He who knowingly affords his activity to an undertaking that he judges to be disastrous, cannot shirk his responsibility. He may find attenuating circumstances, not a justification. It is still more serious when it involves killing people, tracking rebels whose cause one cannot disavow. It is somewhat as if you were asked to go and hunt peasants of the Massif Central, or of Auvergne, who did not want to pay their taxes; or else to go and evict some workers' families who had moved into some empty buildings in order to escape from their hovels.

For an extremist of my type, it is impossible to consider as enemies these young ragamuffins, rebelling at the sight of their children's hunger and the constant humiliation of their parents. This ignoble war will remain as a spot on France. At a given moment the Germans should have said no to Hitler's Naziism. I have believed and I still believe that the moment has come to say no to this abomination.

This, of course, brings up the delicate problem of obedience to a State. But one must not make a divinity out of the State. The misfortune of France, in my opinion, comes from the fact that too many Frenchmen, without batting an eye, accepted the idea of serving a cause which they knew was unjust. How many officers have accepted and are accepting torture, condemned by the clearest passages in the regulations!

I don't know what this will cost me. Two years in prison or more. But that is only of little importance. I don't think that it will get you into any trouble. For the time being, I am not unhappy. All of my friends are backing me up and will not let me down. The only thing that bothers me is the solitude. . . .

Taberdga, All Saints' Day, 1958

. . . I am writing to you from my basement room which looks out on the South through a vent about half a meter square. At times the sun slips a few rays through and I can catch a glimpse of a piece of sky. I am half-way through a few books and I lead the very shut-in life of a serious student-candidate for a doctoral degree. They bring me my meals scrupulously and the mail is like a visit to me. I suppose some day they will pay attention to me, if only to give me a little less comfortable prison. For the moment, it is not too serious, and I have the impression of being in a "hide-out." I sleep my fill, my food allowance is very decent since it is the same as the officers', and my activities are only of the spare-time type. I don't deserve to be pitied, as you well see. Mme I.'s solicitude distressed her too quickly. One or two years in prison are not sufficient to "spoil a life." Sometimes it is even a very good opportunity to put your ideas in order, to learn to reflect, to get rid of the accessories, and gauge from the wrong side how good life is and how much one needs one's friends. On my optimistic days I congratulate myself on having performed a good operation by taking this "stupid long shot."

From time to time I feel less swell-headed and then I scratch my curly head and tell myself that, anyway, this will contribute the weight of a very tiny hair toward changing the face of things. So it's really your fault a little, of people like you and my parents, if certain boys get the feeling very early of being privileged persons, and the desire to be not too unfaithful to what they have received. Before changing the face of the globe (we think about it very seriously), one should, first of all, no longer contribute to its disfigurement. . . .

Taberdga, November 13, 1958

Dear little V.,

       *   *   *

By dint of coming to my situation again and again, I finally find it natural. I have been brought to this point of view not by the masochism of a martyr, nor by superacute heroism, but by the simple refusal to accept injustice set up as a system. All those people who cannot condemn quickly enough the Germans' docility toward Naziism take on an air of shock and offense when, for very definite arguments which they share, someone refuses to bow before the exigencies of a policy that has gone astray. When one reflects on it, one cannot help feeling a vague terror because all the evidence points to the fact that France is ripe for a totalitarianism in which it is already swimming and which it is unable to recognize. In Lyons, the people living near the Police Station complain "about being unable to sleep." The progressive curés of the Prado are reproached for crying "torture" when it was only a matter of a "light going-over." Certain of my friends are supplying the torture chambers with suspects; I mean they take prisoners, and believe that integrity boils down to not actually turning on the switch yourself.

There is an undeniable degeneration of conscience. What can one say about intellectuals of the left who have gone through it all, washing their hands of everything, without getting wet! And the priests! The capacity for indignation is completely debilitated, dulled by the habit of comfort, intellectual conformity, and forgetting responsibility in an amoral life. Where are Péguy and Bernanos?

You talk about the high command who would indeed like to do something and are full of good intentions. It is enough to make you vomit. If they disapprove, let them get the hell out, if they are incapable of preventing such things. A company sergeant-major knows how to make himself obeyed. They have only to take some lessons.

But each one takes refuge behind his impotence, gets under cover: "What do you want me to do?" Let them at least be responsible for themselves.

I am launching into grand speeches. What I am serving you are warmed-over monologues. I have few opportunities to chat. It is two months now that I have been eating my meals all alone, that the only company I have is the printed paper or manuscript. Fortunately, I still don't have to be afraid of boredom. Sometimes it is lucky to be an intellectual and a literary man. The difficulty lies elsewhere and is, moreover, intermittent. X. scolds me for speaking about "the sadness of my adventure." It is sad because it is solitary and based on the condemnation of my community. Even if it were necessary, it is no less painful. All that remains is certitude and a timid pride.

*   *   *

I am still at Taberdga, a picture of which I am sending you. I have had no news about my story. The procedure is long. I have paid off forty days of confinement for my refusal to obey and thirty days mandatory for not being in agreement with the fellow who "didn't want any prisoners."

Taberdga, Monday, November 24, 1958

Very dear Francis,

*   *   *

An important change has occurred in my story. On October 21, I completed my series of sentences. But since I could not be kept in Taberdga on vacation, the Colonel asked me to command a patrol in the neighborhood. I was completely dumbfounded and naturally, I refused. So I pulled some new arrests and a new request to be brought up for court-martial. I thought the sole objective of this show was to make my legal situation here clear again. But a few days ago, I learned that my first indictment has been dismissed for insufficient cause and that now it was my second case of disobedience (of October 21) that was at the bar. I have received no official notification of the dismissal of charges and I did not expect it. I suppose that the second complaint, offense against army morale, is not unrelated to the decision. It is, as a matter of fact, properly inadmissible. All the same, it is reassuring that the military jurisdiction did not sustain it. And now, we start over again on solid ground with "disobedience in the presence of rebels," in good and due form, sanctioned by Article 205 of the code of military justice (an article which provides a sentence of imprisonment for this infraction).

This is why even the pedagogical solution seems to me to be an alibi and a challenge, besides: what sense does our language still hold? I would like to be able to explain Montesquieu, Voltaire, Hugo, and Péguy.

*   *   *

You understand, I am fed up with seminarians, who, on their return, come and weep on the bosom of their director of conscience and tell their confidential thoughts to their bishops, and who, for their contribution, are satisfied to offer ejaculatory prayers. I am just sick and tired of those who condemned Nazism so roundly once it was laid low—and of the complacency of those who, in other days, fought it. I have friends who could write Alleg's book, if they knew how to write. I have others who play the part of game-beaters. In these conditions humor becomes acrobatics, juggling; a swindle.

Biskra, Tuesday, December 23, 1958

Dear Francis,

They are "working" in the premises of the C.C.S. of the 24th R.I.C. Demented screams are the signal. You ask me if such should prove to be the case, would I accept questionable jobs "with a good future." Here the essential things are these racked bodies, these enraged interrogations. As long as they wage this war, I refuse to participate in anything whatsoever. Besides, could I do it without becoming an advocate of nationalism? I want to have nothing in common with the rabid beasts who represent France here. I wonder how long Frenchmen will thus accept being sowers of dread. The saddest thing is to discover that everyone accepts the use of these methods without raising an eyebrow and that people talk about it as if it were a natural thing. My poor friend, one feels cowardly and shaky when one skirts the torments of agony. One sees no other solution but in the extremism of despair. It is a fact that when I left Officers Training School, I naively expected that my services would be used to limit the damage. Now I no longer see such a possibility. One would have to collaborate or subscribe with ease to dirty deeds without number. The evil is fundamental and the general hypocrisy disgusts me. The bards of grandeur are seated solidly among the ignoble. I am fed up with this country endowed with patent killers and torturers and I want no part in complicity, even diluted. On the contrary, I insist on remaining on the plane of a contestation, an absolute protestation. . . .

Biskra, December 24, 1958

Dear Maurice,

*   *   *

They have not succeeded in shaking me, not by a long shot, those who are nostalgic for the inquisition, nor the restorers of the question extraordinary. No more than the prophets of Psychological Action. Backing me into a corner, they asked me to repudiate just about everything on which I have decided to

stake my life. I preferred prison. As for distinguishing the influences in this adventure, they are multiple, for it involves everything that has contributed toward giving me what is best in me.
But I am so conscious of this act, it is so much my own (if it
had to be done over again, I would take the same road) that I
accept the full responsibility for it. Except for discharging my
debt subsequently by thanking those who helped me, far from
dreaming of blaming them.

You have given me the example and perhaps the taste for a
stern thought: intellectual rigor is already a form of honesty.
But if in your card you allude to your own political positions
and are afraid of their repercussions, you should be reassured.
The time when we were seen together most frequently was in
Paris and I was a rare ninny about these matters then. You could
have made observations on the subject whose meaning would
have totally escaped me. It was only later, through the bias of
trade-union action, that I felt concerned with history and thereby responsible as a citizen. Then, the Algerian rebellion, Gaby's
military service crystallized or precipitated things. I don't know
if in all this there is a question of kissing lepers. But at no
price do I want to be one of those who apply the whip to
them. That certainly is worth a few sacrifices.

*   *   *

It was a matter of basing "justice" on the crushing of Spartacus
the Servant. When I think it over, I realize that I have definitely
not made a choice: there was no plurality of solutions. Prison
was the only way for me to refuse a form of suicide: the instinct
of self-preservation. Auto-defensive reflex!

*   *   *

Constantine, January 12, 1959

Dear little one,
In prison we are cut off from current events and censorship
removes writings of a political order. One very rapidly becomes a creature without any history, detemporized at the very
moment when one is dependent on what is happening. One is
enclosed in parentheses and defined solely in relation to a completed past. The situation of an accused person marks a stoppage
of time, reduces the human being to a particular act which these
gentlemen of the court myopically pick to pieces.

*   *   *

Constantine, January 19, 1959

Dear friends,

... For more than three months now I have been without any news from Philippe. You are the ones who keep me informed about his health troubles and the imprudent ideas that run through his head. I am not too surprised, as you can imagine, but, in my opinion, this is too serious a question for me to dare to influence his decision in one direction or the other. I only know that he will comply with the deepest exigencies, and whatever he chooses, I am with him. One would simply like to bring less weight to bear on another person's life, not be the source of any blackmail. I ask your forgiveness for any supplementary trouble that I might cause you indirectly.

I think I have answered in my preceding letters the reproaches stemming from the ridiculous uselessness of such an adventure: it is not certain that it is useless but that is a secondary point. What is essential is to know whether, yes or no, one will participate in a thing that one judges to be fundamentally unjust, whether one will be willing to put up with a few minor worries in order to conserve what could be called honor. That is an old-fashioned notion, you say? It is one of those things that we found in our inheritance because our "old" parents put it there or transmitted it to us. What would our children say if we lost it on the way? And then, if we do not take certain risks for the sake of ideas that are good and fine and fecund, who else will take them, the risks?

What I am telling you is not of a nature to reassure you. But have confidence. Even so, peace is not a chimera; in any case, it is our only hope. From having desired it so much, we shall perhaps be able to use it advantageously to ward off new menaces or render them less terrible. And your children will give you still more consolation. Will you please send me the works of Valéry-Larbaud in the Pléiade edition? It is a costly book but it tells of happiness. It is in prison that one believes in happiness the most, and you are going to consider me naive again.

Constantine, February 1, 1959

Dear Parents,

*   *   *

I have a cell, a bed, a writing-table, all that I need except the freedom to go where I please. ...

The procedure is very simple: the examining magistrate will summon me a certain number of times. The court is two hundred meters from the prison. You go there accompanied by a gendarme. You sniff the outdoor air. You look around with wide-open eyes. Then the examining magistrate will confess me thoroughly, ask me at what age I learned to ride a bike, whether I like jazz, and what my political opinions are. Then he will send out some juridical commissions to conduct an inquiry on my behalf, verify my statements. We will chat very courteously. Then, in a few months, the court will judge and convict me in the name of discipline which it is important to safeguard, and without going into the fundamental issue. It is very simple, as you see, and all I need to do is to let things happen and wait until it is all over. No more gray hairs than are usual in the course of everyday life. Why should they exonerate me when I condemn them.

*   *   *

Constantine, March 27, 1959

Philippe,

I am finishing the *Memoirs of a Well Bred Young Girl.* Primarily to find a common ground, to have something in common, by some magic to reduce distance, which at times seems more than geographical. At times I catch myself bawling people out. "Certainly, the peasant is pig-headed, he gets himself into impossible situations, just a case of trying to act like somebody interesting. He makes everything complicated. But at least, write to him and give him a lecture. Even if he discourages friendship, we can still pity him or help his morale. It takes very little to brighten up the gray light of prison."

For the time being, it is the only serious difficulty. Here it takes on a purely chemical aggressiveness, while in ordinary life it is diluted by little daily worries: the dread of the absence of others to which I cannot resign myself and the disillusionment of seeing that people adjust themselves to my departure rather easily, that they are willing to become strangers; and then I tell myself that this is a poor time to let me down. You are going to assume a pitying air: "But this is childishness. What is one letter more or less? You well know that nothing has changed." Well no, I don't know. I know that I am not the same.

Easter Sunday. Confitemini Domino quoniam bonus, quoniam in saeculum misericordia ejus. Sometimes I find that God's pity is very slow in showing itself and that Easter is a sham holiday: it is still the week of the Passion.

If others are not around, I am encumbered with myself and obsessed with my relations toward them. I do nothing but scrutinize phantoms. What can I expect to find in those tightly shut faces except reprobation, irritation, indifference? Impatience germinates quickly here in the faults of indolence. A little indulgence, s.v.p., for the jailbird: he's mentally disturbed.

*   *   *

Will you please sketch for me the main lines of your plans for the immediate future, so that I can place them in a proper frame of reference. Many things may seem trifling to you which to me have great value. Prison, nevertheless, is a desert isle where references are lacking and history stops. One lives in reprieve. Society identifies each person for a certain amount of time with such and such an infraction. Its revenge consists in inflicting a nul and negative slice of life. It is a system of vindicative repression, a hypocritical avatar of the law of retaliation.

I have probably abused Corneille's vocabulary up to this point. You will pardon me for this grandiloquence that fits the situation better than the individual. I should like so much to talk about it with you, just to talk with you. This feeling takes hold of me violently, for example, when I look at little Jean-Francois' picture. It's the promised land, the return to prose, to dialogue, to daily virtues, unflinching fidelity rewarded. But I dream of rewards too soon.

*   *   *

Constantine, April 25, 1959

My examining magistrate wants to coach me, too, and play both ends against the middle. He might as well have been a psychoanalyst from the way he makes it his duty to probe to the bottom of things. What zeal! The same indiscretion everywhere, the lack of discernment. It would be nice if this incoherence were only the sign of confusion. But one becomes entangled in a web of contradictions with the greatest of arrogance. That's why it becomes necessary to put away those who try to understand.

Here silence is more compact than elsewhere, and what may seem to you to be empty chatter and frivolity is for me the long-awaited sign of an existence, the solvent of monologue which too often gives shelter to pride, scorn, or despair. There is nothing surprising about the first of these. The last is familiar to me in connection with the thought of these thoroughly nazified people. I thought that I didn't know what contempt was, but I must also defend myself on this score. Along with bitterness, this is the feeling inspired in me by the malice and pettiness that proliferate in the boredom of prisons. Contagion spreads quickly, even where one might believe that sympathy would offer resistance. My protected youth had remained singularly candid and I had rarely experienced the need to "defend" myself. It is a depressing occupation that takes too much time. One becomes hardened.

Conflicts like these, anodyne at first, thus bring about the Hundred Years War. They manifest real and irreducible tensions, their gratuity is only apparent. Racism is a reality, wickedness too. One would like not to know of the existence of these misdemeanors, remain vulnerable and exposed, and perhaps in this way disarm animosities that are as yet hardly substantial. But it is also necessary to limit the field of arrogance, cut back the impudence of rodents. It is a dangerous exercise in which I am clumsy and somewhat of a novice. I do not seek to master it and I see only too clearly the dangers of a pride in love with itself: you run the risk of closing all doors, and especially, your own.

I am telling you unreliable and muddled secrets in many and fancy words. Simplicity is not the fruit of solitude. But perhaps, the capacity to welcome, the desire to understand? But jeopardized by atrophy and sclerosis. Thus I take inventory of the riches I lack and which freedom promises me. I am counting greatly on you—and the others—to help me endure the trauma of that new birth.

*   *   *

May 1st

Some time ago I took a psychiatric test or what was supposed to be one. I expected something intelligent, to enjoy this little diversion and perhaps have a chat with some people. I had to deal with a wellfed gentleman who was about as much of a psychiatrist as a veterinary. No method, a bonesetter's scorn for psychoanalysis, bizarre questions, as strait-laced as a gendarme. I am still absolutely scandalized about it and I kick myself for having spoken to him as to a broadminded man.

May 2nd

I can't write to you very well. I am disturbed about the hermetic parentheses by which I am isolated from history and forced to invent my own language and the rhythm of my obsolescence. I am deprived of the friendship of children and I am advancing toward an unknown world where I shall constantly have to present myself, explain complicated stories to inattentive people. An exercise in lucidity, in epitome. The risk of inflexibility. Do tell the others that I am relying on them and that they are, to some extent, responsible. . . . Too bad for them.

You speak of attitudes that construe personal experiences. But, in my opinion, it is not a matter of setting up an experiment and working it out but of responding to a given situation which can be described in what amounts to a limited number of broad outlines. The alibi of the experience allows one to postpone a decision indefinitely. Military action transforms the world into a Manichean universe. If I am writing this to you, it is not for the purpose of winning you over summarily to my theses. But I am no more clever than anyone else: the major and minor premises of the syllogism were given to me before my arrival here. I assure you that it is not so easy to draw the conclusion, but how can I avoid it? I am a little tired of grand shattering speeches: sheep who make believe they are freedmen.

Constantine, June 1, 1959

Dear Maître,*

From my cell, in the evening, I hear all too often cries and screams that are doubtless wrung by torture: the Casbah barracks are contiguous to the prison. For me it is a source of permanent anguish. Every vibration of silence, every unidentified cry grips and maddens me. This obsession exhausts and monopolizes me. It keeps me in a state close to hopelessness. And in a cowardly way, I pray for miracles to happen, since man has given rein to what is ignoble. This anxiety preserves me from a somewhat facile serenity that could very easily be spread out in the comfort and ennui of prisons. But I am not sure of

* This letter was addressed by J. Le Meur to his lawyer.

coming out of it intact. I feel that my capacity for indignation is still brand new, but what if the mainspring should happen to break? I don't see the great mainsprings of society and I have only discovered little banal truths, that are everywhere, which is why no one notices them. The abuses stem from the fact that people do not have the courage to defend their rights. Such resignation can only encourage the riffraff. We must be intransigent and also make the rights of our neighbor our responsibility. We must claim and use legal appeals, no matter how much repugnance we may have toward doing so. If I permit my neighbor to be pummeled, the next time the blows will fall on me. We must deflate the goldbeater's skins and repulse the arrogance of foolishness, impose some modesty on it. Sometimes it is necessary to shock in order to expose what is shocking. It is a meager harvest that I have gleaned, you see. But then, our misfortunes are not new; we don't have to fight an unknown virus. Strength is formed out of our weaknesses.

Constantine, June 25, 1959

Dear little jellyfish,
I come out of court with a sentence of two years in prison. Which I shall finish on October 10, 1960. I saved my head, as you see, and it is no meager result, for I have the weakness of being fond of this appendage. I also keep my bars after expecting for a long time to go into mourning for them. From a strictly hedonistic point of view, I don't know if it is an advantage. The government's commissioner treated me as if I were a coward, hiding out, reproving me for fleeing from my responsibilities in the security and comfort of prison. I did not think it wise to undeceive him. I am not very satisfied with myself because my explanations were confused. Next time (?) I shall go about it better. This time I really was a virgin. At any rate, these gentlemen were in a hurry to get it over with; all this is so complicated! Afterward, my lawyer buttered me up to try to compensate for the unfortunate impression. As for me, I would have liked above all to have been ironical and chatted about this and that, without malice. A man is judged quickly. A fine birthday present!

Now I must get back to living. I am not very optimistic and yet I am far from being prostrate with grief. I can't say that I was surprised. All I have to do now is get over the sterile torpor and useless nervous tension that I have been experiencing for the last two months and which, I assure you, have in no way been caused by apprehension about the trial.

Constantine, August 24, 1959

Dear Maître,

D. said that I made my decision "as a Christian," but the reasons I had are more strictly of a human order and perfectly accessible, I think, to a Freemason or a Buddhist.

Conscientious objectors who are not scatterbrains are those who in a general and permanent way refuse to perform any military activity out of faithfulness to the precept, "Thou shalt not kill," without considering the political significance of each conflict. If I am not mistaken, they still have no status, at least in France, "the most civilized country in the world" as they keep drilling into us at the Psychological Action meetings at Cherchell. In other countries, instead of putting them in prison to grow moldy for n years, they are asked to work for the same length of time in a "civil service," which is no doubt better for everyone concerned. Such ideas can only occur in backward countries.

I am surprised that they are asking for precise details about my attitude, whereas for a year I have been explaining myself quite abundantly. The label "conscientious objector" does not fit because it has a very precise meaning that does not apply to me, and it is very obvious that this is "an" objection of conscience, but one should not use words that lend themselves to confusion. It is just as easy to say: he refused to do this because he thinks it is unjust. . . .

ROBERT PAUL WOLFF

An Analysis of the Concept of Political Loyalty

———————————————————————————◆

The diffident and ineffectual response of American liberals to the attacks of the political right in the 1950's revealed a deep confusion over the concept of "loyalty." Liberals were uncertain

Written especially for this volume.

about the propriety of the Federal loyalty and security program, and confused over the legitimacy of judging a man's loyalty by his "associations." The government itself seemed not to know what was meant by "loyalty to the United States." The standards of loyalty defined by the various executive orders were either vague or else hodgepodges of inspirational exhortations and injunctions against acts which were already crimes under existing laws. The questions raised by the loyalty program were many and difficult to answer: Could a man have done nothing for which any court might try him, and yet be disloyal to his country? Should the determination of loyalty be a quasi-legal procedure subject to the restrictions of due process and protected by constitutional guarantees? Were a man's tastes, interests, personal associations, or family ties relevant data for a judgment of loyalty? Was loyalty anything more than the mere negation of disloyalty?

The literature provoked by the loyalty crisis discusses these issues heatedly, but without very much illuminating them. The problem seems to lie in the incoherence of the concept of "loyalty" rather than in the lack of pertinent information or even of agreed-upon moral principles. What I propose, therefore, is to attempt a formal analysis of "loyalty" in order to prepare the way for a more useful debate over substantive issues. Since I aim only at distinguishing the different concepts which are confused together under the title "loyalty," my analysis will produce no answers. Nevertheless, I am convinced that many questions will lose their urgency once it is seen that they grow from conceptual unclarity rather than genuine disagreement over facts or values.

I.

When we say of a man that he is *loyal*, there are at least four quite distinct things that we may mean to assert. First, we may intend to attribute to him a certain disposition of character, in much the way that we might say that he was courageous, generous, or industrious. In other words, loyalty may be conceived as a personality trait, and disloyalty either as the absence of that trait, or as a contrary trait.* Character traits are habits or propensities; they are tendencies of the person to behave in certain

---

*That is to say, we would still have to decide whether disloyalty was to loyalty as a lack of courage to courage, or as cowardliness to courage. The distinction is involved in the explosive issue of "positive loyalty." See below, section II.

ways when confronted with certain sorts of situations. For example, physical courage is the disposition to do such things as stand and fight when attacked on the battlefield, risk one's life in the performance of duty, and suffer pain without losing self-control or being deterred from one's purpose.

The relation between a character trait and individual acts may take one of two forms, according to the analysis one adopts. The simpler view is that the acts are consequences of the disposition and hence evidences of its existence. They may, indeed, be the only evidence which is logically possible. That is to say, how a man acts (including what he says) may be the sole way of discovering how he is prone to act. The second, and more complex, theory is that the performance of some acts or other of the appropriate sort is part of what it means to have a character trait. To be courageous, for example, is to have the tendency to do brave deeds and also to do them on at least some occasions. According to the first view, if a man has never acted courageously (or cowardly either), we simply lack the information to decide whether he is brave or not. On the second view, however, a man who never acts courageously or cowardly during his life is *not* courageous or cowardly. It is therefore analytically false, or self-contradictory, to say that he lived and died a coward but never actually showed it.

How shall we describe the character trait called loyalty? First of all, a loyal person is loyal to something. The proper object of loyalty is either another person, a group of persons, or an institution. The loyal man comes to the aid of the object of his loyalty when its interests are threatened; he identifies himself with its career, making its successes his successes and its enemies his enemies. He is prepared to sacrifice for it, even to the extent of giving his life in order that it may be safe-guarded. The loyal man takes pride in his loyalty object and expresses solidarity with it through ritual acts which evoke and reinforce his emotional identification with it. Frequently he focuses his feelings through symbols such as a song, a flag, or a name.

In a second sense of the term, to say that a man is "loyal" is to ascribe to him a certain status defined by law. The notion of a legal status needs elucidating, for it is neither descriptive nor normative, but what has been called "ascriptive" in character. When we say that a man has killed someone, we assert a causal connection between some act of his and the other's death. But when we call him a murderer, we are strictly speaking asserting that a duly constituted court of law has tried him for the crime of murder, that it has found him guilty, and perhaps also that he has appealed and lost. In short, the term "murderer" is a legal term, and we use it to ascribe a legal status to a man, one which makes him liable to certain punishments and disabilities determined by law. A killer who has been acquitted is not a murderer, in the proper sense of the term. When we call him such, we usually mean that he is morally reprehensible and deserves to be punished in the way that the law customarily punishes murderers. Speaking quixotically, we mean that he ought to be a murderer—ought, that is, to have the legal status of murderer imposed upon him.

The notion of a legal status is easily illustrated from the law of property. The thought which first comes to mind when one thinks about property is that ownership is based upon some natural relationship, such as actual physical possession, as when a squatter claims to own the land he sits on or as in the saying, "possession is nine points of the law." But a little reflection reveals that there is no natural relation between a man and a piece of land, object, or economic right, which is either sufficient or necessary to his ownership of it. To own something, it is not necessary to have one's hands on it, nor even to be in its vicinity. One can own something without ever having seen it, or even knowing of its existence. Ownership usually does not carry an absolute right to do with the property as one wills, or to destroy it if one chooses. Ownership is a complex set of legally determined rights and responsibilities which cannot be reduced to a natural relationship. The legal fact of ownership is determined by a court of law, just as is the status of murderer. The court does not discover ownership; it determines it, in the proper sense of the term. Until the court has handed down an opinion, there is strictly speaking no ownership at all. Here again, however, we may assert moral principles which we believe ought to find expression in the laws of property. A classic example is John Locke's argument that a man gains a proprietary right to an object through mixing his labor with it and fitting it for human use.

The interpretation of loyalty as a legal status has historical antecedents in the medieval concept of a "legal" man, which is to say a man who was entitled to appear in court as a free man, possessed of the full rights and protections of the law. A legal man was contrasted either with a serf, who could not for example serve on a jury, or with an alien who stood outside the normal processes of law. In modern times, as in classical Athens, the concept of legality is submerged in that of citizenship, or perhaps "full" citizenship, to distinguish it from the disadvantaged status of criminals and others who have lost some of their political rights. On this interpretation of "loyalty," then, to say that a man is loyal is to say that he is legally a citizen in good standing, and fully possessed of the rights of citizenship as defined by law.

Loyalty so understood is a status to be ascribed by the decision of a legal or quasi-legal body. As a man in medieval England might go to law to establish that he was a free man and hence entitled to own land, marry whom he chose, or inherit property, so an individual accused of disloyalty would come before a court to have the charge adjudicated. Calling a man disloyal would, in the first instance, be equivalent to asserting that he had been denied the status of citizen for one or more of a number of specified causes. In a precisely analogous manner, when we call a man an alien, we assert that he has a legal status and imply that it has been ascribed to him (by law) for one of the causes laid down by law (such as foreign birth, conflicting citizenship, falsification of naturalization papers, etc.). Needless to say, we may charge a man with disloyalty just as we may charge him with murder, meaning thereby that by his acts or omissions he has in our opinion earned the status of "disloyal." We may by extension mean that although the law does not now proscribe such acts as his, it ought to do so. But strictly, to call a man disloyal is to assert that he has been adjudged disloyal by an appropriate tribunal. Loyalty, on this second interpretation, is precisely what the law says it is.

I have dwelt at length on this technical sense of "loyalty" despite its relative unfamiliarity to modern ears because only in terms of it can we make sense of the insistence that loyalty investigations be governed by the legal protections of the Constitution. I shall return to this point later.

In addition to naming a character trait and a legal status, "loyalty" may also mean "orthodoxy" with regard to some set of political or philosophical principles. Calling a man disloyal can be a way of saying that he has dissented from a dogma or perhaps merely that he has failed to confess it with sufficient frequency and vigor. Disloyalty is thus assimilated to heresy or apostasy.

As with religious orthodoxy, so with the political variety. The creed may consist either of factual assertions or of moral principles. The loyal man is one who believes *that* the assertions are true, or who believes *in* the principles. In political life, there is no limit to what may come to be either a test or a component of doctrinal loyalty. To be a loyal American, on the view of some people, one must believe that the theory of laissez-faire capitalism is an adequate analysis of industrial life. Others demand that one believe in the equality of man, which still others interpret as the belief that intelligence is not genetically linked to skin color.

It is useful for analytical purposes to treat the identification of loyalty with orthodoxy as a distinct meaning of the term, but its connections with the first two meanings are of course very close. Beliefs, as motives of action, are evidence for the existence of character traits, though experience teaches us not to take them at face value without some corroborating support from behavior. Beliefs also may be among the criteria for the ascription of a legal status. The history of religious persecutions has made Anglo-American law wary of test oaths and other enforced expressions of belief, but in principle there is no legal impossibility in requiring a confession of faith as a condition of obtaining or preserving one's status as a citizen. (The oath of allegiance is not such a confession, as we shall see presently.)

The last sense of "loyal" is that in which to be loyal is to remain true, to be faithful, to honor a moral commitment. This is probably the predominant use today, as well as the original meaning of the term. Loyalty as the honoring of a moral commitment must be distinguished from loyalty as a character trait, though the two are obviously very closely related. To have a character trait is to be disposed to respond in certain ways to situations of a specific type. These responses are spontaneous and issue from inclination, not an awareness of duty. A man may be of a faithful disposition without having contracted a moral commitment to the object of his loyalty; conversely, he may loyally fulfill his obligation without feeling an unforced inclination to do so. Some philosophers argue that in fact the fulfillment of moral commitments—the doing of one's duty—psychologically must involve habits of character. Aristotle and Plato may both be read in this way. But since the concepts of loyalty as a disposition and loyalty as the honoring of a commitment are logically distinct, it is as well for our purposes to treat them separately.

There are many sorts of moral commitments, and most are not entitled "loyalty." Strictly, men are said to be loyal either to individuals, to groups, or to institutions (as in the case of loyalty as a character trait). By extension, we sometimes speak of being loyal to a principle or an ideal, and some philosophers have made a great deal of this sort of abstract loyalty. I shall not treat it in this paper, save insofar as it can be subsumed under the heading, loyalty-as-a-belief. To be "true to one's principles" is either a metaphor or else an elliptical way of describing loyalty to other men who share those principles and are relying upon you to observe them. With regard to moral commitments to men or institutions, the term "loyalty" is usually reserved for a *total commitment* to the interests, safety, and preservation of the loyalty-object. We can see here one source of the confusion between the concepts of loyalty as a disposition and as a commitment. Speaking loosely, there may be little difference between a man who lays down his life out of love for his country and another who makes the same sacrifice in fulfillment of his sworn promise of loyalty. When we come to consider the limits of the demands which a state may make upon its subjects, the distinction is quite material indeed.

For convenience we may use a two-dimensional matrix to classify types of total commitments. Loyalty may in the first place be to a single individual, a group, or an institution.* We may also distinguish between contractual obligations explicitly entered into and so-called natural obligations arising from some human relationship such as that of a child to its parent. These two sets of alternatives generate six kinds of total commitments, all of which have been termed loyalty in the history of discussion on the topic. The diagram summarizes the classification:

*There is an important difference between obligation to an institution and obligation to a group of individuals who may be organized institutionally. This point arises in discussions of social contract theories of political obligation, where the question is whether the original promise of all to all remains in force after some of the original contracting parties have died and others have taken their places.

TYPE OF OBLIGATION	OBJECT OF LOYALTY		
	Individual	*Group*	*Institution*
Natural	Subject to king; child to parent	Clansman to clan; individual to human race	Native-born to motherland
	Paternal theory of kingship; "family loyalty"	Tribal view of loyalty; World Federalism	Plato's *Crito;* nationalist ideologies
Contractual	Vassal to liege lord	Social Contract	Loyalty oath; naturalization; "implicit contract"
	Medieval theory of feudal king	Locke; Rousseau	Locke; modern legal concept of loyalty

Each box contains examples of a kind of loyalty and authors who have defended such a conception or theories in which it figures. Thus in the middle box of the lower line we have an example of contractual total commitment of an individual to a group, namely the social contract, followed by two authors— Locke and Rousseau—who have offered a group-contractual analysis of political loyalty.

1. Natural Moral Obligation to an Individual: Under this heading we find the form of authority, and its correlative loyalty, often cited by traditional authors as the prototype of all political authority, namely that of a father over his sons. The obligation of the sons is supposed to stem from the debt they owe their father for having given them existence. The analogy is frequently drawn by Judeo-Christian writers between the paternal authority of God and that of the head of the family. From extended family to tribe to nation, so Aristotle for example tells us, paternal authority and the duty of filial obedience grow into kingly authority and the subject's duty of loyalty. Although sovereignty has been rationalized and rulers institutionalized, a tendency can still be seen in even the most advanced democracies to invest the political leader with an aura of paternal majesty. Thence comes the horror we feel at the assassination of a Prime Minister or President.

2. Contractual Moral Obligation to an Individual: As the tra-

dition of patriarchal tribes gives us the model of natural loyalty to an individual, so the equally ancient institution of the *comitatus* exemplifies contractual loyalty to an individual. In early Germanic culture, it was the practice for an outstanding warrior to gather about him a band of comrades who swore a personal oath to follow him, fight at his side, and lay down their lives for him if necessary. In return they received a share of the booty from the raids which constituted the principal occupation of the group. The custom was fused in early medieval times with Roman practices to form the characteristic feudal relation of vassal to lord. Both parties to the ceremony of fealty were free men, and though the vassal submitted himself to the lord in postures of humility, he might be, and often was, a count or bishop or even king. In late medieval times, with the growth of mercenary armies and the centralization of political authority, the relationship became more and more an economic contract, and the notion of loyalty to a national king took the place of the old individual fealty.

3. Natural Moral Obligation to a Group: The most ancient and the most modern conceptions of loyalty fall into this category. The loyalty of a clansman to his people is one of the earliest moral obligations to be recognized by society. It is based on the ties of kinship, frequently extended and indirect, which unite a tribe into a single "in-group." The idea has been universalized in the modern concept of loyalty to the whole human race. Opponents of nationalism argue that the same obligation which all men acknowledge to their kinsmen or fellow-citizens is owed by each of us to the human race taken collectively. As with the loyalty of son to father, our obligation to mankind is said to rest on a natural relation, that of a common humanity. In the absence of an adequate analysis of the concept of a collective humanity, it is not clear how we are to distinguish this special debt of loyalty from the general moral obligation to treat all men as ends and take cognizance of their needs and rights.

4. Contractual Moral Obligation to a Group: The principal example of this sort of obligation of loyalty is the social contract which, according to political philosophers in the democratic tradition, first creates and defines the political community and gathers together the individual moral authority of the separate individuals into the collective sovereignty of the society. As the name itself implies, the social contract is modeled upon the con-

cept of a legal contract. Several consequences follow from this legal metaphor. First, the parties to the contract are equal before the law, although of course some may be wealthier, more powerful, or of higher status than others. Second, the contract is a self-interested agreement from which each party expects to gain and under which each party must give. Third, the contract is limited in its scope and force by the terms of the original agreement. Its goals and methods of implementation are more or less explicitly spelled out and there may even be stated circumstances in which the contract is void and the parties have the right to violate it.

5. Natural Moral Obligation to an Institution: In the past century and a half political loyalty has by and large been understood as a natural tie binding the individual to his native land. The concept is as old as Socrates, who argues in the *Crito* that he owes a debt of filial obedience to the Athenian Laws which have raised and cared for him. Socrates makes it clear that his obligation is to the laws (i.e., the state) and not to his fellow Athenians. In like manner, many a modern patriot conceives himself as protecting his nation against its present inhabitants and recalling them to its historic faith or mission. In a world which has seen the demystification of authority and the demythologization of Christianity, a religious horror is still felt at the traitor. He is viewed not as a man who has broken a contract or reneged on a debt but as a defiler of sacred things.

6. Contractual Moral Obligation to an Institution: As the natural authority of father over son is the original of all political authority, so the most recent variety is the last of our six types, the contractual debt owed to a political institution such as the state. Social contract theory holds that the authority created by the original contract is vested in the state. Thereafter it remains the possession of the state even though the original contracting parties die out and are replaced. New citizens either take a formal oath of allegiance upon admission to the status of citizen or else—as in the case of native-born children who achieve legal maturity—are considered to have made an implicit contract with the state by remaining in the country and accepting the benefits of citizenship. The voluntary character of contractual political obligation is preserved in most social contract theories by the fiction that the citizen may leave the country and annul his contract if he is no longer able to support his government in

good conscience. There may just barely have been some reality in this notion in the seventeenth century, when Locke advanced it. Today, with the earth's surface exhaustively divided into sovereign nations, not even the wealthy man can escape submission to some state or other. The only sizeable group of people in the modern world who owe no political allegiance are the displaced persons and refugees who live a life of bare subsistence and wait for a chance to return to their native land.

II.

In addition to identifying four separate meanings of the term "loyal," it will be helpful to make two other distinctions before going on to use this conceptual apparatus. First let us recall Aristotle's distinction between the contrary and the contradictory of a term. The contradictory of, for example, "black," is simply the negation of the term "not black." To say of anything that it is not black is to deny it the property of blackness. Nothing positive can be inferred from the assertion, not even that the thing exists. The contrary of a term, on the other hand, is a distinct term which is in some sense the opposite of the first, in our case "white." A pair of contraries are conceived as lying at opposite ends of a spectrum which is defined by the presence or absence of some characteristic. Black and white, for example, were thought by the ancients to lie at opposite ends of a spectrum of varying degrees of color, from the least (black) to the most color (white).

"Disloyalty" can be taken either as the contradictory or as the contrary of "loyalty." Disloyalty as the contradictory would be simply the denial of loyalty. Disloyalty, understood as the contrary of loyalty, would be a character trait, legal status, belief, or moral condition, in some sense opposite to loyalty. There would presumably be a middle ground which was defined neither as loyalty nor as disloyalty. The point appears quibbling, but it has far-reaching consequences. There is all the difference in the world between a government which demands that its citizens be loyal in the sense of simply not being disloyal, and a government which requires active, positive displays of adherence to official dogmas and support for official positions. The difference is expressed by the two sayings, "Everyone who is not against us is with us!" and "Anyone who is not with us is against us!"

The issue of "positive loyalty" can make an appearance in

democracies as well as in totalitarian states. For example the Supreme Court decisions concerning flag-salutes and pledges of allegiance turn on whether a government has the right to demand oaths and other signs of positive loyalty beyond a mere obedience to the laws.

If loyalty is conceived as a character trait, then disloyalty will be either the mere lack of that trait or a distinct and opposite trait disposing the individual to betray his nation, fail to come to its defense, and so forth. Loyalty as a legal status has as its opposites the lack of that status (contradictory) or another status, like that of criminal, carrying various penalties and determined by law (contrary). In the case of loyalty as a belief, disloyalty is either absence of the belief (contradictory) or a conflicting belief (contrary). The analogy in religion is agnosticism versus atheism. Finally, if loyalty is interpreted as the honoring of a total commitment, then disloyalty is either the mere failure to keep the commitment or else the deliberate breach of it for some conflicting purpose, not necessarily self-regarding.

The second distinction we need is that between actual and potential loyalty or disloyalty. The concept of potential loyalty is rather complex, and it will help to consider it in connection with each of our four senses of loyalty in turn.

1. If loyalty is a character trait, then it is already in a certain sense a potentiality. Courage is the disposition, or potentiality, to act bravely when faced with danger. As Aristotle pointed out, a man may be potentially courageous either in the sense that he now has the disposition to act bravely, or in the sense that he has the capacity to develop that disposition. Analogously, a child is said to have musical talent, meaning that he has it within him to become a fine musician; an accomplished musician, by contrast, is said to be a fine pianist, meaning that although he is not now performing, he can do so (actualize his potentiality) when he chooses. As I mentioned in my discussion of loyalty as a character trait, one analysis of such traits makes the performance of some characteristic acts or other a necessary condition of having the trait, while a second analysis does not. The former will apply the concept of potential loyalty to persons who have not yet given evidence of their loyal disposition; the latter will employ the concept of actual loyalty rather more widely.

There is a certain asymmetry in the interpretation of the concept of disloyalty by the loyalty-as-character-trait school.

Whereas a man is said to be loyal insofar as he is disposed to act in defense of his nation, etc., he is often said to be disloyal only when he has actually committed a breach of faith. In that sense, "loyalty" is what Gilbert Ryle has called a disposition-term, and disloyalty is what he calls an occurrence-term. Nevertheless, one can find some instances in which a man's loyalty is questioned not because he has committed some act, but because he is likely to do so. A man might be called chronically disloyal, despite the fact that he has not in the present instance broken faith, because he is thought to be prone to disloyalty. This, indeed, is one of the grounds on which alcoholics and homosexuals were denied security clearance by the State Department.

2. Strictly speaking, there is no valid use of the concept of potential loyalty in the case of loyalty-as-a-legal-status. Either a man has the status of citizen in good standing or he has not. We may of course predict the outcome of a loyalty hearing, just as we may predict the outcome of a murder trial, but the injunction to treat a man as innocent until proven guilty holds good in all cases of ascription of legal status. It may be reasonable to bar a man from government employ because he is thought likely to commit acts which would ordinarily be punished by a judgment of disloyalty. However, if disloyalty is a legal status, then a man is not disloyal until he has been so judged by an appropriate tribunal.

3. The distinction between actual and potential loyalty has an equally dubious application in the case of loyalty-as-a-belief. One could think up some meaning for the term "potential belief," but in general it hardly seems a useful concept to define. One might imagine cases, for example, in which a religious or political leader, alert to the dangers of heresy in his flock, came to recognize certain types as prone to heterodoxy. He could then say of someone, "He is one of the faithful at present, but his sort is prone to fall away, he is potentially unfaithful."

4. Moral commitments are in some respects like character traits, in that a man may correctly be said to have and honor a moral commitment even when, at the moment, he is doing nothing which relates to it in any way. If I have sworn to defend my country in time of war, and if I remain so resolved, then I am a loyal citizen even though my country is at peace and I am quietly minding my business. To acknowledge and honor a commitment is to do what is required by the commitment

when the occasion arises. Save in odd cases like keeping a secret, where not doing something moment by moment is what is required, moral commitments are operative only intermittently. It would be absurd to say that between wars, the valiant soldier is not loyal because he is not then fighting.

We encounter once again the asymmetry in the concepts of loyalty and disloyalty which appeared in the case of loyalty-as-a-character-trait. When a man is called "loyal" it is never meant simply that he has committed certain acts, although those acts may be evidence of his loyalty. Whether loyalty is conceived as a character trait, a legal status, a belief, or the fulfillment of an obligation, it is something more than any number of specific acts. (Namely, a proneness to commit acts of that sort, or a legal status ascribed because of those acts, or a belief which issues in acts like those, or a moral commitment which those acts serve to honor.) Disloyalty, however, is sometimes treated not as a proneness to certain acts, or a legal status ascribed because of certain acts, etc., but simply as the performance of those acts themselves. In part this follows from the fact that a single counter-instance refutes a universal judgment. Hence, if "disloyal" simply means "not loyal," any disloyal act is enough to destroy the implied universality of "He is (unfailingly) loyal." In part, however, it is a reflection of the fact that whereas "loyal" is most often taken to mean "having the character trait of loyalty" or "honoring a total commitment," the contrary term "disloyal" usually has the legalistic sense of having broken some law or security regulation.

III.

The time has come at last to apply the system of categories and distinctions developed so far. My aim is not to elaborate a theory of loyalty, but simply to clear the way for a theory by untangling some of the confusions in which the subject lies ensnarled. My program is to take up three questions around which controversy has centered in the loyalty debates, and ask in each case what sorts of answers would be appropriate to each of the senses of "loyalty" analyzed in sections I and II.

1. Let us begin with the question which lies at the base of all discussions of political loyalty: Does a nation-state have the right to demand that its subjects be loyal? What sorts of answers make sense according to the different meanings of "loyalty"? If

we understand loyalty as a character trait, then the state clearly never has the right to demand that its subjects be loyal, for one can justly require of a man only what it is within his power to give, and it is psychologically impossible to alter one's personality by an act of will. On the other hand, the state might (depending on other moral considerations) have the right to require ceremonies, courses of education, salutes of the flag, and other acts designed to create and sustain loyalty in the citizenry. In the United States, the public schools at the elementary and secondary levels are avowedly committed to the goal of creating loyal citizens. From the nature of the activities which are directed to this end in the schools, we can infer that the schools view loyalty—albeit somewhat confusedly—as a trait of character like honesty, industry, or generosity. It is clear, I take it, that the attempt to instill loyalty in the hearts of young Americans is directly in conflict with the liberal ideal of non-interference in the internal life of the individual.

In sum, if we claim both that loyalty is a character trait and that the state has a right to attempt to instill it in citizens, then we allow the state to decide what is best for its subjects. In the manner of Plato's philosopher-king or Dostoyevsky's Grand Inquisitor, the state is permitted to shape the souls of the young by patriotic myths or religious rituals. This consequence, it seems to me, is one of the strong reasons for *not* treating political loyalty as a character trait.

If loyalty is equated with the legal status of full citizenship, then the state by definition has the right to require it of all citizens. However the method of ascertaining loyalty will be hedged round with all the safeguards which go by the title "due process." No *a priori* restriction on the criteria of citizenship can be deduced from the mere interpretation of loyalty as a legal status. The procedural restrictions, however, would obviously have far-reaching implications for a loyalty program or other quasi-judicial operation.

Beliefs, like traits of character, cannot be commanded. If being loyal to a nation-state means believing in some political ideology which it is supposed to embody, then no state can ever order its subjects to be loyal. It can, to be sure, require them to utter ritual words ("I pledge allegiance . . .") or sign oaths promising never to falter in their faith, but the effort will be fruitless.

The interpretation of loyalty as orthodoxy leads quite naturally to censorship, inquisitions, and all the hated concommitances of an established religious or political dogma. One would suppose, therefore, that men of a liberal persuasion would be careful to avoid such an interpretation and fix instead upon one of the other possibilities. Nevertheless, there are a great many liberals who argue that in order to be accorded the rights of citizenship, a man must believe in the principles or ground-rules of democratic politics. The implication, of course, is that individuals who find themselves in all honesty unable to confess the democratic faith must be politically excommunicated. There is, I suppose, an alternative possibility. Following the wise and forgiving practice of the Catholic Church, the state might announce itself willing to gather to its bosom all those souls who, though unable to believe, nevertheless submitted themselves to the authority of the government.

Finally, if loyalty is the honoring of a total moral commitment, then we can make sense of the government's requiring that all its subjects be loyal. In the case of loyalty-as-a-natural-obligation, the government would, like the Laws in the *Crito,* demand that the citizen acknowledge the debt he had incurred to the state by living within its territory, accepting its protection, and benefiting from its institutions. In the case of loyalty-as-a-contractual-obligation, the state would either remind the citizen of the agreement he had made, or appeal to the concept of an implicit contract to prove that every adult citizen had made a quasi-contract with the state.

The essence of a moral commitment is that it be freely made. In political terms, this means that the citizens have an alternative to binding themselves to the state, namely emigration. Most social contract theorists include an emigration clause in order to make sense of the notion of an implicit contract. The theory of contracts in law posits two free and legally equal parties who come together in agreement for mutual benefit. If one of the parties has no choice in the matter—if there is coercion—then the contract is not binding. The analogous argument is presupposed in political theories. In the modern world, as I have remarked, emigration is in general impossible. The question inevitably arises, therefore, whether a state can have the right to demand a total moral commitment from what is essentially a captive citizenry. I am not asking here whether it is wise or just for the state to make such a demand but only whether it makes sense for it to do so. The answer clearly is that when an individual has no choice in the matter, it is illogical to ask him to choose. Hence, insofar as loyalty is viewed as a total moral commitment of the citizen to the state (or of the citizen to his fellow-citizens), the state cannot have even the possibility of a right to demand that commitment save in the most special of circumstances which rarely exist in the modern world.

It would appear that the state can require loyalty of its citizens only if loyalty is understood to mean "full citizenship." In that case, attention shifts from the definition of loyalty to the criteria which the law employs in ascribing citizenship. Whatever they are, the determination of loyalty will be a legal matter. If character traits, beliefs, or moral commitments are made criteria of citizenship, then we will once more encounter the objections which have just been rehearsed. The appropriate sorts of criteria, I would suggest, are qualifications such as birthplace, parentage, and residence, together with the absence of any defeating facts such as conflicting citizenship, past convictions for specified crimes, and so forth. Loyalty so conceived is purely a function of behavior; it does not involve the inner man, neither his beliefs nor his inclinations and character. It also does not place him in the false position of having to announce a moral commitment as though he had freely chosen it when in fact it has been forced upon him.

Insofar as other conceptions of loyalty do not spring from a fundamentally illiberal orientation, I suggest that they originate in a false and idyllic image of the political sphere. Those who call for unanimity on the ideological ground-work of democracy and equally those who appeal to the legal fiction of a quasi-contract presuppose a non-existent escape hatch of emigration. They are frequently critical of the simpler, more sentimental souls who would identify loyalty with an abiding attachment to the patriotic symbols of the homeland, but the mistake they make is fully as great.

2. A subsidiary question over which debate has raged is what sort of evidence is relevant to a determination of loyalty. One phrase, "guilt by association," has come to epitomize all the most odious features of the "red hunt" which was waged during the height of the loyalty crisis. Many an individual's loyalty was called into question because he was friendly with

a member of the Communist Party, had been part of a social circle of people with left-wing politics, was the son or father or brother of a suspicious person, or even because he liked the ballet and subscribed to foreign (non-Communist) publications. There was a great deal of know-nothing parochial stupidity in the administration of the loyalty program, as many of the more sophisticated red-hunters themselves complained. It was therefore dangerously easy for at least some liberals to concentrate their attacks on instances of crudity or ignorance and so avoid a direct confrontation with the principles which underlay the program. It was outrageous to brand a man disloyal because of the friends he made and the journals he read. And yet, the spy trials revealed that a distressingly high proportion of those convicted were intellectuals, former adherents of left-wing causes, friends or relations of Communists, and even readers of foreign publications. Liberals found themselves in the impossible position of maintaining that who a man knew and what he read would give no clue to his political convictions or probable future behavior.

If loyalty is indeed a character trait, then nothing could be more relevant to its discovery than associations, interests, and ties of kinship. According to many social psychologists, the personality develops and takes shape through a process of identification and internalization. The individual identifies himself with a person or group in his immediate environment; he looks to them for praise, fears their disapproval, imitates their behavior, and copies a life-style from them. They are what sociologists call his primary group. Through the processes of identification, the individual adopts the value attitudes of his primary group and internalizes them. He comes to approve what they approve, to desire what they desire. Most individuals are unable to sustain a life-style and set of values for more than a short while without some reinforcement from a primary group of like-minded persons. The group may be small, and it may be outcast from the larger society, but so long as it provides each member with psychological "feedback," it can survive considerable external pressure. Clearly, on this theory of personality formation, the best—indeed sometimes the only—way to discover an individual's character traits is to observe whom he associates with, what his family is like, how he dresses, where he comes from, and even whether he attends the ballet regularly. "Where there's smoke, there's fire!" may be a bad rule of law, but it is the first principle of social psychology.

This point is extremely important and worth exploring further. A man's interests, actions, associations, are influenced by his personality (and his beliefs—the argument holds for loyalty-as-a-belief with only minor changes). Therefore it is perfectly reasonable to infer his traits of character or beliefs from any data we have about his associations. Of course we may make mistakes, as with all inferences from effects to causes, but the mode of reasoning is in principle legitimate.

The term "security risk" is used to denote the degree of probability that an individual will, at some time in the future, reveal secret information to unauthorized persons or in some other way undermine the security precautions of the government. A man's decision to commit a breach of security is obviously influenced by many things, including his political beliefs, the character of his friendships, his susceptibility to pressures, the probability that he will encounter an alien agent, and so forth. Experience shows that persons who possess certain characteristics commit breaches of security in a higher proportion of cases than those who lack them. Therefore, by the laws of probability, those with the characteristics are greater "security risks." Characterologically, such people are either actually or potentially disloyal —they are prone to commit disloyal acts, or prone to develop such tendencies. If disloyalty is interpreted as a character trait or belief, then it will be perfectly reasonable to judge men's loyalty by the principle of "guilt by association."

It is clear, I think, that in arguing against the practice of condemning a man for his beliefs or associations, it is foolish to do so on the grounds that those data bear no relation to his probable actions. Palpably they do. The best line is to say that loyalty, insofar as it is required by the government, is not a belief or character trait, but a legal status or moral commitment, and hence that all the intimate details which fill the secret files of the F.B.I. are simply irrelevant.

3. Finally, let us give some consideration to the "loyalty oath" which has played so prominent a role in American political debates. There are two distinct sorts of depositions which are both somewhat confusedly referred to as "loyalty oaths." The first, the loyalty oath proper, is a pledge to uphold the Constitution of the United States (or of one of the fifty states) and protect it

from its enemies "both foreign and domestic." The second is an affidavit swearing to certain matters of fact, such as that one is not now and never has been a member of the Communist Party, or that one is not a member of some other organization proscribed by the Federal Government. The affidavit is quite clearly a dubious legal instrument. If the activities to which it refers are against the law, then it invades the constitutional protection against self-incrimination; if the activities are legal, then the affidavit is a method of punishing an individual nonjudicially. In practice the affidavit is an unsavory device for transforming a legal act into an illegal one. A man is asked to swear that he has not done X, an act which is perfectly legal. He knows that if he refuses to swear, he will suffer the loss of a job, social and professional ostracism, and other quasi-punishments. If he lies to avoid those sanctions, he can then be prosecuted for perjury, even though not for the original act. All in all, not a pretty business.

The loyalty oath is quite another matter. If the state is conceived to be founded upon a social contract, then the original promise of each to all *is* a loyalty oath. It is a pledge to accept the decisions of the duly constituted government as one's own, to make such sacrifices for the good of all as may be demanded, and to defend the political community against its enemies. Thus, if loyalty is interpreted as honoring a contractual total commitment, then every citizen is assumed to have taken an oath of loyalty and to be bound by its conditions. It may be doubted whether anything is gained from constant reiterations of the pledge, but no social contract theorist could ever deny the government's right to require it.

The matter is rather different once we acknowledge the inapplicability of the social contract model to contemporary politics. When a man has no real choice but to live in the country of his birth, the demand that he swear loyalty to it has the quality of a coerced promise which is morally worthless. States can perhaps require their subjects to obey the laws and punish them for not doing so. But it makes no sense, in addition, for the government to exact the lip-service of a loyalty oath.

Loyalty oaths are inappropriate as well in the cases of loyalty-as-a-character-trait and loyalty-as-a-belief. In the former, a willingness to take the oath may be one sign of a loyal disposition, but since one cannot acquire a new personality trait by an act of will, the oath is not morally binding. As for loyalty-as-a-belief, the appropriate instrument would be a confession of faith or catechism rather than an oath of loyalty.

There is one other case in which a loyalty oath seems to me a reasonable requirement. If loyalty is conceived as a natural moral obligation of an individual to the state, total in character and arising from the quasi-parental protective and educative role which the state has played, then the absence of an escape or emigration provision would have no effect on the binding character of the obligation. In these days of contractual rather than natural human relationships, there are few serious political thinkers who could straight-facedly argue that the state stands *in loco parentis* to the subject and possesses those rights which were once vested in the head of the family. Nevertheless, the belief in a natural obligation to the motherland is very widespread and plays an important role in determining popular attitudes toward loyalty.

Suggestions for Further Reading

*(Books marked with * are available in paperback editions.)*

In addition to the *Crito*, students interested in Plato's political theory should read *The Republic, Gorgias,* and *Laws.* Cornford's translation of *The Republic,* parts of which have been reproduced in this book, contains extremely valuable notes and comments. A. E. Taylor's *The Mind of Plato* (Ann Arbor, 1960)* is a good general summary and analysis of the dialogues. An anarchist attack on all governments and state power can be found in *The Political Philosophy of Bakunin* (New York, 1953), edited by G. P. Maximoff, as well as in *The Philosophy of Anarchism* (London, 1944) by the English philosopher of art, Sir Herbert Read. The conflict between state authority and individual liberty has been a major theme in most political philosophy. John of Salisbury's vigorous defense of tyrannicide in *Policraticus,* translated in part as *The Statesman's Book of John of Salisbury,* by John Dickenson (New York, 1963), can be contrasted with the strongly authoritarian position of Jean Bodin in his *Six Bookes of a Commonweale* (Cambridge, Eng., 1962). In the English tradition, Thomas Hobbes, *Leviathan,* stands opposed to John Milton, *The Ready and Easy Way to Establish a Commonwealth.* Thomas Paine, in his strongly individualistic *The Rights of Man,* enunciated many of the arguments which swayed the revolutionary Americans and Frenchmen of the late eighteenth century. Shortly thereafter, William Godwin took a strong libertarian anti-statist line in *Political Justice.* More recently, the American philosopher Josiah Royce argued in *The Philosophy of Loyalty* (New York, 1908) that the concept of loyalty—to friends, family, community, even to a principle or idea—could be made the foundation of a social and moral philosophy.

The traitor has always been a morally ambiguous figure, simultaneously reviled as the lowest of criminals and exalted as the most selfless of heroes. Among the studies of treason and traitors, Margret Boveri's *Treason in the Twentieth Century* (New York, 1962) is the most comprehensive. Rebecca West offers case studies in *The Meaning of Treason* (New York, 1947). For an American experience, there is no more vivid account than Whittaker Chambers' *Witness* (New York, 1952).

Contemporary theoretical accounts include A. D. Lindsay, *The Modern Democratic State* (New York, 1961), Harold Laski, *Authority in the Modern State* (New Haven, 1919), and André Thérive's *Essai sur les Trahisons* (Paris, 1951).

The controversy over the loyalty-security programs of the United States government in the 1950's resulted in a large number of books, some tailored to the problems of the moment and others seeking to set the debate in a broader context. In addition to John Schaar's very fine book, which has been excerpted here, the student can follow the debate in Sidney Hook's *Heresy, Yes—Conspiracy, No!* (New York, 1953), Alan Barth's *The Loyalty of Free Men* (New York, 1952), and Henry Steele Commager's *Freedom, Loyalty, Dissent* (New York, 1954). Eleanor Bontecou has gathered together a good deal of factual material on the government's program in *The Federal Loyalty-Security Program* (Ithaca,

1953). Somewhat specialized, but of considerable background interest for the subject of loyalty oaths, is H. Silving's article on "Oaths" in the *Yale Law Review* for 1958–1959. Morton Grodzins, in *The Loyal and the Disloyal* (Chicago, 1956), builds a general theory of loyalty on his earlier study of the fate of the Japanese-Americans during World War II.

The concept of personality traits as dispositions is explored at length in Gilbert Ryle's *Concept of Mind* (New York, 1950),* as well as in Aristotle's *On the Soul.* The notion of a legal status is clarified by H. L. A. Hart's essay "On the Ascription of Rights and Responsibilities," reprinted in *Logic and Language* (Oxford, 1955), first series, edited by A. G. N. Flew. Other examples of analytical political philosophy, done in the Anglo-American linguistic style, can be found in the two volumes of essays entitled *Philosophy, Politics, and Society,* edited by Peter Laslett (New York, 1963).

PART TWO

The Individual
and Society

CLASSICAL IMAGES
OF MAN

A consideration of the relationship between the individual and society must begin with some conception of the nature of man. If we suppose that men are rational, calculating, egoistic seekers after pleasure, that they enter into social or political intercourse with other men deliberately and prudentially, that each man treats his fellows purely as a means to his own ends—if we adopt this image, then political society will look to us much like a joint-stock corporation in which the investor gives only so that he may get and guides his decisions by a calculus of profit and loss. If, on the other hand, men appear to us as emotional, altruistic, naturally social creatures; if we see human relationships as among the ends of life, valuable simply for themselves; if we view the individual as an abstraction from society, rather than society as a collection of atomic individuals; then we shall very likely treat the political community as an organism in which each part depends upon the other, and the good of the whole takes precedence over the good of any single member.

Strictly speaking, of course, no statement about the way men *are* can contradict a statement about the way they *ought to be,* and it might therefore be supposed that the new sciences of psychology and sociology cannot offer any challenge to classical political theory. It is obvious, however, that no serious philosopher will cling to a utopian model of an ideal society once he discovers that it requires an impossible breed of men as its citizens. For example, if Aristotle were right that only a few men have the native capacity to rule themselves, and hence to rule others as well, then democracy would cease to be an ideal for which men could strive and become instead an idle dream, akin to the fantasy of eternal youth. To be sure, democratic theorists could go on saying that a political society of equals was the best of all imaginable worlds, but they could no longer call it the best of all possible worlds.

In their contrasting theories of man, Jeremy Bentham and Karl Marx raise a problem which lies at the heart of social philosophy. Bentham describes men simply as seekers of pleasure and avoiders of pain. From the point of view of a given individual, other men can be helps or hindrances in this search, but in either case they are only instrumental. Social solidarity for Bentham is a matter of mutual self-interest. Marx rejects this image as a caricature which reflects the economic interests of the bourgeoisie rather than the real nature of man. For him, the activity which distinguishes man from other creatures—namely production—is inherently social. In order to develop themselves spiritually and materially, men must engage in co-operative social labor, molding nature to produce objects of use or beauty. If men are thwarted in their labor, then no matter how much pleasure they absorb, their personalities will be warped and their lives unfulfilled.

Here again we must grant that Bentham's utilitarian moral philosophy cannot be *deduced* from his psychological hedonism, nor is Marx's ideal of the communist society a logical conse-quence of the theory of alienation. Nevertheless, it is easy to see why both authors begin their social philosophies with portraits of human nature. Psychology is the natural prolegomenon to moral philosophy.

Political Man

———————————————————————————◆

Aristotle, 384–322 B.C., begins his treatise on politics in characteristic fashion with a definition of the term "state" (polis), and an analysis of man as a political animal. In contrast with later political theorists such as Locke and Hobbes, Aristotle views the state as both natural and desirable. Political activity is an essential component of the good life, not an unpleasant necessity thrust upon men by civil disorder or unchecked avarice and aggression. It is easy to view Aristotle's famous defense of slavery as a curious—perhaps notorious—historical oddity, of little relevance in the twentieth century. If one removes the word "slave" however, and substitutes for it some euphemism like "passive citizen," Aristotle's theory bears a disturbing resemblance to some recent accounts of American politics. The fundamental question is whether all men, or only a select few, have a right to govern themselves.

Every state is a community of some kind, and every community is established with a view to some good; for mankind always act in order to obtain that which they think good. But, if all communities aim at some good, the state or political community, which is the highest of all, and which embraces all the rest, aims, and in a greater degree than any other, at the highest good.

Now there is an erroneous opinion* that a statesman, king, householder, and master are the same, and that they differ, not in kind, but only in the number of their subjects. For example, the ruler over a few is called a master; over more, the manager of a household; over a still larger number, a statesman or king, as if there were no difference between a great household and a small state. The distinction which is made between the king and the statesman is as follows: When the government is personal, the ruler is a king; when, according to the principles of

—————————————————

Reprinted from Aristotle, *Politics*, translated by B. Jowett (Oxford, Eng.: Clarendon Press, 1885).

* Plato Politicus, 258 E foll.—Trans.

the political science, the citizens rule and are ruled in turn, then he is called a statesman.

But all this is a mistake; for governments differ in kind, as will be evident to any one who considers the matter according to the method which has hitherto guided us. As in other departments of science, so in politics, the compound should always be resolved into the simple elements or least parts of the whole. We must therefore look at the elements of which the state is composed, in order that we may see in what they differ from one another, and whether any scientific distinction can be drawn between the different kinds of rule.*

He who thus considers things in their first growth and origin, whether a state or anything else, will obtain the clearest view of them. In the first place (1) there must be a union of those who cannot exist without each other; for example, of male and female, that the race may continue; and this is a union which is formed, not of deliberate purpose, but because, in common with other animals and with plants, mankind have a natural desire to leave behind them an image of themselves. And (2) there must be a union of natural ruler and subject, that both may be preserved. For he who can foresee with his mind is by nature intended to be lord and master, and he who can work with his body is a subject, and by nature a slave; hence master and slave have the same interest. Nature, however, has distinguished between the female and the slave. For she is not niggardly, like the smith who fashions the Delphian knife for many uses; she makes each thing for a single use, and every instrument is best made when intended for one and not for many uses. But among barbarians no distinction is made between women and slaves, because there is no natural ruler among them: they are a community of slaves, male and female. Wherefore the poets say,—

"It is meet that Hellenes should rule over barbarians,"†

as if they thought that the barbarian and the slave were by nature one.

Out of these two relationships between man and woman,

---

* Or, with Bernays, "how the different kinds of rule differ from one another, and generally whether any scientific result can be attained about each one of them."—Trans.

† Eurip. Iphig. in Aulid. 1400.—Trans.

master and slave, the family first arises, and Hesiod is right
when he says,—

"First house and wife and an ox for the plough,"*

for the ox is the poor man's slave. The family is the association
established by nature for the supply of men's every day wants,
and the members of it are called by Charondas "companions of
the cupboard" [ὁμοσιπύους], and by Epimenides the Cretan, "companions of the manger" [ὁμοκάπους].† But when several families
are united, and the association aims at something more than the
supply of daily needs, then comes into existence the village. And
the most natural form of the village appears to be that of a colony from the family, composed of the children and grandchil-
dren, who are said to be "suckled with the same milk." And this
is the reason why Hellenic states were originally governed by
kings; because the Hellenes were under royal rule before they
came together, as the barbarians still are. Every family is ruled
by the eldest, and therefore in the colonies of the family the
kingly form of government prevailed because they were of the
same blood. As Homer says [of the Cyclopes]:—

"Each one gives law to his children and to his wives." ‡

For they lived dispersedly, as was the manner in ancient times.
Wherefore men say that the Gods have a king, because they
themselves either are or were in ancient times under the rule of
a king. For they imagine, not only the forms of the Gods, but
their ways of life to be like their own.

When several villages are united in a single community, perfect and large enough to be nearly or quite self-sufficing, the
state comes into existence, originating in the bare needs of life,
and continuing in existence for the sake of a good life. And
therefore, if the earlier forms of society are natural, so is the
state, for it is the end of them, and the [completed] nature is
the end. For what each thing is when fully developed, we call
its nature, whether we are speaking of a man, a horse, or a family. Besides, the final cause and end of a thing is the best, and
to be self-sufficing is the end and the best.

* Op. et Di. 405.—Trans.
† Or, reading with the old translator (William of Moerbek) ὁμοκάπνους,
"companions of the hearth."—Trans.
‡ Od. ix. 114, quoted by Plato Laws, iii. 680, and in N. Eth. x. 9. § 13.—
Trans.

Hence it is evident that the state is a creation of nature, and that man is by nature a political animal. And he who by nature and not by mere accident is without a state, is either above humanity, or below it; he is the

"Tribeless, lawless, hearthless one,"

whom Homer denounces—the outcast who is a lover of war; he may be compared to a bird which flies alone.

Now the reason why man is more of a political animal than bees or any other gregarious animals is evident. Nature, as we often say, makes nothing in vain, and man is the only animal whom she has endowed with the gift of speech. And whereas mere sound is but an indication of pleasure or pain, and is therefore found in other animals (for their nature attains to the perception of pleasure and pain and the intimation of them to one another, and no further), the power of speech is intended to set forth the expedient and inexpedient, and likewise the just and the unjust. And it is a characteristic of man that he alone has any sense of good and evil, of just and unjust, and the association of living beings who have this sense makes a family and a state.

Thus the state is by nature clearly prior to the family and to the individual, since the whole is of necessity prior to the part; for example, if the whole body be destroyed, there will be no foot or hand, except in an equivocal sense, as we might speak of a stone hand; for when destroyed the hand will be no better. But things are defined by their working and power; and we ought not to say that they are the same when they are no longer the same, but only that they have the same name. The proof that the state is a creation of nature and prior to the individual is that the individual, when isolated, is not self-sufficing; and therefore he is like a part in relation to the whole. But he who is unable to live in society, or who has no need because he is sufficient for himself, must be either a beast or a god: he is no part of a state. A social instinct is implanted in all men by nature, and yet he who first founded the state was the greatest of benefactors. For man, when perfected, is the best of animals, but, when separated from law and justice, he is the worst of all; since armed injustice is the more dangerous, and he is equipped at birth with the arms of intelligence and with moral qualities which he may use for the worst ends. Wherefore, if he have not virtue, he is the most unholy and the most savage of animals, and the most full of lust and gluttony. But justice is the bond of men in states, and the administration of justice, which is the determination of what is just, is the principle of order in political society.

Seeing then that the state is made up of households, before speaking of the state, we must speak of the management of the household. The parts of the household are the persons who compose it, and a complete household consists of slaves and freemen. Now we should begin by examining everything in its least elements; and the first and least parts of a family are master and slave, husband and wife, father and children. We have therefore to consider what each of these three relations is and ought to be:—I mean the relation of master and servant, of husband and wife, and thirdly of parent and child. [I say γαμική and τεκνοποιητική, there being no words for the two latter notions which adequately represent them.] And there is another element of a household, the so-called art of money-making, which, according to some, is identical with household management, according to others, a principal part of it; the nature of this art will also have to be considered by us.

Let us first speak of master and slave, looking to the needs of practical life and also seeking to attain some better theory of their relation than exists at present. For some are of opinion that the rule of a master is a science, and that the management of a household, and the mastership of slaves, and the political and royal rule, as I was saying at the outset, are all the same. Others affirm that the rule of a master over slaves is contrary to nature, and that the distinction between slave and freeman exists by law only, and not by nature; and being an interference with nature is therefore unjust.

Property is a part of the household, and therefore the art of acquiring property is a part of the art of managing the household; for no man can live well, or indeed live at all, unless he be provided with necessaries. And as in the arts which have a definite sphere the workers must have their own proper instruments for the accomplishment of their work, so it is in the management of a household. Now, instruments are of various sorts; some are living, others lifeless; in the rudder, the pilot of a ship has a lifeless, in the look-out man, a living instrument; for in the arts the servant is a kind of instrument. Thus, too, a possession is an instrument for maintaining life. And so, in the arrangement of the family, a slave is a living possession, and property a number of such instruments; and the servant is himself an instrument, which takes precedence of all other instruments. For if every instrument could accomplish its own work, obeying or anticipating the will of others, like the statues of Daedalus, or the tripods of Hephaestus, which, says the poet

"of their own accord entered the assembly of the Gods;"

if, in like manner, the shuttle would weave and the plectrum touch the lyre without a hand to guide them, chief workmen would not want servants, nor masters slaves. Here, however, another distinction must be drawn: the instruments commonly so called are instruments of production, whilst a possession is an instrument of action. The shuttle, for example, is not only of use; but something else is made by it, whereas of a garment or of a bed there is only the use. Further, as production and action are different in kind, and both require instruments, the instruments which they employ must likewise differ in kind. But life is action and not production, and therefore the slave is the minister of action [for he ministers to his master's life]. Again, a possession is spoken of as a part is spoken of; for the part is not only a part of something else, but wholly belongs to it; and this is also true of a possession. The master is only the master of the slave; he does not belong to him, whereas the slave is not only the slave of his master, but wholly belongs to him. Hence we see what is the nature and office of a slave; he who is by nature not his own but another's and yet a man, is by nature a slave; and he may be said to belong to another who, being a human being, is also a possession. And a possession may be defined as an instrument of action, separable from the possessor.

But is there any one thus intended by nature to be a slave, and for whom such a condition is expedient and right, or rather is not all slavery a violation of nature?

There is no difficulty in answering this question, on grounds both of reason and of fact. For that some should rule, and others be ruled is a thing, not only necessary, but expedient; from the hour of their birth, some are marked out for subjection, others for rule.

And whereas there are many kinds both of rulers and subjects, that rule is the better which is exercised over better subjects—

for example, to rule over men is better than to rule over wild
beasts. The work is better which is executed by better workmen;
and where one man rules and another is ruled, they may be said
to have a work. In all things which form a composite whole and
which are made up of parts, whether continuous or discrete, a
distinction between the ruling and the subject element comes to
light. Such a duality exists in living creatures, but not in them
only; it originates in the constitution of the universe; even in
things which have no life, there is a ruling principle, as in musical harmony.* But we are wandering from the subject. We will,
therefore, restrict ourselves to the living creature which, in the
first place, consists of soul and body: and of these two, the one
is by nature the ruler, and the other the subject. But then we
must look for the intentions of nature in things which retain their
nature, and not in things which are corrupted. And therefore
we must study the man who is in the most perfect state both of
body and soul, for in him we shall see the true relation of the
two; although in bad or corrupted natures the body will often
appear to rule over the soul, because they are in an evil and
unnatural condition. First then we may observe in living creatures both a despotical and a constitutional rule; for the soul
rules the body with a despotical rule, whereas the intellect rules
the appetites with a constitutional and royal rule. And it is clear
that the rule of the soul over the body, and of the mind and the
rational element over the passionate is natural and expedient;
whereas the equality of the two or the rule of the inferior is always hurtful. The same holds good of animals as well as of
men; for tame animals have a better nature than wild, and all
tame animals are better off when they are ruled by man; for
then they are preserved. Again, the male is by nature superior,
and the female inferior; and the one rules, and the other is ruled;
this principle, of necessity, extends to all mankind. Where then
there is such a difference as that between soul and body, or between men and animals (as in the case of those whose business
is to use their body, and who can do nothing better), the lower
sort are by nature slaves, and it is better for them as for all
inferiors that they should be under the rule of a master. For he
who can be, and therefore is another's, and he who participates
in reason enough to apprehend, but not to have, reason, is a
slave by nature. Whereas the lower animals cannot even appre-

* Or, "of harmony [in music]."—Trans.

hend reason; they obey their instincts. And indeed the use made of slaves and of tame animals is not very different; for both with their bodies minister to the needs of life. Nature would like to distinguish between the bodies of freemen and slaves, making the one strong for servile labour, the other upright, and although useless for such services, useful for political life in the arts both of war and peace. But this does not hold universally: for some slaves have the souls and others have the bodies of freemen. And doubtless if men differed from one another in the mere forms of their bodies as much as the statues of the Gods do from men, all would acknowledge that the inferior class should be slaves of the superior. And if there is a difference in the body, how much more in the soul? but the beauty of the body is seen, whereas the beauty of the soul is not seen. It is clear, then, that some men are by nature free, and others slaves, and that for these latter slavery is both expedient and right.

But that those who take the opposite view have in a certain way right on their side, may be easily seen. For the words slavery and slave are used in two senses. There is a slave or slavery by law as well as by nature. The law of which I speak is a sort of convention, according to which whatever is taken in war is supposed to belong to the victors. But this right many jurists impeach, as they would an orator who brought forward an unconstitutional measure: they detest the notion that, because one man has the power of doing violence and is superior in brute strength, another shall be his slave and subject. Even among philosophers there is a difference of opinion. The origin of the dispute, and the reason why the arguments cross, is as follows: Virtue, when furnished with means, may be deemed to have the greatest power of doing violence: and as superior power is only found where there is superior excellence of some kind, power is thought to imply virtue. But does it likewise imply justice?—that is the question. And, in order to make a distinction between them, some assert that justice is benevolence: to which others reply that justice is nothing more than the rule of a superior. If the two views are regarded as antagonistic and exclusive [i.e. if the notion that justice is benevolence excludes the idea of a just rule of a superior], the alternative [viz. that no one should rule over others] has no force or plausibility, because it implies that not even the superior in virtue ought to rule, or be master. Some, clinging, as they think, to a principle of justice (for law and custom are a sort of justice), assume that slavery in war is justified by law, but they are not consistent. For what if the cause of the war be unjust? No one would ever say that he is a slave who is unworthy to be a slave. Were this the case, men of the highest rank would be slaves and the children of slaves if they or their parents chance to have been taken captive and sold. Wherefore Hellenes do not like to call themselves slaves, but confine the term to barbarians. Yet, in using this language, they really mean the natural slave of whom we spoke at first; for it must be admitted that some are slaves everywhere, others nowhere. The same principle applies to nobility. Hellenes regard themselves as noble everywhere, and not only in their own country, but they deem the barbarians noble only when at home, thereby implying that there are two sorts of nobility and freedom, the one absolute, the other relative. The Helen of Theodectes says:—

"Who would presume to call me servant who am on both sides sprung from the stem of the Gods?"

What does this mean but that they distinguish freedom and slavery, noble and humble birth, by the two principles of good and evil? They think that as men and animals beget men and animals, so from good men a good man springs. But this is what nature, though she may intend it, cannot always accomplish.

We see then that there is some foundation for this difference of opinion, and that all are not either slaves by nature or freemen by nature, and also that there is in some cases a marked distinction between the two classes, rendering it expedient and right for the one to be slaves and the others to be masters: the one practising obedience, the others exercising the authority which nature intended them to have. The abuse of this authority is injurious to both; for the interests of part and whole, of body and soul, are the same, and the slave is a part of the master, a living but separated part of his bodily frame. Where the relation between them is natural they are friends and have a common interest, but where it rests merely on law and force the reverse is true.

The previous remarks are quite enough to show that the rule of a master is not a constitutional rule, and therefore that all the different kinds of rule are not, as some affirm, the same with each other. For there is one rule exercised over subjects who are by nature free, another over subjects who are by nature slaves. The rule of a household is a monarchy, for every house is under one head: whereas constitutional rule is a government of free-men and equals. The master is not called a master because he has science, but because he is of a certain character, and the same remark applies to the slave and the freeman. Still there may be a science for the master and a science for the slave. The science of the slave would be such as the man of Syracuse taught, who made money by instructing slaves in their ordinary duties. And such a knowledge may be carried further, so as to include cookery and similar menial arts. For some duties are of the more necessary, others of the more honourable sort; as the proverb says, "slave before slave, master before master." But all such branches of knowledge are servile. There is likewise a science of the master, which teaches the use of slaves; for the master as such is concerned, not with the acquisition, but with the use of them. Yet this so-called science is not anything great or wonderful; for the master need only know how to order that which the slave must know how to execute. Hence those who are in a position which places them above toil, have stewards who attend to their households while they occupy themselves with philosophy or with politics. But the art of acquiring slaves, I mean of justly acquiring them, differs both from the art of the master and the art of the slave, being a species of hunting or war. Enough of the distinction between master and slave.

THOMAS HOBBES

Man in a State of Nature

Thomas Hobbes, 1588–1679, is one of the small company of western thinkers who have espoused the doctrine known as materialism. In Leviathan, *before discussing political questions, Hobbes lays the groundwork for a materialistic psychology by translating into his atomistic framework the terms with which we describe human per-*

Reprinted from Thomas Hobbes, *Leviathan,* ed. Sir William Molesworth, 1839.

sonalities and actions. Hobbes is not strictly a hedonist, as some of his statements might suggest, for it is fear, more than desire for pleasure, which according to him motivates man. In reading Hobbes' pessimistic descriptions of man's natural condition, one must bear in mind the civil turmoil of England in his lifetime. Hobbes' discussion of power is especially noteworthy for its awareness of the many forms —other than physical force or wealth—which power may take.

Of the Interior Beginnings of Voluntary Motions; Commonly Called the Passions; and the Speeches by Which They Are Expressed

There be in animals, two sorts of *motions* peculiar to them: one called *vital;* begun in generation, and continued without interruption through their whole life; such as are the *course* of the *blood,* the *pulse,* the *breathing,* the *concoction, nutrition, excretion,* &c. to which motions there needs no help of imagination: the other is *animal motion,* otherwise called *voluntary motion;* as to *go,* to *speak,* to *move* any of our limbs, in such manner as is first fancied in our minds. That sense is motion in the organs and interior parts of man's body, caused by the action of the things we see, hear, &c.; and that fancy is but the relics of the same motion, remaining after sense, has been already said in the first and second chapters. And because *going, speaking,* and the like voluntary motions, depend always upon a precedent thought of *whither, which way,* and *what;* it is evident, that the imagination is the first internal beginning of all voluntary motion. And although unstudied men do not conceive any motion at all to be there, where the thing moved is invisible; or the space it is moved in is, for the shortness of it, insensible; yet that doth not hinder, but that such motions are. For let a space be never so little, that which is moved over a greater space, whereof that little one is part, must first be moved over that. These small beginnings of motion, within the body of man, before they appear in walking, speaking, striking, and other visible actions, are commonly called ENDEAVOUR.

This endeavour, when it is toward something which causes it, is called APPETITE, or DESIRE; the latter, being the general name; and the other oftentimes restrained to signify the desire of food, namely *hunger* and *thirst.* And when the endeavour is fromward something, it is generally called AVERSION. These words, *appetite* and *aversion*, we have from the Latins; and they both of them signify the motions, one of approaching, the other of retiring. So also do the Greek words for the same, which are ὁρμή and ἀφορμή. For nature itself does often press upon men those truths, which afterwards, when they look for somewhat beyond nature, they stumble at. For the Schools find in mere appetite to go, or move, no actual motion at all: but because some motion they must acknowledge, they call it metaphorical motion; which is but an absurd speech: for though words may be called metaphorical; bodies and motions can not.

That which men desire, they are also said to LOVE: and to HATE those things for which they have aversion. So that desire and love are the same thing; save that by desire, we always signify the absence of the object; by love, most commonly the presence of the same. So also by aversion, we signify the absence; and by hate, the presence of the object.

Of appetites and aversions, some are born with men; as appetite of food, appetite of excretion, and exoneration, which may also and more properly be called aversions, from somewhat they feel in their bodies; and some other appetites, not many. The rest, which are appetites of particular things, proceed from experience, and trial of their effects upon themselves or other men. For of things we know not at all, or believe not to be, we can have no further desire, than to taste and try. But aversion we have for things, not only which we know have hurt us, but also that we do not know whether they will hurt us, or not.

Those things which we neither desire, nor hate, we are said to *contemn*; CONTEMPT being nothing else but an immobility, or contumacy of the heart, in resisting the action of certain things; and proceeding from that the heart is already moved otherwise, by other more potent objects; or from want of experience of them.

And because the constitution of a man's body is in continual mutation, it is impossible that all the same things should always cause in him the same appetites, and aversions: much less can all men consent, in the desire of almost any one and the same object.

But whatsoever is the object of any man's appetite or desire, that is it which he for his part calleth *good*: and the object of his hate and aversion, *evil*; and of his contempt, *vile* and *inconsiderable*. For these words of good, evil, and contemptible, are ever used with relation to the person that useth them: there being nothing simply and absolutely so; nor any common rule of good and evil, to be taken from the nature of the objects themselves; but from the person of the man, where there is no common-wealth; or, in a commonwealth, from the person that repre-senteth it; or from an arbitrator or judge, whom men disagree-ing shall by consent set up, and make his sentence the rule thereof.

* * *

Of Power, Worth, Dignity, Honour, and Worthiness

The power *of a man,* to take it universally, is his present means; to obtain some future apparent good; and is either *original* or *instrumental.*

Natural power, is the eminence of the faculties of body, or mind: as extraordinary strength, form, prudence, arts, eloquence, liberality, nobility. *Instrumental* are those powers, which ac-quired by these, or by fortune, are means and instruments to acquire more: as riches, reputation, friends, and the secret work-ing of God, which men call good luck. For the nature of power, is in this point, like to fame, increasing as it proceeds; or like the motion of heavy bodies, which the further they go, make still the more haste.

The greatest of human powers, is that which is compounded of the powers of most men, united by consent, in one person, natural, or civil, that has the use of all their powers depending on his will; such as is the power of a common-wealth: or de-pending on the wills of each particular; such as is the power of a faction or of divers factions leagued. Therefore to have ser-vants, is power; to have friends, is power: for they are strengths united.

Also riches joined with liberality, is power; because it pro-cureth friends, and servants: without liberality, not so; because in this case they defend not; but expose men to envy, as a prey.

Reputation of power, is power; because it draweth with it the adherence of those that need protection.

So is reputation of love of a man's country, called popularity, for the same reason.

Also, what quality soever maketh a man beloved, or feared of many; or the reputation of such quality, is power; because it is a means to have the assistance, and service of many.

Good success is power; because it maketh reputation of wisdom, or good fortune; which makes men either fear him, or rely on him.

Affability of men already in power, is increase of power; because it gaineth love.

Reputation of prudence in the conduct of peace or war, is power; because to prudent men, we commit the government of ourselves, more willingly than to others.

Nobility is power, not in all places, but only in those commonwealths, where it has privileges; for in such privileges, consisteth their power.

Eloquence is power, because it is seeming prudence.

Form is power; because being a promise of good, it recommendeth men to the favour of women and strangers.

The sciences, are small power; because not eminent; and therefore, not acknowledged in any man; nor are at all, but in a few, and in them, but of a few things. For science is of that nature, as none can understand it to be, but such as in a good measure have attained it.

Arts of public use, as fortification, making of engines, and other instruments of war; because they confer to defence, and victory, are power: and though the true mother of them, be science, namely the mathematics; yet, because they are brought into the light, by the hand of the artificer, they be esteemed, the midwife passing with the vulgar for the mother, as his issue.

*   *   *

Of the Natural Condition of Mankind as Concerning Their Felicity, and Misery

Nature hath made men so equal, in the faculties of the body, and mind; as that though there be found one man sometimes manifestly stronger in body, or of quicker mind than another; yet when all is reckoned together, the difference between man, and man, is not so considerable, as that one man can thereupon claim to himself any benefit, to which another may not pretend, as well as he. For as to the strength of body, the weakest has strength enough to kill the strongest, either by secret machination, or by confederacy with others, that are in the same danger with himself.

And as to the faculties of the mind, setting aside the arts grounded upon words, and especially that skill of proceeding upon general, and infallible rules, called science; which very few have, and but in few things; as being not a native faculty, born with us; nor attained, as prudence, while we look after somewhat else, I find yet a greater equality amongst men, than that of strength. For prudence, is but experience; which equal time, equally bestows on all men, in those things they equally apply themselves unto. That which may perhaps make such equality incredible, is but a vain conceit of one's own wisdom, which almost all men think they have in a greater degree, than the vulgar; that is, than all men but themselves, and a few others, whom by fame, or for concurring with themselves, they approve. For such is the nature of men, that howsoever they may acknowledge many others to be more witty, or more eloquent, or more learned; yet they will hardly believe there be many so wise as themselves; for they see their own wit at hand, and other men's at a distance. But this proveth rather that men are in that point equal, than unequal. For there is not ordinarily a greater sign of the equal distribution of any thing, than that every man is contented with his share.

From this equality of ability, ariseth equality of hope in the attaining of our ends. And therefore if any two men desire the same thing, which nevertheless they cannot both enjoy, they become enemies; and in the way to their end, which is principally their own conservation, and sometimes their delectation only, endeavour to destroy, or subdue one another. And from hence it comes to pass, that where an invader hath no more to fear, than another man's single power; if one plant, sow, build, or possess a convenient seat, others may probably be expected to come prepared with forces united, to dispossess, and deprive him, not only of the fruit of his labour, but also of his life, or liberty. And the invader again is in the like danger of another.

And from this diffidence of one another, there is no way for any man to secure himself, so reasonable, as anticipation; that is, by force, or wiles, to master the persons of all men he can, so long, till he see no other power great enough to endanger him: and this is no more than his own conservation requireth, and is generally allowed. Also because there be some, that taking pleasure in contemplating their own power in the acts of conquest, which they pursue farther than their security requires;

if others, that otherwise would be glad to be at ease within modest bounds, should not by invasion increase their power, they would not be able, long time, by standing only on their defence, to subsist. And by consequence, such augmentation of dominion over men being necessary to a man's conservation, it ought to be allowed him.

Again, men have no pleasure, but on the contrary a great deal of grief, in keeping company, where there is no power able to over-awe them all. For every man looketh that his companion should value him, at the same rate he sets upon himself: and upon all signs of contempt, or undervaluing, naturally endeavours, as far as he dares, (which amongst them that have no common power to keep them in quiet, is far enough to make them destroy each other), to extort a greater value from his contemners, by damage; and from others, by the example.

So that in the nature of man, we find three principal causes of quarrel. First, competition; secondly, diffidence; thirdly, glory.

The first, maketh men invade for gain; the second, for safety; and the third, for reputation. The first use violence, to make themselves masters of other men's persons, wives, children, and cattle; the second, to defend them; the third, for trifles, as a word, a smile, a different opinion, and any other sign of undervalue, either direct in their persons, or by reflection in their kindred, their friends. their nation, their profession, or their name.

Hereby it is manifest, that during the time men live without a common power to keep them all in awe, they are in that condition which is called war; and such a war, as is of every man, against every man. For WAR, consisteth not in battle only, or the act of fighting; but in a tract of time, wherein the will to contend by battle is sufficiently known: and therefore the notion of *time*, is to be considered in the nature of war; as it is in the nature of weather. For as the nature of foul weather, lieth not in a shower or two of rain; but in an inclination thereto of many days together: so the nature of war, consisteth not in actual fighting; but in the known disposition thereto, during all the time there is no assurance to the contrary. All other time is PEACE.

Whatsoever therefore is consequent to a time of war, where every man is enemy to every man; the same is consequent to the time, wherein men live without other security, than what their own strength, and their own invention shall furnish them withal. In such condition, there is no place for industry; because the fruit thereof is uncertain: and consequently no culture of the earth; no navigation, nor use of the commodities that may be imported by sea; no commodious building; no instruments of moving, and removing, such things as require much force; no knowledge of the face of the earth; no account of time; no arts; no letters; no society; and which is worst of all, continual fear, and danger of violent death; and the life of man, solitary, poor, nasty, brutish, and short.

It may seem strange to some man, that has not well weighed these things; that nature should thus dissociate, and render men apt to invade, and destroy one another: and he may therefore, not trusting to this inference, made from the passions, desire perhaps to have the same confirmed by experience. Let him therefore consider with himself, when taking a journey, he arms himself, and seeks to go well accompanied; when going to sleep, he locks his doors; when even in his house he locks his chests; and this when he knows there be laws, and public officers, armed, to revenge all injuries shall be done him; what opinion he has of his fellow-subjects, when he rides armed; of his fellow citizens, when he locks his doors; and of his children, and servants, when he locks his chests. Does he not there as much accuse mankind by his actions, as I do by my words? But neither of us accuse man's nature in it. The desires, and other passions of man, are in themselves no sin. No more are the actions, that proceed from those passions, till they know a law that forbids them: which till laws be made they cannot know: nor can any law be made, till they have agreed upon the person that shall make it.

It may peradventure be thought, there was never such a time, nor condition of war as this; and I believe it was never generally so, over all the world: but there are many places, where they live so now. For the savage people in many places of America, except the government of small families, the concord whereof dependeth on natural lust, have no government at all; and live at this day in that brutish manner, as I said before. Howsoever, it may be perceived what manner of life there would be, where there were no common power to fear, by the manner of life, which men that have formerly lived under a peaceful government, use to degenerate into, in a civil war.

But though there had never been any time, wherein particular men were in a condition of war one against another; yet in all times, kings, and persons of sovereign authority, because of their independency, are in continual jealousies, and in the state and posture of gladiators; having their weapons pointing, and their eyes fixed on one another; that is, their forts, garrisons, and guns upon the frontiers of their kingdoms; and continual spies upon their neighbours; which is a posture of war. But because they uphold thereby, the industry of their subjects; there does not follow from it, that misery, which accompanies the liberty of particular men.

To this war of every man, against every man, this also is consequent; that nothing can be unjust. The notions of right and wrong, justice and injustice have there no place. Where there is no common power, there is no law: where no law, no injustice. Force, and fraud, are in war the two cardinal virtues. Justice, and injustice are none of the faculties neither of the body, nor mind. If they were, they might be in a man that were alone in the world, as well as his senses, and passions. They are qualities, that relate to men in society, not in solitude. It is consequent also to the same condition, that there be no propriety, no dominion, no *mine* and *thine* distinct; but only that to be every man's, that he can get; and for so long, as he can keep it. And thus much for the ill condition, which man by mere nature is actually placed in; though with a possibility to come out of it, consisting partly in the passions, partly in his reason.

The passions that incline men to peace, are fear of death; desire of such things as are necessary to commodious living; and a hope by their industry to obtain them. And reason suggesteth convenient articles of peace, upon which men may be drawn to agreement. These articles, are they, which otherwise are called the Laws of Nature: whereof I shall speak more particularly, in the two following chapters.

The Principle of Utilitarianism

———————————————————————————◆

Jeremy Bentham, 1748–1832, is the author of the ethical theory called "utilitarianism." In the first chapter of his Introduction to the Principles of Morals and Legislation, *he presents an image of man as a rational value calculator, maximizing the sum total of pleasure over pain as though they were profit and loss. Critics of Bentham frequently point out that men do not go through life adding and subtracting quantities of pleasure. But whenever we defend a government measure to reduce unemployment, or give medical care to the sick, or clean up our cities, we are appealing implicitly to Bentham's "greatest happiness" principle. Notice that Bentham distinguishes between the psychological tendency of all human beings to seek their own happiness, and the moral principle that they ought to seek the happiness of everyone.*

Of the Principle of Utility

I. Nature has placed mankind under the governance of two sovereign masters, *pain* and *pleasure*. It is for them alone to point out what we ought to do, as well as to determine what we shall do. On the one hand the standard of right and wrong, on the other the chain of causes and effects, are fastened to their throne. They govern us in all we do, in all we say, in all we think: every effort we can make to throw off our subjection, will serve but to demonstrate and confirm it. In words a man may pretend to abjure their empire: but in reality he will remain subject to it all the while. The *principle of utility* * recognises this subjection,

Reprinted from Jeremy Bentham, *An Introduction to the Principles of Morals and Legislation*, 1789. First printed in 1780.

* Note by the Author, July 1822.

To this denomination has of late been added, or substituted, the *greatest happiness* or *greatest felicity* principle: this for shortness, instead of saying at length *that principle* which states the greatest happiness of all those whose interest is in question, as being the right and proper, and only right and proper and universally desirable, end of human action: of human action in every situation, and in particular in that of a functionary or set of functionaries exercising the powers of Government. The word *utility* does and assumes it for the foundation of that system, the object of which is to rear the fabric of felicity by the hands of reason and of law. Systems which attempt to question it, deal in sounds instead of sense, in caprice instead of reason, in darkness instead of light.

But enough of metaphor and declamation: it is not by such means that moral science is to be improved.

II. The principle of utility is the foundation of the present work: it will be proper therefore at the outset to give an explicit and determinate account of what is meant by it. By the principle* of utility is meant that principle which approves or disapproves of every action whatsoever, according to the tendency which it appears to have to augment or diminish the happiness of the party whose interest is in question: or, what is the same thing in other words, to promote or to oppose that happiness. I say of every action whatsoever; and therefore not only of every action of a private individual, but of every measure of government.

III. By utility is meant that property in any object, whereby it tends to produce benefit, advantage, pleasure, good, or happiness, (all this in the present case comes to the same thing) or (what comes again to the same thing) to prevent the happening of mischief, pain, evil, or unhappiness to the party whose interest is considered: if that party be the community in general,

---

not so clearly point to the ideas of *pleasure* and *pain* as the words *happiness* and *felicity* do: nor does it lead us to the consideration of the *number*, of the interests affected; to the *number*, as being the circumstance, which contributes, in the largest proportion, to the formation of the standard here in question; the *standard of right and wrong*, by which alone the propriety of human conduct, in every situation, can with propriety be tried. This want of a sufficiently manifest connexion between the ideas of *happiness* and *pleasure* on the one hand, and the idea of *utility* on the other, I have every now and then found operating, and with but too much efficiency, as a bar to the acceptance, that might otherwise have been given, to this principle.

* The word principle is derived from the Latin principium: which seems to be compounded of the two words *primus*, first, or chief, and *cipium*, a termination which seems to be derived from *capio*, to take, as in *mancipium, municipium;* to which are analogous, *auceps, forceps,* and others. It is a term of very vague and very extensive signification: it is applied to any thing which is conceived to serve as a foundation or beginning to any series of operations: in some cases, of physical operations; but of mental operations in the present case.

The principle here in question may be taken for an act of the mind; a sentiment; a sentiment of approbation; a sentiment which, when applied to an action, approves of its utility, as that quality of it by which the measure of approbation or disapprobation bestowed upon it ought to be governed.

then the happiness of the community: if a particular individual, then the happiness of that individual.

IV. The interest of the community is one of the most general expressions that can occur in the phraseology of morals: no wonder that the meaning of it is often lost. When it has a meaning, it is this. The community is a fictitious *body*, composed of the individual persons who are considered as constituting as it were its *members*. The interest of the community then is, what? —the sum of the interests of the several members who compose it.

V. It is in vain to talk of the interest of the community, without understanding what is the interest of the individual.* A thing is said to promote the interest, or to be *for* the interest, of an individual, when it tends to add to the sum total of his pleasures: or, what comes to the same thing, to diminish the sum total of his pains.

VI. An action then may be said to be conformable to the principle of utility, or, for shortness sake, to utility, (meaning with respect to the community at large) when the tendency it has to augment the happiness of the community is greater than any it has to diminish it.

VII. A measure of government (which is but a particular kind of action, performed by a particular person or persons) may be said to be conformable to or dictated by the principle of utility, when in like manner the tendency which it has to augment the happiness of the community is greater than any which it has to diminish it.

VIII. When an action, or in particular a measure of government, is supposed by a man to be conformable to the principle of utility, it may be convenient, for the purposes of discourse, to imagine a kind of law or dictate, called a law or dictate of utility: and to speak of the action in question, as being conformable to such law or dictate.

IX. A man may be said to be a partizan of the principle of utility, when the approbation or disapprobation he annexes to any action, or to any measure, is determined by and proportioned to the tendency which he conceives it to have to augment or to diminish the happiness of the community: or in other words, to its conformity or unconformity to the laws or dictates of utility.

* Interest is one of those words, which not having any superior *genus*, cannnot in the ordinary way be defined.

X. Of an action that is conformable to the principle of utility one may always say either that it is one that ought to be done, or at least that it is not one that ought not to be done. One may say also, that it is right it should be done; at least that it is not wrong it should be done: that it is a right action; at least that it is not a wrong action. When thus interpreted, the words *ought*, and *right* and *wrong*, and others of that stamp, have a meaning: when otherwise, they have none.

XI. Has the rectitude of this principle been ever formally contested? It should seem that it had, by those who have not known what they have been meaning. Is it susceptible of any direct proof? it should seem not: for that which is used to prove every thing else, cannot itself be proved: a chain of proofs must have their commencement somewhere. To give such proof is as impossible as it is needless.

XII. Not that there is or ever has been that human creature breathing, however stupid or perverse, who has not on many, perhaps on most occasions of his life, deferred to it. By the natural constitution of the human frame, on most occasions of their lives men in general embrace this principle, without thinking of it: if not for the ordering of their own actions, yet for the trying of their own actions, as well as of those of other men. There have been, at the same time, not many, perhaps, even of the most intelligent, who have been disposed to embrace it purely and without reserve. There are even few who have not taken some occasion or other to quarrel with it, either on account of their not understanding always how to apply it, or on account of some prejudice or other which they were afraid to examine into, or could not bear to part with. For such is the stuff that man is made of: in principle and in practice, in a right track and in a wrong one, the rarest of all human qualities is consistency.

XIII. When a man attempts to combat the principle of utility, it is with reasons drawn, without his being aware of it, from that very principle itself.* His arguments, if they prove any

---

* "The principle of utility, (I have heard it said) is a dangerous principle: it is dangerous on certain occasions to consult it." This is as much as to say, what? that it is not consonant to utility, to consult utility: in short, that it is *not* consulting it, to consult it.

Addition by the Author, July 1822.

Not long after the publication of the Fragment on Government, anno 1776, in which, in the character of an all-comprehensive and all-command-

thing, prove not that the principle is *wrong*, but that, according
to the applications he supposes to be made of it, it is *misapplied*.
Is it possible for a man to move the earth? Yes; but he must first
find out another earth to stand upon.

XIV. To disprove the propriety of it by arguments is impossible; but, from the causes that have been mentioned, or from
some confused or partial view of it, a man may happen to be
disposed not to relish it. Where this is the case, if he thinks the
settling of his opinions on such a subject worth the trouble, let
him take the following steps, and at length, perhaps, he may
come to reconcile himself to it.

1. Let him settle with himself, whether he would wish to dis-

---

ing principle, the principle of *utility* was brought to view, one person by
whom observation to the above effect was made was *Alexander Wedderburn*, at that time Attorney or Solicitor General, afterwards successively
Chief Justice of the Common Pleas, and Chancellor of England, under the
successive titles of Lord Loughborough and Earl of Rosslyn. It was made—
not indeed in my hearing, but in the hearing of a person by whom it was
almost immediately communicated to me. So far from being self-contradictory, it was a shrewd and perfectly true one. By that distinguished
functionary, the state of the Government was thoroughly understood: by
the obscure individual, at that time not so much as supposed to be so: his
disquisitions had not been as yet applied, with any thing like a comprehensive view, to the field of Constitutional Law, nor therefore to those features
of the English Government, by which the greatest happiness of the ruling
one with or without that of a favoured few, are now so plainly seen to be
the only ends to which the course of it has at any time been directed. The
principle of utility was an appellative, at that time employed—employed by
me, as it had been by others, to designate that which, in a more perspicuous
and instructive manner, may, as above, be designated by the name of the
greatest happiness principle. "This principle (said Wedderburn) is a dangerous one." Saying so, he said that which, to a certain extent, is strictly
true: a principle, which lays down, as the only *right* and justifiable end of
Government, the greatest happiness of the greatest number—how can it be
denied to be a dangerous one? dangerous it unquestionably is, to every
government which has for its *actual* end or object, the greatest happiness
of a certain *one*, with or without the addition of some comparatively small
number of others, whom it is matter of pleasure or accommodation to him
to admit, each of them, to a share in the concern, on the footing of so
many junior partners. *Dangerous* it therefore really was, to the interest—
the sinister interest—of all those functionaries, himself included, whose
interest it was, to maximize delay, vexation, and expense, in judicial and
other modes of procedure, for the sake of the profit, extractible out of the
expense. In a Government which had for its end in view the greatest
happiness of the greatest number, Alexander Wedderburn might have been
Attorney General and then Chancellor: but he would not have been Attorney General with £15,000 a year, nor Chancellor, with a peerage with
a veto upon all justice, with £25,000 a year, and with 500 sinecures at his
disposal, under the name of Ecclesiastical Benefices, besides *et cœteras*.

card this principle altogether; if so, let him consider what it is that all his reasonings (in matters of politics especially) can amount to?

2. If he would, let him settle with himself, whether he would judge and act without any principle, or whether there is any other he would judge and act by?

3. If there be, let him examine and satisfy himself whether the principle he thinks he has found is really any separate intelligible principle; or whether it be not a mere principle in words, a kind of phrase, which at bottom expresses neither more nor less than the mere averment of his own unfounded sentiments; that is, what in another person he might be apt to call caprice?

4. If he is inclined to think that his own approbation or disapprobation, annexed to the idea of an act, without any regard to its consequences, is a sufficient foundation for him to judge and act upon, let him ask himself whether his sentiment is to be a standard of right and wrong, with respect to every other man, or whether every man's sentiment has the same privilege of being a standard to itself?

5. In the first case, let him ask himself whether his principle is not despotical, and hostile to all the rest of human race?

6. In the second case, whether it is not anarchial, and whether at this rate there are not as many different standards of right and wrong as there are men? and whether even to the same man, the same thing, which is right to-day, may not (without the least change in its nature) be wrong to-morrow? and whether the same thing is not right and wrong in the same place at the same time? and in either case, whether all argument is not at an end? and whether, when two men have said, "I like this," and "I don't like it," they can (upon such a principle) have anything more to say?

7. If he should have said to himself, No: for that the sentiment which he proposes as a standard must be grounded on reflection, let him say on what particulars the reflection is to turn? if on particulars having relation to the utility of the act, then let him say whether this is not deserting his own principle, and borrowing assistance from that very one in opposition to which he sets it up: or if not on those particulars, on what other particulars?

8. If he should be for compounding the matter, and adopting

his own principle in part, and the principle of utility in part, let him say how far he will adopt it?

9. When he has settled with himself where he will stop, then let him ask himself how he justifies to himself the adopting it so far? and why he will not adopt it any farther?

10. Admitting any other principle than the principle of utility to be a right principle, a principle that it is right for a man to pursue; admitting (what is not true) that the word *right* can have a meaning without reference to utility, let him say whether there is any such thing as a *motive* that a man can have to pursue the dictates of it: if there is, let him say what that motive is, and how it is to be distinguished from those which enforce the dictates of utility: if not, then lastly let him say what it is this other principle can be good for?

KARL MARX

Alienated Labor

Karl Marx, 1818–1883, has until recently been known best for the writings of his middle and later years. In the past several decades, a number of manuscripts have come to light which date from Marx's early formative years. They contain a systematic exposition of his theory of human nature, on which much of the later more technically economic work was grounded. The theory of alienation presented here is the basis for Marx's bitter attack upon capitalism. Worse even than the economic or political injustice of capitalism, Marx argues, is the warping and corrupting effect on all those— capitalists as well as workers—who become caught up in it. The dream of a good society, in which men can fulfill themselves through creative labor, serves as a pleasant relief from Marx's harsh picture of the realities of industrial capitalism. The technical terms used by Marx here reflect the philosophy of Hegel, a German philosopher who was at that time the major intellectual influence in Europe.

* * *

Reprinted by permission of the publishers from Karl Marx, *Economic and Philosophic Manuscripts of 1844*, ed. with an introduction by Dirk J. Struik (New York: International Publishers Co., Inc., 1964).

The worker becomes all the poorer the more wealth he produces, the more his production increases in power and size. The worker becomes an ever cheaper commodity the more commodities he creates. With the *increasing value* of the world of things proceeds in direct proportion the *devaluation* of the world of men. Labor produces not only commodities: it produces itself and the worker as a *commodity*—and this in the same general proportion in which it produces commodities.

This fact expresses merely that the object which labor produces—labor's product—confronts it as *something alien*, as a *power independent* of the producer. The product of labor is labor which has been embodied in an object, which has become material: it is the *objectification* of labor. Labor's realization is its objectification. In the sphere of political economy this realization of labor appears as *loss of realization* for the workers; objectification as *loss of the object* and *bondage to it*; appropriation as *estrangement*, as *alienation*.

So much does labor's realization appear as loss of realization that the worker loses realization to the point of starving to death. So much does objectification appear as loss of the object that the worker is robbed of the objects most necessary not only for his life but for his work. Indeed, labor itself becomes an object which he can obtain only with the greatest effort and with the most irregular interruptions. So much does the appropriation of the object appear as estrangement that the more objects the worker produces the less he can possess and the more he falls under the sway of his product, capital.

All these consequences result from the fact that the worker is related to the *product of his labor* as to an *alien* object. For on this premise it is clear that the more the worker spends himself, the more powerful becomes the alien world of objects which he creates over and against himself, the poorer he himself—his inner world—becomes, the less belongs to him as his own. It is the same in religion. The more man puts into God, the less he retains in himself. The worker puts his life into the object; but now his life no longer belongs to him but to the object. Hence, the greater this activity, the greater is the worker's lack of objects. Whatever the product of his labor is, he is not. Therefore the greater this product, the less is he himself. The *alienation* of the worker in his product means not only that his labor becomes an object, an *external* existence, but that it exists *outside him*, independently, as something alien to him, and that it becomes a power on its own confronting him. It means that the life which he has conferred on the object confronts him as something hostile and alien.

Let us now look more closely at the *objectification,* at the production of the worker; and in it at the *estrangement,* the *loss* of the object, of his product.

The worker can create nothing without *nature,* without the *sensuous external world.* It is the material on which his labor is realized, in which it is active, from which and by means of which it produces.

But just as nature provides labor with the *means of life* in the sense that labor cannot *live* without objects on which to operate, on the other hand, it also provides the *means of life* in the more restricted sense, i.e., the means for the physical subsistence of the *worker* himself.

Thus the more the worker by his labor *appropriates* the external world, hence sensuous nature, the more he deprives himself of *means of life* in a double manner: first, in that the sensuous external world more and more ceases to be an object belonging to his labor—to be his labor's *means of life;* and secondly, in that it more and more ceases to be *means of life* in the immediate sense, means for the physical subsistence of the worker.

In both respects, therefore, the worker becomes a slave of his object, first, in that he receives an *object of labor,* i.e., in that he receives *work;* and secondly, in that he receives *means of subsistence.* Therefore, it enables him to exist, first, as a *worker;* and, second as a *physical subject.* The height of this bondage is that it is only as a *worker* that he continues to maintain himself as a *physical subject,* and that it is only as a *physical subject* that he is a *worker.*

(The laws of political economy express the estrangement of the worker in his object thus: the more the worker produces, the less he has to consume; the more values he creates, the more valueless, the more unworthy he becomes; the better formed his product, the more deformed becomes the worker; the more civilized his object, the more barbarous becomes the worker; the more powerful labor becomes, the more powerless becomes the worker; the more ingenious labor becomes, the less ingenious becomes the worker and the more he becomes nature's bondsman.)

Political economy conceals the estrangement inherent in the nature of labor by not considering the direct relationship between the worker (labor) *and production.* It is true that labor produces for the rich wonderful things—but for the worker it produces privation. It produces palaces—but for the worker, hovels. It produces beauty—but for the worker, deformity. It replaces labor by machines, but it throws a section of the workers back to a barbarous type of labor, and it turns the other workers into machines. It produces intelligence—but for the worker stupidity, cretinism.

The direct relationship of labor to its products is the relationship of the worker to the objects of his production. The relationship of the man of means to the objects of production and to production itself is only a *consequence* of this first relationship—and confirms it. We shall consider this other aspect later.

When we ask, then, what is the essential relationship of labor we are asking about the relationship of the *worker* to production.

Till now we have been considering the estrangement, the alienation of the worker only in one of its aspects, i.e., the worker's *relationship to the products of his labor.* But the estrangement is manifested not only in the result but in the *act of production,* within the *producing activity,* itself. How could the worker come to face the product of his activity as a stranger, were it not that in the very act of production he was estranging himself from himself? The product is after all but the summary of the activity, of production. If then the product of labor is alienation, production itself must be active alienation, the alienation of activity, the activity of alienation. In the estrangement of the object of labor is merely summarized the estrangement, the alienation, in the activity of labor itself.

What, then, constitutes the alienation of labor?

First, the fact that labor is *external* to the worker, i.e., it does not belong to his essential being; that in his work, therefore, he does not affirm himself but denies himself, does not feel content but unhappy, does not develop freely his physical and mental energy but mortifies his body and ruins his mind. The worker therefore only feels himself outside his work, and in his work feels outside himself. He is at home when he is not working, and when he is working he is not at home. His labor is therefore not voluntary, but coerced; it is *forced labor.* It is therefore not the satisfaction of a need; it is merely a *means* to satisfy needs external to it. Its alien character emerges clearly in the fact that as soon as no physical or other compulsion exists, labor is shunned like the plague. External labor, labor in which man alienates himself, is a labor of self-sacrifice, of mortification. Lastly, the external character of labor for the worker appears in the fact that it is not his own, but someone else's, that it does not belong to him, that in it he belongs, not to himself, but to another. Just as in religion the spontaneous activity of the human imagination, of the human brain and the human heart, operates independently of the individual—that is, operates on him as an alien, divine or diabolical activity—so is the worker's activity not his spontaneous activity. It belongs to another; it is the loss of his self.

As a result, therefore, man (the worker) only feels himself freely active in his animal functions—eating, drinking, procreating, or at most in his dwelling and in dressing-up, etc.; and in his human functions he no longer feels himself to be anything but an animal. What is animal becomes human and what is human becomes animal.

Certainly eating, drinking, procreating, etc., are also genuinely human functions. But abstractly taken, separated from the sphere of all other human activity and turned into sole and ultimate ends, they are animal functions.

We have considered the act of estranging practical human activity, labor, in two of its aspects. (1) The relation of the worker to the *product of labor* as an alien object exercising power over him. This relation is at the same time the relation to the sensuous external world, to the objects of nature, as an alien world inimically opposed to him. (2) The relation of labor to the *act of production* within the *labor* process. This relation is the relation of the worker to his own activity as an alien activity not belonging to him; it is activity as suffering, strength as weakness, begetting as emasculating, the worker's *own* physical and mental energy, his personal life indeed, what is life but activity?—as an activity which is turned against him, independent of him and not belonging to him. Here we have *self-estrangement*, as previously we had the estrangement of the *thing*.

We have still a third aspect of *estranged labor* to deduce from the two already considered.

Man is a species being, not only because in practice and in theory he adopts the species as his object (his own as well as those of other things), but—and this is only another way of expressing it—also because he treats himself as the actual, living species; because he treats himself as a *universal* and therefore a free being.

The life of the species, both in man and in animals, consists physically in the fact that man (like the animal) lives on inorganic nature; and the more universal man is compared with an animal, the more universal is the sphere of inorganic nature on which he lives. Just as plants, animals, stones, air, light, etc., constitute theoretically a part of human consciousness, partly as objects of natural science, partly as objects of art—his spiritual inorganic nature, spiritual nourishment which he must first prepare to make palatable and digestible—so also in the realm of practice they constitute a part of human life and human activity. Physically man lives only on these products of nature, whether they appear in the form of food, heating, clothes, a dwelling, etc. The universality of man appears in practice precisely in the universality which makes all nature his *inorganic* body—both inasmuch as nature is (1) his direct means of life, and (2) the material, the object, and the instrument of his life activity. Nature is man's *inorganic body*—nature, that is, in so far as it is not itself the human body. Man *lives* on nature—means that nature is his *body*, with which he must remain in continuous interchange if he is not to die. That man's physical and spiritual life is linked to nature means simply that nature is linked to itself, for man is a part of nature.

In estranging from man (1) nature, and (2) himself, his own active functions, his life activity, estranged labor estranges the *species* from man. It changes for him the *life of the species* into a means of individual life. First it estranges the life of the species and individual life, and secondly it makes individual life in its abstract form the purpose of the life of the species, likewise in its abstract and estranged form.

Indeed, labor, *life-activity, productive life* itself, appears in the first place merely as a *means* of satisfying a need—the need to maintain physical existence. Yet the productive life is the life of the species. It is life-engendering life. The whole character of a species—its species character—is contained in the character of its life activity; and free, conscious activity is man's species character. Life itself appears only as a *means to life*.

The animal is immediately one with its life activity. It does not distinguish itself from it. It is *its life activity*. Man makes his life activity itself the object of his will and of his consciousness. He has conscious life activity. It is not a determination with which he directly merges. Conscious life activity distinguishes man immediately from animal life activity. It is just because of this that he is a species being. Or rather, it is only because he is a species being that he is a conscious being, i.e., that his own life is an object for him. Only because of that is his activity free activity. Estranged labor reverses this relationship, so that it is just because man is a conscious being that he makes his life activity, his *essential* being, a mere means to his *existence*.

In creating a *world of objects* by his practical activity, in *his work upon* inorganic nature, man proves himself a conscious species being, i.e., as a being that treats the species as its own essential being, or that treats itself as a species being. Admittedly animals also produce. They build themselves nests, dwellings, like the bees, beavers, ants, etc. But an animal only produces what it immediately needs for itself or its young. It produces one-sidedly, whilst man produces universally. It produces only under the dominion of immediate physical need, whilst man produces even when he is free from physical need and only truly produces in freedom therefrom. An animal produces only itself, whilst man reproduces the whole of nature. An animal's product belongs immediately to its physical body, whilst man freely confronts his product. An animal forms things in accordance with the standard and the need of the species to which it belongs, whilst man knows how to produce in accordance with the standard of every species, and knows how to apply everywhere the inherent standard to the object. Man therefore also forms things in accordance with the laws of beauty.

It is just in his work upon the objective world, therefore, that man first really proves himself to be a *species being*. This production is his active species life. Through and because of this production, nature appears as *his* work and his reality. The object of labor is, therefore, the *objectification of man's species life:* for he duplicates himself not only, as in consciousness, intellectually, but also actively, in reality, and therefore he contemplates himself in a world that he has created. In tearing away from man the object of his production, therefore, estranged labor tears from him his *species life*, his real objectivity as a member of the species and transforms his advantage over animals into the disadvantage that his inorganic body, nature, is taken away from him.

Similarly, in degrading spontaneous, free, activity, to a means, estranged labor makes man's species life a means to his physical existence.

The consciousness which man has of his species is thus transformed by estrangement in such a way that species life becomes for him a means.

Estranged labor turns thus:

(3) *Man's species being,* both nature and his spiritual species property, into a being *alien* to him, into a *means* to his *individual existence.* It estranges from man his own body, as well as external nature and his spiritual essence, his *human* being.

(4) An immediate consequence of the fact that man is estranged from the product of his labor, from his life activity, from his species being is the *estrangement of man* from *man.* When man confronts himself, he confronts the *other* man. What applies to a man's relation to his work, to the product of his labor and to himself, also holds of a man's relation to the other man, and to the other man's labor and object of labor.

In fact, the proposition that man's species nature is estranged from him means that one man is estranged from the other, as each of them is from man's essential nature.

The estrangement of man, and in fact every relationship in which man stands to himself, is first realized and expressed in the relationship in which a man stands to other men.

Hence within the relationship of estranged labor each man views the other in accordance with the standard and the relationship in which he finds himself as a worker.

We took our departure from a fact of political economy—the estrangement of the worker and his production. We have formulated this fact in conceptual terms as *estranged, alienated* labor. We have analyzed this concept—hence analyzing merely a fact of political economy.

Let us now see, further, how the concept of estranged, alienated labor must express and present itself in real life.

If the product of labor is alien to me, if it confronts me as an alien power, to whom, then, does it belong?

If my own activity does not belong to me, if it is an alien, a coerced activity, to whom, then, does it belong?

To a being *other* than myself.

Who is this being?

The *gods?* To be sure, in the earliest times the principal production (for example, the building of temples, etc., in Egypt, India and Mexico) appears to be in the service of the gods, and the product belongs to the gods. However, the gods on their own were never the lords of labor. No more was *nature.* And what a contradiction it would be if, the more man subjugated nature by his labor and the more the miracles of the gods were rendered superfluous by the miracles of industry, the more man were to renounce the joy of production and the enjoyment of the product in favor of these powers.

The *alien* being, to whom labor and the product of labor belongs, in whose service labor is done and for whose benefit the product of labor is provided, can only be *man* himself.

If the product of labor does not belong to the worker, if it confronts him as an alien power, then this can only be because it belongs to some *other man than the worker.* If the worker's activity is a torment to him, to another it must be *delight* and his life's joy. Not the gods, not nature, but only man himself can be this alien power over man.

We must bear in mind the previous proposition that man's relation to himself only becomes for him *objective* and *actual* through his relation to the other man. Thus, if the product of his labor, his labor *objectified*, is for him an *alien*, hostile, powerful object independent of him, then his position towards it is such that someone else is master of this object, someone who is alien, hostile, powerful, and independent of him. If his own activity is to him related as an unfree activity, then he is related to it as an activity performed in the service, under the dominion, the coercion, and the yoke of another man.

Every self-estrangement of man, from himself and from nature, appears in the relation in which he places himself and nature to men other than and differentiated from himself. For this reason religious self-estrangement necessarily appears in the relationship of the layman to the priest, or again to a mediator, etc., since we are here dealing with the intellectual world. In the real practical world self-estrangement can only become manifest through the real practical relationship to other men. The medium through which estrangement takes place is itself *practical.* Thus through estranged labor man not only creates his relationship to the object and to the act of production as to

men that are alien and hostile to him; he also creates the relationship in which other men stand to his production and to his
product, and the relationship in which he stands to these other
men. Just as he creates his own production as the loss of his
reality, as his punishment; his own product as a loss, as a product not belonging to him; so he creates the domination of the
person who does not produce over production and over the
product. Just as he estranges his own activity from himself, so
he confers to the stranger an activity which is not his own.

*   *   *

MARX AND ENGELS

Man as a Productive Animal

◆

*Marx and Engels broke with their German compatriots, a group of
intellectuals known as the Young Hegelians, in a long, rambling, high-
spirited work called* The German Ideology. *Most of the book, which
the two young authors never published, is an attack on their former
friends, but the opening section is an extended exposition of the
theory of historical materialism. In this selection, Marx and Engels
enter the long lists of those who have defined man in terms of one
of his functions or activities. Man, the philosophers have said, is a
rational animal, a spiritual animal, a conscious animal, the only animal
who laughs or plays. Man, Marx and Engels reply, is truly to be defined as an animal who produces. It is in this sense that Marxism is
an economic theory of man.*

*   *   *

The premises from which we begin are not arbitrary ones, not
dogmas, but real premises from which abstraction can only be
made in the imagination. They are the real individuals, their
activity and the material conditions under which they live, both
those which they find already existing and those produced by

Reprinted by permission of the publishers from Karl Marx and Friedrich
Engels, *The German Ideology*, ed. with an introduction by R. Pascal (New
York: International Publishers Co., Inc., 1947).

their activity. These premises can thus be verified in a purely empirical way.

The first premise of all human history is, of course, the existence of living human individuals. Thus the first fact to be established is the physical organization of these individuals and their consequent relation to the rest of nature. Of course, we cannot here go either into the actual physical nature of man, or into the natural conditions in which man finds himself— geological, orohydrographical, climatic and so on. The writing of history must always set out from these natural bases and their modification in the course of history through the action of man.

Men can be distinguished from animals by consciousness, by religion or anything else you like. They themselves begin to distinguish themselves from animals as soon as they begin to *produce* their means of subsistence, a step which is conditioned by their physical organization. By producing their means of subsistence men are indirectly producing their actual material life.

The way in which men produce their means of subsistence depends first of all on the nature of the actual means they find in existence and have to reproduce. This mode of production must not be considered simply as being the reproduction of the physical existence of the individuals. Rather it is a definite form of activity of these individuals, a definite form of expressing their life, a definite *mode of life* on their part. As individuals express their life, so they are. What they are, therefore, coincides with their production, both with *what* they produce and with *how* they produce. The nature of individuals thus depends on the material conditions determining their production.

*   *   *

The fact is therefore that definite individuals who are productively active in a definite way enter into these definite social and political relations. Empirical observation must in each separate instance bring out empirically, and without any mystification and speculation, the connection of the social and political structure with production. The social structure and the State are continually evolving out of the life-process of definite individuals, but of individuals, not as they may appear in their own or other people's imagination, but as they really are; i.e. as they are effective, produce materially, and are active under definite material limits, presuppositions and conditions independent of their will.

The production of ideas, of conceptions, of consciousness, is at first directly interwoven with the material activity and the material intercourse of men, the language of real life. Conceiving, thinking, the mental intercourse of men, appear at this stage as the direct efflux of their material behaviour. The same applies to mental production as expressed in the language of the politics, laws, morality, religion, metaphysics of a people. Men are the producers of their conceptions, ideas, etc.—real, active men, as they are conditioned by a definite development of their productive forces and of the intercourse corresponding to these, up to its furthest forms. Consciousness can never be anything else than conscious existence, and the existence of men is their actual life-process. If in all ideology men and their circumstances appear upside down as in a *camera obscura,* this phenomenon arises just as much from their historical life-process as the inversion of objects on the retina does from their physical life-process.

In direct contrast to German philosophy which descends from heaven to earth, here we ascend from earth to heaven. That is to say, we do not set out from what men say, imagine, conceive, nor from men as narrated, thought of, imagined, conceived, in order to arrive at men in the flesh. We set out from real, active men, and on the basis of their real life-process we demonstrate the development of the ideological reflexes and echoes of this life-process. The phantoms formed in the human brain are also, necessarily, sublimates of their material life-process, which is empirically verifiable and bound to material premises. Morality, religion, metaphysics, all the rest of ideology and their corresponding forms of consciousness, thus no longer retain the semblance of independence. They have no history, no development; but men, developing their material production and their material intercourse, alter, along with this their real existence, their thinking and the products of their thinking. Life is not determined by consciousness, but consciousness by life. In the first method of approach the starting-point is consciousness taken as the living individual; in the second it is the real living individuals themselves, as they are in actual life, and consciousness is considered solely as *their* consciousness.

This method of approach is not devoid of premises. It starts out from the real premises and does not abandon them for a moment. Its premises are men, not in any fantastic isolation or abstract definition, but in their actual, empirically perceptible process of development under definite conditions. As soon as this active life-process is described, history ceases to be a collection of dead facts as it is with the empiricists (themselves still abstract), or an imagined activity of imagined subjects, as with the idealists.

Where speculation ends—in real life—there real, positive science begins: the representation of the practical activity, of the practical process of development of men. Empty talk about consciousness ceases, and real knowledge has to take its place. When reality is depicted, philosophy as an independent branch of activity loses its medium of existence. At the best its place can only be taken by a summing-up of the most general results, abstractions which arise from the observation of the historical development of men. Viewed apart from real history, these abstractions have in themselves no value whatsoever. They can only serve to facilitate the arrangement of historical material, to indicate the sequence of its separate strata.

* * *

Suggestions for Further Reading

Virtually every major philosopher and political theorist presents or presupposes some theory of the nature of man. I will suggest some supplementary and secondary readings of assistance in understanding the selections included in this section, and then mention a few additional classical and contemporary works.

Ernest Barker's edition of Aristotle's *Politics* (New York, 1946) * contains very useful notes and introductions, particularly with regard to the historical context of Aristotle's discussion. W. D. Ross's *Aristotle* (New York, 1955) * remains the best work-by-work summary and analysis of all Aristotle's writings. Michael Oakeshott's edition (New York, 1955) of the *Leviathan* contains an introductory essay which makes an impressive case for Hobbes' political theory. Other useful commentaries are John Laird's *Hobbes* (London, 1934) and Leslie Stephen's work by the same name (London, 1928). For a brilliant but idiosyncratic interpretation, see Leo Strauss' *The Political Philosophy of Hobbes, Its Basis and Its Genesis* (Chicago, 1963).* A provocative Marxist interpretation of the tradition of political theory in England from Hobbes to Locke can be found in C. B. Macpherson's recent work, *The Political Theory of Possessive Individualism* (Oxford, 1962). John Stuart Mill's *Utilitarianism* expounds that doctrine more systematically—and convincingly—than perhaps Bentham ever did, though with important alterations. Leslie Stephen is again useful, this time with *The English Utilitarians* (New York, 1912). The literature on Marx is enormous, although only recently have the early philosophical writings received great attention. Erich Fromm's edition of the *Economic-Philosophic Manuscripts* under the title *Marx's Concept of Man* (New York, 1961) * has a long interpretative introduction. Karl Popper's *The Open Society and Its Enemies* (London, 1962, fourth edition) states the case against the Marxian doctrine. Fritz Pappenheim's little book on *The Alienation of Modern Man* (New York, 1959) * summarizes the major developments in the history of Marx's seminal notion of alienation. A wide variety of materials, old and new, on that topic is gathered together in a convenient paperback, *Man Alone* (New York, 1962) * edited by E. and M. Josephson.

Among the countless classical texts which one might read for a theory of man, let me simply mention Plato's *The Republic*, Epictetus' *Discourses*, St. Augustine's *Confessions*, Machiavelli's *The Prince*, Mandeville's *Fable of the Bees*, Hume's *Treatise of Human Nature*, Book II, Spinoza's *Ethics*, Part Four, and Pope's *Essay on Man*.

Contemporary historical studies have added much to our understanding of the growth of the concept of man. Two exciting books on the Greek image of the human personality are Bruno Snell's *The Discovery of the Mind* (New York, 1960)* and E. R. Dodds' *The Greeks and the Irrational* (Berkeley, 1960).* Johan Huizinga's *Homo Ludens* (Boston, 1955) * is an intellectual *jeu d'esprit*, displaying man as a creature who plays, rather than as a creature who thinks or produces. Somewhat peripheral to the subject of human nature, but always useful for its account of a major tradition in western thought, is Arthur Lovejoy's *The Great Chain of Being* (New York, 1960).*

PERSONALITY
AND SOCIETY

Political philosophy can produce useful and important results only insofar as it relies upon the best social science available for its images of man and society. Philosophers who employ the psychology of ancient Greece or an eighteenth century notion of economics in their analyses of political problems will have little of value to say. In this section we pursue this theme by studying the relationship between the structure of individual personality on the one hand and the organization of political attitudes and institutions on the other. The first selection is an early and very famous attempt to establish a correlation between types of personality and types of political orders. Plato traces the military state of the Spartan sort to the predominance in the community of men ambitious for honor; the oligarchical state is linked to the ascendency of merchants whose sole end is the accumulation of wealth; in like manner Plato accounts for the democratic and tyrannical states. Unfortunately, the analogy between man and the state which Plato and others have employed is far too simple to be successful as an explanation of political reality, for the personality patterns of the individuals who comprise a state are only indirectly reflected in the political organizations of the state.

The complexity of the relationship between personality and politics is exhibited in Erik Erikson's study of Hitler and the appeal of naziism to the German people. Erikson shows that in the figure of Hitler German men could see the realization of their fantasies of unending adolescent rebellion against the world of their fathers. Erikson's work, together with the psychoanalytical analyses of naziism by Theodor Adorno, Bertram Schaffner, and others, constitutes one of the most impressive contributions of modern psychoanalysis to the study of politics.

Emile Durkheim raises questions of a quite different sort in his pioneering study of suicide. Durkheim's statistics of the variations in the incidence of suicide among different social groups seem to prove that society is not just the sum of the individuals in it, but is itself an independent entity to be studied by the science of sociology. Innumerable studies of voting behavior, consumer preference, automobile accidents, death rates, and marriage customs have substantiated Durkheim's claim that social groups behave according to laws of their own which cannot be inferred or predicted from any amount of knowledge about the psychology of individuals. In the light of this fact, can political philosophers go on assuming that the proper object of study is the individual rather than the community or nation?

David Riesman offers some insight into this problem with his typology of tradition-directed, inner-directed, and other-directed personalities. Riesman suggests that the autonomous individual of classical political philosophy, capable of taking responsibility for his acts in a society of free men, is the product of a specific stage in the economic and demographic development of industrial society. If this is so, then it may be fruitless to issue repeated calls for citizen participation in politics and a return to the spirit of the New England town meeting while pressing forward with socio-economic changes which make those old-fashioned virtues psychologically impossible.

Social philosophy comes here to the edge of pessimism and despair. We cannot debate the issues of political theory without assuming that we are masters of our fate and that the course of political life is the direct consequence of the decisions— well- or ill-considered—of those who rule and those who are ruled. Yet what Durkheim, Riesman, and Erikson are telling us in their different ways is that the broad patterns of social existence, which affect even the structure of the individual personality itself, are shaped in ways that we can scarcely recognize, let alone control. Nor does knowledge necessarily bring power, as Francis Bacon argued, for one of the first discoveries we make is that the very values which guide our use of that power are themselves instilled in us by the society we are attempting to change.

The Fall of the Ideal State

◆

The Republic, Plato's longest and most complex dialogue, is a systematic examination of the nature of the good society and the good life. The dialogue begins with the problem, what is justice? Very quickly, however, it broadens into a discussion of virtue in general. After an account of the philosopher's pursuit of wisdom, Plato offers a vivid description of the ideal state, in which wise men rule for the good of the whole community and the other citizens willingly accept their appropriate subordinate functions. In the selection presented here, various imperfect political orders are portrayed as corruptions or fallings away from the ideal. Plato traces the causal links between family life and individual psychology on the one hand, and the public life of the state on the other.

The Fall of the Ideal State.
Timocracy and the Timocratic Man

[*'In the infinity of time, past or future' the Ideal State may never have existed or be destined to exist; but if we suppose it realised, nothing in this world of mortality and change can last for ever. Most students of history would admit that the flow and ebb of collective vitality which accompany the rise and fall of successive forms of culture has not yet been explained. Aware that here is an equally unanswerable question, Plato veils his account in poetical and even mock-heroic language, hinting at some predestined correspondence between the cycle of life in animals and plants and the periodicity of the heavenly bodies. The wisest of Rulers, entrusted with the regulation of marriage and childbirth, may well fail to understand and observe this principle, and then children will be born who are worse than their parents. The decline of society will set in with the out-

Reprinted by permission of the publishers from Plato, *The Republic*, translated by F. M. Cornford (Oxford, Eng.: Clarendon Press, 1941).

* The bracketed material throughout this selection is the introductory summary of F. M. Cornford.

break of dissension within the ruling order. This is at all times the cause of revolution.

The first degenerate form of constitution is called Timocracy, a state in which the ambitious man's love of honour *(timé)*, the motive of the 'spirited' part, usurps the rule of reason. Plato expressly regards this principle as exemplified in Spartan institutions, from which he had borrowed several features in prescribing the mode of life of his Auxiliaries (Chap. X). But at Sparta private property had nourished the secret growth of avarice, intellect was distrusted, and an exaggerated cult of military efficiency aimed at holding down a population of helots. (Aristotle describes Spartan and Cretan institutions in the *Politics, Bk. ii. Chap. 9–10.*) This type of state might emerge, if Plato's Auxiliaries should begin to oust the philosophic Rulers from supreme control. The history and character of the timocratic individual closely reflect those of the state.

The argument here goes back to the point, at the beginning of Chapter XV, where Socrates professed to be 'within sight of the clearest possible proof' of the superiority of the just life to the unjust—the proof which will be given at the end of this Part. The whole of Part III, the central and most important section of the *Republic*, is treated as if it were a digression.]

Very well, I continued. So far, then, Glaucon, we agree that in a state destined to reach the height of good government wives and children must be held in common; men and women must have the same education throughout and share all pursuits, warlike or peaceful; and those who have proved themselves the best both in philosophy and in war are to be kings among them. Further, the Rulers, as soon as they are appointed, will lead the soldiers and settle them in quarters such as we prescribed, common to all, with nothing private about them; and besides these dwellings we agreed, if you remember, how far they should have anything they could call their own.

Yes, I remember we thought they should have no property in the ordinary sense, but, as Guardians in training for war, they should receive as wages from the other citizens enough to keep them for the year while they fulfilled their duty of watching over the community, themselves included.

That is right. But when we had done with those matters, we went off into the digression which has brought us to this point.

Let us go back now into our old path. Where did we leave it?

That is easy to remember. You were talking, very much as you are now, as if your description of the state were complete, and telling us that such a constitution and the corresponding type of man were what you would call good; although, as it now appears, you had it in your power to tell of a state and an individual of a still higher quality.* But at any rate you said that, if this constitution were right, all others must be wrong, mentioning, if I remember, four varieties as worth considering with an eye to their defects. We were also to look at all the corresponding types of individual character, decide which was the best and which the worst, and then consider whether or not the best is also the happiest, the worst the most miserable. I was asking what these four constitutions were, when Polemarchus and Adeimantus interrupted us; and so you entered on the discussion which has brought us to this point.

Your memory is very accurate, I replied.

Let us be like wrestlers, then, who go back to the same grip after an indecisive fall. If I repeat my question, try to give me the answer you were going to make.

I will do my best.

Well, I am just as eager to hear what are the four types of government you meant.

There is no difficulty about that; they are the types which have names in common use. First there is the constitution of Crete and Sparta, which is so commonly admired; second and next in esteem oligarchy, as it is called, a constitution fraught with many evils; next follows its antagonist, democracy; then despotism, which is thought so glorious and goes beyond them all as the fourth and final disease of society. Can you mention any other type of government, I mean any that is obviously a distinct species? There are, of course, types like hereditary monarchy, and states where the highest offices can be bought; † but these are rather intermediate forms, to be found quite as frequently outside Greece as within it.

True, one hears of many strange varieties.

Do you see, then, that there must be as many types of human character as there are forms of government? Constitutions can-

---

* Plato speaks as if the account of the philosophic ruler had brought out the full merits of the ideal state outlined in the earlier part.—Trans.

† This was so at Carthage, according to Aristotle, *Pol.* 1273 a 36, and Polybius vi. 56, 4. Plato confines himself to Greek institutions.—Trans.

not come out of sticks and stones; they must result from the preponderance of certain characters which draw the rest of the community in their wake. So if there are five forms of government, there must be five kinds of mental constitution among individuals.

Naturally.

Now we have already described the man whom we regard as in the full sense good and just and who corresponds to aristocracy, the government of the best. We have next to consider the inferior types: the competitive and ambitious temperament, answering to the Spartan constitution, and then the oligarchic, democratic, and despotic characters, in order that, by setting the extreme examples in contrast, we may finally answer the question how pure justice and pure injustice stand in respect of the happiness or misery they bring, and so decide to pursue the one or the other, according as we listen to Thrasymachus or to the argument we are now developing.

Yes, that is the next thing to be done.

When we were studying moral qualities earlier, we began with the state, because they stood out more clearly there than in the individual. On the same principle we had better now take, in each case, the constitution first, and then, in the light of our results, examine the corresponding character. We shall start with the constitution dominated by motives of ambition—it has no name in common use that I know of; let us call it timarchy or timocracy—and then go on to oligarchy and democracy, and lastly visit a state under despotic government and look into the despot's soul. We ought then to be in a position to decide the question before us.

Yes, such a systematic review should give us the materials for judgement.

Come then, let us try to explain how the government of the best might give place to a timocracy. Is it not a simple fact that in any form of government revolution always starts from the outbreak of internal dissension in the ruling class? The constitution cannot be upset so long as that class is of one mind, however small it may be.

That is true.

Then how, Glaucon, will trouble begin in our commonwealth? How will our Auxiliaries and Rulers come to be divided against each other or among themselves? Shall we, like Homer, invoke the Muses to tell us 'how first division came,' and imagine them amusing themselves at our expense by talking in high-flown language, as one teases a child with a pretence of being in earnest?

What have they to say?

Something of this sort. 'Hard as it may be for a state so framed to be shaken, yet, since all that comes into being must decay, even a fabric like this will not endure for ever, but will suffer dissolution. In this manner: not only for plants that grow in the earth, but also for all creatures that move thereon, there are seasons of fruitfulness and unfruitfulness for soul and body alike, which come whenever a certain cycle is completed, in a period * short or long according to the length of life of each species. For your own race, the rulers you have bred for your commonwealth, wise as they are, will not be able, by observation and reckoning, to hit upon the times propitious or otherwise for birth; some day the moment will slip by and they will beget children out of due season. For the divine creature there is a period embraced by a perfect number; † while for the human there is a geometrical number determining the better or worse quality of the births. ‡ When your Guardians, from ignorance of this, bring together brides and bridegrooms out of season, their

* This period has been taken to be the period of gestation, at the end of which the seed of the living creature ('soul and body') either comes successfully to birth or miscarries. Aristotle (*On the Generation of Animals*, iv. 10, 777 b 16) remarks: 'In all animals the time of gestation and development and the length of life aim at being measured by naturally complete periods. By a natural period I mean, e.g. a day and night, a month, a year, and the greater times measured by these, and also the periods (phases) of the moon.'

† The 'divine creature' is the visible universe, which is called a "created god" in the cosmological myth of the *Timaeus*. The perfect number is probably the number of days in a Great Year, which is completed when all the heavenly bodies come back to the same relative positions (*Tim.* 39 D).

‡ The extremely obscure description of this number, which has been variously interpreted, is omitted. Ancient evidence points to some relation between two numbers, both ultimately based on the factors 3, 4, 5, representing the sides of the "Pythagorean" or "zoogonic" right-angled triangle. (1) One is $216 = 3^8 + 4^8 + 5^3 = 6^3$. This was called the 'psychogonic cube,' as expressing the number of days in the gestation period of the seven-months' child. The period of the nine-months' child was obtained by adding $60 = 3 \times 4 \times 5$. (2) The other number is $12,960,000 = 3,600^2 = (3 \times 4 \times 5)^4$, the number of days in a Great Year, reckoned as 36,000 solar years of 360 days each. If Plato does describe two numbers, and not (as some hold) the second only, he has not explained how the two should be brought into relation. The serious idea behind this seemingly fanciful passage is the affinity and correspondence of macrocosm and microcosm and the embodiment of mathematical principles in both.—Trans.

children will not be well-endowed or fortunate. The best of
these may be appointed by the elder generation; but when they
succeed to their fathers' authority as Guardians, being unworthy,
they will begin to neglect us and to think too lightly first of the
cultivation of the mind, and then of bodily training, so that your
young men will come to be worse educated. Then Rulers appointed from among them will fail in their duty as Guardians to
try the mettle of your citizens, those breeds of gold and silver,
brass and iron that Hesiod told of; and when the silver is alloyed
with iron and the gold with brass, diversity, inequality, and dis-
harmony will beget, as they always must, enmity and war. Such,
everywhere, is the birth and lineage of civil strife.'

Yes, we will take that as a true answer to our question.

How could it be otherwise, when it comes from the Muses?

And what will they go on to tell us?

Once civil strife is born, the two parties begin to pull different
ways: the breed of iron and brass towards money-making and
the possession of house and land, silver and gold; while the
other two, wanting no other wealth than the gold and silver
in the composition of their souls, try to draw them towards
virtue and the ancient ways. But the violence of their contention
ends in a compromise: they agree to distribute land and houses
for private ownership; they enslave their own people who
formerly lived as free men under their guardianship and gave
them maintenance; and, holding them as serfs and menials, devote themselves to war and to keeping these subjects under
watch and ward.

I agree: that is how the transition begins.

And this form of government will be midway between the
rule of the best and oligarchy, will it not?

Yes.

Such being the transition, how will the state be governed after
the change? Obviously, as intermediate between the earlier
constitution and oligarchy, it will resemble each of these in some
respects and have some features of its own.

True.

It will be like the earlier constitution in several ways. Authority will be respected; the fighting class will abstain from any
form of business, farming, or handicrafts; they will keep up their
common meals and give their time to physical training and martial exercises.

Yes.

On the other hand, it will have some peculiar characteristics. It will be afraid to admit intellectuals to office. The men of that quality now at its disposal will no longer be single-minded and sincere; it will prefer simpler characters with plenty of spirit, better suited for war than for peace. War will be its constant occupation, and military tricks and stratagems will be greatly admired.

Yes.

At the same time, men of this kind will resemble the ruling class of an oligarchy in being avaricious, cherishing furtively a passionate regard for gold and silver; for they will now have private homes where they can hoard their treasure in secret and live ensconced in a nest of their own, lavishing their riches on their women or whom they please. They will also be miserly, prizing the money they may not openly acquire, though prodigal enough of other people's wealth for the satisfaction of their desires. They will enjoy their pleasures in secret, like truant children, in defiance of the law; because they have been educated not by gentle influence but under compulsion, cultivating the body in preference to the mind and caring nothing for the spirit of genuine culture which seeks truth by the discourse of reason.

The society you describe is certainly a mixture of good and evil.

Yes, it is a mixture; but, thanks to the predominance of the spirited part of our nature, it has one most conspicuous feature: ambition and the passion to excel.

Quite so.

Such, then, is the origin and character of this form of government. We have given only an outline, for no more finished picture is needed for the purpose of setting before our eyes the perfect types of just and unjust men. It would be an endless task to go through all the forms of government and of human character without omitting any detail.

True.

And now what of the corresponding individual? How does he come into being, and what is he like?

I imagine, said Adeimantus, his desire to excel, so far as that goes, would make him rather like Glaucon.

Perhaps, said I; but in other ways the likeness fails. He must be more self-willed than Glaucon and rather uncultivated, though fond of music; one who will listen readily, but is no speaker. Not having a properly educated man's consciousness of superiority to slaves, he will treat them harshly; though he will be civil to free men, and very obedient to those in authority. Ambitious for office, he will base his claims, not on any gifts of speech, but on his exploits in war and the soldierly qualities he has acquired through his devotion to athletics and hunting. In his youth he will despise money, but the older he grows the more he will care for it, because of the touch of avarice in his nature; and besides his character is not thoroughly sound, for lack of the only safeguard that can preserve it throughout life, a thoughtful and cultivated mind.*

Quite true.

If that is the sort of young man whose character reflects a timocratical régime, his history will be something like this. He may be the son of an excellent father who, living in an ill-governed state, holds aloof from public life because he would sooner forgo some of his rights than take part in the scramble for office or be troubled with going to law. His son's character begins to take shape when he hears his mother complaining that she is slighted by the other women because her husband has no official post. She sees too that he cares little for money, and is indifferent to all the scurrilous battle of words that goes on in the Assembly and the law-courts; and she finds him always absorbed in his thoughts, without much regard for her, or disregard either. Nursing all these grievances, she tells her son that his father is not much of a man and far too easy-going, and has all the other weaknesses that the wives of such men are fond of harping on.

Yes, we hear plenty of these feminine complaints.

Besides, as you know, servants who are esteemed loyal to the family sometimes talk privately to the sons in the same way. If they see the father taking no action against a swindler or a defaulting debtor, they urge the son, when he is grown up, to stand up for his rights and be more of a man than his father. When the boy goes out, he sees and hears the same sort of thing: one man is made light of as a fool for minding his own business, whereas another who has a finger in every pie is praised and respected. All this experience affects the young man, and on the other hand he listens to his father's conversation and can see at close quarters how his way of life compares

---

* This speech represents an Athenian's view of a typical Spartan.—Trans.

with other people's; and so he is pulled both ways. His father tends the growth of reason in his soul, while the rest of the world is fostering the other two elements, ambition and appetite. By temperament he is not a bad man, but he has fallen into bad company, and the two contrary influences result in a compromise: he gives himself up to the control of the middle principle of high-spirited emulation and becomes an arrogant and ambitious man.

That is a good account of his history, I think.

So now we have an idea of the second form of government and the corresponding individual.

Yes.

Oligarchy (Plutocracy) and the Oligarchic Man

[In Timocracy the illegitimate institution of private property for the Guardians stimulated ambition, under cover of which the still lower passion for wealth was released from the control of reason. The love of money is the most reputable motive characterizing the third element in human nature, the 'multifarious' group of appetites for the satisfactions, necessary or unnecessary, which money can buy. Oligarchy, the 'government of the few,' or, as Xenophon (Mem. iv, 6, 12) calls it, Plutocracy, is the constitution which results when power passes into the hands of men for whom wealth is the end of life. The state now suffers a further loss of unity by the outbreak of that class war of rich against poor which Plato sought to avert by denying all private property to the ruling order and limiting the acquisition of wealth by tradesmen and farmers (Chap. XI). The plutocrat, as a mere consumer of goods, is compared to the drone; and when he has squandered his money he sinks into the dangerous class of paupers and criminals (sting-drones).

In the oligarchic individual, the drone-like appetites have gained some ground against reason; but they are still held in check by the dominant passion for wealth, which calls for an outward respectability.]

Shall we go on then, as Aeschylus might say, to tell of 'another man, matched with another state,' * or rather keep to our plan of taking the state first?

---

* Alludes to the messenger's descriptions of the champions who appeared before the gates of Thebes in Aeschylus' Seven against Thebes.

By all means.

Then I suppose the next type of constitution will be oligarchy.

What sort of régime do you mean?

The one which is based on a property qualification, where the rich are in power and the poor man cannot hold office.

I see.

We must start, then, by describing the transition from timoc-racy to oligarchy. No one could fail to see how that happens. The downfall of timocracy is due to the flow of gold into those private stores we spoke of. In finding new ways of spending their money, men begin by stretching the law for that purpose, until they and their wives obey it no longer. Then, as each keeps an envious eye on his neighbour, their rivalry infects the great mass of them; and as they go to further lengths in the pursuit of riches, the more they value money and the less they care for virtue. Virtue and wealth are balanced against one another in the scales; as the rich rise in social esteem, the virtuous sink. These changes of valuation, moreover, are always reflected in practice. So at last the competitive spirit of ambi-tion in these men gives way to the passion for gain; they despise the poor man and promote to power the rich, who wins all their praise and admiration. At this point they fix by statute the qual-ification for privilege in an oligarchy, an amount of wealth which varies with the strength of the oligarchical principle; no one may hold office whose property falls below the prescribed sum. This measure is carried through by armed force, unless they have already set up their constitution by terrorism. That, then, is how an oligarchy comes to be established.

Yes, said Adeimantus; but what is the character of this régime, and what are the defects we said it would have?

In the first place, I replied, the principle on which it limits privilege. How would it be, if the captain of a ship were ap-pointed on a property qualification, and a poor man could never get a command, though he might know much more about sea-manship?

The voyage would be likely to end in disaster.

Is not the same true of any position of authority? Or is the government of a state an exception?

Anything but an exception, inasmuch as a state is the hardest thing to govern and the most important.

So this is one serious fault of oligarchy.

Evidently.

Is it any less serious that such a state must lose its unity and become two, one of the poor, the other of the rich, living together and always plotting against each other?

Quite as serious.

Another thing to its discredit is that they may well be unable to carry on a war. Either they must call out the common people or not. If they do, they will have more to fear from the armed multitude than from the enemy; and if they do not, in the day of battle these oligarchs will find themselves only too literally a government of the few. Also, their avarice will make them unwilling to pay war-taxes.

True.

And again, is it right that the same persons should combine many occupations, agriculture, business, and soldiering? We condemned that practice some time ago.

No, not at all right.

Worst of all, a man is allowed to sell all he has to another and then to go on living in a community where he plays no part as tradesman or artisan or as a soldier capable of providing his own equipment; he is only what they call a pauper. This is an evil which first becomes possible under an oligarchy, or at least there is nothing to prevent it; otherwise there would not be some men excessively wealthy and others destitute.

True.

Now think of this pauper in his earlier days when he was well off. By spending his money, was he doing any more good to the community in those useful ways I mentioned? He seemed to belong to the ruling class, but really he was neither ruling the state nor serving it; he was a mere consumer of goods. His house might be compared to one of those cells in the honeycomb where a drone is bred to be the plague of the hive. Some drones can fly, and these were all created without stings; others, which cannot fly, are of two sorts: some have formidable stings, the rest have none.* In society, the stingless drones end as beggars in their old age; the ones which have stings become what is known as the criminal class. It follows that, in any community

* Aristotle, *Hist. Anim.* ix. 40, describes drones as living on the honey made by the working bees. If the king-bee dies, drones are said to be reared by the workers in their own cells and to become more spirited; hence they are called sting-drones, though they really have no stings, but only the wish to use such weapons. Drones and robber-bees, if caught damaging the work of the other bees, are killed or driven from the hive.—Trans.

where beggers are to be seen, there are also thieves and pick-pockets and temple-robbers and other such artists in crime concealed somewhere about the place. And you will certainly see beggars in any state governed by an oligarchy.

Yes, nearly everywhere, outside the ruling class.

Then we may assume that there are also plenty of drones with stings, criminals whom the government takes care to hold down by force; and we shall conclude that they are bred by lack of education, bad upbringing, and a vicious form of government.

Yes.

Such, then, is the character of a state ruled by an oligarchy. It has all these evils and perhaps more.

Very likely.

We have finished, then, with the constitution known as oligarchy, where power is held on a property qualification, and we may turn now to the history and character of the corresponding individual.

Yes, let us do so.

The transition from the timocratic type to the oligarchical happens somewhat in this way. The timocratical man has a son, who at first emulates his father and follows in his steps. Then suddenly he sees him come up against society, like a ship striking a sunken rock, and founder with all his possessions; he may have held some high office or command and then have been brought to trial by informers and put to death or banished or outlawed with the loss of all his property.

All this might well happen.

The son is terror-stricken at the sight of this ruin, in which his own fortunes are involved. At once that spirit of eager ambition which hitherto ruled in his heart is thrust headlong from the throne. Humbled by poverty, he turns to earning his living and, little by little, through hard work and petty savings, scrapes together a fortune. And now he will instal another spirit on the vacant throne, the money-loving spirit of sensual appetite, like an eastern monarch with diadem and golden chain and scimitar girt at his side. At its footstool, on either hand, will crouch the two slaves he has forced into subjection: Reason, whose thought is now confined to calculating how money may breed more money, and Ambition, suffered to admire and value nothing but wealth and its possessors and to excel in nothing but the struggle to gain money by any and every means.

There is no swifter and surer way by which an ambitious young man may be transformed into a lover of money.

Is this, then, our oligarchical type?

Well, at any rate, the type from which he has developed corresponded to the constitution from which oligarchy arose.

Let us see, then, whether he will not have the same sort of character. The first point of resemblance is that he values wealth above everything. Another is that he is niggardly and a worker who satisfies only his necessary wants and will go to no further expense; his other desires he keeps in subjection as leading nowhere. There is something squalid about him, with his way of always expecting to make a profit and add to his hoard—the sort of person who is much admired by the vulgar. Surely there is a likeness here to the state under an oligarchy?

I think there is, especially in the way that money is valued above everything.

Because, I suspect, he has never thought of cultivating his mind.

Never; or he would not have promoted the blind god of Wealth * to lead the dance.

Good; and here is another point. As a consequence of his lack of education, appetites will spring up in him, comparable to those drones in society whom we classified as either beggars or criminals, though his habitual carefulness will keep them in check. If you want to see his criminal tendencies at work, you must look to any occasions, such as the guardianship of orphans, where he has a chance to be dishonest without risk. It will then be clear that in his other business relations, where his apparent honesty gives him a good reputation, he is only exercising a sort of enforced moderation. The base desires are there, not tamed by a reasonable conviction that it is wrong to gratify them, but only held down under stress of fear, which makes him tremble for the safety of his whole fortune. Moreover, you may generally be sure of discovering these drone-like appetites whenever men of this sort have other people's money to spend.

That is very true.

Such a man, then, will not be single-minded but torn in two by internal conflict, though his better desires will usually keep

* Plutus is blind in Aristophanes' play of that name and elsewhere.—Trans.

the upper hand over the worse. Hence he presents a more decent appearance than many; but the genuine virtue of a soul in peace and harmony with itself will be utterly beyond his reach.

I agree.

Further, his stinginess weakens him as a competitor for any personal success or honourable distinction. He is unwilling to spend his money in a struggle for that sort of renown, being afraid to stir up his expensive desires by calling upon them to second his ambition. So, like a true oligarch, fighting with only a small part of his forces, he is usually beaten and remains a rich man.

Quite so.

Have we any further doubts, then, about the likeness between a state under an oligarchy and this parsimonious money-getter?

None at all.

Democracy and the Democratic Man

[The type of democracy whose defects Plato has in view could exist only in a small city-state like Athens. It was not the rule of the majority through elected representatives, but was based on the theory that every adult male citizen had an equal right to take a personal part in the government through the Assembly and the law-courts and was capable of holding any office. (It must be remembered that more than half the population were either slaves with no civic rights or resident aliens.) At Athens the members of the Council of five hundred, which prepared the business and carried out the resolutions of the Assembly, were appointed by lot from among the candidates who presented themselves. The Assembly was nominally the whole body of citizens over eighteen, a quorum of 6,000 being required for certain purposes. It was the sovereign administrative power, though it could not alter the constitutional laws, under whose impersonal sovereignty the Greek citizen conceived himself to live, without the co-operation of another popular judicial body, the *Heliaea*, composed nominally of all citizens over thirty who had taken an oath to observe the constitution and been declared by the nine Archons to be duly qualified. The ideals of Athenian democracy are set down in the Funeral Speech of Pericles (*Thuc. ii*, 35). In Plato's view, the direct rule of the many violated the fundamental principle of 'justice,' that men, being born with different capacities, should do only the work for which they are fitted. Fitness to govern is, he has argued, the last achievement of the highest natures.

Oligarchy, by making wealth the end of life and failing to check the accumulation of property in a few hands and the ravages of usury, so weakens itself that the poor see their opportunity to wrest power from the degenerate rich.

In the democratic temperament the principle of freedom and equal rights for all is applied to the whole mob of appetites in the lowest part of the soul. Ignoring the distinction between the necessary, profitable desires, indulged by the thrifty plutocrat without loss of respectability, and the unnecessary, prodigal desires, the democratic man gives himself up to the pleasures of the moment, everything by turns and nothing long.

In a later dialogue, *The Statesman,* Plato regards even the more lawless type of democracy as superior to oligarchy, though not to timocracy.]

Democracy, I suppose, should come next. A study of its rise and character should help us to recognize the democratic type of man and set him beside the others for judgement.

Certainly that course would fit in with our plan.

If the aim of life in an oligarchy is to become as rich as possible, that insatiable craving would bring about the transition to democracy. In this way: since the power of the ruling class is due to its wealth, they will not want to have laws restraining prodigal young men from ruining themselves by extravagance. They will hope to lend these spendthrifts money on their property and buy it up, so as to become richer and more influential than ever. We can see at once that a society cannot hold wealth in honour and at the same time establish a proper self-control in its citizens. One or the other must be sacrificed.

Yes, that is fairly obvious.

In an oligarchy, then, this neglect to curb riotous living sometimes reduces to poverty men of a not ungenerous nature. They settle down in idleness, some of them burdened with debt, some disfranchised, some both at once; and these drones are armed and can sting. Hating the men who have acquired their property and conspiring against them and the rest of society, they long for a revolution. Meanwhile the usurers, intent upon their own business, seem unaware of their existence; they are too busy planting their own stings into any fresh victim who offers them an opening to inject the poison of their money; and while they multiply their capital by usury, they are also multiplying the drones and the paupers. When the danger threatens to break out, they will do nothing to quench the flames, either in the way we mentioned, by forbidding a man to do what he likes with his own, or by the next best remedy, which would be a law enforcing a respect for right conduct. If it were enacted that, in general, voluntary contracts for a loan should be made at the lender's risk,* there would be less of this shameless pursuit of wealth and a scantier crop of those evils I have just described.

Quite true.

But, as things are, this is the plight to which the rulers of an oligarchy, for all these reasons, reduce their subjects. As for themselves, luxurious indolence of body and mind makes their young men too lazy and effeminate to resist pleasure or to endure pain; and the fathers, neglecting everything but money, have no higher ideals in life than the poor. Such being the condition of rulers and subjects, what will happen when they are thrown together, perhaps as fellow-travellers by sea or land to some festival or on a campaign, and can observe one another's demeanour in a moment of danger? The rich will have no chance to feel superior to the poor. On the contrary, the poor man, lean and sunburnt, may find himself posted in battle beside one who, thanks to his wealth and indoor life, is panting under his burden of fat and showing every mark of distress. 'Such men,' he will think, 'are rich because we are cowards'; and when he and his friends meet in private, the word will go round: 'These men are no good: they are at our mercy.'

Yes, that is sure to happen.

This state, then, is in the same precarious condition as a person so unhealthy that the least shock from outside will upset the balance or, even without that, internal disorder will break out. It falls sick and is at war with itself on the slightest occasion, as soon as one party or the other calls in allies from a

---

* At *Laws* 742 E, Plato proposes a law: 'No one shall deposit money with anyone he does not trust, nor lend at interest, since it is permissible for the borrower to refuse entirely to pay back either interest or principal' (trans. R. G. Bury).—Trans.

neighbouring oligarchy or democracy; and sometimes civil war begins with no help from without.

Quite true.

And when the poor win, the result is a democracy. They kill some of the opposite party, banish others, and grant the rest an equal share in civil rights and government, officials being usually appointed by lot.

Yes, that is how a democracy comes to be established, whether by force of arms or because the other party is terrorized into giving way.

Now what is the character of this new régime? Obviously the way they govern themselves will throw light on the democratic type of man.

No doubt.

First of all, they are free. Liberty and free speech are rife everywhere; anyone is allowed to do what he likes.

Yes, so we are told.

That being so, every man will arrange his own manner of life to suit his pleasure. The result will be a greater variety of individuals than under any other constitution. So it may be the finest of all, with its variegated pattern of all sorts of characters. Many people may think it the best, just as women and children might admire a mixture of colours of every shade in the pattern of a dress. At any rate if we are in search of a constitution, here is a good place to look for one. A democracy is so free that it contains a sample of every kind; and perhaps anyone who intends to found a state, as we have been doing, ought first to visit this emporium of constitutions and choose the model he likes best.

He will find plenty to choose from.

Here, too, you are not obliged to be in authority, however competent you may be, or to submit to authority, if you do not like it; you need not fight when your fellow citizens are at war, nor remain at peace when they do, unless you want peace; and though you may have no legal right to hold office or sit on juries, you will do so all the same if the fancy takes you. A wonderfully pleasant life, surely, for the moment.

For the moment, no doubt.

There is a charm, too, in the forgiving spirit shown by some who have been sentenced by the courts. In a democracy you must have seen how men condemned to death or exile stay on and go about in public, and no one takes any more notice than he would of a spirit that walked invisible. There is so much tolerance and superiority to petty considerations; such a contempt for all those fine principles we laid down in founding our commonwealth, as when we said that only a very exceptional nature could turn out a good man, if he had not played as a child among things of beauty and given himself only to creditable pursuits. A democracy tramples all such notions under foot; with a magnificent indifference to the sort of life a man has led before he enters politics, it will promote to honour anyone who merely calls himself the people's friend.

Magnificent indeed.

These then, and such as these, are the features of a democracy, an agreeable form of anarchy with plenty of variety and an equality of a peculiar kind for equals and unequals alike.

All that is notoriously true.

Now consider the corresponding individual character. Or shall we take his origin first, as we did in the case of the constitution?

Yes.

I imagine him as the son of our miserly oligarch, brought up under his father's eye and in his father's ways. So he too will enforce a firm control over all such pleasures as lead to expense rather than profit—unnecessary pleasures, as they have been called. But, before going farther, shall we draw the distinction between necessary and unnecessary appetites, so as not to argue in the dark? *

Please do so.

There are appetites which cannot be got rid of, and there are all those which it does us good to fulfil. Our nature cannot help seeking to satisfy both these kinds; so they may fairly be described as necessary. On the other hand, 'unnecessary' would be the right name for all appetites which can be got rid of by early training and which do us no good and in some cases do harm. Let us take an example of each kind, so as to form a general idea of them. The desire to eat enough plain food—

---

* A classification of appetites is needed because oligarchy, democracy, and despotism are based on the supremacy of three sorts of appetite: (1) the necessary, (2) the unnecessary and spendthrift, and (3) the lawless, distinguished later at 571 A. p. 315 ff.—Trans.

just bread and meat—to keep in health and good condition may
be called necessary. In the case of bread the necessity is twofold, since it not only does us good but is indispensable to life;
whereas meat is only necessary in so far as it helps to keep
us in good condition. Beyond these simple needs the desire for
a whole variety of luxuries is unnecessary. Most people can get
rid of it by early discipline and education; and it is as preju-
dicial to intelligence and self-control as it is to bodily health.
Further, these unnecessary appetites might be called expensive,
whereas the necessary ones are rather profitable, as helping a
man to do his work. The same distinctions could be drawn in
the case of sexual appetite and all the rest.

Yes.

Now, when we were speaking just now of drones, we meant
the sort of man who is under the sway of a host of unnecessary
pleasures and appetites, in contrast with our miserly oligarch,
over whom the necessary desires are in control. Accordingly, we
can now go back to describe how the democratic type develops
from the oligarchical. I imagine it usually happens in this way.
When a young man, bred, as we were saying, in a stingy and
uncultivated home, has once tasted the honey of the drones and
keeps company with those dangerous and cunning creatures,
who know how to purvey pleasures in all their multitudinous
variety, then the oligarchical constitution of his soul begins to
turn into a democracy. The corresponding revolution was effected in the state by one of the two factions calling in the help
of partisans from outside. In the same way one of the conflicting sets of desires in the soul of this youth will be reinforced
from without by a group of kindred passions; and if the resistance of the oligarchical faction in him is strengthened by remon-
strances and reproaches coming from his father, perhaps, or his
friends, the opposing parties will soon be battling within him.
In some cases the democratic interest yields to the oligarchical:
a sense of shame gains a footing in the young man's soul, and
some appetites are crushed, others banished, until order is
restored.

Yes, that happens sometimes.

But then again, perhaps, owing to the father's having no
idea how to bring up his son, another brood of desires, akin
to those which were banished, are secretly nursed up until they
become numerous and strong. These draw the young man back

into clandestine commerce with his old associates, and between them they breed a whole multitude. In the end, they seize the citadel of the young man's soul, finding it unguarded by the trusty sentinels which keep watch over the minds of men favoured by heaven. Knowledge, right principles, true thoughts, are not at their post; and the place lies open to the assault of false and presumptuous notions. So he turns again to those lotus-eaters and now throws in his lot with them openly. If his family send reinforcements to the support of his thrifty instincts, the impostors who have seized the royal fortress shut the gates upon them, and will not even come to parley with the fatherly counsels of individual friends. In the internal conflict they gain the day; modesty and self-control, dishonoured and insulted as the weaknesses of an unmanly fool, are thrust out into exile; and the whole crew of unprofitable desires take a hand in banishing moderation and frugality, which, as they will have it, are nothing but churlish meanness. So they take possession of the soul which they have swept clean, as if purified for initiation into higher mysteries; and nothing remains but to marshal the great procession * bringing home Insolence, Anarchy, Waste, and Impudence, those resplendent divinities crowned with garlands, whose praises they sing under flattering names: Insolence they call good breeding, Anarchy freedom, Waste magnificence, and Impudence a manly spirit. Is not that a fair account of the revolution which gives free rein to unnecessary and harmful pleasures in a young man brought up in the satisfaction only of the necessary desires?

Yes, it is a vivid description.

In his life thenceforward he spends as much time and pains and money on his superfluous pleasures as on the necessary ones. If he is lucky enough not to be carried beyond all bounds, the tumult may begin to subside as he grows older. Then perhaps he may recall some of the banished virtues and cease to give himself up entirely to the passions which ousted them; and now he will set all his pleasures on a footing of equality, denying to none its equal rights and maintenance, and allowing each in turn, as it presents itself, to succeed, as if by the chance of the lot, to the government of his soul until it is satis-

---

* Using once more the imagery of the Eleusinian Mysteries, Plato alludes to the evening procession which conducted the image of Iacchus from Athens home to Eleusis.—Trans.

fied. When he is told that some pleasures should be sought and valued as arising from desires of a higher order, others chastised and enslaved because the desires are base, he will shut the gates of the citadel against the messengers of truth, shaking his head and declaring that one appetite is as good as another and all must have their equal rights. So he spends his days indulging the pleasure of the moment, now intoxicated with wine and music, and then taking to a spare diet and drinking nothing but water; one day in hard training, the next doing nothing at all, the third apparently immersed in study. Every now and then he takes a part in politics, leaping to his feet to say or do whatever comes into his head. Or he will set out to rival someone he admires, a soldier it may be, or, if the fancy takes him, a man of business. His life is subject to no order or restraint, and he has no wish to change an existence which he calls pleasant, free, and happy.

That well describes the life of one whose motto is liberty and equality.

Yes, and his character contains the same fine variety of pattern that we found in the democratic state; it is as multifarious as that epitome of all types of constitution. Many a man, and many a woman too, will find in it something to envy. So we may see in him the counterpart of democracy, and call him the democratic man.

We may.

Despotism and the Despotic Man

[The Greeks called an absolute, unconstitutional ruler a 'tyrant,' but the word by no means always bore the sinister associations which are now gathering round its modern equivalent, the once honourable name of 'dictator.' A tyrant might be, like Peisistratus at Athens, a comparatively benevolent champion of the common people against the oppression of a landed aristocracy; but then, as now, Acton's saying was true: 'all power corrupts; absolute power corrupts absolutely.' Little as Plato valued what he has described as democratic liberty, no democrat could surpass him in detestation of the despotism which is the triumph of injustice and the very negation of the liberty he did believe in.

Democratic anarchy, carried to the extreme, divides society into three classes: a growing number of ruined spendthrift and desperadoes; capitalists, quietly amassing wealth; and the mass of country people, working their own small farms and uninterested in politics. The most unscrupulous 'drones' lead an attack upon property, which drives the capitalists in self-defence to form a reactionary party. The people then put forward a champion who, having tasted blood, is fated to become a human wolf, the enemy of mankind. Threatened with assassination, he successfully demands a bodyguard or private army, seizes absolute power, and makes the people his slaves. This account of the rise of despotism is adapted to Plato's psychological standpoint, rather than to the normal course of Greek history. At Athens, for example, the 'tyranny' of Peisistratus broke the power of the landed nobility and prepared the way for democracy. On the other hand democracy sometimes passed into despotism, as at Syracuse in Plato's time.

A picture follows of the miserable condition to which the despot is driven to reduce himself by murdering his opponents and possible rivals, till he is left with only scoundrels for company and loathed by the people when they realize how they have been enslaved.

In the individual soul despotism means the dominion of one among those unlawful appetites whose existence, even in decent people, is revealed in dreams. The democratic man allowed equal rights to all his desires; but this balance is easily destroyed by the growth of a master passion, which will gradually enslave every other element in the soul. So at last the portrait of the perfectly unjust man is completed for comparison with the perfectly just philosopher-king.]

Now there remains only the most admired of all constitutions and characters—despotism and the despot. How does despotism arise? That it comes out of democracy is fairly clear. Does the change take place in the same sort of way as the change from oligarchy to democracy? Oligarchy was established by men with a certain aim in life: the good they sought was wealth, and it was the insatiable appetite for money-making to the neglect of everything else that proved its undoing. Is democracy likewise ruined by greed for what it conceives to be the supreme good?

What good do you mean?

Liberty. In a democratic country you will be told that liberty is its noblest possession, which makes it the only fit place for a free spirit to live in.

True; that is often said.

Well then, as I was saying, perhaps the insatiable desire for this good to the neglect of everything else may transform a democracy and lead to a demand for despotism. A democratic state may fall under the influence of unprincipled leaders, ready to minister to its thirst for liberty with too deep draughts of this heady wine; and then, if its rulers are not complaisant enough to give it unstinted freedom, they will be arraigned as accursed oligarchs and punished. Law-abiding citizens will be insulted as nonentities who hug their chains; and all praise and honour will be bestowed, both publicly and in private, on rulers who behave like subjects and subjects who behave like rulers. In such a state the spirit of liberty is bound to go to all lengths.

Inevitably.

It will make its way into the home, until at last the very animals catch the infection of anarchy. The parent falls into the habit of behaving like the child, and the child like the parent: the father is afraid of his sons, and they show no fear or respect for their parents, in order to assert their freedom. Citizens, resident aliens, and strangers from abroad are all on an equal footing. To descend to smaller matters, the schoolmaster timidly flatters his pupils, and the pupils make light of their masters as well as of their attendants. Generally speaking, the young copy their elders, argue with them, and will not do as they are told; while the old, anxious not to be thought disagreeable tyrants, imitate the young and condescend to enter into their jokes and amusements. The full measure of popular liberty is reached when the slaves of both sexes are quite as free as the owners who paid for them; and I had almost forgotten to mention the spirit of freedom and equality in the mutual relations of men and women.

Well, to quote Aeschylus, we may as well speak 'the word that rises to our lips.'

Certainly; so I will. No one who had not seen it would believe how much more freedom the domestic animals enjoy in a democracy than elsewhere. The very dogs behave as if the proverb 'like mistress, like maid' applied to them; and the horses and donkeys catch the habit of walking down the street with all the dignity of freemen, running into anyone they meet who does not get out of their way. The whole place is simply bursting with the spirit of liberty.

No need to tell me that. I have often suffered from it on my way out of the town.

Putting all these items together, you can see the result: the citizens become so sensitive that they resent the slightest application of control as intolerable tyranny, and in their resolve to have no master they end by disregarding even the law, written or unwritten.

Yes, I know that only too well.

Such then, I should say, is the seed, so full of fair promise, from which springs despotism.

Promising indeed. But what is the next stage?

The same disease that destroyed oligarchy breaks out again here, with all the more force because of the prevailing licence, and enslaves democracy. The truth is that, in the constitution of society, quite as much as in the weather or in plants and animals, any excess brings about an equally violent reaction. So the only outcome of too much freedom is likely to be excessive subjection, in the state or in the individual; which means that the culmination of liberty in democracy is precisely what prepares the way for the cruellest extreme of servitude under a despot. But I think you were asking rather about the nature of that disease which afflicts democracy in common with oligarchy and reduces it to slavery.

Yes, I was.

What I had in mind was that set of idle spendthrifts, among whom the bolder spirits take the lead. We compared these leaders, if you remember, to drones armed with stings, the stingless drones being their less enterprising followers. In any society where these two groups appear they create disorder, as phlegm and bile do in the body. Hence the lawgiver, as a good physician of the body politic, should take measures in advance, no less than the prudent bee-keeper who tries to forestall the appearance of drones, or, failing that, cuts them out, cells and all, as quickly as he can.

Quite true.

Then, to gain a clearer view of our problem, let us suppose the democratic commonwealth to be divided into three parts, as in fact it is. One consists of the drones we have just described. Bred

by the spirit of licence, in a democracy this class is no less numerous and much more energetic than in an oligarchy, where it
is despised and kept out of office and so remains weak for lack
of exercise. But in a democracy it furnishes all the leaders, with
a few exceptions; its keenest members make the speeches and
transact the business, while the other drones settle on the
benches round, humming applause to drown any opposition.
Thus nearly the whole management of the commonwealth is in
its hands.

Quite true.

Meanwhile, a second group is constantly emerging from the
mass. Where everyone is bent upon making money, the steadiest
characters tend to amass the greatest wealth. Here is a very convenient source from which the drones can draw an abundance
of honey.

No doubt; they cannot squeeze any out of men of small means.

'The rich,' I believe, is what they call this class which provides
provender for the drones.

Yes.

The third class will be the 'people,' comprising all the peasantry who work their own farms, with few possessions and no
interest in politics. In a democracy this is the largest class and,
when once assembled, its power is supreme.

Yes, but it will not often meet, unless it gets some share of the
honey.

Well, it always does get its share, when the leaders are distributing to the people what they have taken from the well-to-do,
always provided they can keep the lion's share for themselves.*
The plundered rich are driven to defend themselves in debate
before the Assembly and by any measures they can compass; and
then, even if they have no revolutionary designs, the other party
accuse them of plotting against the people and of being reactionary oligarchs. At last, when they see the people unwittingly mis-
led by such denunciation into attempts to treat them unjustly,
then, whether they wish it or not, they become reactionaries in
good earnest. There is no help for it; the poison is injected by the

---

* Pericles had introduced the payment of a small fee to enable country
people to come to Athens for service on juries. This was later increased to
an amount compensating for the loss of a day's work. After the Pelopon-
nesian War, citizens were paid for attending the Assembly. There were
also distributions of surplus revenue, corn-doles, and payments for festivals.
—Trans.

sting of those drones we spoke of. Then follow impeachments
and trials, in which each party arraigns the other.

Quite so.

And the people always put forward a single champion of their
interests, whom they nurse to greatness. Here, plainly enough,
is the root from which despotism invariably springs.*

Yes.

How does the transformation of the people's champion into a
despot begin? You have heard the legend they tell of the shrine
of Lycaean Zeus in Arcadia: how one who tastes a single piece
of human flesh mixed in with the flesh of the sacrificial victims
is fated to be changed into a wolf. In the same way the people's
champion, finding himself in full control of the mob, may not
scruple to shed a brother's blood; dragging him before a tribunal
with the usual unjust charges, he may foully murder him, blot-
ting out a man's life and tasting kindred blood with unhallowed
tongue and lips; he may send men to death or exile with hinted
promises of debts to be cancelled and estates to be redistributed.
Is it not thenceforth his inevitable fate either to be destroyed by
his enemies or to seize absolute power and be transformed from
a human being into a wolf?

It is.

Here, then, we have the party-leader in the civil war against
property. If he is banished, and then returns from exile in despite
of his enemies, he will come back a finished despot. If they cannot procure his banishment or death by denouncing him to the
state, they will conspire to assassinate him. Then comes the notorious device of all who have reached this stage in the despot's
career, the request for a bodyguard to keep the people's champion safe for them. The request is granted, because the people,
in their alarm on his account, have no fear for themselves.

Quite true.

This is a terrifying sight for the man of property, who is
charged with being not merely rich but the people's enemy. He
will follow the oracle's advice to Croesus,

> To flee by Hermus' pebbly shore,
> Dreading the coward's shame no more.[1]

Well, he would have little chance to dread it a second time.

True; if he is caught, no doubt he will be done to death;

* Aristotle (*Politics*, v. 5) observes that in the old days most despots had
risen from being demagogues. Cf. Herod. iii. 82.—Trans.

whereas our champion himself does not, like Hector's charioteer,[2] 'measure his towering length in dust,' but on the contrary, overthrows a host of rivals and stands erect in the chariot of the state, no longer protector of the people, but its absolute master.

Yes, it must come to that.

And now shall we describe the happy condition of the man and of the country which harbours a creature of this stamp?

By all means.

In the early days he has a smile and a greeting for everyone he meets; disclaims any absolute power; makes large promises to his friends and to the public; sets about the relief of debtors and the distribution of land to the people and to his supporters; and assumes a mild and gracious air towards everybody. But as soon as he has disembarrassed himself of his exiled enemies by coming to terms with some and destroying others, he begins stirring up one war after another, in order that the people may feel their need of a leader, and also be so impoverished by taxation that they will be forced to think of nothing but winning their daily bread, instead of plotting against him. Moreover, if he suspects some of cherishing thoughts of freedom and not submiting to his rule, he will find a pretext for putting them at the enemy's mercy and so making away with them. For all these reasons a despot must be constantly provoking wars.

He must.

This course will lead to his being hated by his countrymen more and more. Also, the bolder spirits among those who have helped him to power and now hold positions of influence will begin to speak their mind to him and among themselves and to criticize his policy. If the despot is to maintain his rule, he must gradually make away with all these malcontents, until he has not a friend or an enemy left who is of any account. He will need to keep a sharp eye open for anyone who is courageous or highminded or intelligent or rich; it is his happy fate to be at war with all such, whether he likes it or not, and to lay his plans against them until he has purged the commonwealth.*

* At *Gorg.* 510 B Socrates remarks that a despot cannot make friends with his betters, whom he will fear, or with his inferiors, whom he will despise, but only with men of like character, who will truckle to him. In *Ep.* vii 332 C Plato says that Dionysius I was too clever to trust anyone, and 'there is no surer sign of moral character than the lack of trustworthy friends.'—Trans.

A fine sort of purgation!

Yes, the exact opposite of the medical procedure, which removes the worst elements in the bodily condition and leaves the best.

There seems to be no choice, if he is to hold his power.

No; he is confined to the happy alternatives of living with people most of whom are good for nothing and who hate him into the bargain, or not living at all. And the greater the loathing these actions inspire in his countrymen, the more he will need trustworthy recruits to strengthen his bodyguard. Where will he turn to find men on whom he can rely?

They will come flocking of their own accord, if he offers enough pay.

Foreigners of all sorts, you mean—yet another swarm of drones. But why not draw upon the home supply? He could rob the citizens of their slaves, emancipate them, and enroll them in his bodyguard.

No doubt they would be the most faithful adherents he could find.

What an enviable condition for the despot, to put his trust in such friends as these, when he has made away with his earlier supporters! He will, of course, be the admiration of all this band of new-made citizens, whose company he will enjoy when every decent person shuns him with loathing. It is not for nothing that the tragic drama is thought to be a storehouse of wisdom, and above all Euripides, whose profundity of thought appears in the remark that 'despots grow wise by converse with the wise,' meaning no doubt by the wise these associates we have described.

Yes, and Euripides praises absolute power as godlike, with much more to the same effect. So do the other poets.*

That being so, the tragedians will give a further proof of their wisdom if they will excuse us and all states whose constitution resembles ours, when we deny them admittance on the ground that they sing the praises of despotism. At the same time, I expect they will go the round of other states, where they will hire actors with fine sonorous voices to sway the inclination of the assembled crowd towards a despotic or a democratic constitution. Naturally they are honoured and well paid for these serv-

* The ancients often quote lines from the tragedians, as many people now quote Shakespeare, without regard to the context or the fact that a dramatist is not responsible for all the sentiments expressed by his characters.—Trans.

ices, by despots chiefly, and in a less degree by democracies. But the higher they mount up the scale of commonwealths, the more their reputation flags, like a climber who gives in for lack of breath. However, we are wandering from our subject. Let us go back to the despot's army. How is he to maintain this fine, ever-shifting array of nondescripts?

No doubt he will spend any treasure there may be in the temples,* so long as it will last, as well as the property of his victims, thus lightening the war-taxes imposed on the people.

And when that source fails?

Clearly he will support himself, with his boon-companions, minions, and mistresses, from his parent's estate.

I understand: the despot and his comrades will be maintained by the common people which gave him birth.

Inevitably.

But how if the people resent this and say it is not right for the father to support his grown-up son—it ought to be the other way about; they did not bring him into being and set him up in order that, when he had grown great, they should be the slaves of their own slaves and support them together with their master and the rest of his rabble; he was to be the champion to set them free from the rich and the so-called upper class. Suppose they now order him and his partisans to leave the country, as a father might drive his son out of the house along with his riotous friends?

Then, to be sure, the people will learn what sort of a creature it has bred and nursed to greatness in its bosom, until now the child is too strong for the parent to drive out.

Do you mean that the despot will dare to lay violent hands on this father of his and beat him if he resists?

Yes, when once he has disarmed him.

So the despot is a parricide, with no pity for the weakness of age. Here, it seems, is absolutism openly avowed. The people, as they say, have escaped the smoke only to fall into the fire, exchanging service to free men for the tyranny of slaves. That freedom which knew no bounds must now put on the livery of the most harsh and bitter servitude, where the slave has become the master.

Yes, that is what happens.

---

* In the ancient world temples were to some extent used like banks for the safe deposit of valuables, since robbery would involve the additional guilt of sacrilege.—Trans.

May we say, then, that we have now sufficiently described the transition from democracy to despotism, and what despotism is like when once established?

Yes, quite sufficiently.

Last comes the man of despotic character. It remains to ask how he develops from the democratic type, what he is like, and whether his life is one of happiness or of misery.

Yes.

Here I feel the need to define, more fully than we have so far done, the number and nature of the appetites. Otherwise it will not be so easy to see our way to a conclusion.

Well, it is not too late.

Quite so. Now, about the appetites, here is the point I want to make plain. Among the unnecessary pleasures and desires, some, I should say, are unlawful. Probably they are innate in everyone; but when they are disciplined by law and by the higher desires with the aid of reason, they can in some people be got rid of entirely, or at least left few and feeble, although in others they will be comparatively strong and numerous.

What kind of desires do you mean?

Those which bestir themselves in dreams, when the gentler part of the soul slumbers and the control of reason is withdrawn; then the wild beast in us, full-fed with meat or drink, becomes rampant and shakes off sleep to go in quest of what will gratify its own instincts. As you know, it will cast away all shame and prudence at such moments and stick at nothing. In phantasy it will not shrink from intercourse with a mother or anyone else, man, god, or brute, or from forbidden food or any deed of blood. In a word, it will go to any length of shamelessness and folly.

Quite true.

It is otherwise with a man sound in body and mind, who, before he goes to sleep, awakens the reason within him to feed on high thoughts and questionings in collected meditation. If he has neither starved nor surfeited his appetites, so that, lulled to rest, no delights or griefs of theirs may trouble that better part, but leave it free to reach out, in pure and independent thought, after some new knowledge of things past, present, or to come; if, likewise, he has soothed his passions so as not to fall asleep with his anger roused against any man; if, in fact, he does not take his rest until he has quieted two of the three elements in his soul and awakened the third wherein wisdom dwells, then he is in a fair way to grasp the truth of things, and the visions of his dreams will not be unlawful. However, we have been carried away from our point, which is that in every one of us, even those who seem most respectable, there exist desires, terrible in their untamed lawlessness, which reveal themselves in dreams. Do you agree?

I do.

Remember, then, our account of the democratic man, how his character was shaped by his early training under a parsimonious father, who respected only the businesslike desires, dismissing the unnecessary ones as concerned with frivolous embellishments. Then, associating with more sophisticated people who were a prey to those lawless appetites we have just described, he fell into their ways, and hatred of his father's miserliness drove him into every sort of extravagance. But, having a better disposition than his corrupters, he came to a compromise between the two conflicting ways of life, making the best of both with what he called moderation and avoiding alike the meanness of the one and the licence of the other. So the oligarchical man was transformed into the democratic type.

Yes, I hold by that description.

Now imagine him grown old in his turn, with a young son bred in his ways, who is exposed to the same influences, drawn towards the utter lawlessness which his seducers call perfect freedom, while on the other side his father and friends lend their support to the compromise. When those terrible wizards who would conjure up an absolute ruler in the young man's soul begin to doubt the power of their spells, in the last resort they contrive to engender in him a master passion, to champion the mob of idle appetites which are for dividing among themselves all available plunder—a passion that can only be compared to a great winged drone. Like a swarm buzzing round this creature, the other desires come laden with incense and perfumes, garlands and wine, feeding its growth to the full on the pleasures of a dissolute life, until they have implanted the sting of a longing that cannot be satisfied.* Then at last this passion, as leader of the soul, takes madness for the captain of its guard and breaks out in frenzy; if it can lay hold upon any thoughts or desires that are of good report and still capable of shame, it kills them or

* The winged drone, it will be remembered, is naturally stingless. The word translated by 'passion' is *Eros*, and Eros was commonly pictured with wings.—Trans.

drives them forth, until it has purged the soul of all sobriety and called in the partisans of madness to fill the vacant place.

That is a complete picture of how the despotic character develops.

Is not this the reason why lust has long since been called a tyrant? A drunken man, too, has something of this tyrannical spirit; and so has the lunatic who dreams that he can lord it over all mankind and heaven besides. Thus, when nature or habit or both have combined the traits of drunkenness, lust, and lunacy, then you have the perfect specimen of the despotic man.

Quite true.

Such, then, being his origin and character, what will his life be like?

I give it up. You must tell me.

I will. When a master passion is enthroned in absolute dominion over every part of the soul, feasting and revelling with courtesans and all such delights will become the order of the day. And every day and night a formidable crop of fresh appetites springs up, whose numerous demands quickly consume whatever income there may be. Soon he will be borrowing and trenching on his capital; and when all resources fail, the lusty brood of appetites will crowd about him clamouring. Goaded on to frenzy by them and above all by that ruling passion to which they serve as a sort of bodyguard, he will look out for any man of property whom he can rob by fraud or violence. Money he must have, no matter how, if he is not to suffer torments.

All that is inevitable.

Now, just as a succession of new pleasures asserted themselves in his soul at the expense of the older ones, so this young man will claim the right to live at his parents' expense and help himself to their property when his own portion is spent. If they resist, he will first try to cheat them; and failing that, he will rob them by force. If the old people still hold out, will any scruple restrain him from behaving like a despot?

I should not have much hope for the parents of such a son.

And yet consider, Adeimantus: his father and mother have been bound to him by the closest ties all his life; and now that they are old and faded, would he really be ready to beat them for the sake of the charms of some new-found mistress or favourite who has no sort of claim on him? Is he going to bring these creatures under the same roof and let them lord it over his parents?

I believe he would.

It is no very enviable lot, then, to give birth to a despotic son.

It is not.

And now suppose that his parents' resources begin to fail, while his appetites for new pleasures have mustered into a great swarm in his soul; he will begin by breaking into someone's house or robbing a traveller by night, and go on to sweep some temple clean of its treasures. Meanwhile, the old approved beliefs about right and wrong which he had as a child will be overpowered by thoughts, once held in subjection, but now emancipated to second that master passion whose bodyguard they form. In his democratic days when he was still under the control of his father and of the laws, they broke loose only in sleep; but now that this passion has set up an absolute dominion, he has become for all his waking life the man he used to be from time to time in his dreams, ready to shed blood or eat forbidden food or do any dreadful deed. The desire that lives in him as sole ruler in a waste of lawless disrule will drive him, as a tyrant would drive his country, into any desperate venture which promises to maintain it with its horde of followers, some of whom evil communication has brought in from without, while others have been released from bondage by the same evil practices within. Is that a fair account of his manner of life?

Yes.

If there are a few such characters in a country where most men are law-abiding, they will go elsewhere to join some despot's bodyguard or serve as mercenaries in any war that is toward. In quiet times of peace, they stay at home and commit crimes on a small scale, as thieves, burglars, pickpockets, temple-robbers, kidnappers; or, if they have a ready tongue, they may take to selling their services as informers and false witnesses.

Such crimes will be a small matter, you mean, so long as the criminals are few in number.

Small is a relative term; and all of them put together do not, as they say, come within sight of the degradation and misery of society under a despot. When the number of such criminals and their hangers-on increases and they become aware of their strength, then it is they who, helped by the folly of the common people, create the despot out of that one among their number whose soul is itself under the most tyrannical despotism.

Yes, such a state of mind would naturally be his best qualification.

All goes smoothly if men are ready to submit. But the country may resist; and then, just as he began by calling his father and mother to order, so now he will discipline his once loved fatherland, or motherland as the Cretans call it, and see that it shall live in subjection to the new-found partisans he has called in to enslave it. So this man's desires come to their fulfilment.

Yes, that is true.

In private life, before they gain power, men of this stamp either consort with none but parasites ready to do them any service, or, if they have a favour to beg, they will not hesitate themselves to cringe and posture in simulated friendliness, which soon cools off when their end is gained. So, throughout life, the despotic character has not a friend in the world; he is sometimes master, sometimes slave, but never knows true friendship or freedom. There is no faithfulness in him; and, if we were right in our notion of justice, he is the perfect example of the unjust man.

Certainly.

*   *   *

Notes

1. Herodotus, i. 55.
2. *Iliad*, xvi. 776.

EMILE DURKHEIM

Three Types of Suicide

◆

Emile Durkheim, 1858–1917, was one of the founders of sociology. His primary interest was in the forms and causes of social cohesion, the forces that hold a community together and make it a group rather than merely a number of isolated individuals. In Suicide, *Durkheim employs the brilliant device of investigating social unity by focusing*

Reprinted with permission of The Free Press of Glencoe and Routledge & Kegan Paul Ltd. from Emile Durkheim, *Suicide,* translated by J. A. Spaulding and G. Simpson (New York: Free Press of Glencoe, 1951). Copyright 1951 by The Free Press, A Corporation.

attention upon the most dramatic kind of failure of that unity. If we understand under what conditions a man will sever connection with his social group, Durkheim thought, we will come closer to learning what normally binds him to it. Note carefully the definitions given by Durkheim of altruism, egoism, and anomie. Durkheim's collectivist conception of social man can be contrasted with the individualist portraits offered by Hobbes and Bentham.

Egoistic Suicide

We have thus successively set up the three following propositions:

Suicide varies inversely with the degree of integration of religious society.

Suicide varies inversely with the degree of integration of domestic society.

Suicide varies inversely with the degree of integration of political society.

This grouping shows that whereas these different societies have a moderating influence upon suicide, this is due not to special characteristics of each but to a characteristic common to all. Religion does not owe its efficacy to the special nature of religious sentiments, since domestic and political societies both produce the same effects when strongly integrated. This, moreover, we have already proved when studying directly the manner of action of different religions upon suicide. Inversely, it is not the specific nature of the domestic or political tie which can explain the immunity they confer, since religious society has the same advantage. The cause can only be found in a single quality possessed by all the social groups, though perhaps to varying degrees. The only quality satisfying this condition is that they are all strongly integrated social groups. So we reach the general conclusion: suicide varies inversely with the degree of integration of the social groups of which the individual forms a part.

But society cannot disintegrate without the individual simultaneously detaching himself from social life, without his own goals becoming preponderant over those of the community, in a word without his personality tending to surmount the collective personality. The more weakened the groups to which he belongs, the less he depends on them, the more he consequently depends only on himself and recognizes no other rules of conduct than what are founded on his private interests. If we agree to call this state egoism, in which the individual ego asserts itself to excess in the face of the social ego and at its expense, we may call egoistic the special type of suicide springing from excessive individualism.

But how can suicide have such an origin?

First of all, it can be said that, as collective force is one of the obstacles best calculated to restrain suicide, its weakening involves a development of suicide. When society is strongly integrated, it holds individuals under its control, considers them at its service and thus forbids them to dispose wilfully of themselves. Accordingly it opposes their evading their duties to it through death. But how could society impose its supremacy upon them when they refuse to accept this subordination as legitimate? It no longer then possesses the requisite authority to retain them in their duty if they wish to desert; and conscious of its own weakness, it even recognizes their right to do freely what it can no longer prevent. So far as they are the admitted masters of their destinies, it is their privilege to end their lives. They, on their part, have no reason to endure life's sufferings patiently. For they cling to life more resolutely when belonging to a group they love, so as not to betray interests they put before their own. The bond that unites them with the common cause attaches them to life and the lofty goal they envisage prevents their feeling personal troubles so deeply. There is, in short, in a cohesive and animated society a constant interchange of ideas and feelings from all to each and each to all, something like a mutual moral support, which instead of throwing the individual on his own resources, leads him to share in the collective energy and supports his own when exhausted.

But these reasons are purely secondary. Excessive individualism not only results in favoring the action of suicidogenic causes, but it is itself such a cause. It not only frees man's inclination to do away with himself from a protective obstacle, but creates this inclination out of whole cloth and thus gives birth to a special suicide which bears its mark. This must be clearly understood for this is what constitutes the special character of the type of suicide just distinguished and justifies the name we have given it. What is there then in individualism that explains this result?

It has been sometimes said that because of his psychological constitution, man cannot live without attachment to some object which transcends and survives him, and that the reason for this necessity is a need we must have not to perish entirely. Life is said to be intolerable unless some reason for existing is involved, some purpose justifying life's trials. The individual alone is not a sufficient end for his activity. He is too little. He is not only hemmed in spatially; he is also strictly limited temporally. When, therefore, we have no other object than ourselves we cannot avoid the thought that our efforts will finally end in nothingness, since we ourselves disappear. But annihilation terrifies us. Under these conditions one would lose courage to live, that is, to act and struggle, since nothing will remain of our exertions. The state of egoism, in other words, is supposed to be contradictory to human nature and, consequently, too uncertain to have chances of permanence.

In this absolute formulation the proposition is vulnerable. If the thought of the end of our personality were really so hateful, we could consent to live only by blinding ourselves voluntarily as to life's value. For if we may in a measure avoid the prospect of annihilation we cannot extirpate it; it is inevitable, whatever we do. We may push back the frontier for some generations, force our name to endure for some years or centuries longer than our body; a moment, too soon for most men, always comes when it will be nothing. For the groups we join in order to prolong our existence by their means are themselves mortal; they too must dissolve, carrying with them all our deposit of ourselves. Those are few whose memories are closely enough bound to the very history of humanity to be assured of living until its death. So, if we really thus thirsted after immortality, no such brief perspectives could ever appease us. Besides, what of us is it that lives? A word, a sound, an imperceptible trace, most often anonymous,* therefore nothing comparable to the violence of our efforts or able to justify them to us. In actuality, though a child is naturally an egoist who feels not the slightest craving to survive himself, and the old man is very often a child in this and so many other respects, neither ceases to cling to life as

---

* We say nothing of the ideal protraction of life involved in the belief in immortality of the soul, for (1) this cannot explain why the family or attachment to political society preserves us from suicide; and (2) it is not even this belief which forms religion's prophylactic influence, as we have shown above.

much or more than the adult; indeed we have seen that suicide is very rare for the first fifteen years and tends to decrease at the other extreme of life. Such too is the case with animals, whose psychological constitution differs from that of men only in degree. It is therefore untrue that life is only possible by its possessing its rationale outside of itself.

Indeed, a whole range of functions concern only the individual; these are the ones indispensable for physical life. Since they are made for this purpose only, they are perfected by its attainment. In everything concerning them, therefore, man can act reasonably without thought of transcendental purposes. These functions serve by merely serving him. In so far as he has no other needs, he is therefore self-sufficient and can live happily with no other objective than living. This is not the case, however, with the civilized adult. He has many ideas, feelings and practices unrelated to organic needs. The roles of art, morality, religion, political faith, science itself are not to repair organic exhaustion nor to provide sound functioning of the organs. All this supra-physical life is built and expanded not because of the demands of the cosmic environment but because of the demands of the social environment. The influence of society is what has aroused in us the sentiments of sympathy and solidarity drawing us toward others; it is society which, fashioning us in its image, fills us with religious, political and moral beliefs that control our actions. To play our social role we have striven to extend our intelligence and it is still society that has supplied us with tools for this development by transmitting to us its trust fund of knowledge.

Through the very fact that these superior forms of human activity have a collective origin, they have a collective purpose. As they derive from society they have reference to it; rather they are society itself incarnated and individualized in each one of us. But for them to have a raison d'etre in our eyes, the purpose they envisage must be one not indifferent to us. We can cling to these forms of human activity only to the degree that we cling to society itself. Contrariwise, in the same measure as we feel detached from society we become detached from that life whose source and aim is society. For what purpose do these rules of morality, these precepts of law binding us to all sorts of sacrifices, these restrictive dogmas exist, if there is no being outside us whom they serve and in whom we participate? What is the purpose of science itself? If its only use is to increase our chances for survival, it does not deserve the trouble it entails. Instinct acquits itself better of this role; animals prove this. Why substitute for it a more hesitant and uncertain reflection? What is the end of suffering, above all? If the value of things can only be estimated by their relation to this positive evil for the individual, it is without reward and incomprehensible. This problem does not exist for the believer firm in his faith or the man strongly bound by ties of domestic or political society. Instinctively and unreflectively they ascribe all that they are and do, the one to his Church or his God, the living symbol of the Church, the other to his family, the third to his country or party. Even in their sufferings they see only a means of glorifying the group to which they belong and thus do homage to it. So, the Christian ultimately desires and seeks suffering to testify more fully to his contempt for the flesh and more fully resemble his divine model. But the more the believer doubts, that is, the less he feels himself a real participant in the religious faith to which he belongs, and from which he is freeing himself; the more the family and community become foreign to the individual, so much the more does he become a mystery to himself, unable to escape the exasperating and agonizing question: to what purpose?

If, in other words, as has often been said, man is double, that is because social man superimposes himself upon physical man. Social man necessarily presupposes a society which he expresses and serves. If this dissolves, if we no longer feel it in existence and action about and above us, whatever is social in us is deprived of all objective foundation. All that remains is an artificial combination of illusory images, a phantasmagoria vanishing at the least reflection; that is, nothing which can be a goal for our action. Yet this social man is the essence of civilized man; he is the masterpiece of existence. Thus we are bereft of reasons for existence; for the only life to which we could cling no longer corresponds to anything actual; the only existence still based upon reality no longer meets our needs. Because we have been initiated into a higher existence, the one which satisfies an animal or a child can satisfy us no more and the other itself fades and leaves us helpless. So there is nothing more for our efforts to lay hold of, and we feel them lose themselves in emptiness. In this sense it is true to say that our activity needs an object transcending it. We do not need it to maintain ourselves in the illusion of an impossible immortality; it is implicit in our moral constitution and cannot be even partially lost without this losing its raison d'etre in the same degree. No proof is needed that in such a state of confusion the least cause of discouragement may easily give birth to desperate resolutions. If life is not worth the trouble of being lived, everything becomes a pretext to rid ourselves of it.

But this is not all. This detachment occurs not only in single individuals. One of the constitutive elements of every national temperament consists of a certain way of estimating the value of existence. There is a collective as well as an individual humor inclining peoples to sadness or cheerfulness, making them see things in bright or sombre lights. In fact, only society can pass a collective opinion on the value of human life; for this the individual is incompetent. The latter knows nothing but himself and his own little horizon; thus his experience is too limited to serve as a basis for a general appraisal. He may indeed consider his own life to be aimless; he can say nothing applicable to others. On the contrary, without sophistry, society may generalize its own feeling as to itself, its state of health or lack of health. For individuals share too deeply in the life of society for it to be diseased without their suffering infection. What it suffers they necessarily suffer. Because it is the whole, its ills are communicated to its parts. Hence it cannot disintegrate without awareness that the regular conditions of general existence are equally disturbed. Because society is the end on which our better selves depend, it cannot feel us escaping it without a simultaneous realization that our activity is purposeless. Since we are its handiwork, society cannot be conscious of its own decadence without the feeling that henceforth this work is of no value. Thence are formed currents of depression and disillusionment emanating from no particular individual but expressing society's state of disintegration. They reflect the relaxation of social bonds, a sort of collective asthenia, or social malaise, just as individual sadness, when chronic, in its way reflects the poor organic state of the individual. Then metaphysical and religious systems spring up which, by reducing these obscure sentiments to formulae, attempt to prove to men the senselessness of life and that it is self-deception to believe that it has purpose. Then new moralities originate which, by elevating facts to ethics, commend suicide or at least tend in that direction by suggesting a minimal existence. On their appearance they seem to have been created out of whole cloth by their makers who are sometimes blamed for the pessimism of their doctrines. In reality they are an effect rather than a cause; they merely symbolize in abstract language and systematic form the physiological distress of the body social.* As these currents are collective, they have, by virtue of their origin, an authority which they impose upon the individual and they drive him more vigorously on the way to which he is already inclined by the state of moral distress directly aroused in him by the disintegration of society. Thus, at the very moment that, with excessive zeal, he frees himself from the social environment, he still submits to its influence. However individualized a man may be, there is always something collective remaining—the very depression and melancholy resulting from this same exaggerated individualism. He effects communion through sadness when he no longer has anything else with which to achieve it.

Hence this type of suicide well deserves the name we have given it. Egoism is not merely a contributing factor in it; it is its generating cause. In this case the bond attaching man to life relaxes because that attaching him to society is itself slack. The incidents of private life which seem the direct inspiration of suicide and are considered its determining causes are in reality only incidental causes. The individual yields to the slightest shock of circumstance because the state of society has made him a ready prey to suicide.

Several facts confirm this explanation. Suicide is known to be rare among children and to diminish among the aged at the last confines of life; physical man, in both, tends to become the whole of man. Society is still lacking in the former, for it has not had the time to form him in its image; it begins to retreat from the latter or, what amounts to the same thing, he retreats from it. Thus both are more self-sufficient. Feeling a lesser need for self-completion through something not themselves, they are also less exposed to feel the lack of what is necessary for living. The immunity of an animal has the same causes. We shall likewise see in the next chapter that, though lower societies practice a form of suicide of their own, the one we have just discussed is almost unknown to them. Since their social life is very simple, the social inclinations of individuals are simple also and thus they need little for satisfaction. They readily find external objectives to which they become attached. If he can carry with

---

* This is why it is unjust to accuse these theorists of sadness of generalizing personal impressions. They are the echo of a general condition.

him his gods and his family, primitive man, everywhere that he goes, has all that his social nature demands.

This is also why woman can endure life in isolation more easily than man. When a widow is seen to endure her condition much better than a widower and desires marriage less passionately, one is led to consider this ease in dispensing with the family a mark of superiority; it is said that woman's affective faculties, being very intense, are easily employed outside the domestic circle, while her devotion is indispensable to man to help him endure life. Actually, if this is her privilege it is because her sensibility is rudimentary rather than highly developed. As she lives outside of community existence more than man, she is less penetrated by it; society is less necessary to her because she is less impregnated with sociability. She has few needs in this direction and satisfies them easily. With a few devotional practices and some animals to care for, the old unmarried woman's life is full. If she remains faithfully attached to religious traditions and thus finds ready protection against suicide, it is because these very simple social forms satisfy all her needs. Man, on the contrary, is hard beset in this respect. As his thought and activity develop, they increasingly overflow these antiquated forms. But then he needs others. Because he is a more complex social being, he can maintain his equilibrium only by finding more points of support outside himself, and it is because his moral balance depends on a larger number of conditions that it is more easily disturbed.

Altruistic Suicide [1]

In the order of existence, no good is measureless. A biological quality can only fulfill the purposes it is meant to serve on condition that it does not transgress certain limits. So with social phenomena. If, as we have just seen, excessive individuation leads to suicide, insufficient individuation has the same effects. When man has become detached from society, he encounters less resistance to suicide in himself, and he does so likewise when social integration is too strong.

I.

It has sometimes [2] been said that suicide was unknown among lower societies. Thus expressed, the assertion is inexact. To be sure, egoistic suicide, constituted as has just been shown, seems not to be frequent there. But another form exists among them in an endemic state.

Bartholin, in his book, *De Causis contemptae mortis a Danis,* reports that Danish warriors considered it a disgrace to die in bed of old age or sickness, and killed themselves to escape this ignominy. The Goths likewise believed that those who die a natural death are destined to languish forever in caverns full of venomous creatures.[3] On the frontier of the Visigoths' territory was a high pinnacle called *The Rock of the Forefathers,* from the top of which old men would throw themselves when weary of life. The same custom was found among the Thracians, the Heruli, etc. Silvius Italicus says of the Spanish Celts: "They are a nation lavish of their blood and eager to face death. As soon as the Celt has passed the age of mature strength, he endures the flight of time impatiently and scorns to await old age; the term of his existence depends upon himself." [4] Accordingly they assigned a delightful abode to those who committed suicide and a horrible subterranean one to those who died of sickness or decrepitude. The same custom has long been maintained in India. Perhaps this favorable attitude toward suicide did not appear in the Vedas, but it was certainly very ancient. Plutarch says concerning the suicide of the brahmin Calanus: "He sacrificed himself with his own hands as was customary with sages of this country." [5] And Quintus Curtius: "Among them exists a sort of wild and bestial men to whom they give the name of sages. The anticipation of the time of death is a glory in their eyes, and they have themselves burned alive as soon as age or sickness begins to trouble them. According to them, death, passively awaited, is a dishonor to life; thus no honors are rendered those bodies which old age has destroyed. Fire would be contaminated did it not receive the human sacrifice still breathing." [6] Similar facts are recorded at Fiji,[7] in the New Hebrides, Manga, etc.[8] At Ceos, men who had outlived a certain age used to unite in a solemn festival where with heads crowned with flowers they joyfully drank the hemlock.[9] Like practices were found among the Troglodytes [10] and the Seri, who were nevertheless renowned for their morality.[11]

Besides the old men, women are often required among the same peoples to kill themselves on their husbands' death. This barbarous practice is so ingrained in Hindu customs that the efforts of the English are futile against it. In 1817, 706 widows killed themselves in the one province of Bengal and in 1821, 2,366 were found in all India. Moreover, when a prince or chief dies, his followers are forced not to survive him. Such was the case in Gaul. The funerals of chiefs, Henri Martin declares, were bloody hecatombs where their garments, weapons, horses and favorite slaves were solemnly burned, together with the personal followers who had not died in the chief's last battle.[12] Such a follower was never to survive his chief. Among the Ashantis, on the king's death his officers must die.[13] Observers have found the same custom in Hawaii.[14]

Suicide, accordingly, is surely very common among primitive peoples. But it displays peculiar characteristics. All the facts above reported fall into one of the following three categories:

1. Suicides of men on the threshold of old age or stricken with sickness.

2. Suicides of women on their husbands' death.

3. Suicides of followers or servants on the death of their chiefs.

Now, when a person kills himself, in all these cases, it is not because he assumes the right to do so but, on the contrary, *because it is his duty*. If he fails in this obligation, he is dishonored and also punished, usually, by religious sanctions. Of course, when we hear of aged men killing themselves we are tempted at first to believe that the cause is weariness or the sufferings common to age. But if these suicides really had no other source, if the individual made away with himself merely to be rid of an unendurable existence, he would not be required to do so; one is never obliged to take advantage of a privilege. Now, we have seen that if such a person insists on living he loses public respect; in one case the usual funeral honors are denied, in another a life of horror is supposed to await him beyond the grave. The weight of society is thus brought to bear on him to lead him to destroy himself. To be sure, society intervenes in egoistic suicide, as well; but its intervention differs in the two cases. In one case, it speaks the sentence of death; in the other it forbids the choice of death. In the case of egoistic suicide it suggests or counsels at most; in the other case it compels and is the author of conditions and circumstances making this obligation coercive.

This sacrifice then is imposed by society for social ends. If the follower must not survive his chief or the servant his prince, this is because so strict an interdependence between followers and chiefs, officers and king, is involved in the constitution of the society that any thought of separation is out of the question. The destiny of one must be that of the others. Subjects as well as clothing and armor must follow their master wherever he goes, even beyond the tomb; if another possibility were to be admitted social subordination would be inadequate.* Such is the relation of the woman to her husband. As for the aged, if they are not allowed to await death, it is probably, at least in many instances, for religious reasons. The protecting spirit of a family is supposed to reside in its chief. It is further thought that a god inhabiting the body of another shares in his life, enduring the same phases of health and sickness and aging with him. Age cannot therefore reduce the strength of one without the other being similarly weakened and consequently without the group existence being threatened, since a strengthless divinity would be its only remaining protector. For this reason, in the common interest, a father is required not to await the furthest limit of life before transferring to his successors the precious trust that is in his keeping.[15]

This description sufficiently defines the cause of these suicides. For society to be able thus to compel some of its members to kill themselves, the individual personality can have little value. For as soon as the latter begins to form, the right to existence is the first conceded it; or is at least suspended only in such unusual circumstances as war. But there can be only one cause for this feeble individuation itself. For the individual to occupy so little place in collective life he must be almost completely absorbed in the group and the latter, accordingly, very highly integrated. For the parts to have so little life of their own, the whole must indeed be a compact, continuous mass. And we have shown elsewhere that such massive cohesion is indeed that of societies where the above practices obtain.[16] As they consist of few elements, everyone leads the same life; everything is common to all, ideas, feelings, occupations. Also, because of the small size of the group it is close to everyone and loses no one from sight; consequently collective supervision is constant, extending to every-

* At the foundation of these practices there is probably also the desire to prevent the spirit of the dead man from returning to earth to revisit the objects and persons closely associated with him. But this very desire implies that servants and followers are strictly subordinated to their master, inseparable from him, and, furthermore, that to avoid the disaster of the spirit's remaining on earth they must sacrifice themselves in the common interest.

thing, and thus more readily prevents divergences. The individual thus has no way to set up an environment of his own in the shelter of which he may develop his own nature and form a physiognomy that is his exclusively. To all intents and purposes indistinct from his companions, he is only an inseparable part of the whole without personal value. His person has so little value that attacks upon it by individuals receive only relatively weak restraint. It is thus natural for him to be yet less protected against collective necessities and that society should not hesitate, for the very slightest reason, to bid him end a life it values so little.

We thus confront a type of suicide differing by incisive qualities from the preceding one. Whereas the latter is due to excessive individuation, the former is caused by too rudimentary individuation. One occurs because society allows the individual to escape it, being insufficiently aggregated in some parts or even in the whole; the other, because society holds him in too strict tutelage. Having given the name of *egoism* to the state of the ego living its own life and obeying itself alone, that of *altruism* adequately expresses the opposite state, where the ego is not its own property, where it is blended with something not itself, where the goal of conduct is exterior to itself, that is, in one of the groups in which it participates. So we call the suicide caused by intense altruism *altruistic suicide*. But since it is also characteristically performed as a duty, the terminology adopted should express this fact. So we will call such a type *obligatory altruistic suicide*.

The combination of these two adjectives is required to define it; for not every altrustic suicide is necessarily obligatory. Some are not so expressly imposed by society, having a more optional character.

*   *   *

II.

No living being can be happy or even exist unless his needs are sufficiently proportioned to his means. In other words, if his needs require more than can be granted, or even merely something of a different sort, they will be under continual friction and can only function painfully. Movements incapable of production without pain tend not to be reproduced. Unsatisfied tendencies atrophy, and as the impulse to live is merely the result of all the rest, it is bound to weaken as the others relax.

In the animal, at least in a normal condition, this equilibrium is established with automatic spontaneity because the animal depends on purely material conditions. All the organism needs is that the supplies of substance and energy constantly employed in the vital process should be periodically renewed by equivalent quantities; that replacement be equivalent to use. When the void created by existence in its own resources is filled, the animal, satisfied, asks nothing further. Its power of reflection is not sufficiently developed to imagine other ends than those implicit in its physical nature. On the other hand, as the work demanded of each organ itself depends on the general state of vital energy and the needs of organic equilibrium, use is regulated in turn by replacement and the balance is automatic. The limits of one are those of the other; both are fundamental to the constitution of the existence in question, which cannot exceed them.

This is not the case with man, because most of his needs are not dependent on his body or not to the same degree. Strictly speaking, we may consider that the quantity of material supplies necessary to the physical maintenance of a human life is subject to computation, though this be less exact than in the preceding case and a wider margin left for the free combinations of the will; for beyond the indispensable minimum which satisfies nature when instinctive, a more awakened reflection suggests better conditions, seemingly desirable ends craving fulfillment. Such appetites, however, admittedly sooner or later reach a limit which they cannot pass. But how determine the quantity of well-being, comfort or luxury legitimately to be craved by a human being? Nothing appears in man's organic nor in his psychological constitution which sets a limit to such tendencies. The functioning of individual life does not require them to cease at one point rather than at another; the proof being that they have constantly increased since the beginnings of history, receiving more and complete satisfaction, yet with no weakening of average health. Above all, how establish their proper variation with different conditions of life, occupations, relative importance of services, etc.? In no society are they equally satisfied in the different stages of the social hierarchy. Yet human nature is substantially the same among all men, in its essential qualities. It is not human nature which can assign the variable limits necessary to our needs. They are thus unlimited so far as they depend on the individual alone. Irrespective of any external regulatory force, our capacity for feeling is in itself an insatiable and bottomless abyss.

But if nothing external can restrain this capacity, it can only be a source of torment to itself. Unlimited desires are insatiable by definition and insatiability is rightly considered a sign of morbidity. Being unlimited, they constantly and infinitely surpass the means at their command; they cannot be quenched. Inextinguishable thirst is constantly renewed torture. It has been claimed, indeed, that human activity naturally aspires beyond assignable limits and sets itself unattainable goals. But how can such an undetermined state be any more reconciled with the conditions of mental life than with the demands of physical life? All man's pleasure in acting, moving and exerting himself implies the sense that his efforts are not in vain and that by walking he has advanced. However, one does not advance when one walks toward no goal, or—which is the same thing—when his goal is infinity. Since the distance between us and it is always the same, whatever road we take, we might as well have made the motions without progress from the spot. Even our glances behind and our feeling of pride at the distance covered can cause only deceptive satisfaction, since the remaining distance is not proportionately reduced. To pursue a goal which is by definition unattainable is to condemn oneself to a state of perpetual unhappiness. Of course, man may hope contrary to all reason, and hope has its pleasures even when unreasonable. It may sustain him for a time; but it cannot survive the repeated disappointments of experience indefinitely. What more can the future offer him than the past, since he can never reach a tenable condition nor even approach the glimpsed ideal? Thus, the more one has, the more one wants, since satisfactions received only stimulate instead of filling needs. Shall action as such be considered agreeable? First, only on condition of blindness to its uselessness. Secondly, for this pleasure to be felt and to temper and half veil the accompanying painful unrest, such unending motion must at least always be easy and unhampered. If it is interfered with only restlessness is left, with the lack of ease which it, itself, entails. But it would be a miracle if no insurmountable obstacle were never encountered. Our thread of life on these conditions is pretty thin, breakable at any instant.

To achieve any other result, the passions first must be limited.

Only then can they be harmonized with the faculties and satisfied. But since the individual has no way of limiting them, this must be done by some force exterior to him. A regulative force must play the same role for moral needs which the organism plays for physical needs. This means that the force can only be moral. The awakening of conscience interrupted the state of equilibrium of the animal's dormant existence; only conscience, therefore, can furnish the means to re-establish it. Physical restraint would be ineffective; hearts cannot be touched by physiochemical forces. So far as the appetites are not automatically restrained by physiological mechanisms, they can be halted only by a limit that they recognize as just. Men would never consent to restrict their desires if they felt justified in passing the assigned limit. But, for reasons given above, they cannot assign themselves this law of justice. So they must receive it from an authority which they respect, to which they yield spontaneously. Either directly and as a whole, or through the agency of one of its organs, society alone can play this moderating role; for it is the only moral power superior to the individual, the authority of which he accepts. It alone has the power necessary to stipulate law and to set the point beyond which the passions must not go. Finally, it alone can estimate the reward to be prospectively offered to every class of human functionary, in the name of the common interest.

As a matter of fact, at every moment of history there is a dim perception, in the moral consciousness of societies, of the respective value of different social services, the relative reward due to each, and the consequent degree of comfort appropriate on the average to workers in each occupation. The different functions are graded in public opinion and a certain coefficient of well-being assigned to each, according to its place in the hierarchy. According to accepted ideas, for example, a certain way of living is considered the upper limit to which a workman may aspire in his efforts to improve his existence, and there is another limit below which he is not willingly permitted to fall unless he has seriously bemeaned himself. Both differ for city and country workers, for the domestic servant and the day-laborer, for the business clerk and the official, etc. Likewise the man of wealth is reproved if he lives the life of a poor man, but also if he seeks the refinements of luxury overmuch. Economists may protest in vain; public feeling will always be scandalized if an individual spends too much wealth for wholly superfluous use, and it even seems that this severity relaxes only in times of moral disturbance.* A genuine regimen exists, therefore, although not always legally formulated, which fixes with relative precision the maximum degree of ease of living to which each social class may legitimately aspire. However, there is nothing immutable about such a scale. It changes with the increase or decrease of collective revenue and the changes occurring in the moral ideas of society. Thus what appears luxury to one period no longer does so to another; and the well-being which for long periods was granted to a class only by exception and supererogation, finally appears strictly necessary and equitable.

Under this pressure, each in his sphere vaguely realizes the extreme limit set to his ambitions and aspires to nothing beyond. At least if he respects regulations and is docile to collective authority, that is, has a wholesome moral constitution, he feels that it is not well to ask more. Thus, an end and goal are set to the passions. Truly, there is nothing rigid nor absolute about such determination. The economic ideal assigned each class of citizens is itself confined to certain limits, within which the desires have free range. But it is not infinite. This relative limitation and the moderation it involves, make men contented with their lot while stimulating them moderately to improve it; and this average contentment causes the feeling of calm, active happiness, the pleasure in existing and living which characterizes health for societies as well as for individuals. Each person is then at least, generally speaking, in harmony with his condition, and desires only what he may legitimately hope for as the normal reward of his activity. Besides, this does not condemn man to a sort of immobility. He may seek to give beauty to his life; but his attempts in this direction may fail without causing him to despair. For, loving what he has and not fixing his desire solely on what he lacks, his wishes and hopes may fail of what he has happened to aspire to, without his being wholly destitute. He has the essentials. The equilibrium of his happiness is secure because it is defined, and a few mishaps cannot disconcert him.

But it would be of little use for everyone to recognize the justice of the hierarchy of functions established by public opin-

---

* Actually, this is a purely moral reprobation and can hardly be judicially implemented. We do not consider any reestablishment of sumptuary laws desirable or even possible.

ion, if he did not also consider the distribution of these functions just. The workman is not in harmony with his social position if he is not convinced that he has his deserts. If he feels justified in occupying another, what he has would not satisfy him. So it is not enough for the average level of needs for each social condition to be regulated by public opinion, but another, more precise rule, must fix the way in which these conditions are open to individuals. There is no society in which such regulation does not exist. It varies with times and places. Once it regarded birth as the almost exclusive principle of social classification; today it recognizes no other inherent inequality than hereditary fortune and merit. But in all these various forms its object is unchanged. It is also only possible, everywhere, as a restriction upon individuals imposed by superior authority, that is, by collective authority. For it can be established only by requiring of one or another group of men, usually of all, sacrifices and concessions in the name of the public interest.

Some, to be sure, have thought that this moral pressure would become unnecessary if men's economic circumstances were only no longer determined by heredity. If inheritance were abolished, the argument runs, if everyone began life with equal resources and if the competitive struggle were fought out on a basis of perfect equality, no one could think its results unjust. Each would instinctively feel that things are as they should be.

Truly, the nearer this ideal equality were approached, the less social restraint will be necessary. But it is only a matter of degree. One sort of heredity will always exist, that of natural talent. Intelligence, taste, scientific, artistic, literary or industrial ability, courage and manual dexterity are gifts received by each of us at birth, as the heir to wealth receives his capital or as the nobleman formerly received his title and function. A moral discipline will therefore still be required to make those less favored by nature accept the lesser advantages which they owe to the chance of birth. Shall it be demanded that all have an equal share and that no advantage be given those more useful and deserving? But then there would have to be a discipline far stronger to make these accept a treatment merely equal to that of the mediocre and incapable.

But like the one first mentioned, this discipline can be useful only if considered just by the peoples subject to it. When it is maintained only by custom and force, peace and harmony are illusory; the spirit of unrest and discontent are latent; appetites superficially restrained are ready to revolt. This happened in Rome and Greece when the faiths underlying the old organization of the patricians and plebeians were shaken, and in our modern societies when aristocratic prejudices began to lose their old ascendancy. But this state of upheaval is exceptional; it occurs only when society is passing through some abnormal crisis. In normal conditions the collective order is regarded as just by the great majority of persons. Therefore, when we say that an authority is necessary to impose this order on individuals, we certainly do not mean that violence is the only means of establishing it. Since this regulation is meant to restrain individual passions, it must come from a power which dominates individuals; but this power must also be obeyed through respect, not fear.

It is not true, then, that human activity can be released from all restraint. Nothing in the world can enjoy such a privilege. All existence being a part of the universe is relative to the remainder; its nature and method of manifestation accordingly depend not only on itself but on other beings, who consequently restrain and regulate it. Here there are only differences of degree and form between the mineral realm and the thinking person. Man's characteristic privilege is that the bond he accepts is not physical but moral; that is, social. He is governed not by a material environment brutally imposed on him, but by a conscience superior to his own, the superiority of which he feels. Because the greater, better part of his existence transcends the body, he escapes the body's yoke, but is subject to that of society.

But when society is disturbed by some painful crisis or by beneficent but abrupt transitions, it is momentarily incapable of exercising this influence; thence come the sudden rises in the curve of suicides which we have pointed out above.

In the case of economic disasters, indeed, something like a declassification occurs which suddenly casts certain individuals into a lower state than their previous one. Then they must reduce their requirements, restrain their needs, learn greater self-control. All the advantages of social influence are lost so far as they are concerned; their moral education has to be recommenced. But society cannot adjust them instantaneously to this new life and teach them to practice the increased self-repression to which they are unaccustomed. So they are not adjusted to the condition forced on them, and its very prospect is intolerable; hence the suffering which detaches them from a reduced existence even before they have made trial of it.

It is the same if the source of the crisis is an abrupt growth of power and wealth. Then, truly, as the conditions of life are changed, the standard according to which needs were regulated can no longer remain the same; for it varies with social resources, since it largely determines the share of each class of producers. The scale is upset; but a new scale cannot be immediately improvised. Time is required for the public conscience to reclassify men and things. So long as the social forces thus freed have not regained equilibrium, their respective values are unknown and so all regulation is lacking for a time. The limits are unknown between the possible and the impossible, what is just and what is unjust, legitimate claims and hopes and those which are immoderate. Consequently, there is no restraint upon aspirations. If the disturbance is profound, it affects even the principles controlling the distribution of men among various occupations. Since the relations between various parts of society are necessarily modified, the ideas expressing these relations must change. Some particular class especially favored by the crisis is no longer resigned to its former lot, and, on the other hand, the example of its greater good fortune arouses all sorts of jealousy below and about it. Appetites, not being controlled by a public opinion become disoriented, no longer recognize the limits proper to them. Besides, they are at the same time seized by a sort of natural erethism simply by the greater intensity of public life. With increased prosperity desires increase. At the very moment when traditional rules have lost their authority, the richer prize offered these appetites stimulates them and makes them more exigent and impatient of control. The state of de-regulation or anomy is thus further heightened by passions being less disciplined, precisely when they need more disciplining.

But then their very demands make fulfillment impossible. Over-weening ambition always exceeds the results obtained, great as they may be, since there is no warning to pause here. Nothing gives satisfaction and all this agitation is uninterruptedly maintained without appeasement. Above all, since this race for an unattainable goal can give no other pleasure but that of the race itself, if it is one, once it is interrupted the participants are left empty-handed. At the same time the struggle grows more violent and painful, both from being less controlled and because competition is greater. All classes contend among themselves because no established classification any longer exists. Effort grows, just when it becomes less productive. How could the desire to live not be weakened under such conditions?

This explanation is confirmed by the remarkable immunity of poor countries. Poverty protects against suicide because it is a restraint in itself. No matter how one acts, desires have to depend upon resources to some extent; actual possessions are partly the criterion of those aspired to. So the less one has the less he is tempted to extend the range of his needs indefinitely. Lack of power, compelling moderation, accustoms men to it, while nothing excites envy if no one has superfluity. Wealth, on the other hand, by the power it bestows, deceives us into believing that we depend on ourselves only. Reducing the resistance we encounter from objects, it suggests the possibility of unlimited success against them. The less limited one feels, the more intolerable all limitation appears. Not without reason, therefore, have so many religions dwelt on the advantages and moral value of poverty. It is actually the best school for teaching self-restraint. Forcing us to constant self-discipline, it prepares us to accept collective discipline with equanimity, while wealth, exalting the individual, may always arouse the spirit of rebellion which is the very source of immorality. This, of course, is no reason why humanity should not improve its material condition. But though the moral danger involved in every growth of prosperity is not irremediable, it should not be forgotten.

III.

If anomy never appeared except, as in the above instances, in intermittent spurts and acute crisis, it might cause the social suicide-rate to vary from time to time, but it would not be a regular, constant factor. In one sphere of social life, however—the sphere of trade and industry—it is actually in a chronic state.

For a whole century, economic progress has mainly consisted in freeing industrial relations from all regulation. Until very recently, it was the function of a whole system of moral forces to exert this discipline. First, the influence of religion was felt alike by workers and masters, the poor and the rich. It consoled the former and taught them contentment with their lot by informing them of the providential nature of the social order, that the share of each class was assigned by God himself, and by holding out the hope for just compensation in a world to come in return for the inequalities of this world. It governed the latter, recalling that worldly interests are not man's entire lot, that they must be subordinate to other and higher interests, and that they should therefore not be pursued without rule or measure. Temporal power, in turn, restrained the scope of economic functions by its supremacy over them and by the relatively subordinate role it assigned them. Finally, within the business world proper, the occupational groups by regulating salaries, the price of products and production itself, indirectly fixed the average level of income on which needs are partially based by the very force of circumstances. However, we do not mean to propose this organization as a model. Clearly it would be inadequate to existing societies without great changes. What we stress is its existence, the fact of its useful influence, and that nothing today has come to take its place.

Actually, religion has lost most of its power. And government, instead of regulating economic life, has become its tool and servant. The most opposite schools, orthodox economists and extreme socialists, unite to reduce government to the role of a more or less passive intermediary among the various social functions. The former wish to make it simply the guardian of individual contracts; the latter leave it the task of doing the collective bookkeeping, that is, of recording the demands of consumers, transmitting them to producers, inventorying the total revenue and distributing it according to a fixed formula. But both refuse it any power to subordinate other social organs to itself and to make them converge toward one dominant aim. On both sides nations are declared to have the single or chief purpose of achieving industrial prosperity; such is the implication of the dogma of economic materialism, the basis of both apparently opposed systems. And as these theories merely express the state of opinion, industry, instead of being still regarded as a means to an end transcending itself, has become the supreme end of individuals and societies alike. Thereupon the appetites thus excited have become freed of any limiting authority. By sanctifying them, so to speak, this apotheosis of well-being has placed them above all human law. Their restraint seems like a sort of sacrilege. For this reason, even the purely utilitarian regulation of them exercised by the industrial world itself through the medium of occupational groups has been unable to persist. Ultimately, this liberation of desires has been made worse by the very development of industry and the almost infinite extension of the market. So long as the producer could gain his profits only in his immediate neighborhood, the restricted amount of possible gain could not much overexcite ambition. Now that he may assume to have almost the entire world as his customer, how could passions accept their former confinement in the face of such limitless prospects?

Such is the source of the excitement predominating in this part of society, and which has thence extended to the other parts. There, the state of crisis and anomy is constant and, so to speak, normal. From top to bottom of the ladder, greed is aroused without knowing where to find ultimate foothold. Nothing can calm it, since its goal is far beyond all it can attain. Reality seems valueless by comparison with the dreams of fevered imaginations; reality is therefore abandoned, but so too is possibility abandoned when it in turn becomes reality. A thirst arises for novelties, unfamiliar pleasures, nameless sensations, all of which lose their savor once known. Henceforth one has no strength to endure the least reverse. The whole fever subsides and the sterility of all the tumult is apparent, and it is seen that all these new sensations in their infinite quantity cannot form a solid foundation of happiness to support one during days of trial. The wise man, knowing how to enjoy achieved results without having constantly to replace them with others, finds in them an attachment to life in the hour of difficulty. But the man who has always pinned all his hopes on the future and lived with his eyes fixed upon it, has nothing in the past as a comfort against the present's afflictions, for the past was nothing to him but a series of hastily experienced stages. What blinded him to himself was his expectation always to find further on the happiness he had so far missed. Now he is stopped in his tracks; from now on nothing remains behind or ahead of him to fix his gaze upon. Weariness alone, moreover, is enough to bring disillusionment, for he cannot in the end escape the futility of an endless pursuit.

We may even wonder if this moral state is not principally what makes economic catastrophes of our day so fertile in suicides. In societies where a man is subjected to a healthy discipline, he submits more readily to the blows of chance. The necessary effort for sustaining a little more discomfort costs him relatively little, since he is used to discomfort and constraint. But when every constraint is hateful in itself, how can closer constraint not seem intolerable? There is no tendency to resignation in the feverish impatience of men's lives. When there is no other aim but to outstrip constantly the point arrived at, how painful to be thrown back! Now this very lack of organization characterizing our economic condition throws the door wide to every sort of adventure. Since imagination is hungry for novelty, and ungoverned, it gropes at random. Setbacks necessarily increase with risks and thus crises multiply, just when they are becoming more destructive.

Yet these dispositions are so inbred that society has grown to accept them and is accustomed to think them normal. It is everlastingly repeated that it is man's nature to be eternally dissatisfied, constantly to advance, without relief or rest, toward an indefinite goal. The longing for infinity is daily represented as a mark of moral distinction, whereas it can only appear within unregulated consciences which elevate to a rule the lack of rule from which they suffer. The doctrine of the most ruthless and swift progress has become an article of faith. But other theories appear parallel with those praising the advantages of instability, which, generalizing the situation that gives them birth, declare life evil, claim that it is richer in grief than in pleasure and that it attracts men only by false claims. Since this disorder is greatest in the economic world, it has most victims there.

Industrial and commercial functions are really among the occupations which furnish the greatest number of suicides (see Table, p. 343). Almost on a level with the liberal professions, they sometimes surpass them; they are especially more afflicted than agriculture, where the old regulative forces still make their appearance felt most and where the fever of business has least penetrated. Here is best recalled what was once the general constitution of the economic order. And the divergence would be yet greater if, among the suicides of industry, employers were distinguished from workmen, for the former are probably most stricken by the state of anomy. The enormous rate of those with independent means (720 per million) sufficiently shows that the possessors of most comfort suffer most. Everything that enforces subordination attenuates the effects of this state. At least the horizon of the lower classes is limited by those above them, and for this same reason their desires are more modest. Those who have only empty space above them are almost inevitably lost in it, if no force restrains them.

TABLE: SUICIDES PER MILLION PERSONS OF DIFFERENT
OCCUPATIONS

	Trade	Trans- portation	Industry	Agricul- ture	Liberal* Pro- fessions
France (1878–87) †	440	. . . . .	340	240	300
Switzerland (1876)	664	1,514	577	304	558
Italy (1866–76)	277	152.6	80.4	26.7	618 ‡
Prussia (1883–90)	754	. . . . .	456	315	832
Bavaria (1884–91)	465	. . . . .	369	153	454
Belgium (1886–90)	421	. . . . .	160	160	100
Wurttemberg (1873–78)	273	. . . . .	190	206	. . .
Saxony (1878)		341.59 §		71.17	. . .

* When statistics distinguish several different sorts of liberal occupations, we show as a specimen the one in which the suicide-rate is highest.

† From 1826 to 1880 economic functions seem less affected (see *Compte-rendu* of 1880); but were occupational statistics very accurate?

‡ This figure is reached only by men of letters.

§ Figure represents Trade, Transportation and Industry combined for Saxony. Ed.

Anomy, therefore, is a regular and specific factor in suicide in our modern societies; one of the springs from which the annual contingent feeds. So we have here a new type to distinguish from the others. It differs from them in its dependence, not on the way in which individuals are attached to society, but on how it regulates them. Egoistic suicide results from man's no longer finding a basis for existence in life; altruistic suicide, because this basis for existence appears to man situated beyond life itself. The third sort of suicide, the existence of which has just been shown, results from man's activity's lacking regulation and his consequent sufferings. By virtue of its origin we shall assign this last variety the name of *anomic suicide*.

Certainly, this and egoistic suicide have kindred ties. Both spring from society's insufficient presence in individuals. But the sphere of its absence is not the same in both cases. In egoistic suicide it is deficient in truly collective activity, thus depriving the latter of object and meaning. In anomic suicide, society's influence is lacking in the basically individual passions, thus leaving them without a check-rein. In spite of their relationship, therefore, the two types are independent of each other. We may offer society everything social in us, and still be unable to control our desires; one may live in an anomic state without being egoistic, and vice versa. These two sorts of suicide therefore do not draw their chief recruits from the same social environments; one has its principal field among intellectual careers, the world of thought—the other, the industrial or commercial world.

Notes

1. Bibliography.—Steinmetz, *Suicide Among Primitive Peoples*, in *American Anthropologist*, January 1894.—Waitz, *Anthropologie der Naturvoelker, passim.—Suicides dans les Armées*, in *Journal de la société de statistique*, 1874, p. 250.—Millar, *Statistic of military suicide*, in *Journal of the Statistical Society*, London, June 1874.—Mesnier, *Du suicide dans l'Armée*, Paris 1881.—Bournet, *Criminalité en France et en Italie*, p. 83 ff.—Roth, *Die Selbstmorde in der K. u. K. Armee, in den Jahren 1873–80*, in *Statistische Monatschrift*, 1892.—Rosenfeld, *Die Selbstmorde in der Preussischen Armee, in Militarwochenblatt*, 1894, 3. supplement.—By the same, *Der Selbstmord in der K. u. K. oesterreichischen Heere*, in *Deutsche Worte*, 1893.—Anthony, *Suicide dans l'armée allemande*, in *Arch. de med. et de phar. militaire*, Paris. 1895.
2. Oettingen, *Moralstatistik*, p. 762.
3. Quoted from Brierre de Boismont, p. 23.
4. *Punica*, I, 225 and ff.
5. *Life of Alexander*, CXIII.
6. VIII, 9.
7. Cf. Wyatt Gill, *Myths and Songs of the South Pacific*, p. 163.
8. Frazer, *Golden Bough*, vol. I, p. 216 and ff.
9. Strabo, par. 486.—Elian, V. H., 337.
10. Diodorus Sicilus, III, 33, pars. 5 and 6.
11. Pomponius Mela, III, 7.
12. *Histoire de France*, I, 81, c. Caesar, *de Bello Gallico*, VI, 19.
13. See Spencer, *Sociology*, vol. II, p. 146.
14. See Jarves, *History of the Sandwich Islands*, 1843, p. 108.
15. See Frazer, *Golden Bough, loc. cit.,* and *passim.*
16. See *Division du travail social, passim.*

DAVID RIESMAN

Three Types of
Character and Society

◆

*David Riesman, 1909–   , is Henry Ford II Professor of Social
Sciences at Harvard University. Trained as a lawyer, Riesman turned
to the social sciences and gained wide attention with his provocative
study of American life, The Lonely Crowd. Riesman is the creator of
a genre of "popular sociology" which brings the tradition and insights
of Marx, Durkheim, Weber, and Freud to bear on the broad problems
of contemporary American society. The theory of character types developed in this selection has passed into our language in the phrases
"tradition-directed," "inner-directed," and "other-directed." Note that
Riesman does not intend the three types as portraits of actual people.
Rather he has constructed them as analytical models which are useful
in describing certain kinds of character patterns.*

> *. . . nor can the learned reader be ignorant, that in human
> nature, though here collected under one general name, is such
> prodigious variety, that a cook will sooner have gone through
> all the several species of animal and vegetable food in the
> world, than an author will be able to exhaust so extensive a
> subject.*
>
> FIELDING, *Tom Jones*

Social character is the product of social forms; in that sense,
man is made by his society. Yet we know that social forms
change; sometimes men change them; and character changes
with them. What part does character play, then, in the initiation
of change?

Let us take political apathy as an illustration. The complexity
of society, its segmentation, the difficulty of comprehending it,
the consistent failure to have it act the way people say they
would like it to act—all these factors induce political apathy.

At the same time general political apathy is itself one of the main factors "causing" the apparent inelasticity of society.

The relations between political apathy and social change are actually more complicated even than this, once unconscious interconnections are recognized. For example, uncertainty as to social position, combined with the possibility or hope of rapid social advance, leads parents in certain middle social strata to largely unconscious changes in their child-rearing practices. The child is no longer trained to an unquestioned ideal as perhaps his parents were; he is trained to do the "best possible" in any situation. The decline of specifically defined goals and clear purposes, for this and other reasons, can easily have the effect of making the person more vulnerable to apathy. This in turn may lead him to interpret the world in such a way as to justify his apathy and to mold it into a political style. He says, "No one can do anything in politics anyway," when the point is, "I cannot imagine myself doing anything, in politics or elsewhere."

The complexity of such interconnections is so great that we must recognize very clearly the limitations of historical analysis pursued according to *any* method we now have; the *Kultur-kampf* aroused by Max Weber's magnificent essay on *The Protestant Ethic and the Spirit of Capitalism* indicates both the controversiality and the possible fruitfulness of pursuing a typological method to see where it leads. Hence the place given to character in this book is heuristic; it is an effort to find something out, not a conviction as to *the* road for overcoming the elusiveness of history.

Let us begin by defining character structure as the more or less permanent, socially and historically conditioned organization of an individual's drives and satisfactions. The term as thus defined is less inclusive than "personality," the word which in current usage denotes the total self, with its inherited temperament and talents, its biological as well as psychological components, its evanescent as well as more or less permanent attributes.[1] My reason for selecting from this complex the abstraction called "character" is that in this book I propose to deal with those components of personality that also play the principal role in the maintenance of social forms—those that are *learned* in the lifelong process of socialization.

As soon as we begin to speak of character as related to social forms we make, in effect, a still further selection from the matrix of personality. For we begin to isolate for inspection those components of character that are shared among significant social groups. And to speak of character in these terms is to speak of character as "social character." This notion of social character, the character that is clearly generalized in a society, permits us to speak elliptically but meaningfully of the character of classes, groups, regions, and nations.

The assumption that a social character exists has always been a more or less invisible premise in ordinary parlance; and it is becoming a more or less visible premise in the language of the social sciences. Its importance as a premise in the social sciences stands in direct proportion to the uncertainty that the social sciences feel about the nonsocial, or less obviously social, aspects of personality that are rooted in temperament. Under "temperament" we may lump together the constitutional or physiological determinants of behavior—such matters as hormones, metabolism, blood pressure as well as "temperament" in the sense of cheerfulness, dourness, peppiness, etc. We know little about the causes or consequences of differences of temperament in individuals and groups; and hence they are excluded from the scope of this study, although this is not intended to deny their importance.

Why should there be a social character? Psychoanalysts have given an answer explaining it on the basis of the society's needs. Thus Erik H. Erikson writes, speaking of child socialization in preliterate groups: ". . . systems of child training . . . represent unconscious attempts at creating out of human raw material that configuration of attitudes which is (or once was) the optimum under the tribe's particular natural conditions and economic-historic necessities." [2]

Likewise, Erich Fromm declares:

In order that any society may function well, its members must acquire the kind of character which makes them *want* to act in the way they *have* to act as members of the society or of a special class within it. They have to *desire* what objectively is *necessary* for them to do. *Outer force* is replaced by *inner compulsion*, and by the particular kind of human energy which is channeled into character traits. [3]

By implication these writers are saying that if human beings lived at random—in an inconceivable pure contingency—their drives could not be harnessed to perform the culturally required tasks.

The individual undoubtedly gets some benefit out of living in the more or less confining strait jacket of the social character which is imposed on him. It is one of the ambiguities of human existence, as it is of art, that personal life flourishes within the forms provided for it by tradition and necessity. Character structure, like social structure, serves not only to limit choice but also to channel action by foreclosing some of the otherwise limitless behavior choices of human beings. We are familiar enough with the compulsive person, who feels he must decide, without the aid of habitual conformity, which shoe to put on first, whether to take the local or the express, whether to order eggs boiled or scrambled. Since life is too short for such overworked elaboration of choice, the social character permits it to be lived in some sort of working harness.

The danger is not of having too much leeway but of having too little. This is the constriction of choice range against which Freud eloquently warned mankind—character and culture can overreach themselves and thus swallow up all of life in enterprises whose only virtue is that they are shared.

Character and Society

Since this study assumes that character is socially conditioned, it also takes for granted that there is some observable relation between a particular society and the kind of social character it produces. What is the best way to define this relation? Since the social function of character is to insure or permit conformity, it appears that the various types of social character can be defined most appropriately in terms of the modes of conformity that are developed in them. Finally, any prevalent mode of conformity may itself be used as an index to characterize a whole society.

Having said this, we must not overestimate the role of character in the social process. It is not a sufficient explanation, for instance, to say, as some students have said, that the German army held together because "the Germans" had an authoritarian character, since armies of very diverse character type do in fact hold together under given conditions of battle and supply. Nor will it do to assume, as American aptitude-testers sometimes do, that certain jobs can be successfully handled only by a narrowly limited range of character types: that we need "extrovert" or "oral" salesmen and administrators, and "introvert" or "anal" chemists and accountants. Our conventions on this score may make an introvert administrator feel inadequate because he does not fit the stereotype that patterns the narrow judgment passed on him by others and, through their eyes, by himself.

Actually, people of radically different types can adapt themselves to perform, adequately enough, a wide variety of complex tasks. Or, to put the same thing in another way, social institutions can harness a gamut of different motivations, springing from different character types, to perform very much the same kinds of socially demanded jobs. And yet, of course, this is not to say that character is merely a shadowy factor in history, like some Hegelian spirit. Character will affect the style and psychic costs of job performances that, in economic or political analysis, look almost identical.

Thus we are forced to take account of the possibility that people may be compelled to behave in one way although their character structure presses them to behave in the opposite way. Society may change more rapidly than character, or vice versa. Indeed, this disparity between socially required behavior and characterologically compatible behavior is one of the great levers of change. Fortunately we know of no society like the one glumly envisaged by Aldous Huxley in *Brave New World,* where the social character types have been completely content in their social roles and where consequently, barring accident, no social change exists. Thus while we shall be talking hereafter of social character types we must try to remember that these types are constructions and that the richness of human potentiality, human discontent, and human variety cannot be imprisoned within a typology.

As there are numberless ways of classifying people, none of them definitive, none of them more than approximations, none of them useful for more than a limited range of analytic purposes, so there exists in the social science literature an enormous number of different ways of classifying societies. I myself have chosen to emphasize some possible relationships between the population growth of a society and the historical sequence of character types. For I think it fruitful in developing a historical characterology to explore the correlations between the conformity demands put on people in a society and the broadest of

the social indexes that connect men with their environment—
the demographic indexes. A useful key to those indexes is the
theory developed by modern students of population who see
all societies as located in and moving along a *curve of population
growth and distribution.*

Actually there is no single curve of population, but a variety.
We are interested here in a particular kind of S-shaped curve
that appears in the history of the long-industrialized countries,
as well as in the projected populations of certain other countries as they are expected to take shape in the future. The
S-shaped curve begins at a point where the number of births
and deaths are fairly equal (both birth rates and death rates
being high) and moves through a period of rapid population
increase to a new plateau where births and deaths are again
equal (both rates being low).

As Malthus gloomily observed one hundred and fifty years
ago, populations are capable of growing at a geometric rate.
A slight rate of increase of births over deaths per annum means
that in fifteen or twenty years there will be more women of
childbearing age who are able in turn to swell the birth rate
in comparison with the death rate. In a short time, moreover,
such a development can change the age composition of a society
—just as in the postwar years in America some of the consequences of an upward spurt in births are visible.

Societies at an early place on the S-curve are heavily weighted
toward the younger age groups, which means that birth rates
and death rates are high: the turnover of generations is rapid.
Societies at a late place on the curve are weighted toward the
middle-aged groups, which ordinarily means that birth rates
and death rates are low. These vital statistics (we are ignoring
the many technical indeterminates that haunt work with population figures) are in their turn dependent on many subtle social
and psychological factors: attitudes toward sanitation and toward
children, cultural beliefs about the standard of living appropriate
to different classes, food and sex taboos—these merely begin
the list.

Population theorists* distinguish three phases on the population S-curve. Societies of high birth rate and equally high
death rate are said to be in the phase of "high growth poten-

* We have relied here chiefly on the terminology and theory of Frank W.
Notestein.

tial": their population would increase with great rapidity if the death rate were lowered by, say, a sudden advance in hygiene. Societies which have passed into the phase of decreased death rate are said to be in the phase of "transitional growth." Finally, societies which have passed through both these earlier phases and are beginning to move toward a net decrease in population are said to be in the phase of "incipient population decline." (It should be noted that all references to the population phase of a society are to averages which do not take account of the very different rates that may characterize classes or ethnic groups within the society—our treatment is highly generalized.)

It would be very surprising if variations in the basic conditions of reproduction, livelihood, and survival chances, that is, in the supply of and demand for human beings, failed to influence character. My thesis is, in fact, that each of these three different phases on the population curve appears to be occupied by a society that enforces conformity and molds social character in a definably different way.

The society of high growth potential develops in its typical members a social character whose conformity is insured by their tendency to follow tradition: these I shall term *tradition-directed* people and the society in which they live *a society dependent on tradition-direction.*

The society of transitional population growth develops in its typical members a social character whose conformity is insured by their tendency to acquire early in life an internalized set of goals. These I shall term *inner-directed* people and the society in which they live *a society dependent on inner-direction.*

Finally, the society of incipient population decline develops in its typical members a social character whose conformity is insured by their tendency to be sensitized to the expectations and preferences of others. These I shall term *other-directed* people and the society in which they live one *dependent on other-direction.*

Let me point out, however, before embarking on a description of these three "ideal types" of character and society, that I am not concerned here with making a detailed demographic analysis such as would be necessary before one could prove that a link exists between population phase and character type. Rather, the theory of the curve of population provides me with a kind of shorthand for referring to the myriad institutional elements that are also—though usually more heatedly—symbolized by such words as "industrialism," "folk society," "monopoly capitalism," "urbanization," "rationalization," and so on. Hence when I speak here of transitional growth or incipient decline of population in conjunction with shifts in character and conformity, these phrases should not be taken as magical and comprehensive explanations.[4]

I am sure that change in the population age distribution, even with all it implies in change of the spacing of people, the size of markets, the role of children, the society's feeling of vitality or senescence, and many other intangibles, cannot determine character all by itself. It is a necessary but not a sufficient condition. What matters, too, is the *rate* of change, the size of the country or other unit of organization, the distribution of the change among social classes, a group's reaction to its density, the persistence of traditions because (as in the case of Japan) they can be made compatible with industrialization.

HIGH GROWTH POTENTIAL: TRADITION-DIRECTED TYPES

It has already been stated that a society characterized by high birth rates and high death rates is in the stage of high growth potential. The mortality rates are so high that any decline in them permits a very rapid expansion of the population. This is the situation of more than half the world's population: in India, Egypt, and China (which have already grown immensely in recent generations), for most preliterate peoples in Central Africa, parts of Central and South America, in fact in most areas of the world relatively untouched by industrialization. Here death rates are so high that if birth rates were not also high the populations would die out.

Regions where the population is in this stage of growth may be sparsely populated, as in the areas occupied by many primitive tribes and as in parts of Central and South America. They may be densely populated, as in India, China, and Egypt. In either case, the society achieves a Malthusian bargain with the limited food supply by killing off, in one way or another, some of the potential surplus of births over deaths—the enormous trap which, in Malthus' view, nature sets for man and which can be peaceably escaped only by prudent cultivation of the soil and prudent uncultivation of the species through the delay of marriage. Without the prevention of childbirth by means of marriage postponement or other contraceptive measures, the population must be limited by taking the life of living beings. And so other societies have "invented" cannibalism, induced abortion, organized wars, made human sacrifice, and practiced infanticide (especially female) as means of avoiding periodic famine and epidemics.

Though this settling of accounts with the contradictory impulses of hunger and sex is accompanied often enough by upheaval and distress, these societies in the stage of high growth potential tend to be stable at least in the sense that their social practices, including the "crimes" that keep population down, are institutionalized and patterned. Generation after generation people are born, are weeded out, and die to make room for others. The net rate of natural increase fluctuates only within narrow limits, as is true also of societies in the stage of incipient decline. But unlike the latter, the average life expectancy in the former is characteristically low: the population is heavily weighted on the side of the young, and generation replaces generation far more rapidly and less "efficiently" than in those industrialized societies of incipient population decline.

In viewing such a society we inevitably associate the relative stability of the man-land ratio, whether high or low, with the tenacity of custom and social structure. However, we must not equate stability of social structure over historical time with psychic stability in the life span of an individual: the latter may subjectively experience much violence and disorganization. In the last analysis, however, he learns to deal with life by adaptation, not by innovation. With certain exceptions conformity is largely given in the "self-evident" social situation. Of course nothing in human life is ever really self-evident; where it so appears it is because perceptions have been narrowed by cultural conditioning. As the precarious relation to the food supply is built into the going culture, it helps create a pattern of conventional conformity which is reflected in many, if not in all, societies in the stage of high growth potential. This is what we mean when we speak of tradition-direction.

A definition of tradition-direction. Since the type of social order we have been discussing is relatively unchanging, the conformity of the individual tends to be dictated to a very large degree by power relations among the various age and sex groups, the clans, castes, professions, and so forth—relations which have endured for centuries and are modified but slightly, if at all, by successive generations. The culture controls behavior minutely, and, while the rules are not so complicated that the young cannot learn them during the period of intensive socialization, careful and rigid etiquette governs the fundamentally influential sphere of kin relationships. Moreover, the culture, in addition to its economic tasks, or as part of them, provides ritual, routine, and religion to occupy and to orient everyone. Little energy is directed toward finding new solutions of the age-old problems, let us say, of agricultural technique or "medicine," the problems to which people are acculturated.

It is not to be thought, however, that in these societies, where the activity of the individual member is determined by characterologically grounded obedience to traditions, the individual may not be highly prized and, in many instances, encouraged to develop his capabilities, his initiative, and even, within very narrow time limits, his aspirations. Indeed, the individual in some primitive societies is far more appreciated and respected than in some sectors of modern society. For the individual in a society dependent on tradition-direction has a well-defined functional relationship to other members of the group. If he is not killed off, he "belongs"—he is not "surplus," as the modern unemployed are surplus, nor is he expendable as the unskilled are expendable in modern society. But by very virtue of his "belonging," life goals that are *his* in terms of conscious choice appear to shape his destiny only to a very limited extent, just as only to a limited extent is there any concept of progress for the group.

In societies in which tradition-direction is the dominant mode of insuring conformity, relative stability is preserved in part by the infrequent but highly important process of fitting such deviants as there are into institutionalized roles. In such societies a person who might have become at a later historical stage an innovator or rebel, whose belonging, as such, is marginal and problematic, is drawn instead into roles like those of the shaman or sorcerer. That is, he is drawn into roles that make a socially acceptable contribution, while at the same time they provide the individual with a more or less approved niche. The medieval monastic orders may have served in a similar way to absorb many characterological mutations.

In some of these societies certain individuals are encouraged toward a degree of individuality from childhood, especially if they belong to families of high status. But, since the range of choice, even for high-status people, is minimal, the apparent social need for an individuated type of character is also minimal. It is probably accurate to say that character structure in these societies is very largely "adjusted," in the sense that for most people it appears to be in tune with social institutions. Even the few misfits "fit" to a degree; and only very rarely is one driven out of his social world.

This does not mean, of course, that the people are happy; the society to whose traditions they are adjusted may be a miserable one, ridden with anxiety, sadism, and disease. The point is rather that change, while never completely absent in human affairs, is slowed down as the movement of molecules is slowed down at low temperature; and the social character comes as close as it ever does to looking like the matrix of the social forms themselves.

In western history the Middle Ages can be considered a period in which the majority were tradition-directed. But the term tradition-directed refers to a common element, not only among the people of precapitalist Europe but also among such enormously different types of people as Hindus and Hopi Indians, Zulus and Chinese, North African Arabs and Balinese. There is comfort in relying on the many writers who have found a similar unity amid diversity, a unity they express in such terms as "folk society" (as against "civilization"), a "status society" (as against a "contract society"), *"Gemeinschaft"* (as against *"Gesellschaft"*), and so on. Different as the societies envisaged by these terms are, the folk, status, and *Gemeinschaft* societies resemble each other in their relative slowness of change, their dependence on family and kin organization, and—in comparison with later epochs—their tight web of values. And, as is now well recognized by students, the high birth rate of these societies in the stage of high growth potential is not merely the result of a lack of contraceptive knowledge or techniques. A whole way of life—an outlook on chance, on children, on the place of women, on sexuality, on the very meaning of existence—lies between the societies in which human fertility is allowed to take its course and toll and those which prefer to pay other kinds of toll to cut down on fertility by calculation, and, conceivably, as Freud and other observers have suggested, by a decline in sexual energy itself.

TRANSITIONAL GROWTH: INNER-DIRECTED TYPES

The emergence of transitional growth. Except for the west, we know very little about the cumulation of small changes that can eventuate in a breakup of the tradition-directed type of society, leading it to realize its potential for high population growth. As for the west, however, much has been learned about the slow decay of feudalism and the subsequent rise of a type of society in which inner-direction is the dominant mode of insuring conformity. Such a society is likely to be found in the phase of transitional growth of population.

Many writers are apt to view the situation of the tradition-directed peasant as idyllic and to exaggerate by comparison the anomie, the rootlessness, the trapped malaise, of the modern city dweller. There is more than a hint of this in the work of many contemporary social scientists. On the other hand, critical historians, pushing the Renaissance ever back into the Middle Ages, seem sometimes to deny that any decisive change occurred. On the whole, it makes sense to suppose that the greatest social and characterological shift of recent centuries did indeed come when men were driven out of the primary ties that bound them to the western medieval version of tradition-directed society. All later shifts, including the shift from inner-direction to other-direction, seem unimportant by comparison, although of course this latter shift is still under way and we cannot tell what it will look like when complete.

A change in the relatively stable ratio of births to deaths, which characterizes the period of high growth potential, is both the cause and consequence of other profound social changes. In most of the cases known to us a decline takes place in mortality prior to a decline in fertility; hence there is some period in which the population expands rapidly. The drop in death rate occurs as the result of many interacting factors, among them sanitation, improved communications (which permit government to operate over a wider area and also permit easier transport of food to areas of shortage from areas of surplus), the decline, forced or otherwise, of infanticide, cannibalism, and other inbred kinds of violence. Because of improved methods of agriculture the land is able to support more people, and these in turn produce still more people.

As a result population begins increasing nearly in geometric ratio, as it did in Europe between 1650 and 1900 and as it has in recent years been doing in countries like India. Notestein's phrase "transitional growth," is a mild way of putting it. The "transition" is likely to be violent, disrupting the stabilized paths of existence in societies in which tradition-direction has been the principal mode of insuring conformity. The imbalance of births and deaths puts pressure on the society's customary ways. A new slate of character structures is called for or finds its opportunity in coping with the rapid changes—and the need for still more changes—in the social organization.

A definition of inner-direction. In western history the society that emerged with the Renaissance and Reformation and that is only now vanishing serves to illustrate the type of society in which inner-direction is the principal mode of securing conformity. Such a society is characterized by increased personal mobility, by a rapid accumulation of capital (teamed with devastating technological shifts), and by an almost constant *expansion:* intensive expansion in the production of goods and people, and extensive expansion in exploration, colonization, and imperialism. The greater choices this society gives—and the greater initiatives it demands in order to cope with its novel problems—are handled by character types who can manage to live socially without strict and self-evident tradition-direction. These are the inner-directed types.

The concept of inner-direction is intended to cover a very wide range of types. Thus, while it is essential for the study of certain problems to differentiate between Protestant and Catholic countries and their character types, between the effects of the Reformation and the effects of the Renaissance, between the puritan ethic of the European and American north and west and the somewhat more hedonistic ethic of the European east and south, while all these are valid and, for certain purposes, important distinctions, the concentration of this study on the development of modes of conformity permits their neglect. It allows the grouping together of these otherwise distinct developments because they have one thing in common: *the source of direction for the individual is "inner" in the sense that it is*

implanted early in life by the elders and directed toward gen-
eralized but nonetheless inescapably destined goals.

We can see what this means when we realize that, in societies
in which tradition-direction is the dominant mode of insuring
conformity, attention is focused on securing external *behavioral*
conformity. While behavior is minutely prescribed, individuality
of character need not be highly developed to meet prescriptions
that are objectified in ritual and etiquette—though to be sure,
a social character *capable* of such behavioral attention and
obedience is requisite. By contrast, societies in which inner-
direction becomes important, though they also are concerned
with behavioral conformity, cannot be satisfied with behavioral
conformity alone. Too many novel situations are presented, situations which a code cannot encompass in advance. Consequently
the problem of personal choice, solved in the earlier period of
high growth potential by channeling choice through rigid social
organization, in the period of transitional growth is solved by
channeling choice through a rigid though highly individualized
character.

This rigidity is a complex matter. While any society dependent on inner-direction seems to present people with a wide
choice of aims—such as money, possessions, power, knowledge,
fame, goodness—these aims are ideologically interrelated, and
the selection made by any one individual remains relatively
unalterable throughout his life. Moreover, the means to those
ends, though not fitted into as tight a social frame of reference
as in the society dependent on tradition-direction, are nevertheless limited by the new voluntary associations—for instance, the
Quakers, the Masons, the Mechanics' Associations—to which
people tie themselves. Indeed, the term "tradition-direction"
could be misleading if the reader were to conclude that the
force of tradition has no weight for the inner-directed character.
On the contrary, he is very considerably bound by traditions:
they limit his ends and inhibit his choice of means. The point is
rather that a splintering of tradition takes place, connected in
part with the increasing division of labor and stratification of
society. Even if the individual's choice of tradition is largely
determined for him by his family, as it is in most cases, he
cannot help becoming aware of the existence of competing
traditions—hence of tradition as such. As a result he possesses
a somewhat greater degree of flexibility in adapting himself to

ever changing requirements and in return requires more from his environment.

As the situational controls of the primary group are loosened—the group that both socializes the young and controls the adult in the earlier era—a new psychological mechanism appropriate to the more open society is "invented"; it is a psychological gyroscope.[5] This instrument, once it is set by the parents and other authorities, keeps the inner-directed person, as we shall see, "on course" even when tradition, as responded to by his character, no longer dictates his moves. The inner-directed person becomes capable of maintaining a delicate balance between the demands upon him of his life goal and the buffetings of his external environment.

This metaphor of the gyroscope, like any other, must not be taken literally. It would be a mistake to see the inner-directed man as incapable of learning from experience or as insensitive to public opinion in matters of external conformity. He can receive and utilize certain signals from outside, provided that they can be reconciled with the limited maneuverability that his gyroscope permits him. His pilot is not quite automatic.

Huizinga's *The Waning of the Middle Ages* gives a picture of the anguish and turmoil, the conflict of values, out of which the new forms slowly emerged. As early as the late Middle Ages people were forced to live under new conditions of awareness. As their self-consciousness and their individuality developed, they had to make themselves at home in the world in novel ways. They still have to.

INCIPIENT DECLINE OF POPULATION: OTHER-DIRECTED TYPES

The emergence of the next phase: incipient decline. The problem facing the societies in the stage of transitional growth is that of reaching a point at which resources become plentiful enough or are utilized effectively enough to permit a rapid accumulation of capital. This rapid accumulation has to be achieved even while the social product is being drawn on at an accelerated rate to satisfy the consumer demands that go with the way of life that has already been adopted. For most countries, unless capital and techniques can be imported from other countries in still later phases of the population curve, every effort to increase national resources at a rapid rate must actually be at the expense of current standards of living. We have seen this occur in the U.S.S.R., now in the stage of transitional growth. Only a fantastically large increase in productive capacity will, without a prolonged period of misery, permit an increase in the supply of food and other commodities sufficient to stimulate migration from country to city and at the same time to accommodate the change from large-family to small-family ideational patterns. For Europe this transition was long, drawn out, and painful; and this may be one reason that countries such as France, despite their demographic transformation into the third stage of incipient decline, still retain modes of conformity appropriate to an economy in the second stage or even earlier. For America, Canada, and Australia—at once beneficiaries of European technique and native resources—the transition was rapid and relatively easy.

As has been said, the tradition-directed character hardly thinks of himself as an individual. Still less does it occur to him that he might shape his own destiny in terms of personal, lifelong goals or that the destiny of his children might be separate from that of the family group. He is not sufficiently separated psychologically from himself (or, therefore, sufficiently close to himself), his family, or group to think in these terms. In the phase of transitional growth, however, people of inner-directed character do gain a feeling of control over their own lives and see their children also as individuals with careers to make. At the same time, with the shift out of agriculture and, later, with the banning of child labor in factories (a humanitarian measure both needed and possible because of the altered social relations introduced by industrialization), children no longer become an unequivocal economic asset. And with the growth of habits of scientific thought, religious and magical views of human fertility—views that in an earlier phase of the population curve made sense for the culture if it was to reproduce itself—give way to "rational," individualistic attitudes. Indeed, just as the rapid accumulation of productive capital requires that people be imbued with the "Protestant ethic" (as Max Weber characterized one manifestation of what is here termed inner-direction), so also the decreased number of progeny requires a profound change in values—a change so deep that, in all probability, it has to be rooted in character structure.

As the birth rate begins to follow the death rate downward, societies move toward the epoch of incipient decline of population—the prelude to the time when the birth rate will plunge below the already lowered death rate, so that total population will decline.

This problem of incipient population decline has been much discussed in the western countries, notably in France, Britain, and the Scandinavian countries, where the population is nearing stability or hovering on the verge of actual decrease. Production here has at last outrun even greatly expanded consumption, and the standard of living, which Malthus already realized was a cultural and psychological index, has completed its work by subtle psychological pressures on fertility—though not every social class shares equally in these developments. Fewer and fewer people work on the land or in the extractive industries or even in manufacturing. Hours are short. People may have material abundance and leisure besides. They pay for these changes however—here, as always, the solution of old problems gives rise to new ones—by finding themselves in a centralized and bureaucratized society and a world shrunken and agitated by the contact—accelerated by industrialization—of races, nations, and cultures.

The hard enduringness and enterprise of the inner-directed types are somewhat less necessary under these new conditions. Increasingly, *other people* are the problem, not the material environment. And as people mix more widely and become more sensitive to each other, the surviving traditions from the stage of high growth potential—much disrupted, in any case, during the violent spurt of industrialization—become still further attenuated. Gyroscopic control is no longer sufficiently flexible, and a new psychological mechanism is called for.

Furthermore, the "scarcity psychology" of many inner-directed people, which was socially adaptive during the period of heavy capital accumulation that accompanied transitional growth of population, needs to give way to an "abundance psychology" capable of "wasteful" luxury consumption of leisure and of the surplus product. Unless people want to destroy the surplus product in war, which still does require heavy capital equipment, they must learn to enjoy and engage in those services that are expensive in terms of man power but not of capital —poetry and philosophy, for instance.[6] Indeed, in the period of incipient decline, nonproductive consumers, both the increasing number of old people and the diminishing number of as yet untrained young, form a high proportion of the population, and these need both the economic opportunity to be prodigal and the character structure to allow it.

Has this need for still another slate of character types actually been acknowledged to any degree? My observations lead me to believe that in America it has.

A definition of other-direction. The type of character I shall describe as other-directed seems to be emerging in very recent years in the upper middle class of our larger cities: more prominent in New York than in Boston, in Los Angeles than in Spokane, in Cincinnati than in Chillicothe. Yet in some respects this type is strikingly similar to *the* American, whom Tocqueville and other curious and astonished visitors from Europe, even before the Revolution, thought to be a new kind of man. Indeed, travelers' reports on America impress us with their unanimity. The American is said to be shallower, freer with his money, friendlier, more uncertain of himself and his values, more demanding of approval than the European. It all adds up to a pattern which, without stretching matters too far, resembles the kind of character that a number of social scientists have seen as developing in contemporary, highly industrialized, and bureaucratic America: Fromm's "marketer," Mills's "fixer," Arnold Green's "middle class male child." [7]

This raises several questions which, as I said earlier, I have not been able to answer. It is my impression that the middle-class American of today is decisively different from those Americans of Tocqueville's writings who strike us as so contemporary, and much of this book will be devoted to discussing these differences.* It is also my impression that the conditions I believe

---

* I have tried to discover, by reading the eyewitness social observers of the early nineteenth century in America, whether Tocqueville "saw" America or "foresaw" it, to what extent he was influenced—as visiting firemen of today also are—by American snobs who take their image of Europe as the norm in describing their own countrymen. And to what extent, in establishing America's polarity from Europe, he tendentiously noticed those things that were different rather than those that were the same. From conversations with Phillips Bradley and Arthur Schlesinger, Jr., and from G. W. Pierson, *Tocqueville and Beaumont in America* (New York, Oxford University Press, 1938) I get the impression that all these qualifications must be put on Tocqueville's picture of America in the 1830's. On the general problem of whether there is an American character, and if so what are its sources, and how such questions might be investigated, I have profited from the work of Oscar Handlin, and from suggestions made by him. Thomas

to be responsible for other-direction are affecting increasing numbers of people in the metropolitan centers of the advanced industrial countries. However, the available comparative studies of European "national character," broken down by social class, are not yet sufficiently inclusive to permit comparison. Given impetus by the late Ruth Benedict, Gorer, Kardiner, Kluckhohn, Margaret Mead, and others, such studies are now under way. Meanwhile, my analysis of the other-directed character is at once an analysis of the American and of contemporary man. Much of the time I find it hard or impossible to say where one ends and the other begins. Tentatively, I am inclined to think that the other-directed type does find itself most at home in America, due to certain constant elements in American society, such as its recruitment from Europe and its lack of any seriously feudal past. As against this, I am also inclined to put more weight on capitalism, industrialism, and urbanization— these being international tendencies—than on any character-forming peculiarities of the American scene.

Bearing these qualifications in mind, it seems appropriate to treat contemporary metropolitan America as our illustration of a society—so far, perhaps, the only illustration—in which other-direction is the dominant mode of insuring conformity. It would be premature, however, to say that it is already the dominant mode in America as a whole. But since the other-directed types are to be found among the young, in the larger cities, and among the upper income groups, we may assume that, unless present trends are reversed, the hegemony of other-direction lies not far off.

If we wanted to cast our social character types into social class molds, we could say that inner-direction is the typical character of the "old" middle class—the banker, the tradesman, the small entrepreneur, the technically oriented engineer, etc.— while other-direction is becoming the typical character of the "new" middle class—the bureaucrat, the salaried employee in business, etc. Many of the economic factors associated with the recent growth of the "new" middle class are well known. They have been discussed by James Burnham, Colin Clark, Peter Drucker, and others. There is a decline in the numbers

and Znaniecki's *Polish Peasant* may be thought of as a pioneer effort, unfortunately too little followed up, to attack the problem in terms of the experience of a particular ethnic group.

and in the proportion of the working population engaged in production and extraction—agriculture, heavy industry, heavy transport—and an increase in the numbers and the proportion engaged in white-collar work and the service trades.

Furthermore, societies in the phase of incipient decline (societies, that is, in which we expect other-directed types to come to the fore) are not only highly urbanized but have a high level of capital equipment and technological skill built up during the period of transitional growth. People who are literate, educated, and provided with the necessities of life by machine industry and agriculture, turn increasingly to the "tertiary" economic realm. The service industries prosper among the people as a whole and no longer only in court circles. Education, leisure, services, these go together with an increased consumption of words and images from the mass media of communications in societies that have moved into the incipient decline stage via the route of industrialization. Hence, while societies in the phase of transitional growth begin the process of distributing words from urban centers, the flow becomes a torrent in the societies of incipient population decline. This process, while modulated by profound national and class differences, connected with differences in literacy and loquacity, takes place everywhere in the industrialized lands. Increasingly, relations with the outer world and with oneself are mediated by the flow of mass communication. For the other-directed types political events are likewise experienced through a screen of words by which the events are habitually atomized and personalized—or pseudopersonalized. For the inner-directed person who remains still extant in this period the tendency is rather to systematize and moralize this flow of words.

These developments lead, for large numbers of people, to changes in paths to success and to the requirement of more "socialized" behavior both for success and for marital and personal adaptation. Connected with such changes are changes in the family and in child-rearing practices. In the smaller families of urban life, and with the spread of "permissive" child care to ever wider strata of the population, there is a relaxation of older patterns of discipline. Under these newer patterns the peer-group (the age- and class-graded group in a child's school and neighborhood) becomes much more important to the child, while the parents make him feel guilty not so much about violation of inner standards as about failure to be popular or otherwise to manage his relations with these other children. Moreover, the pressures of the school and the peer-group are reinforced and continued—in a manner whose inner paradoxes I shall discuss later—by the mass media: movies, radio, comics, and popular culture media generally. Under these conditions types of character emerge that we shall here term other-directed. To them much of the discussion in the ensuing chapters is devoted. *What is common to all other-directeds is that their contemporaries are the source of direction for the individual— either those known to him or those with whom he is indirectly acquainted, through friends and through the mass media. This source is of course "internalized" in the sense that dependence on it for guidance in life is implanted early. The goals toward which the other-directed person strives shift with that guidance: it is only the process of striving itself and the process of paying close attention to the signals from others that remain unaltered throughout life.* This mode of keeping in touch with others permits a close behavioral conformity, not through drill in be-havior itself, as in the tradition-directed character, but rather through an exceptional sensitivity to the actions and wishes of others.

Of course, it matters very much who those "others" are: whether they are the individual's immediate circle or a "higher" circle or the anonymous voices of the mass media; whether the individual fears the hostility of chance acquaintances or only of those who "count." But his need for approval and direction from others—and contemporary others rather than ancestors— goes beyond the reasons that lead most people in any era to care very much what others think of them. While all people want and need to be liked by some of the people some of the time, it is only the modern other-directed types who make this their chief source of direction and chief area of sensitivity.[8]

It is perhaps the insatiable force of this psychological need for approval that differentiates people of the metropolitan, Amer-ican upper middle class, whom we regard as other-directed, from very similar types that have appeared in capital cities and among other classes in previous historical periods, whether in Imperial Canton, in eighteenth- and nineteenth-century Europe, or in ancient Athens, Alexandria, or Rome. In all these groups fashion not only ruled as a substitute for morals and customs, but it was a rapidly changing fashion that held sway. It could do so because, although the mass media were in their infancy, the group corresponding to the American upper middle class was comparably small and the elite structure was extremely reverberant. It can be argued, for example, that a copy of *The Spectator* covered its potential readership about as thoroughly in the late eighteenth century as *The New Yorker* covers its readership today. In eighteenth- and nineteenth-century English and French writing as well as in Tolstoy we find portraits of the sort of people who operated in the upper reaches of bureaucracy and had to be prepared for rapid changes of signals. Stepan Arkadyevitch Oblonsky in *Anna Karenina* is one of the more likeable and less opportunistic examples, especially striking because of the way Tolstoy contrasts him with Levin, a moralizing, inner-directed person. At any dinner party Stepan manifests exceptional social skills; his political skills as described in the following quotation are also highly social:

Stepan Arkadyevitch took in and read a liberal newspaper, not an extreme one, but one advocating the views held by the majority. And in spite of the fact that science, art, and politics had no special interest for him, he firmly held those views on all subjects which were held by the majority and by his paper, and he only changed them when the majority changed them—or, more strictly speaking, he did not change them, but they imperceptibly changed of themselves within him.

Stepan Arkadyevitch had not chosen his political opinions or his views; these political opinions and views had come to him of themselves, just as he did not choose the shapes of his hats or coats, but simply took those that were being worn. And for him, living in a certain society—owing to the need, ordinarily developed at years of discretion, for some degree of mental activity—to have views was just as indispensable as to have a hat. If there was a reason for his preferring liberal to conservative views, which were held also by many of his circle, it arose not from his considering liberalism more rational, but from its being in closer accord with his manner of life . . . And so liberalism had become a habit of Stepan Arkadyevitch's, and he liked his newspaper, as he did his cigar after dinner, for the slight fog it diffused in his brain.

It would, of course, be better if there were space for more than one such description to reinforce my point that Stepan, while his good-natured gregariousness makes him seem like a modern middle-class American, is not fully other-directed. This gregariousness alone, without a certain sensitivity to others as individuals and as a source of direction, is not the identifying trait. Just so, we must differentiate the nineteenth-century American, gregarious and subservient to public opinion though he was found to be by Tocqueville, Bryce, and others, from the other-directed American as he emerges today, an American who in his character is more capable of and more interested in maintaining responsive contact with others both at work and at play. This point needs to be emphasized, since the distinction is easily misunderstood. The inner-directed person, though he often sought and sometimes achieved a relative independence of public opinion and of what the neighbors thought of him, was in most cases very much concerned with his good repute and, at least in America, with "keeping up with the Joneses." These conformities, however, were primarily external, typified in such details as clothes, curtains, and bank credit. For, indeed, the conformities were to a standard, evidence of which was provided by the "best people" in one's milieu. In contrast with this pattern, the other-directed person, though he has his eye very much on the Joneses, aims to keep up with them not so much in external details as in the quality of his inner experience. That is, his great sensitivity keeps him in touch with others on many more levels than the externals of appearance and propriety. Nor does any ideal of independence or of reliance on God alone modify his desire to look to the others—and the "good guys" as well as the best people—for guidance in what experiences to seek and in how to interpret them.

The three types compared. While for analytic purposes it is sound to visualize all these differences sharply, it would be a mistake to expect to find such a sharp separation in the world of living people. In one respect all human behavior is inner-directed, in the sense that it is motivated, and all human behavior is other-directed, in the sense that it results from the process of socialization by others. And, of course, neither the tradition-directed nor the inner-directed person is immune to the impact of the opinions and directions of others. Nevertheless, one way to see the structural differences between the three types is to see the differences—again, as a matter of degree only —in the emotional sanction, control, or "tuning" in each type.

The tradition-directed person feels the impact of his culture as a unit, but it is nevertheless mediated through the specific, small number of individuals with whom he is in daily contact. These expect of him not so much that he be a certain type of person but that he behave in the approved way. Consequently the sanction for behavior tends to be the fear of being *shamed*.

The inner-directed person has early incorporated a psychic gyroscope which is set going by his parents and can receive signals later on from other authorities who resemble his parents. He goes through life less independent than he seems, obeying this internal piloting. Getting off course, whether in response to inner impulses or to the fluctuating voices of contemporaries, may lead to the feeling of *guilt*.

Since the direction to be taken in life has been learned in the privacy of the home from a small number of guides and since principles, rather than details of behavior, are internalized, the inner-directed person is capable of great stability. Especially so when it turns out that his fellows have gyroscopes too, spinning at the same speed and set in the same direction. But many inner-directed individuals can remain stable even when the reinforcement of social approval is not available—as in the upright life of the stock Englishman in the tropics.

Contrasted with such a type as this, the other-directed person learns to respond to signals from a far wider circle than is constituted by his parents. The family is no longer a closely knit unit to which he belongs but merely part of a wider social environment to which he early becomes attentive. In these respects the other-directed person resembles the tradition-directed person: both live in a group milieu and lack the inner-directed person's capacity to go it alone. The nature of this group milieu, however, differs radically in the two cases. The other-directed person is cosmopolitan. For him the border between the familiar and the strange—a border clearly marked in the societies depending on tradition-direction—has broken down. As the family continuously absorbs the strange and so reshapes itself, so the strange becomes familiar. While the inner-directed person could be "at home abroad" by virtue of his relative insensitivity to others, the other-directed person is, in a sense, at home everywhere and nowhere, capable of a superficial intimacy with and response to everyone.

The tradition-directed person takes his signals from others, but they come in a cultural monotone; he needs no complex receiving equipment to pick them up. The other-directed person must be able to receive signals from far and near; the sources are many, the changes rapid. What can be internalized, then, is not a code of behavior but the elaborate equipment needed to attend to such messages and occasionally to participate in their circulation. As against guilt-and-shame controls, though of course these survive, one prime psychological lever of the other-directed person is a diffuse *anxiety*. This control equipment, instead of being like a gyroscope, is like a radar.[9]

*　　*　　*

Notes

1. See Erich Fromm, *Man for Himself* (New York, Rinehart, 1947), pp. 50–61; see also, Gardner Murphy, *Personality: A Biosocial Approach to Origins and Structure* (New York, Harper, 1947), pp. 1–11; *Culture and Personality*, ed. S. Stansfeld Sargent and Marian W. Smith (Viking Fund, 1949).
2. "Observations on the Yurok: Childhood and World Image," *University of California Publications in American Archaeology and Ethnology*, XXXV (1943), iv.
3. "Individual and Social Origins of Neurosis," *American Sociological Review*, IX (1944), 380; reprinted in *Personality in Nature, Society, and Culture*, ed. Clyde Kluckhohn and Henry Murray (New York, Alfred A. Knopf, 1948), pp. 407, 409–410.
4. See the incisive discussion of the psychological appeal and social menace of deterministic theories of history by Jerome Frank, *Fate and Freedom* (New York, Simon & Schuster, 1945). I am indebted to Judge Frank for a number of helpful suggestions.
5. Since writing the above I have discovered Gardner Murphy's use of the same metaphor in his volume *Personality*.
6. These examples are given by Allan G. B. Fisher, *The Clash of Progress and Security* (London, Macmillan, 1935).
7. See Erich Fromm, *Man for Himself;* C. Wright Mills, "The Competitive Personality," *Partisan Review*, XIII (1946), 433; Arnold Green, "The Middle Class Male Child and Neurosis," *American Sociological Review*, XI (1946), 31. See also the work of Jurgen Ruesch, Martin B. Loeb, and co-workers on the "infantile personality."
8. This picture of the other-directed person has been stimulated by, and developed from, Erich Fromm's discussion of the "marketing orientation" in *Man for Himself*, pp. 67–82. I have also drawn on my portrait of "The Cash Customer," *Common Sense*, XI (1942), 183.
9. The "radar" metaphor was suggested by Karl Wittfogel.

The Legend of Hitler's Youth

*Erik Homburger Erikson, 1902–   , is Professor of Human Develop-
ment at Harvard University. Artist, sociologist, lay analyst, and psychologist, Erikson has ranged over the entire spectrum of the social
sciences and humanities in his search for a theory of human development. He is the author of the concept of adolescent identity crisis, set
forth in his psychoanalytic study of Martin Luther. In that and other
works, he emphasizes the impact of conscious, post-infantile experiences on the formation of the adult personality. Much of Erikson's
work deals with the complex interrelationships between the individual personality and the cultural patterns of the society. This study of
naziism and German national character can be compared with Plato's
account of the despotic man in the* Republic.

The most ruthless exploiters of any nation's fight for a safe identity have been Adolf Hitler and his associates, who for a decade
were the undisputed political and military masters of a great, industrious, and studious people. To stop these experts of the cheap
word from becoming a threat to the whole of Western civilization the combined resources of the industrial nations of the world
were mobilized.

The West would now prefer to ignore the question mark
which thus challenges the idea of unilinear progress. It hopes
that, after some feeding and policing by occupation troops, these
same Germans will once more emerge as good customers, easily
domesticated; that they will return to the pursuit of *Kultur,* and
forever forget the martial foolishness they were once more
trapped into.

Men of good will must believe in psychological as well as in
economic miracles. Yet I do not think that we are improving the
chances of human progress in Germany or anywhere else by for-

getting too soon what happened. Rather, it is our task to recognize that the black miracle of Naziism was only the German version—superbly planned and superbly bungled—of a universal contemporary potential. The trend persists; Hitler's ghost is counting on it.

For nations, as well as individuals, are not only defined by their highest point of civilized achievement, but also by the weakest one in their collective identity: they are, in fact, defined by the distance, and the quality of the distance, between these points. National Socialist Germany has provided a clear-cut illustration of the fact that advancing civilization is potentially endangered by its own advance, in that it splits ancient conscience, endangers incomplete identities, and releases destructive forces which now can count on the cold efficiency of the super-managers. I shall therefore go back this one step in our history and restate here a few formulations written for a U.S. government agency at the beginning of World War II, in preparation for the arrival of the—oh, so arrogant—first Nazi prisoners. Some of these formulations may already sound dated. Yet the psychological problems presented here do not vanish overnight either from Germany proper, or from the continent of which she is the center. At any rate, history only teaches those who are not over-eager to forget.

I shall take as my text the Brown Piper's sweetest, most alluring tune: the account of his childhood, in *Mein Kampf*.

In this little town on the river Inn, Bavarian by blood and Austrian by nationality, gilded by the light of German martyrdom, there lived, at the end of the eighties of last century, my parents: the father a faithful civil servant, the mother devoting herself to the cares of the household and looking after her children with eternally the same loving care.[1]

The sentence structure, the tone quality, indicate that we are to hear a fairy tale; and indeed we shall analyze it as part of a modern attempt to create a myth. But a myth, old or modern, is not a lie. It is useless to try to show that it has no basis in fact; nor to claim that its fiction is fake and nonsense. A myth blends historical fact and significant fiction in such a way that it "rings true" to an area or an era, causing pious wonderment and burning ambition. The people affected will not question truth or logic;

the few who cannot help doubting will find their reason paralyzed. To study a myth critically, therefore, means to analyze its images and themes in their relation to the culture area affected.

1. GERMANY

"This little town. . . . Bavarian by blood and Austrian by nationality, gilded by the light of German martyrdom. . . ."

Hitler was born in the Austrian town of Braunau, near the German border. He thus belonged to the Austrian Empire's German minority.

It had been in Braunau, he records, that a man named Palm was shot by Napoleon's soldiers for printing a pamphlet: *In the Hour of Germany's Deepest Humiliation.* Palm's memorial stands in the center of the town.

There was, of course, no German Reich in Palm's time. In fact, some of the German states were Napoleon's military allies. But having used the all-inclusive, the magic term "Germany," Palm, when delivered to Napoleon by the Austrian police, became the idol of the nationalist movement calling for a greater Germany.

Having pointed to Palm's resistance to and martyrdom under the sinister *Bonaparte,* the story proceeds to describe young Adolf's heroic opposition to his *father,* and tells of the German minority's hatred of the Austrian *emperor.* Little Adolf belonged, so he says, to "those who in painful emotion long for the hour that will allow them to return to the arms of the beloved mother" —Germany.

It is here that his imagery begins to involve terms of family relations which openly identify his "oedipus" situation with his country's national problems. He complains that this "beloved mother, . . . the *young* Reich," by her "tragic alliance with the *old Austrian sham state* . . . herself sanctioned the slow extermination of the German nationality."

Hitler's mother was twenty-three years younger than his father; and, as we shall see, the mother, as a good woman of her day, valiantly stood up for the man who beat her. The father was a drunkard and a tyrant. The equation suggests itself that in Hitler's national as well as domestic imagery, the young mother betrays the longing son for a senile tyrant. Little Adolf's personal experience thus blends with that of the German minority which refuses to sing "God Save Emperor Francis," when the Austrian

anthem is sung and substitutes for it "Germany over All." Hitler
continues: "The direct result of this period was: first, I became
a nationalist; second, I learned to grasp and to understand the
meaning of history . . . so that at fifteen, I already understood
the difference between dynastic patriotism and popular nationalism."

Such seemingly naïve coincidence of themes lends itself easily
—much too easily—to a psychoanalytic interpretation of the first
chapter of *Mein Kampf* as an involuntary confession of Hitler's
oedipus complex. This interpretation would suggest that in Hitler's case the love for his young mother and the hate for his old
father assumed morbid proportions, and that it was this conflict
which drove him to love and to hate and compelled him to save
or destroy people and peoples who really "stand for" his mother
and his father. There have been articles in psychoanalytic literature which claim such simple causality. But it obviously takes
much more than an individual complex to make a successful
revolutionary. The complex creates the initial fervor; but if
it were too strong it would paralyze the revolutionary, not inspire him. The striking use of parental and familial images in
Hitler's public utterances has that strange mixture of naïve confession and shrewd propaganda which characterizes the histrionic genius. Goebbels knew this and he guided his barking
master well—until very close to the end.

I shall not now review the psychiatric literature which has
described Hitler as a "psychopathic paranoid," an "amoral
sadistic infant," an "overcompensatory sissy," or "a neurotic labor-
ing under the compulsion to murder." At times, he undoubtedly
was all of that. But, unfortunately, he was something over and
above it all. His capacity for acting and for creating action was
so rare that it seems inexpedient to apply ordinary diagnostic
methods to his words. He was first of all an adventurer, on a
grandiose scale. The personality of the adventurer is akin to that
of an actor, because he must always be ready to personify, as if
he had chosen them, the changing roles suggested by the whims
of fate. Hitler shares with many an actor the fact that he is said
to have been queer and unbearable behind the scenes, to say
nothing of in his bedroom. He undoubtedly had hazardous borderline traits. But he knew how to approach the borderline, to
appear as if he were going too far, and then to turn back on his
breathless audience. Hitler knew how to exploit his own hysteria.

Medicine men, too, often have this gift. On the stage of German history, Hitler sensed to what extent it was safe to let his own personality represent with hysterical abandon what was alive in every German listener and reader. Thus the role he chose reveals as much about his audience as about himself; and precisely that which to the non-German looked queerest and most morbid became the Brown Piper's most persuasive tune for German ears.

2. FATHER

". . . the father a faithful civil servant . . ."

Despite this sentimental characterization of the father, Hitler spends a heated portion of his first chapter in reiterating the assertion that neither his father nor "any power on earth could make an official" out of him. He knew already in earliest adolescence that the life of an official had no appeal for him. How different he was from his father! For though his father, too, had rebelled in early adolescence and at the age of thirteen had run away from home to become "something 'better,' " he had, after twenty-three years, returned home—and become a minor official. And "nobody remembered the little boy of long ago." This futile rebellion, Hitler says, made his father old early. Then, point for point, Hitler demonstrates a rebellious technique superior to that of his father.

Is this the naïve revelation of a pathological father-hate? Or if it is shrewd propaganda, what gave this Austrian German the right to expect that the tale of his boyhood would have a decisive appeal for masses of Reichs-Germans?

Obviously, not all Germans had fathers of the kind Hitler had, although many undoubtedly did. Yet we know that a literary theme, to be convincing, need not be true; it must sound true, as if it reminded one of something deep and past. The question, then, is whether the German father's position in his family made him act—either all of the time, or enough of the time, or at memorable times—in such a way that he created in his son an *inner* image which had some correspondence to that of the older Hitler's publicized image.

Superficially, the position in his family of the German middle-class father of the late nineteenth and the early twentieth century may have been quite similar to other Victorian versions of "life with Father." But patterns of education are elusive. They vary in families and persons; they may remain latent only to appear during memorable crises; they may be counteracted by determined attempts to be different.

I shall present here an impressionistic version of what I consider one pattern of German fatherhood. It is representative in the sense in which Galton's blurred composites of photography are representative of what they are supposed to show.

When the father comes home from work, even the walls seem to pull themselves together (*"nehmen sich zusammen"*). The mother—although often the unofficial master of the house—behaves differently enough to make a baby aware of it. She hurries to fulfill the father's whims and to avoid angering him. The children hold their breath, for the father does not approve of "nonsense"—that is, neither of the mother's feminine moods nor of the children's playfulness. The mother is required to be at his disposal as long as he is at home; his behavior suggests that he looks with disfavor on that unity of mother and children in which they had indulged in his absence. He often speaks to the mother as he speaks to the children, expecting compliance and cutting off any answer. The little boy comes to feel that all the gratifying ties with his mother are a thorn in the father's side, and that her love and admiration—the model for so many later fulfillments and achievements—can be reached only without the father's knowledge, or against his explicit wishes.

The mother increases this feeling by keeping some of the child's "nonsense" or badness from the father—if and when she pleases; while she expresses her disfavor by telling on the child when the father comes home, often making the father execute periodical corporal punishment for misdeeds, the details of which do not interest him. Sons are bad, and punishment is always justified. Later, when the boy comes to observe the father in company, when he notices his father's subservience to superiors, and when he observes his excessive sentimentality when he drinks and sings with his equals, the boy acquires that first ingredient of *Weltschmerz:* a deep doubt of the dignity of man—or at any rate of the "old man." All this, of course, exists concurrently with respect and love. During the storms of adolescence, however, when the boy's identity must settle things with his father image, it leads to that severe German *Pubertät* which is such a strange mixture of open rebellion and "secret sin," cynical delinquency and submissive obedience, romanticism and despondency, and which is apt to break the boy's spirit, once and for all.

In Germany, this pattern had traditional antecedents. It always just happened to happen, although it was, of course, not "planned." Indeed, some fathers who had resented the pattern deeply during their own boyhood wished desperately not to inflict it on their boys. But this wish again and again traumatically failed them in periods of crisis. Others tried to repress the pattern, only to augment both their and their children's neuroticisms. Often the boy sensed that the father himself was unhappy about his inability to break the vicious circle; for this emotional impotence the boy felt pity and disgust.

What, then, made this conflict so universally fateful? What differentiates—in an unconscious but decisive way—the German father's aloofness and harshness from similar traits in other Western fathers? I think the difference lies in the German father's essential lack of true inner authority—that authority which results from an integration of cultural ideal and educational method. The emphasis here definitely lies on *German* in the sense of *Reichs-German*. So often when discussing things German, we think and speak of well-preserved German *regions*, and of "typical" yet isolated instances where the German father's inner authority seemed deeply justified, founded as it was on old rural and small urban *Gemütlichkeit;* on urban *Kultur;* on Christian *Demut;* on professional *Bildung;* or on the spirit of social *Reform*. The important point is that all of this did not assume an integrated meaning on a national scale as the imagery of the Reich became dominant and industrialization undermined the previous social stratification.

Harshness is productive only where there is a sense of obligation in command, a sense of dignity in voluntary obedience. This, however, only an integrating cause can provide: a cause that unites past and present in accord with changes in the economic, political, and spiritual institutions.

The other Western nations had their democratic revolutions. They, as Max Weber demonstrated, by gradually taking over the privileges of their aristocratic classes, had thereby identified with aristocratic ideals. There came to be something of the French chevalier in every Frenchman, of the Anglo-Saxon gentleman in every Englishman, and of the rebellious aristocrat in every American. This something was fused with revolutionary ideals and created the concept of "free man"—a concept which assumes inalienable rights, indispensable self-denial, and unceasing revolutionary watchfulness. For reasons which we shall discuss presently, in connection with the problem of *Lebensraum*, the German identity never quite incorporated such imagery to the extent necessary to influence the unconscious modes of education. The average German father's dominance and harshness was not blended with the tenderness and dignity which comes from participation in an integrating cause. Rather, the average father, either habitually or in decisive moments, came to represent the habits and the ethics of the German top sergeant and petty official who—"dress'd in a little brief authority"—would never be more but was in constant danger of becoming less; and who had sold the birthright of a free man for an official title or a life pension.

In addition, there was the breakdown of the cultural institution which had taken care of the adolescent conflict in its traditional—and regional—forms. In the old days, for example, the custom of *Wanderschaft* existed. The boy left home in order to be an apprentice in foreign lands at about the age—or a little later—at which Hitler announced his opposition, and at which Hitler's father had run away from home. In the immediate pre-Nazi era, some kind of break either still took place, with paternal thunder and maternal tears; or it was reflected in more moderate conflicts which were less effective because more individualized and often neurotic; or it was repressed, in which case not the father-boy relation, but the boy's relation to himself, was broken. Often the—exclusively male—teachers had to bear the brunt of it; while the boy extended his idealistic or cynical hostility over the whole sphere of *Bürgelichkeit*—the German boy's contemptible world of "mere citizens." The connotation of this word *Bürger* is hard to transmit. It is not identical with the solid burgher; nor with the glutted bourgeois of the class-conscious revolutionary youth; and least of all with the proud citoyen or the responsible citizen, who, accepting his equal obligations, asserts his right to be an individual. Rather it means a kind of adult who has betrayed youth and idealism, and has sought refuge in a petty and servile kind of conservatism. This image was often used to indicate that all that was "normal" was corrupt, and that all that was "decent" was weak. As "Wanderbirds," adolescent boys would indulge in a romantic unity with Nature, shared with

many co-rebels and led by special types of youth leaders, professional and confessional adolescents. Another type of adolescent, the "lone genius," would write diaries, poems, and
treatises; at fifteen he would lament with Don Carlos' most
German of all adolescent complaints: "Twenty years old, and as
yet nothing done for immortality!" Other adolescents would form
small bands of intellectual cynics, of delinquents, of homosexuals, and of race-conscious chauvinists. The common feature
of all these activities, however, was the exclusion of the individual fathers as an influence and the adherence to some mystic-
romantic entity: Nature, Fatherland, Art, Existence, etc., which
were super-images of a pure mother, one who would not betray
the rebellious boy to that ogre, the father. While it was sometimes assumed that the mother would openly or secretly favor,
if not envy, such freedom, the father was considered its mortal
foe. If he failed to manifest sufficient enmity, he would be deliberately provoked: for his opposition was the life of the experience.

At this stage, the German boy would rather have died than be
aware of the fact that this misguided, this excessive initiative in
the direction of utter utopianism would arouse deep-seated guilt
and at the end lead to stunned exhaustion. The identification
with the father which in spite of everything had been well established in early childhood would come to the fore. In intricate
ways treacherous Fate (= reality) would finally make a *Bürger*
out of the boy—a "mere citizen" with an eternal sense of sin for
having sacrificed genius for Mammon and for a mere wife and
mere children such as anyone can have.

Naturally, this account is made typical to the point of caricature. Yet I believe that both the overt type and the covert pattern
existed, and that, in fact, this regular split between precocious
individualistic rebellion and disillusioned, obedient citizenship
was a strong factor in the political immaturity of the German:
this adolescent rebellion was an abortion of individualism and of
revolutionary spirit. It is my belief that the German fathers not
only did not oppose this rebellion, but, indeed, unconsciously
fostered it, as one sure way of maintaining their patriarchal hold
over youth. For once a patriarchal superego is firmly established
in early childhood, you can give youth rope: they cannot let
themselves go far.

In the Reichs-German character, this peculiar combination of idealistic rebellion and obedient submission led to a paradox. The German conscience is self-denying and cruel; but its ideals are shifting and, as it were, homeless. The German is harsh with himself and with others; but extreme harshness without inner authority breeds bitterness, fear, and vindictiveness. Lacking coordinated ideals, the German is apt to approach with blind conviction, cruel self-denial, and supreme perfectionism many contradictory and outright destructive aims.

After the defeat and the revolution of 1918 this psychological conflict was increased to the point of catastrophe in the German middle classes; and the middle classes anywhere significantly include the worker class in so far as it aspires to become middle-class. Their servility toward the upper class, which had lost the war, was now suddenly robbed of any resemblance to a meaningful subordination. The inflation endangered pensions. On the other hand, the groping masses were not prepared to anticipate or usurp either the role of free citizens or that of class-conscious workers. It is clear that only under such conditions could Hitler's images immediately convince so many—and paralyze so many more.

I shall not claim, then, that Hitler's father, as described in derogatory accounts, was, in his manifestly rude form, a typical German father. It frequently happens in history that an extreme and even atypical personal experience fits a universal latent conflict so well that a crisis lifts it to a representative position. In fact, it will be remembered here that great nations are apt to choose somebody from just beyond the borders to become their leader: as Napoleon came from Corsica, Stalin came from Georgia. It is a universal childhood pattern, then, which is the basis for the deep wonderment which befell the German man who read about Hitler as a youth. "No matter how firm and determined my father might be . . . his son was just as stubborn and obstinate in rejecting an idea which had little or no appeal for him. I did not want to become an official." This combination of personal revelation and shrewd propaganda (together with loud and determined action) at last carried with it that universal conviction for which the smoldering rebellion in German youth had been waiting: that no old man, be he father, emperor, or god, need stand in the way of his love for his mother Germany. At the same time it proved to the grown-up men that by betraying their rebellious adolescence they had become unworthy of leading Germany's youth, which henceforth would "shape its own destiny." Both fathers and sons now could identify with the Führer, an adolescent who never gave in.

Psychologists overdo the father attributes in Hitler's historical image; Hitler the adolescent who refused to become a father by any connotation, or, for that matter, a kaiser or a president. He did not repeat Napoleon's error. He was the Führer: a glorified older brother, who took over prerogatives of the fathers without overidentifying with them: calling his father "old while still a child," he reserved for himself the new position of the one who remains young in possession of supreme power. He was the unbroken adolescent who had chosen a career apart from civilian happiness, mercantile tranquillity, and spiritual peace: a gang leader who kept the boys together by demanding their admiration, by creating terror, and by shrewdly involving them in crimes from which there was no way back. And he was a ruthless exploiter of parental failures.

"The question of my career was to be settled more quickly than I had anticipated. . . . When I was thirteen my father died quite suddenly. My mother felt the obligation to continue my education for the career of an official." Thus thwarted, Hitler developed a severe pulmonary illness, and "all that I had fought for, all that I had longed for in secret, suddenly became reality. . . ." His mother had to grant the sick boy what she had denied the healthy and stubborn one: he could now go and prepare to be an artist. He did—and failed the entrance examination to the national art school. Then his mother died, too. He was now free —and lonely.

Professional failure followed that early school failure which in retrospect is rationalized as character strength and boyish toughness. It is well known how in picking his sub-leaders Hitler later redeemed similar civilian failures. He got away with this only because of the German habit of gilding school failure with the suspicion of hidden genius: "humanistic" education in Germany suffered all along from the severe split of fostering duty and discipline while glorifying the nostalgic outbreaks of poets.

In his dealings with the "old" generation inside or outside Germany, Hitler consequently played a role as stubborn, as devious, and as cynical as he reports his to have been in relation to his father. In fact, whenever he felt that his acts required public justification and apology, he was likely to set the stage as he did in the first chapter of *Mein Kampf*. His tirades were focused on one foreign leader—Churchill or Roosevelt—and described him as a feudal tyrant and a senile fool. He then created a second image, that of the slick, rich son and decadent cynic: Duff-Cooper and Eden, of all men, are the ones he selected. And, indeed, Germans acquiesced to his broken pledges, as long as Hitler, the tough adolescent, seemed merely to be taking advantage of other men's senility.

3. MOTHER

> ". . . the mother devoting herself to the cares of the household and looking after her children with eternally the same loving care."

Beyond this continuation of his fairy tale, Hitler says little of his mother. He mentions that she was sometimes lovingly worried about the fights he, the boy hero, got into; that after the father's death, she felt "obliged"—out of duty rather than inclination—to have him continue his education; and that soon she, too, died. He had respected his father, he says, but loved his mother.

Of "her children" there is no further word. Hitler never was the brother of anyone.

That Hitler, the histrionic and hysterical adventurer, had a pathological attachment to his mother, there can be little doubt. But this is not the point here. For, pathological or not, he deftly divides his mother image into the two categories which are of the highest propagandistic value: the loving, childlike, and slightly martyred cook who belongs in the warm and cozy background—and the gigantic marble or iron virgin, the monument to the ideal. In contrast to the sparsity of reference to his personal mother, then, there is an abundance of superhuman mother figures in his imagery. His Reichs-German fairy tale does not simply say that Hitler was born in Braunau because his parents lived there; no, it was "Fate which designated my birthplace." This happened when it happened not because of the natural way of things; no, it was an "unmerited mean trick of Fate" that he was "born in a period between two wars, at a time of quiet and order." When he was poor, "Poverty clasped me in her arms"; when sad, "Dame Sorrow was my foster mother." But all this "cruelty of Fate" he later learned to praise as the "wisdom of Providence," for it hardened him for the service of Nature, "the cruel Queen of all wisdom."

When the World War broke out, "Fate graciously permitted"

him to become a German foot soldier, the same "inexorable Goddess of Fate, who uses wars to weigh nations and men." When
after the defeat he stood before a court defending his first revolutionary acts, he felt certain "that the Goddess of History's
eternal judgment will smilingly tear up" the jury's verdict.

Fate, now treacherously frustrating the hero, now graciously
catering to his heroism and tearing up the judgment of the bad
old men: this is the infantile imagery which pervades much of
German idealism; it finds its most representative expression in
the theme of the young hero who becomes great in a foreign
country and returns to free and elevate the "captive" mother:
the romantic counterpart to the saga of King Oedipus.

Behind the imagery of superhuman mothers there thus lurks
a two-faced image of maternity: the mother at one time appears
playful, childlike, and generous; and at another, treacherous, and
in league with sinister forces. This, I believe, is a common set of
images in patriarchal societies where woman, in many ways kept
irresponsible and childlike, becomes a go-between and an in-
between. It thus happens that the father hates in her the elusive
children, and the children hate in her the aloof father. Since "the
mother" regularly becomes and remains the unconscious model
for "the world," under Hitler the ambivalence toward the maternal woman became one of the strongest features of German
official thinking.

The Führer's relationship to motherhood and family remained
ambiguous. In elaboration of a national fantasy he saw in himself
a lonely man fighting and pleasing superhuman mother figures
which now try to destroy him, now are forced to bless him. But
he did not acknowledge women as companions up to the bitter
end, when he insisted on making an honest woman out of Eva
Braun, whom he presently shot with his own hands—or so the
legend ends. But the wives of other men gave birth to their
children in the shelter of the chancellery, while he himself, according to his official biographer, "is the embodiment of the
national will. He does not know any family life; neither does
he know any vice."

Hitler carried this official ambivalence toward women over
into his relationship to Germany as an image. Openly despising
the masses of his countrymen, who, after all, constitute Germany, he stood frenziedly before them, and implored them with
his fanatical cries of "Germany, Germany, Germany" to believe
in a mystical national entity.

But then, the Germans have always been inclined to manifest a comparable attitude of ambivalence toward mankind and the world at large. That the world is essentially perceived as an "outer world" is true for most tribes or nations. But for Germany the world is constantly changing its quality—and always to an extreme. The world is experienced either as vastly superior in age and wisdom, the goal of eternal longing and *Wanderlust;* or as a mean, treacherous, encircling encampment of enemies living for one aim—namely, the betrayal of Germany; or as a mysterious *Lebensraum* to be won by Teutonic courage and to be used for a thousand years of adolescent aggrandizement.

4. ADOLESCENT

In this country, the word "adolescence," to all but those who have to deal with it professionally, has come to mean, at worst, a no man's land between childhood and maturity, and at best, a "normal" time of sports and horseplay, of gangs and cliques and parties. The adolescent in this counrty offers less of a problem and feels less isolated because he has, in fact, become the cultural arbiter; few men in this country can afford to abandon the gestures of the adolescent, along with those of the freeman forever dedicated to the defeat of autocrats.

From here, then, it is hard to see what adolescence may mean in other cultures. In the primitive past, dramatic and bizarre adolescence rites were performed in an endeavor to modify and sublimate the adolescent's budding manhood. In primitive rituals the adolescent was forced to sacrifice some of his blood, some of his teeth, or a part of his genitals; in religious ceremonies he is taught to admit his sinfulness and bow his knee. Ancient rites confirmed the boy's intention of becoming a man in his father's world but at the same time of remaining eternally the modest son of a "Great Father." Leaders of the ritual dance, redeemers, and tragic actors were the representatives of guilt and expiation. Germany's adolescent rebellion was a climactic step in a universal psychological development which parallels the decline of feudalism: the inner emancipation of the sons. For while there are close parallels between primitive adolescence rites and those of National Socialism, there is one most significant difference. In Hitler's world, the adolescent marched with his emancipated equals. Their leader had never sacrificed his will to any father. In fact, he had said that conscience is a blemish like circumcision, and that they both are Jewish blemishes.

Hitler's horror of Jewry—an "emasculating germ" represented by less than 1 per cent of his nation of 70 million—is clothed in the imagery of phobia; he describes the danger emanating from it as a weakening infection and a dirtying contamination. Syphilophobia is the least psychiatry can properly diagnose in his case. But here again, it is hard to say where personal symptom ends and shrewd propaganda begins. For the idealistic adolescent's imagery is typically one of purest white and blackest black. His constant preoccupation is with the attainment of what is white, and the phobic avoidance and extirpation of everything black, in others and in himself. Fears of sexuality, especially, make the adolescent suggestible to words like these: "Alone the loss of purity of the blood destroys the inner happiness forever; it eternally lowers man, and never again can its consequences be removed from body and mind." [2]

The pre-Nazi German adolescent was passionately cruel with himself; it was not in order to indulge himself that he opposed his father. When he "fell," his guilt was great. Hitler, so this adolescent was made to feel, was the man who had the right to be cruel against black everywhere because he was not lenient with himself. What aroused suspicions in sensible non-Germans —namely, Hitler's proclaimed abstinence from meat, coffee, alcohol, and sex—here counted as a heavy propaganda factor. For Hitler thus proved his moral right to free the Germans from their postwar masochism and to convince them that they, in turn, had a right to hate, to torture, to kill.

In the children, Hitler tried to replace the complicated conflict of adolescence as it pursued every German, with simple patterns of hypnotic action and freedom from thought. To do so he established an organization, a training, and a motto which would divert all adolescent energy into National Socialism. The organization was the Hitler Youth; the motto, "Youth shapes its own destiny."

God no longer mattered: "At this hour when the earth is consecrating itself to the sun, we have only one thought. Our sun is Adolph Hitler." [3] Parents did not matter: "All those who from the perspective of their 'experience', and from that alone combat our method of letting youth lead youth, must be silenced. . . ." [4] Ethics did not matter: "An entirely fresh, newborn generation has arisen, free from the preconceived ideas, free from compromises, ready to be loyal to the orders which are its birthright." [5] Brotherhood, friendship did not matter: "I heard not a single song expressing any tender emotion of friendship, love of parents, love for fellow-man, joy of living, hope for future life." [6] Learning did not matter: "National Socialist ideology is to be a sacred foundation. It is not to be degraded by detailed explanation." [7]

What mattered was: to be on the move without looking backward. "Let everything go to pieces, we shall march on. For to-day Germany is ours; tomorrow, the whole world."

On such a foundation Hitler offered a simple racial dichotomy of cosmic dimensions: the German (soldier) versus the Jew. The Jew is described as small, black, and hairy all over; his back is bent, his feet are flat; his eyes squint, and his lips smack; he has an evil smell, is promiscuous, and loves to deflower, impregnate, and infect blond girls. The Aryan is tall, erect, light, without hair on chest and limbs; his glance, walk, and talk are *stramm*, his greeting the outstretched arm. He is passionately clean in his habits. He would not knowingly touch a Jewish girl —except in a brothel.

This antithesis is clearly one of ape man and superman. But while in this country such imagery may have made the comics, in Germany it became official food for adult minds. And let us not forget (for the Germans will not forget) that for long years German youth and the German army seemed to indicate a success for Hitler's imagery. Healthy, hard, calm, obedient, fanatic, they "challenge everything that is weak in body, in intensity, and in loyalty." [8] They were arrogant in the extreme; and it was only in their sneering arrogance that the old German fear of succumbing to foreign "cultured" influence could be recognized.

In women, too, National Socialist race consciousness established a new pride. Girls were taught to accept joyfully the functions of their bodies if mated with selected Aryans. They received sexual enlightenment and encouragement. Childbirth, legitimate or illegitimate, was promoted by propaganda, by subsidies, by the institution of "State children," who were born "for the Führer." Breast feeding was advocated; what American psychiatrists at that time dared suggest only in professional journals, the German state decreed: "Stillfähigkeit ist Stillwille"— ability to nurse is the will to nurse. Thus German babyhood was enriched for the sake of the race and of the Führer.

In his imagery no actor and no effective innovator is really independent, nor can he dare to be entirely original: his originality must consist in the courage and singular concentration with which he expresses an existing imagery—at the proper time. If he does so, however, he is convincing to himself and to others —and paralyzes his adversaries, in so far as they unconsciously partake of his imagery, so that they will wait, become insecure, and finally surrender.

In Germany, then, we saw a highly organized and highly educated nation surrender to the imagery of ideological adolescence. We have indicated that we cannot lay the blame for this on the power of the leaders' individual neuroses. Can we blame the childhood patterns of the led?

5. *Lebensraum,* SOLDIER, JEW

The mere impressionistic comparison of a nation's familial imagery with her national and international attitudes can easily become absurd. It seems to lead to the implication that one could change international attitudes by doctoring a nation's family patterns. Yet nations change only when their total reality changes. In America, the sons and daughters of all nations become Americans, although each remains beset by their specific conflict: and I dare say that many a German-American reader will have recognized some of his own father's problems in this chapter. He will recognize it because there is a lag between his father's world and his: his father lives in a different space-time.

The very ease with which comparisons between childhood patterns and national attitudes can be drawn, and the very absurdity to which they can lead, obscure the important truth which is, nevertheless, involved. We shall therefore use this chapter to illustrate the way in which historical and geographic reality amplify familial patterns and to what extent, in turn, these patterns influence a people's interpretation of reality. It is impossible to characterize what is German without relating Germany's familial imagery to her central position in Europe. For, as we saw, even the most intelligent groups must orient themselves and one another in relatively simple subverbal, magic design. Every person and every group has a limited inventory of historically determined spatial-temporal concepts, which determine the world image, the evil and ideal prototypes, and the unconscious life plan. These concepts dominate a nation's strivings and can lead to high distinction; but they also narrow a people's imagination and thus invite disaster. In German history, such outstanding configurations are encirclement versus *Lebensraum;* and disunity versus unity. Such terms are, of course, so universal that they seem unspecific; the observer who realizes the weight which these words carry in German thinking must suspect them of being insincere propaganda. Yet nothing can be more fatal in international encounters than the attempt to belittle or to argue another nation's mythological space-time. The non-German does not realize that in Germany these words carried a conviction far beyond that of ordinary logic.

The official version of *Lebensraum* stated that the Nazi state must assure, within Europe, military hegemony and armaments monopoly, economic preponderance, and intellectual leadership. Beyond this, *Lebensraum* had an essentially magic meaning. What is this meaning?

At the end of the first World War Max Weber wrote that destiny had decreed [even a realistic German says "destiny," not "geography" or "history"] that Germany alone should have as its immediate neighbors three great land powers and the greatest sea power and that it should stand in their way. No other country on earth, he said, was in this situation.[9]

As Weber saw it, the necessity to create national greatness and security in a thoroughly encircled and vulnerable position left two alternatives: Germany might retain its regional quality and become a modern federation like Switzerland—likable and useful to everybody and a danger to nobody; or it might quickly develop a Reich, fashioned out of quite unfavorable political characteristics, a Reich as mature and powerful as that of England or France, capable of playing power politics, in order to build with the West a cultural and military defense unit against the East. But Weber was a "realist," which meant he considered only what, according to the considered thinking of his conservative mind, seemed "reasonable." * He did not dream that within

---

* A recent publication in this country (H. H. Gerth and C. Wright Mills, *From Max Weber: Essays in Sociology,* Oxford University Press, New York, 1946, pp. 28–29) gives an account of certain events in Weber's life which will be quoted here because they strikingly illustrate the familial patterns under discussion:

"His strong sense of chivalry was, in part, a response to the patriarchal and domineering attitude of his father, who understood his wife's love as a willingness to serve and to allow herself to be exploited and controlled by him. This situation came to a climax when Weber, at the age of 31, in the

a few years a man would stand up and proclaim, even bring to near fulfillment, a third alternative—namely, that Germany would become a nation so powerful and so shrewdly led that the whole encircling combination of Paris, London, Rome, and Moscow could one by one be overrun and occupied long enough to be emasculated "for a thousand years."

This plan still appears fantastic to the non-German. He wonders how such a scheme could live together in one and the same national mind with the simple kindness and the cosmopolitan wisdom representative of the "real" German culture. But, as pointed out, the world meant regional, not national, virtues when it spoke of German culture. It persistently underestimated the desperate German need for unity which, indeed, cannot be appreciated by peoples who in their own land take such unity for granted. The world is apt once more to underestimate the force with which the question of national unity may become a matter of the *preservation of identity*, and thus a matter of (human) life and death, far surpassing the question of political systems.

Throughout her history, the area of Germany has been subjected, or has been potentially vulnerable, to sweeping invasions. It is true that in a hundred-odd years her vital centers had not been occupied by an enemy; but she remained conscious of her vulnerable position, both rationally and irrationally.

The threat of military invasion, however, is not the only one. Whether invading or being invaded by different countries, Germany has been impressed by *foreign values*. Her attitude toward

---

presence of his mother and his wife, saw fit to hold judgment over his father: he would remorselessly break all relations with him unless he met the son's condition: the mother should visit him 'alone' without the father. We have noted that the father died only a short time after this encounter and that Weber came out of the situation with an ineffaceable sense of guilt. One may certainly infer an inordinately strong Oedipus situation.

"Throughout his life, Weber maintained a full correspondence with his mother, who once referred to him as 'an older daughter.' She eagerly sought counsel with him, her first-born, rather than with her husband, in matters concerning the demeanor of her third son. One should also pay heed to what was, to be sure, a passing phase of young Weber's aspiration: his desire to become a real he-man at the university. After only three semesters, he succeeded in changing externally from a slender mother's boy to a massive, beer-drinking, duel-marked, cigar-puffing student of Imperial Germany, whom his mother greeted with a slap in the face. Clearly, this was the father's son. The two models of identification and their associated values, rooted in mother and father, never disappeared from Max Weber's inner life. . . ."

these values, and their relation to her own cultural diversity, constitute a clinical problem hard to define. But one may say that no other young nation of similar size, density, and historical diversity of population, with a similar lack of natural frontiers, is exposed to cultural influences as divergent in their nature and as disturbing in their succession as the influences emanating from Germany's neighbors. As is true for the elements which make for individual anxiety, it is the consistent mutual aggravation of all these items which has never allowed German identity to crystallize or to assimilate economic and social evolution in gradual and logical steps.

The German image of disunity is based on a historical feeling of discomfort which may be called the "Limes complex." The Limes Germanicus was a wall—comparable to the Chinese wall —built by the Romans through western and southern Germany to separate the conquered provinces from those which remained barbaric. This wall was destroyed long ago. But it was replaced by a cultural barrier which separated the area in the south influenced by the Church of Rome from that of Protestant northern Germany. Other empires (military, spiritual, cultural) have thus reached into Germany: from the west, sensual and rational France; from the east, illiterate, spiritual, and dynastic Russia; from the north and northwest, individualistic "protestantism," and from the southeast, oriental easygoingness. All conflicts between east and west, north and south, were fought out in battle somewhere in Germany—and in the German mind.

Germany, from the beginning, was thus constantly disturbed by a traumatic sequence of divergent influences, which aggravated and kept acute a specific form of the universal conflict between suggestibility and defensive stubbornness. Hitler thus promised Germany not only the military conquest of the invasion centers surrounding the Reich, but also a victory of race consciousness over the "bacterial" invasion of foreign aesthetics and ethics within the German mind. His aim was not only the eternal obliteration of Germany's military defeat in the first World War, but also a complete purge of the corrupt foreign values which had invaded German culture. To the tormented Germans this was real "freedom"; other freedoms, in comparison, seemed vague and unessential.

Thus the appeal of Adolf Hitler's violent remedy was directed toward a Reich which was large and felt potentially great; but

which at the same time felt vulnerable in its frontiers and undeveloped in its political core. It was directed toward a national
mind with a great regional heritage and burning spiritual ambitions but with a morbid suggestibility and a deep insecurity in
its basic values. Only an adversary who can fathom the effect of
such a situation on the struggle for identity in a nation's youth
can divine their danger—and his.

Germany's desperate paradoxes led to those extremes of German contradictions which—before Hitler—were considered to
constitute two different Germanies. In reaction to the sense of
cultural encirclement one type of Reichs-German became, as it
were, too broad, while the other became too narrow. That other
nations have analogous conflicts between cosmopolitanism and
provincialism does not remove the necessity of understanding
the German version of this dilemma. The "too broad" type denied
or hated the German paradox and embraced the whole encircling
"outer world"; he became cosmopolitan beyond recognition.
The "narrow" type tried to ignore foreign temptations and became "German" to the point of caricature. The first was always
glad to be mistaken for an Englishman, a Frenchman, or an
American; the second arrogantly overdid the narrow inventory
of his few genuine characteristics. The first felt and thought on
an Olympian scale; the second became obedient and mechanical to the exclusion of all thought and feeling. The first often was
a lifelong nostalgic, a voluntary exile, or a potential suicide or
psychotic; the second remained at home, or wherever he went
made himself at home and, gritting his teeth, remained a German.

The world admired the first type and sneered at the second;
the world ignored, until it was too late, the fact that neither of
these types led to a rebirth on a national level of that maturity
and of that monumental dignity which at times had characterized the burghers and artisans of Germany's regions. The world
ignored the fact that neither type felt sure in himself and safe
in the world, that neither of them accepted a part in man's political emancipation.

It is a fatal error to assume that National Socialism came about
in spite of Germany's intellectual greatness. It was the natural
result of the particular social—or rather asocial—orientation of
its great men.

We need not limit ourselves here to the consideration of such
a lonely hater of man's realities as Nietzsche, who was fortunate

enough to die demented and deluded instead of being forced to witness the stark reality of the uniformed supermen whom he had helped to create. No, we may think of men with an exquisite eye for realities, such as Thomas Mann, who during the first World War is reported to have encouraged the Germans by saying that, after all, the possession of a philosopher such as Kant more than compensated for the French Revolution, and that the *Critique of Pure Reason* was, in fact, a far more radical revolution than was the proclamation of the rights of man.[10]

I realize that this may well have been a great intellectual's way of saying the wrong thing at the right time, which is an intellectual's privilege during his nation's emergencies. But the statement illustrates the German's awe of overpowering, lonely, and often tragic greatness, and his readiness to sacrifice the individual's right in order to emancipate the greatness in his own heart.

Neither as aloof a cosmopolitan as Goethe, nor as aloof a statesman as Bismarck—then the dominant images in the German school's inventory of guiding images—had essentially contributed to a German image of democratic man.

The attempt, after the defeat of 1918, to create a republic led to a temporary dominance of the "too broad" German. The leaders of that era could not prevent the merging of political immaturity and intellectual escapism which combined to create a myth of strange, almost hysterical passion: *Fate* had sent defeat to Germany in order to single her out from among the nations. *Fate* had elected her to be the first great country to accept defeat voluntarily, to shoulder moral blame completely, and to resign political greatness once and for all. Thus *Fate* had used all the Allied countries with all their soldiers, alive and dead, merely to elevate Germany to an exalted existence in an unlimited *spiritual Lebensraum.* Even in this very depth of masochistic self-abasement—impressively decried by Max Weber— world history was still a secret arrangement between the Teutonic spirit and the Goddess of Fate. Germany's basic relationship to history had not changed. The world seems to have been surprised when this spiritual chauvinism gradually turned back into militarism, when it again employed sadistic rather than masochistic images and techniques. The Great Powers at this point failed in their responsibility to "re-educate" Germany in the only way in which one can re-educate peoples—namely, by presenting them with the incorruptible fact of a new identity within a more universal political framework. Instead, they exploited German masochism and increased her universal hopelessness. The too narrow German, in bitter hiding since defeat, now came forward to prepare the wildest possible earthly *Lebensraum* for the narrowest type of German: Aryan world domination.

Caught between the too narrow and the too broad, the few statesmen capable of dignity, realism, and vision broke under the strain or were murdered. The Germans, without work, without food, and without a new integrity, began to listen to Hitler's imagery, which, for the first time in Reichs-German history, gave political expression to the spirit of the German adolescent. There was magic weight in the words, "I, however, resolved now to become a politician," with which the unbroken adolescent closes the seventh chapter of *Mein Kampf*.

When Hitler thus undertook to bring the adolescent imagery of his people to political dominance, a magnificent tool gradually became his—the German army. Book knowledge of the war of 1870-71 had been Hitler's "greatest spiritual experience." In 1914, when he had been permitted to become a Reichs-German soldier, he had moved into the full light of that heroic history. Then had come defeat. Hitler had denied with hysterical fanaticism—he himself had been blinded by gas, some say by emotional exertion—that the light had withdrawn from that image. He had appeared determined to redeem it. His enemies, inside and outside Germany, had shrugged their shoulders.

But here again it is necessary to look beyond the obsessive and to see the ingenious. From the first World War's Thomas Mann to the second's Nazi philosopher, the German soldier was conceived of as a personification, or even the spiritualization, of what is German. He represented "the Watch on the Rhine": the human wall replacing Germany's nonexistent natural frontiers. In him unity through blind obedience proved itself and aspirations toward democratic diversity defeated themselves. It would be dangerous to overlook the fact that this position, exploited as it was by a noisy type of high-stepping young officer, also helped to develop an officer aristocracy which in true absorption of the aristocratic-revolutionary principles of other nations harbored one of the few politically mature European types in Germany. If Hitler, therefore, denied the defeat of this army with all the weapons of self-deception and falsehood, he saved for himself and for German youth the only integrated images that could belong to everybody.

The treaty of Versailles, cleverly exploited, proved helpful in the creation of a new streamlined German soldier. The small army became an army of specialists. Thus the oldest and least modified Reichs-German type was re-created with the insignia of the modern technician. A spirit of teamwork and of personal responsibility replaced that of blind obedience; maturity, instead of caste, became the mark of the officer. With such new material the Blitzkrieg was prepared: not only a technical feat, but also a sweeping solution and salvation for the traumatized German people. For it promised a victory of movement over the Allied superiority in artillery power (and the industrial might behind it) which, during the first World War, had "nailed down" the Germans until they became ready to trust Wilson, to break up, and to attend to higher things. Furthermore, Germany's youth, in the Blitzkrieg, experienced "finalities of a revolution reaching into spiritual, mental and material depths." [11] It relieved the feeling of encirclement and of peripheral vulnerability. And, to quote a Nazi: "The instinctive pleasure which youth finds in the power of engines here divines the expansions of mankind's limitations, which were so narrow from the start and, on the whole, have not been widened by civilization." [12] It would be fatal to brush aside such Nazi mysticism. To defeat motorized Germany, the youth of other countries also had to learn like modern centaurs to grow together with their fighting machines into new restless beings of passionate precision. Hitler tried to anticipate an age that would experience a motorized world as natural; and to fuse it with the image of a totalitarian "state machine." He took it as a personal insult when he saw the industries of the democracies go into high gear (*Gelump*—rubbish—he tried to call their output). When their firepower came on wings right into his cities, and above all, when he saw that Anglo-Saxon youths could identify with their machines without losing their heads, he was incredulous. When he then saw the Russians perform miracles not only of defense but also of offense, his irrational fury knew no bounds, for in his inventory of images he had characterized them not only as unequal to his soldiers, but as people below any possible comparison: men of the mud (*Sumpfmenschen*), he called them, and subhuman. They thus became, toward the end, equivalent to the other subhumans, the Jews:

only the more fortunate Russians had a country and an army.

It is obvious enough that much envy was hidden in Hitler's fantastic overestimation of the Jewish "danger," embodied as it was in such a small part of the population, and a highly intellectualized one at that. But as we have said, the narrow German always felt endangered, denationalized, by information which exposed him to the relativity and diversity of cultural values. The Jew seemed to remain himself despite dispersion over the world, while the German trembled for his identity in his own country. In fact, these mysterious Jews seemed to be making of intellectual relativity a means of racial self-preservation. To some Germans, this was not understandable without assuming an especially devious chauvinism, a hidden Jewish pact with Fate.

*   *   *

Notes

1. Adolf Hitler, *Mein Kampf*, Reynal & Hitchcock edition, New York, 1941, by arrangement with Houghton-Mifflin Company.
2. *Ibid.*
3. Quoted in G. Ziemer, *Education for Death*, Oxford University Press, New York, 1941.
4. Quoted in Hans Siemsen, *Hitler Youth*, Lindsay Drummond, London, 1941.
5. Quoted in Ziemer, *op. cit.*
6. Ziemer, *op. cit.*
7. Quoted in Ziemer, *op. cit.*
8. Ziemer, *op. cit.*
9. Max Weber, *Gesammelte Politische Schriften*, Drei Masken Verlag, Munich, 1921.
10. Janet Flanner, "Goethe in Hollywood," *The New Yorker*, December 20, 1941.
11. W. W. Backhaus, "Ueberwindung der Materialschlacht," *Das Reich*, Berlin, July 13, 1941.
12. *Ibid.*

Suggestions for Further Reading

(*Books marked with* * *are available in paperback editions.*)

A. E. Taylor's *The Mind of Plato* (Ann Arbor, 1960)* offers a careful summary and analysis of the Dialogues. Karl Popper's attack on Plato in *The Open Society and its Enemies* (London, 1962)* is provocative. For a favorable view of Plato's position, John Wild's *Plato's Modern Enemies and the Theory of Natural Law* (Chicago, 1953) will right the balance. In addition to *Suicide*, interested students should also consult Emile Durkheim's famous work on the social psychology of religion, *The Elementary Forms of Religious Life* (New York, 1961).* For a quite different view of the relationship between social structure and religious belief, Max Weber's *The Protestant Ethic and the Spirit of Capitalism* (New York, 1948)* can be read, in conjunction with R. H. Tawney's *Religion and the Rise of Capitalism* (New York, 1953).* A suggestive contemporary case study is Melford Spiro's study of a utopian community, *Kibbutz* (New York, 1963).*

The psychoanalytic approach to the problem of personality and society is found in many of Freud's works, among which *Civilization and its Discontents* is perhaps most famous. Herbert Marcuse's *Eros and Civilization* (Boston, 1955) is a more recent development of Freud's insights. Erik Erikson's *Young Man Luther* (New York, 1958) * is a remarkable study of the psychology of an historic individual. For an entirely different, behaviorist, approach to personality and society, B. F. Skinner's modern utopia, *Walden Two* (New York, 1962)* is irritating and suggestive.

The phenomenon of naziism provoked a flood of brilliant attempts to comprehend the descent of the most cultivated people of Europe into the abyss of bestiality. Franz Neumann's *Behemoth* (New York, 1963), Theodor Adorno's *The Authoritarian Personality* (New York, 1950), and Hannah Arendt's *Origins of Totalitarianism* (New York, 1958), are among the most profound. Bertram Schaffner's *Fatherland; A Study of Authoritarianism in the German Family* (New York, 1948) offers psychoanalytic insight into the causes of the Nazi era.

Anthropologists have been the most active practitioners of the cultural or societal approach to the study of the human personality. Among the countless fine works which could be mentioned, we may note the first of them all, Edward B. Tylor's *Primitive Culture* (New York, 1889), and such well-known introductory works as Ruth Benedict's *Patterns of Culture* (New York, 1934).*

The sociological literature is equally rich. A sophisticated survey and summary can be found in Hans Gerth and C. Wright Mill's *Character and Social Structure* (New York, 1953). The same authors have translated large quantities of Max Weber's theoretical sociology under the title *From Max Weber: Essays in Sociology* (New York, 1958).* The *locus classicus* for the social theory of the self is George Herbert Mead's *Mind, Self and Society* (Chicago, 1934). For a more specifically political study of the relationship between personality and society, William Kornhauser's *Politics of Mass Society* (New York, 1959) advances the theory of mass politics to a new level of systematic clarity. Harold Lasswell has dealt with the subject effectively in several of his books, including *Politics* (New York, 1958), and *Psychopathology and Politics* (New York, 1960).*

Finally, in quite a different direction, let me recommend Erich Auerbach's masterpiece of literary criticism and social theory, *Mimesis* (New York, 1957).* Auerbach demonstrates in a series of close textual analyses that there is an intimate relation between our perception of the social world and the very syntax of our language.

THE PARADOX
OF SOCIAL CONTROL

Does society have the right to interfere with an individual's life purely in order to help him? Ought the state to act toward its citizens as a parent toward his children, guiding them by its superior wisdom and protecting them from the harm which they may do themselves? John Stuart Mill says no, and thereby sets himself against the whole social-democratic tradition which culminates in the modern welfare state. The Grand Inquisitor in Dostoyevsky's famous parable persuasively argues yes, for only a few men he says are capable of bearing the terrible burden of freedom.

Initially, the question was one of law, justice, and the rights of the individual against the state. In Part One we approached the issue first from the perspective of state authority and then from the opposite viewpoint of the individual's loyalty to the state. Clearly, however, the threat to individual liberty lies as much in the pressures of social opinion as in formal acts of government. It becomes necessary, therefore, to look beyond governments to the informal control which society exercises over its members.

George Homans and Erving Goffman, in their accounts of empirical research into forms of social control, demonstrate that the problem is far more complicated than even Mill imagined. It would seem that workers can, at least for a time, be fooled into thinking that the management takes an interest in themselves and their concerns, and thereby be encouraged to increase production purely for the benefit of their bosses. Tricks of human engineering lead them to ignore their own best interests and identify with the owners. This lesson is often enough repeated in modern life, as janitors are placated with the title "superintendent" and old people are reassured of their importance to a society which no longer needs them by means of the empty title "senior citizens."

We have here a picture of social pressure which is very different from that evoked by Mill. The workers in the Western Electric plant experiments discussed by Homans were tricked into raising production by playing on their desire to have an interest taken in them by the previously unconcerned management. In a sad and perverse sense, they received adequate compensation for their increased output, for during the experimental period their labor had at least a superficial significance which until then it had totally lacked. They were not pressured, they were seduced. We return once more to the lesson of David Riesman's theory of character types. In order to feel the approval or disapproval of society as an external pressure, the individual must already have a well-developed sense of the identity and integrity of his own personality. A society which does not foster such personalities may therefore exercise very extensive controls over individual behavior without ever finding it necessary to employ the sort of social pressure which alarmed Mill.

We gain considerable insight into this problem from the final selection, Erving Goffman's account of the threats to ego-identity in such "total institutions" as prisons and mental hospitals. The individual's self-image is sustained by a number of small, daily social acts occurring in a certain setting and requiring material props such as articles of clothing, cigarettes (both for smoking and for offering to others), and money. As Goffman puts the point in another of his works, we are engaged throughout life in playing roles, and the structure of a personality can be analyzed into the repertory of roles which the individual sustains. When these roles are thwarted, when the individual is denied the material props and social responses appropriate to his roles, the integrity of his personality is placed under stress and may be destroyed, thereby also destroying his will to maintain a front. Brainwashing is a particularly dramatic form of this kind of social control. More mundane instances can be found all around us, as in the business executive thrown off stride by a policeman who denies him the customary deference or the wealthy draftee who finds that sloppy fatigues and crewcut do not allow him to maintain a proper social distance from his lower-class sergeant.

Sociology poses for us the perennial problem of lost innocence. Once we understand the ways in which the integrity of personality is sustained or destroyed, we have no choice but to debate the extent and nature of the legitimate uses of that knowledge. The problem is unavoidable, for contrary to Mill, the total absence of all social controls would produce a psychotic or completely undeveloped personality, not a free one.

GEORGE C. HOMANS

The Western Electric Researches

George C. Homans, 1910–   , is Professor of Sociology at Harvard University. This paper is his summary report of a famous series of experiments performed in 1938 under the direction of Elton Mayo and others. The discoveries of Mayo and his colleagues have often been cited as pioneer instances of "human engineering." Some social critics have argued that it is immoral to attempt to control beliefs and attitudes by the sorts of techniques used by Mayo. It is impossible from this essay to tell whether Homans is aware of the moral dimension of the Western Electric experiment. Needless to say, few general conclusions about techniques of social control can be drawn from the quite circumscribed and controlled investigations outlined below. No one, however, will have any difficulty recalling similar instances of human engineering from his own experience.

Perhaps the most important program of research studied by the Committee on Work in Industry of the National Research Council is that which has been carried on at the Hawthorne (Chicago) Works of the Western Electric Company. This program was described by H. A. Wright and M. L. Putnam of the Western Electric Company and by F. J. Roethlisberger, now Professor of Human Relations, Graduate School of Business Administration, Harvard University, particularly at a meeting of the Committee held on March 9, 1938. These men, together with Elton Mayo and G. A. Pennock, both members of the Committee, had been intimately associated with the research.[1]

A word about the Western Electric Company is a necessary introduction to what follows. This company is engaged in manufacturing equipment for the telephone industry. Besides doing this part of its work, it has always shown concern for the welfare of its employees. In the matter of wages and hours, it has maintained a high standard. It has provided good physical conditions

for its employees; and it has tried to make use of every established method of vocational guidance in the effort to suit the
worker to his work. The efforts of the company have been rewarded in good industrial relations: there has been no strike or
other severe symptom of discontent for over twenty years. In
short there is no reason to doubt that while these researches
were being carried out, the morale of the company was high and
that the employees, as a body, had confidence in the abilities and
motives of the company management. These facts had an important bearing on the results achieved.

The program of research which will be described grew out of
a study conducted at Hawthorne by the Western Electric Company in collaboration with the National Research Council, the
aim of which was to determine the relation between intensity of
illumination and efficiency of workers, measured in output. One
of the experiments made was the following: Two groups of employees doing similar work under similar conditions were chosen,
and records of output were kept for each group. The intensity of
the light under which one group worked was varied, while that
under which the other group worked was held constant. By this
method the investigators hoped to isolate from the effect of other
variables the effect of changes in the intensity of illumination
on the rate of output.

In this hope they were disappointed. The experiment failed to
show any simple relation between experimental changes in the
intensity of illumination and observed changes in the rate of
output. The investigators concluded that this result was obtained,
not because such a relation did not exist, but because it was in
fact impossible to isolate it from the other variables entering into
any determination of productive efficiency. This kind of difficulty,
of course, has been encountered in experimental work in many
fields. Furthermore, the investigators were in agreement as to the
character of some of these other variables. They were convinced
that one of the major factors which prevented their securing a
satisfactory result was psychological. The employees being tested
were reacting to changes in light intensity in the way in which
they assumed that they were expected to react. That is, when
light intensity was increased they were expected to produce
more; when it was decreased they were expected to produce less.
A further experiment was devised to demonstrate this point. The
light bulbs were changed, as they had been changed before, and

the workers were allowed to assume that as a result there would be more light. They commented favorably on the increased illumination. As a matter of fact, the bulbs had been replaced with others of just the same power. Other experiments of the sort were made, and in each case the results could be explained as a "psychological" reaction rather than as a "physiological" one.

This discovery seemed to be important. It suggested that the relations between other physical conditions and the efficiency of workers might be obscured by similar psychological reactions. Nevertheless, the investigators were determined to continue in their course. They recognized the existence of the psychological factors, but they thought of them only as disturbing influences. They were not yet ready to turn their attention to the psychological factors themselves. Instead, they were concerned with devising a better way of eliminating them from the experiments, and the experiments they wanted to try by no means ended with illumination. For instance, there was the question of what was called "fatigue." Little information existed about the effect on efficiency of changes in the hours of work and the introduction of rest pauses. The investigators finally came to the conclusion that if a small group of workers were isolated in a separate room and asked to cooperate, the psychological reaction would in time disappear, and they would work exactly as they felt. That is, changes in their rate of output would be the direct result of changes in their physical conditions of work and nothing else.

The decision to organize such a group was in fact taken. A small number of workers was to be selected and placed in a separate room, where experiments were to be made with different kinds of working conditions in order to see if more exact information could be secured. Six questions were asked by those setting up the experiment. They were the following:

1. Do employees actually get tired out?
2. Are rest pauses desirable?
3. Is a shorter working day desirable?
4. What is the attitude of employees toward their work and toward the company?
5. What is the effect of changing the type of working equipment?
6. Why does production fall off in the afternoon?

It is obvious that several of these questions could be answered only indirectly by the proposed experiment, and several of them touched upon the "psychological" rather than the "physiological" factors involved. Nevertheless, all of them arose out of the bewilderment of men of experience faced with the problem of dealing with fellow human beings in a large industrial organization. In fact, one of the executives of the company saw the purpose of the experiment in even simpler and more general terms. He said that the experiment grew out of a desire on the part of the management to "know more about our workers." In this way began the experiment which is referred to as the Relay Assembly Test Room. With this experiment and the others that followed, members of the Department of Industrial Research of the Graduate School of Business Administration, Harvard University, came to be closely associated.

In April, 1927, six girls were selected from a large shop department of the Hawthorne Works. They were chosen as average workers, neither inexperienced nor expert, and their work consisted of the assembling of telephone relays. A coil, armature, contact springs, and insulators were put together on a fixture and secured in position by means of four machine screws. The operation at that time was being completed at the rate of about five relays in six minutes. This particular operation was chosen for the experiment because the relays were being assembled often enough so that even slight changes in output rate would show themselves at once on the output record. Five of the girls were to do the actual assembly work; the duty of the sixth was to keep the others supplied with parts.

The test room itself was an area divided from the main department by a wooden partition eight feet high. The girls sat in a row on one side of a long workbench. Their bench and assembly equipment was identical with that used in the regular department, except in one respect. At the right of each girl's place was a hole in the bench, and into this hole she dropped completed relays. It was the entrance to a chute, in which there was a flapper gate opened by the relay in its passage downward. The opening of the gate closed an electrical circuit which controlled a perforating device, and this in turn recorded the completion of the relay by punching a hole in a tape. The tape moved at the rate of one-quarter of an inch a minute and had space for a separate row of holes for each operator. When punched, it thus constituted a complete output record for each girl for each instant of the day. Such records were kept for five years.

In this experiment then, as in the earlier illumination experiments, great emphasis was laid on the rate of output. A word of caution is needed here. The Western Electric Company was not immediately interested in increasing output. The experiments were not designed for that purpose. On the other hand, output is easily measured, i.e., it yields precise quantitative data, and experience suggested that it was sensitive to at least some of the conditions under which the employees worked. Output was treated as an index. In short, the nature of the experimental conditions made the emphasis on output inevitable.

From their experience in the illumination experiments, the investigators were well aware that factors other than those experimentally varied might affect the output rate. Therefore arrangements were made that a number of other records should be kept. Unsuitable parts supplied by the firm were noted down, as were assemblies rejected for any reason upon inspection. In this way the type of defect could be known and related to the time of day at which it occurred. Records were kept of weather conditions in general and of temperature and humidity in the test room. Every six weeks each operator was given a medical examination by the company doctor. Every day she was asked to tell how many hours she had spent in bed the night before and, during a part of the experiment, what food she had eaten. Besides all these records, which concerned the physical condition of the operators, a log was kept in which were recorded the principal events in the test room hour by hour, including among the entries snatches of conversation between the workers. At first these entries related largely to the physical condition of the operators: how they felt as they worked. Later the ground they covered somewhat widened, and the log ultimately became one of the most important of the test room records. Finally, when the so-called Interviewing Program was instituted at Hawthorne, each of the operators was interviewed several times by an experienced interviewer.

The girls had no supervisor in the ordinary sense, such as they would have had in a regular shop department, but a "test room observer" was placed in the room, whose duty it was to maintain the records, arrange the work, and secure a cooperative spirit on the part of the girls. Later, when the complexity of his work increased, several assistants were assigned to help him.

When the arrangements had been made for the test room, the

operators who had been chosen to take part were called in for an interview in the office of the superintendent of the Inspection Branch, who was in general charge of the experiment and of the researches which grew out of it. The superintendent described this interview as follows: "The nature of the test was carefully explained to these girls and they readily consented to take part in it, although they were very shy at the first conference. An invitation to six shop girls to come up to a superintendent's office was naturally rather startling. They were assured that the object of the test was to determine the effect of certain changes in working conditions, such as rest periods, midmorning lunches, and shorter working hours. They were expressly cautioned to work at a comfortable pace, and under no circumstances to try to make a race out of the test." This conference was only the first of many. Whenever any experimental change was planned, the girls were called in, the purpose of the change was explained to them, and their comments were requested. Certain suggested changes which did not meet with their approval were abandoned. They were repeatedly asked, as they were asked in the first interview, not to strain but to work "as they felt."

The experiment was now ready to begin. Put in its simplest terms, the idea of those directing the experiment was that if an output curve was studied for a long enough time under various changes in working conditions, it would be possible to determine which conditions were the most satisfactory. Accordingly, a number of so-called "experimental periods" were arranged. For two weeks before the operators were placed in the test room, a record was kept of the production of each one without her knowledge. In this way the investigators secured a measure of her productive ability while working in the regular department under the usual conditions. This constituted the first experimental period. And for five weeks after the girls entered the test room no change was made in working conditions. Hours remained what they had been before. The investigators felt that this period would be long enough to reveal any changes in output incidental merely to the transfer. This constituted the second experimental period.

The third period involved a change in the method of payment. In the regular department, the girls had been paid according to a scheme of group piecework, the group consisting of a hundred or more employees. Under these circumstances, variations in an individual's total output would not be immediately reflected in her pay, since such variations tended to cancel one another in a large group. In the test room, the six operators were made a group by themselves. In this way each girl received an amount more nearly in proportion to her individual effort, and her interests became more closely centered on the experiment. Eight weeks later, the directly experimental changes began. An outline will reveal their general character: Period IV: two rest pauses, each five minutes in length, were established, one occurring in midmorning and the other in the early afternoon. Period V: these rest pauses were lengthened to ten minutes each: Period VI: six five-minute rests were established. Period VII: the company provided each member of the group with a light lunch in the midmorning and another in the midafternoon accompanied by rest pauses. This arrangement became standard for subsequent Periods VIII through XI. Period VIII: work stopped a half-hour earlier every day—at 4:30 P.M. Period IX: work stopped at 4 P.M. Period X: conditions returned to what they were in Period VII. Period XI: a five-day work week was established. Each of these experimental periods lasted several weeks.

Period XI ran through the summer of 1928, a year after the beginning of the experiment. Already the results were not what had been expected. The output curve, which had risen on the whole slowly and steadily throughout the year, was obviously reflecting something other than the responses of the group to the imposed experimental conditions. Even when the total weekly output had fallen off, as it could hardly fail to do in such a period as Period XI, when the group was working only five days a week, daily output continued to rise. Therefore, in accordance with a sound experimental procedure, as a control on what had been done, it was agreed with the consent of the operators that in experimental Period XII a return should be made to the original conditions of work, with no rest pauses, no special lunches, and a full-length working week. This period lasted for twelve weeks. Both daily and weekly output rose to a higher point than ever before: the working day and the working week were both longer. The hourly output rate declined somewhat but it did not approach the level of Period III, when similar conditions were in effect.

The conclusions reached after Period XII may be expressed in terms of another observation. Identical conditions of work were repeated in three different experimental periods: Periods VII, X, and XII. If the assumptions on which the study was based had been correct, that is to say, if the output rate were directly related to the physical conditions of work, the expectation would be that in these three experimental periods there would be some similarity in output. Such was not the case. The only apparent uniformity was that in each experimental period output was higher than in the preceding one. In the Relay Assembly Test Room, as in the previous illumination experiments, something was happening which could not be explained by the experimentally controlled conditions of work.

There is no need here to go into the later history of the test room experiment, which came to an end in 1933. It is enough to say that the output of the group continued to rise until it established itself on a high plateau from which there was no descent until the time of discouragement and deepening economic depression which preceded the end of the test. The rough conclusions reached at the end of experimental Period XII were confirmed and sharpened by later research. T. N. Whitehead, Associate Professor of Business in the Graduate School of Business Administration, Harvard University, has made a careful statistical analysis of the output records. He shows that the changes which took place in the output of the group have no simple correlation with the experimental changes in working conditions. Nor can they be correlated with changes in other physical conditions of which records were kept, such as temperature, humidity, hours of rest, and changes of relay type. Even when the girls themselves complained of mugginess or heat, these conditions were not apparently affecting their output. This statement, of course, does not mean that there is never any relation between output rate and these physical conditions. There is such a thing as heat prostration. It means only that, within the limits in which these conditions were varying in the test room, they apparently did not affect the rate of work.

The question remains: with what facts, if any, can the changes in the output rate of the operators in the test room be correlated? Here the statements of the girls themselves are of first importance. Each girl knew that she was producing more in the test room than she ever had in the regular department, and each said that the increase had come about without any conscious effort on her part. It seemed easier to produce at the faster rate in the test room than at the slower rate in the regular department. When questioned further, each girl stated her reasons in slightly different words, but there was uniformity in the answers in two respects. First, the girls liked to work in the test room; "it was fun." Secondly, the new supervisory relation or, as they put it, the absence of the old supervisory control, made it possible for them to work freely without anxiety.

For instance, there was the matter of conversation. In the regular department, conversation was in principle not allowed. In practice it was tolerated if it was carried on in a low tone and did not interfere with work. In the test room an effort was made in the beginning to discourage conversation, though it was soon abandoned. The observer in charge of the experiment was afraid of losing the cooperation of the girls if he insisted too strongly on this point. Talk became common and was often loud and general. Indeed the conversation of the operators came to occupy an important place in the log. T. N. Whitehead has pointed out that the girls in the test room were far more thoroughly supervised than they ever had been in the regular department. They were watched by an observer of their own, an interested management, and outside experts. The point is that the character and purpose of the supervision were different and were felt to be so.

The operators knew that they were taking part in what was considered an important and interesting experiment. They knew that their work was expected to produce results—they were not sure what results—which would lead to the improvement of the working conditions of their fellow employees. They knew that the eyes of the company were upon them. Whitehead has further pointed out that, although the experimental changes might turn out to have no physical significance, their social significance was always favorable. They showed that the management of the company was still interested, that the girls were still part of a valuable piece of research. In the regular department, the girls, like the other employees, were in the position of responding to changes the source and purpose of which were beyond their knowledge. In the test room, they had frequent interviews with the superintendent, a high officer of the company. The reasons for the contemplated experimental changes were explained to them. Their views were consulted and in some instances they were allowed to veto what had been proposed. Professor Mayo has argued that it is idle to speak of an experimental period like Period XII as being in any sense what it purported to be—a return to the original conditions of work. In the meantime, the entire industrial situation of the girls had been reconstructed.

Another factor in what occurred can only be spoken of as the social development of the group itself. When the girls went for the first time to be given a physical examination by the company doctor, someone suggested as a joke that ice cream and cake ought to be served. The company provided them at the next examination, and the custom was kept up for the duration of the experiment. When one of the girls had a birthday, each of the others would bring her a present, and she would respond by offering the group a box of chocolates. Often one of the girls would have some good reason for feeling tired. Then the others would "carry" her. That is, they would agree to work especially fast to make up for the low output expected from her. It is doubtful whether this "carrying" did have any effect, but the important point is the existence of the practice, not its effectiveness. The girls made friends in the test room and went together socially after hours. One of the interesting facts which has appeared from Whitehead's analysis of the output records is that there were times when variations in the output rates of two friends were correlated to a high degree. Their rates varied simultaneously and in the same direction—something, of course, which the girls were not aware of and could not have planned. Also, these correlations were destroyed by such apparently trivial events as a change in the order in which the girls sat at the workbench.

Finally, the group developed leadership and a common purpose. The leader, self-appointed, was an ambitious young Italian girl who entered the test room as a replacement after two of the original members had left. She saw in the experiment a chance for personal distinction and advancement. The common purpose was an increase in the output rate. The girls had been told in the beginning and repeatedly thereafter that they were to work without straining, without trying to make a race of the test, and all the evidence shows that they kept this rule. In fact, they felt that they were working under less pressure than in the regular department. Nevertheless, they knew that the output record was considered the most important of the records of the experiment and was always closely scrutinized. Before long they had committed themselves to a continuous increase in production. In the long run, of course, this ideal was an impossible one, and when the girls found out that it was, the realization was an important element of the change of tone which was noticeable in the second half of the experiment. But for a time they felt that they could achieve the impossible. In brief, the increase in the output rate of the girls in the Relay Assembly Test Room could not be related to any changes in their physical conditions of work, whether experimentally induced or not. It could, however, be related to what can only be spoken of as the development of an organized social group in a peculiar and effective relation with its supervisors.

Many of these conclusions were not worked out in detail until long after the investigators at Hawthorne had lost interest in the Relay Assembly Test Room, but the general meaning of the experiment was clear at least as early as Period XII. A continuous increase in productivity had taken place irrespective of changing physical conditions of work. In the words of a company report made in January, 1931, on all the research which had been done up to that date: "Upon analysis, only one thing seemed to show a continuous relationship with this improved output. This was the mental attitude of the operators. From their conversations with each other and their comments to the test observers, it was not only clear that their attitudes were improving but it was evident that this area of employee reactions and feelings was a fruitful field for industrial research."

At this point the attention of the investigators turned sharply from the test room to the regular department from which the girls had come. Why was the mental attitude of the girls different in the test room from what it had been in the department? In their conversations with one another and in their comments to the observers, the girls were full of comparisons between the test room and the department, very much to the disadvantage of the latter. They felt relief from some form of constraint, particularly the constraint of supervision. They were exceedingly disparaging about the supervisors in the department, although management felt that the department had particularly good supervisory personnel. These facts suggested that the management of the company really knew very little about the attitudes which employees took toward conditions in the plant and very little also about what constituted good supervisory methods. Such was the atmosphere in which the so-called Interviewing Program, the third phase of the work at Hawthorne, was planned. So far the interests of the investigators had been centered on the question of what were good physical conditions of work. Now they shifted definitely in the direction of a study of human relations.

Briefly, the new plan called for interviewing a much larger group of employees than any hitherto studied, with the object of learning more about their feelings and attitudes. A beginning was to be made in the Inspection Branch, representing about 1,600 skilled and unskilled employees in both shop and office work. In the report of January, 1931, the investigators stated that their purposes had been the following: "First, we wanted to know how employees felt about their work and the way they were treated; second, we desired to learn the manner in which the company policies were being applied and the employees' reactions to them; third, we were hopeful that something would come out of these employee expressions which could be used to develop and improve the training of supervisors."

The supervisors in the Inspection organization were called together, and the project was described to them. Their criticism was invited, and various points in the plan were discussed at this meeting. Five interviewers were chosen from among the supervisors to conduct the interviews. Women were selected to interview women, and men to interview men. The interviewers were not to interview employees whom they knew, since their acquaintanceship might influence what was said. In particular, it was obvious that no one should interview any worker over whom he had administrative authority. Records of the interviews were to be kept, and comments on the working situation were to be set down as nearly verbatim as possible, but all records were to be confidential. The names of the persons interviewed were not to be associated with the records, and any identifying statements were to be omitted. This rule was kept so well that it limited the usefulness of the records. It meant that the details of particular interviews could not be put together to give a picture of an entire working group or department.

In accordance with these plans, the interviewing of employees in the Inspection organization was begun in September, 1928, a year and a half after the beginning of the Relay Assembly Test Room experiment. It was completed early in 1929. So favorable were the results that the decision was made to extend the program to the Operating Branch. For this purpose, the Division of

Industrial Research was organized on February 1, 1929, with functions which were stated as follows:

1. To interview annually all employees to find out their likes and dislikes relative to their working status.
2. To study the favorable and unfavorable comments of employees.
   a. To initiate correction or adjustment of causes of unfavorable comments.
   b. To determine upon benefits to be derived from favorable comments and to instigate ways and means of acquiring these benefits.
3. To conduct supervisory training conferences for all supervisors using employee interviews as a basis.
4. To conduct test studies relative to employee relations, fatigue and efficiency.

Obviously a program which called for interviewing annually all employees in a plant in which some 40,000 persons were then working was an ambitious one, and the events showed that it could not be carried through. At the time when the Industrial Research Division was formed, interviews required on the average about a half-hour each. Later, as a result of improvements in the technique of interviewing, they became three times as long. This change alone cut down severely the number of employees who could be interviewed. Nevertheless, in the three years 1928–1930, 21,126 employees were interviewed, more than half of them in the Operating Branch, the rest scattered through other parts of the Hawthorne Works.

The original interviewers had been five in number. The extension of the program made necessary an increase in the staff. For the most part, the new interviewers were chosen from the various branches in which the work was already in progress. In rank they were usually supervisors, and they were taken from their ordinary assignments for a temporary period of about a year. The belief was that such supervisors, with proper instruction, could undertake the interviewing, and that the interviewing experience could be made an important part of their training. Accordingly, as many supervisors as possible were to take part in the work. Besides this temporary personnel, a nucleus staff of permanent investigators was built up, whose duty was to train the new men and take over the more technical aspects of the work, in particular the analysis of the growing body of interview material. The approximate average number of employees involved in the interviewing and analyzing work during 1929 and 1930 was thirty for interviewing and six for analyzing.

The results of the Interviewing Program were interesting from the first. The program was received with enthusiasm by both supervisors and operators. "This is the best thing the Company ever did" and "The Company ought to have done this long ago" were the sort of comments commonly encountered. The employees seemed to enjoy the opportunity of expressing their thoughts. They felt some kind of release, as if feelings which had long been pent up within them had at last found an outlet. Requests for interviews were received, some from the supervisors themselves. Accordingly, the interviewing was extended beyond its original bounds to group and section chiefs, that is, those supervisors immediately in charge of the rank and file.* In the course of their interviews, these supervisors were asked what they thought of the program and its effect. They were in its favor. They felt that it had not embarrassed them, that the employees liked it, and that it ought to be kept up and extended.

Evidence soon accumulated that the interviews not only gave expression to attitudes hitherto pent up but also, in giving them expression, changed them. The report of 1931 explained this rather unexpected result by an analogy: "It has long been known that one who writes a memorandum greatly clarifies his thought upon the material to be presented. Exaggerations, distortions, emotional reactions, defenses, etc., are largely dissolved when thus viewed objectively. In a similar way employees who express their thought and feeling to a critical listener discharge emotional and irrational elements from their minds. Many personal and individual problems and attitudes have been improved by the verbal expression which the interview affords. Taking account of the employees' expressions recorded in twenty thousand interviews, we feel that this value in interviewing cannot be lightly overlooked."

The observation has been made, perhaps too cynically, that in building up good industrial relations it makes little difference what measures are taken to improve working conditions as long

---

* The name "supervisor" is often given at Hawthorne to all ranks of supervision above the worker. The first-line supervisor, in direct contact with the operators, is the group chief. The three ranks above him are section chief, assistant foreman, and foreman. A foreman is in charge of a department.

as the rank and file realize what the purpose of the measures is. The important factor is the conviction of the workers that the management is concerned about their welfare. Something of this sort Whitehead had in mind when he said of the Relay Assembly Test Room that, though the experimental changes might turn out to have no physical significance, their social significance was always favorable. In the same way in the Interviewing Program, the discovery that management was taking an interest in what they thought and felt was new and stimulating for many of the employees. It may be well to repeat here that the Western Electric Company has had a long record of intelligent treatment of its workers, which is reflected in the confidence the workers have in the Company. Without this confidence many of the results of the investigations at Hawthorne could not have been achieved. At the same time the investigations strengthened this confidence.

The effect of the Interviewing Program on the supervisors was not less interesting. The opinion of the management was that supervision improved almost simultaneously with the beginning of interviewing. This improvement was not the result of fear on the part of supervisors that their methods would be disclosed and shown to be faulty. There was apparently no such fear. It was the result rather of an increased knowledge of and interest in workers as individuals and an increased interest in the method of supervision which came from the knowledge that it was being made a subject for research. The records of the interviewers were used as illustrative material for the training of supervisors and for conferences on supervision. An effort was made to see that as many supervisors as possible should have temporary experience as interviewers. Those who took part felt that they acquired a new understanding of the human problems of industry and, not less important, a new understanding of themselves. In fact the two must go together in any study of human behavior. A man can carry his analysis of other men no further than he has carried his analysis of himself. Finally, the men who were most closely associated with the Interviewing Program felt great enthusiasm for the work. They felt that they were acquiring new understanding, that they were free to move wherever the facts led them, and that in the end they would come out with something useful. The Chairman of the Committee pointed out that there seemed to be the same disinterested curiosity among the investigators as there is in any scientific research laboratory when the work is going well.

The investigators came away from the Relay Assembly Test Room with the feeling that management really knew very little about what constituted good supervision or what the employees thought about their conditions of work. The Interviewing Program was designed to provide such knowledge. It is significant that, in the original plan for the interviews, orders were given that comments on the working situation were to be recorded as nearly verbatim as possible. This material was the sort which was supposed to be important. The interviewers went to their early interviews with something like a series of questions in their heads which they expected the employees to answer. The questions concerned such matters as working conditions, job, supervision, and so forth. The interview was to consist in effect of a series of answers to these questions. It is true that the interviewers were cautioned against putting these questions directly to the person being interviewed. Instead they were to enter into conversation with the employee and lead him around to the appropriate subjects only as opportunity served. Nevertheless, the questions existed. Unfortunately for this plan, the discovery was soon made that a series of questions did not form a satisfactory basis for an interview. Questions did produce opinions, but the opinions were of unequal value. For one thing, comments on persons were less likely to produce information on which action could be based than were comments on material conditions of work. Whenever a number of employees working in the same neighborhood complained of cold, smoke and fumes, insufficient locker space, or some other physical source of irritation, an investigation could be made. In many instances the complaints were found to be justified and the conditions were corrected. But complaints about persons and about supervision in general usually had to be disregarded. Investigation showed that they had more reference to the attitudes people took toward situations than to the situations themselves.

An example, of a rather extreme type, will show what this statement means. An employee complained in an interview of one of her supervisors. Complete analysis of the case showed that the supervisor reminded her of a hated stepfather. Her attitude toward the supervisor was conditioned by that fact. In short, the experience of interviewing soon showed that many of the employees' comments, to them the most important, were to be taken as neither true nor false. They were expressions of the attitudes taken by particular persons in particular situations rather than statements of objective truth.

This conclusion led to changes in the method of recording the interviews. To quote once more from the report of 1931: "The original method had been to group employee comments under the heads of working conditions, job, and supervision, with the subclassifications of likes and dislikes under each. This form was supplanted in 1929 because it was found, in attempting to analyze employee comments, that when their expressions were removed from their context they read very similarly and were often meaningless. The method adopted was to reproduce the interview as nearly verbatim as possible, showing both the comments made by the interviewer and those made by the employee. This change had the effect of greatly lengthening the report (from an average of 2½ pages to an average of 10). Furthermore, it somewhat reduced the number of interviews which could be taken by one interviewer, thereby increasing the cost of each interview secured. The added value is that by this means all of the original values of the interviews are preserved and not merely those selected by the first form of analysis."

Another experience of the early interviews was the following. The interviewer would succeed in getting the employee to talk about a particular subject or subjects, but in a few minutes he would be completely off the point. Then the interviewer would try to lead him back, and again he would revert to the topic of his own choosing. It was all very well for the interviewer to have in his mind a set of questions which he hoped to get the employee to answer. Most of them seemed of no importance to the employee, and the answers the interviewer got were at best perfunctory. "It became obvious to the interviewers that, whatever the question, the thoughts of some employees tended to gravitate toward a particular condition or subject; that in these cases something was uppermost in the mind of the employee which completely overshadowed everything else. Cases were found where several subjects predominated in the mind of the employee, and any attempts to lead him away from his line of thought were generally unsuccessful. In other instances the interviewers found that a particularly untalkative person became remarkably communicative if just the right spot could be touched in conversation." These experiences naturally led the interviewers to ask themselves a number of questions. Was there any good reason why they should try, as they had been trying, to lead the employee back to the subjects which they (the interviewer) had particularly in mind? Why should they talk about the matters which were important to them rather than the matters which obviously were important to the employee? Was an employee's preoccupation with a particular subject to be disregarded as a mental aberration or exploited as a latent source of information in the matter of human relations?

Granted it was mental aberration, should it be disregarded even then? The heavy preoccupation characteristic of the thinking of some of the employees struck the investigators by its resemblance to the mental ill called obsession by Pierre Janet and the French School, compulsion neurosis by Freud and his followers. Obsession is a mental ill in the sense that its cause is apparently not physical. It does not arise from any pathological, organic condition, and in some instances it is clearly curable by reeducation or psychological "analysis." Furthermore it differs from hysteria, which may be a mental ill in the same sense, in that its symptoms as well as its causes are mental rather than physical. Hysteria manifests itself in amnesias and also, characteristically, in paralyses and anesthesias; this is not the case in obsession. The chief characteristics of obsession are described in the names given it. The patient is literally besieged, obsessed, by certain ideas; he is compelled to return to them again and again even though he may realize that they are irrational or untrue. He suffers from an inability to control his reflective thinking. This does not mean that he makes no effort to control it. On the contrary, he makes a great effort, but the more he tries the more he fails. With obsessive thinking may go obsessive acts. The patient finds it hard to begin any simple action. He finds it hard to make up his mind. He suffers agonies of indecision, inventing elaborate reasons for and against taking any course which lies before him. But once in action he finds it hard to stop. An obsessive is characteristically the sort of person who goes over his work again and again and yet is never sure that it is done right. Finally, the obsessive may complain of nervousness, tenseness, a pervasive anxiety having no definite object. His is the "nervous temperament."

The work of the psychopathologists, and particularly that of

Freud, has shown that obsession may be the end product of a faulty education, the word "education" being used in its broadest sense to mean the training which an individual receives from earliest childhood and which has the purpose of making him able, as an adult, to take an effective part in society. It may appear also, though in a less extreme degree, in anyone who is in every other sense a normal human being if he cannot respond adequately to the situation in which he finds himself. He will be besieged by the same distorted thoughts about himself and other people. He will suffer from the same inability to act easily and appropriately. He will be aware of the same vague anxiety. A simple example is a person who is, as we say, "overtired." Everyone has had experience with such persons—or has been overtired himself—and knows that for the moment their behavior is quite abnormal.

In short, obsessive behavior may appear in many degrees and under many different conditions. This was the fact which struck the investigators at Hawthorne. Very few of the employees interviewed showed themselves to be candidates for a mental hospital, but the interview records suggested that many of them were elaborating their thinking in a typically obsessive manner. In some instances, the obsessive response could be traced to the home situation of the employee, particularly likely to be disorganized in a large and rapidly growing city, full of unassimilated immigrant groups. But in some cases it could apparently be traced only to the work situation at the plant. Something in their experience of industrial life produced in a number of employees a conviction of personal inadequacy. Nor was this response limited to the rank and file. Members of the top management at Hawthorne were not interviewed, but there is no reason to believe that management is exempt from obsessive thinking or even obsessive actions.

These conclusions were very general and seemed to be rather questions for further investigation than statements of observed fact. Nevertheless, the experience of the interviewers did have one immediate result: a change in the method of interviewing. The report of 1931 described it as follows: "The interviewer is introduced to the employee, and the interviewer 'catches on' in a conversational way at any starting point mentioned by the employee. As long as an employee talks the interviewer follows his comments, displaying a real interest in what the employee has to say and taking sufficient notes to recall the employee's various comments. While the employee continues, no attempt is made on the part of the interviewer to change the subject, because it is a basic assumption of the method that, where the employee chooses his own topics, he chooses them largely in their order of importance to him. If the interviewer were to ask questions or to redirect the employee's comments to other topics or subjects he would in a sense ask the employee to talk about a subject important perhaps to the interviewer, but not necessarily at all important to the employee. The interviewer takes part in the conversation only in so far as it is necessary to keep the employee talking and to stimulate confidence."

It is obvious that the Western Electric researches were all interrelated. One led to another. In planning each experiment, the investigators had in their minds hypotheses which they wished to test; but more important than any hypothesis was the simple desire to find out more about the employees. The factors which led to the next development of the research program were complicated and certainly were not fully realized at the time by the investigating group. The program had begun with a simple attempt to discover by experimentation the effect of changes in physical conditions on efficiency of work. The technique used was a standard one: other factors were to be held constant in order to isolate the effect on the output rate of changes in working conditions. The Relay Assembly Test Room showed that this method would not yield the expected results. In the very process of setting up the experiment, one of the important factors affecting output was being varied rather than held constant. But full realization of this fact did not come until later. The point which emerged at once from the Relay Assembly Test Room was that management really knew very little about the employees' reaction to physical conditions of work and methods of supervision. The Interviewing Program was undertaken with the object of finding out more about these matters, but once more the expectations of the investigators were not realized. The comments elicited from the employees in the interviews were of only limited use in improving working conditions and methods of supervision, and attempts to analyze the material statistically in terms of likes and dislikes came to no significant conclusions.

On the other hand, the comments did acquire meaning if they were taken in their context, as symptoms of sentiments, beliefs, unconscious assumptions held by the persons interviewed; and for a time the investigators were much interested in studying the employees as individuals, each with a personal history which, properly understood, explained much of his behavior. Members of the Department of Industrial Research in the Graduate School of Business Administration, Harvard University, had advised the company in the researches and had followed them closely. The next suggestion came from W. L. Warner, at that time Assistant Professor of Anthropology in Harvard University. It was that the comments secured in the interviews could not be treated as products of individual human beings. They were the precipitate of interaction between people in organized social groups: families, neighborhoods, working groups, and so forth. The investigators were naturally most interested in the social organization of the employees at the Hawthorne Works; and as a result of this new understanding, they gradually lost interest in individual interviews, just as they had lost interest in the Relay Assembly Test Room. They took another step away from their original point of departure and turned to what they were fond of calling the "actual working situation." They were beginning to study the social relations between people actually at work on the job.

Furthermore, the investigators were turned in this direction by certain practical problems which had arisen in the course of the Interviewing Program. The interviewers were receiving a more thorough training. The plan of interviewing all employees once a year had been adopted, but the interviews had grown longer and therefore more expensive. And there were employees who needed interviewing more than once a year. A good picture of their situation could not be secured at a single interview, yet continuous interviewing could not be applied as a regular program all over the plant. There seemed to be a need both to limit and to concentrate the effort of interviewing.

Finally the investigators discovered, in the course of the regular interviews, evidence here and there in the plant of a type of behavior which strongly suggested that the workers were banding together informally in order to protect themselves against practices which they interpreted as a menace to their welfare. This type of behavior manifested itself in (a) "straight-line" output, that is, the operators had adopted a standard of what they felt to be a proper day's work and none of them exceeded it by very much; (b) a resentment of the wage incentive system under which they worked—in most cases, some form of group piece-work; (c) expressions which implied that group piecework as a wage incentive plan was not working satisfactorily; (d) informal practices by which persons who exceeded the accepted standard, that is, "rate killers," could be punished and "brought into line"; (e) informal leadership on the part of individuals who under-took to keep the working group together and enforce its rules; (f) preoccupations of futility with regard to promotion; and (g) extreme likes and dislikes toward immediate superiors, accord-ing to their attitude toward the behavior of the operators. The investigators felt that this complex of behavior deserved further study.

In view of these considerations, the decision was taken in May, 1931, to assign selected interviewers to particular groups of employees and allow them to interview the employees as often as they felt was necessary. The story of one of these groups is characteristic of the findings reached by this new form of inter-viewing. The work of the employees was the adjustment of small parts which went into the construction of telephone equipment. The management thought that the adjustment was a complicated piece of work. The interviewer found that it was really quite simple. He felt that anyone could learn it, but that the operators had conspired to put a fence around the job. They took pride in telling how apparatus which no one could make work properly was sent in from the field for adjustment. Then telephone engi-neers would come in to find out from the operators how the repairs were made. The latter would fool around, doing all sorts of wrong things and taking about two hours to adjust apparatus, and in this way prevented people on the outside from finding out what they really did. They delighted in telling the inter-viewer how they were pulling the wool over everybody's eyes. It followed that they were keeping the management in ignorance as to the amount of work they could do. The output of the group, when plotted, was practically a straight line.

Obviously this result could not have been gained without some informal organization, and such organization in fact there was. The group had developed leadership. Whenever an outsider—engineer, inspector, or supervisor—came into the room, one man always dealt with him. Whenever any technical question was raised about the work, this employee answered it. For other pur-poses, the group had developed a second leader. Whenever a

new man came into the group or a member of the group boosted
output beyond what was considered the proper level, this second
leader took charge of the situation. The group had, so to speak,
one leader for dealing with foreign and one for dealing with
domestic affairs. The different supervisors were largely aware of
the situation which had developed, but they did not try to do
anything about it because in fact they were powerless. Whenever
necessary, they themselves dealt with the recognized leaders of
the group.

Finally, the investigator found that the group was by no means
happy about what it was doing. Its members felt a vague dissatis-
faction or unrest, which showed itself in a demand for advancements and transfers or in complaints about their hard luck in
being kept on the job. This experience of personal futility could
be explained as the result of divided loyalties—divided between
the group and the Company.

In order to study this kind of problem further, to make a more
detailed investigation of social relations in a working group, and
to supplement interview material with direct observation of the
behavior of employees, the Division of Industrial Research decided to set up a new test room. But the investigators remembered what happened in the former test room and tried to
devise an experiment which would not be radically altered by
the process of experimentation itself. They chose a group of men
—nine wiremen, three soldermen, and two inspectors—engaged
in the assembly of terminal banks for use in telephone exchanges,
took them out of their regular department and placed them in a
special room. Otherwise no change was made in their conditions
of work, except that an investigator was installed in the room,
whose duty was simply to observe the behavior of the men.
In the Relay Assembly Test Room a log had been kept of the
principal events of the test. At the beginning it consisted largely
of comments made by the workers in answer to questions about
their physical condition. Later it came to include a much wider
range of entries, which were found to be extremely useful in
interpreting the changes in the output rate of the different
workers. The work of the observer in the new test room was
in effect an expansion of the work of keeping the log in the old
one. Finally an interviewer was assigned to the test room; he was
not, however, one of the population of the room but remained
outside and interviewed the employees from time to time in the

usual manner. No effort was made to get output records other than the ones ordinarily kept in the department from which the group came, since the investigators felt that such a procedure would introduce too large a change from a regular shop situation. In this way the experiment was set up which is referred to as the Bank Wiring Observation Room. It was in existence seven months, from November, 1931, to May, 1932.

The method of payment is the first aspect of this group which must be described. It was a complicated form of group piece-work. The department of which the workers in the observation room were a part was credited with a fixed sum for every unit of equipment it assembled. The amount thus earned on paper by the department every week made up the sum of which the wages of all the men in the department were paid. Each individual was then assigned an hourly rate of pay, and he was guaranteed this amount in case he did not make at least as much on a piece-work basis. The rate was based on a number of factors, including the nature of the job a worker was doing, his efficiency, and his length of service with the Company. Records of the output of every worker were kept, and every six months there was a rate revision, the purpose of which was to make the hourly rates of the different workers correspond to their relative efficiency.

The hourly rate of a given employee, multiplied by the number of hours worked by him during the week, was spoken of as the daywork value of the work done by the employee. The daywork values of the work done by all the employees in the department were then added together, and the total thus obtained was sub-tracted from the total earnings credited to the department for the number of units of equipment assembled. The surplus, divided by the total daywork value, was expressed as a percentage. Each individual's hourly rate was then increased by this percentage, and the resulting hourly earnings figure, multiplied by the number of hours worked, constituted that person's weekly earnings.

Another feature of the system should be mentioned here. Sometimes a stoppage which was beyond the control of the workers took place in the work. For such stoppages the workers were entitled to claim time out, being paid at their regular hourly rates for this time. This was called the "daywork allowance claim." The reason why the employees were paid their hourly rate for such time and not their average hourly wages was a simple one. The

The system was supposed to prevent stalling. The employees could earn more by working than they could by taking time out. As a matter of fact, there was no good definition of what constituted a stoppage which was beyond the control of the workers. All stoppages were more or less within their control. But this circumstance was supposed to make no difference in the working of the system, since the assumption was that in any case the workers, pursuing their economic interests, would be anxious to keep stoppages at a minimum.

This system of payment was a complicated one, but it is obvious that there was a logical reason for every one of its features. An individual's earnings would be affected by changes in his rate or in his output and by changes in the output of the group as a whole. The only way in which the group as a whole could increase its earnings was by increasing its total output. It is obvious also that the experts who designed the system made certain implicit assumptions about the behavior of human beings, or at least the behavior of workers in a large American factory. They assumed that every employee would pursue his economic interest by trying to increase not only his own output but the output of every other person in the group. The group as a whole would act to prevent slacking by any of its members. One possibility, for instance, was that by a few weeks' hard work an employee could establish a high rate for himself. Then he could slack up and be paid out of all proportion to the amount he actually contributed to the wages of the group. Under these circumstances, the other employees were expected to bring pressure to bear to make him work harder.

Such was the way in which the wage incentive scheme ought to have worked. The next question is how it actually did work. At first the workers were naturally suspicious of the observer, but when they got used to him and found that nothing out of the ordinary happened as a result of his presence in the room, they came to take him for granted. The best evidence that the employees were not distrustful of the observer is that they were willing to talk freely to him about what they were doing, even when what they were doing was not in strict accord with what the Company expected. Conversation would die when the group chief entered the room, and when the foreman or the assistant foreman entered everyone became serious. But no embarrassment was felt at the presence of the observer. To avoid misunderstanding, it is important to point out that the observer was in no sense a spy. The employees were deliberately and obviously separated from their regular department. The observer did not, and could not, pass himself off as one of them. And if only from the fact that a special interviewer was assigned to them, the members of the group knew they were under investigation.

The findings reached by the observer were more detailed but in general character the same as those which had emerged from the early interviews of other groups. Among the employees in the observation room there was a notion of a proper day's work. They felt that if they had wired two equipments a day they had done about the right amount. Most of the work was done in the morning. As soon as the employees felt sure of being able to finish what they considered enough for the day, they slacked off. This slacking off was naturally more marked among the faster than among the slower workmen.

As a result, the output graph from week to week tended to be a straight line. The employees resorted to two further practices in order to make sure that it remained so. They reported more or less output than they performed and they claimed more day-work allowances than they were entitled to. At the end of the day, the observer would make an actual count of the number of connections wired—something which was not done by the supervisors—and he found that the men would report to the group chief sometimes more and sometimes less work than they actually had accomplished. At the end of the period of observation, two men had completed more than they ever had reported, but on the whole the error was in the opposite direction. The theory of the employees was that excess work produced on one day should be saved and applied to a deficiency on another day. The other way of keeping the output steady was to claim excessive daywork allowance. The employees saw that the more daywork they were allowed, the less output they would have to maintain in order to keep the average hourly output rate steady. The claims for daywork allowance were reported by the men to their group chief, and he, as will be seen, was in no position to make any check. These practices had two results. In the first place, the departmental efficiency records did not represent true efficiency, and therefore decisions as to grading were subject to errors of considerable importance. In the second place, the group chief was placed in a distinctly awkward position.

The findings of the observer were confirmed by tests which were made as a part of the investigation. Tests of intelligence, finger dexterity, and other skills were given to the workers in the room, and the results of the tests were studied in order to discover whether there was any correlation between output, on the one hand, and earnings, intelligence, or finger dexterity, on the other. The studies showed that there was not. The output was apparently not reflecting the native intelligence or dexterity of the members of the group.

Obviously the wage incentive scheme was not working in the way it was expected to work. The next question is why it was not working. In this connection, the observer reported that the group had developed an informal social organization, such as had been revealed by earlier investigations. The foreman who selected the employees taking part in the Bank Wiring Observation Room was cooperative and had worked with the investigators before. They asked him to produce a normal group. The men he chose all came out of the same regular shop department, but they had not been closely associated in their work there. Nevertheless, as soon as they were thrown together in the observation room, friendships sprang up and soon two well-defined cliques were formed. The division into cliques showed itself in a number of ways: in mutual exclusiveness, in differences in the games played off-hours, and so forth.

What is important here is not what divided the men in the observation room but what they had in common. They shared a common body of sentiments. A person should not turn out too much work. If he did, he was a "rate-buster." The theory was that if an excessive amount of work was turned out, the management would lower the piecework rate so that the employees would be in the position of doing more work for approximately the same pay. On the other hand, a person should not turn out too little work. If he did, he was a "chiseler"; that is, he was getting paid for work he did not do. A person should say nothing which would injure a fellow member of the group. If he did, he was a "squealer." Finally, no member of the group should act officiously.

The working group had also developed methods of enforcing respect for its attitudes. The experts who devised the wage incentive scheme assumed that the group would bring pressure to bear upon the slower workers to make them work faster and so increase the earnings of the group. In point of fact, something like the opposite occurred. The employees brought pressure to bear not upon the slower workers but upon the faster ones, the very ones who contributed most of the earnings of the group. The pressure was brought to bear in various ways. One of them was "binging." If one of the employees did something which was not considered quite proper, one of his fellow workers had the right to "bing" him. Binging consisted of hitting him a stiff blow on the upper arm. The person who was struck usually took the blow without protest and did not strike back. Obviously the virtue of binging as punishment did not lie in the physical hurt given to the worker but in the mental hurt that came from knowing that the group disapproved of what he had done. Other practices which naturally served the same end were sarcasm and the use of invectives. If a person turned out too much work, he was called names, such as "Speed King" or "The Slave."

It is worth while pointing out that the output of the group was not considered low. If it had been, some action might have been taken, but in point of fact it was perfectly satisfactory to the management. It was simply not so high as it would have been if fatigue and skill had been the only limiting factors.

In the matter of wage incentives, the actual situation was quite different from the assumptions made by the experts. Other activities were out of line in the same way. The wiremen and the soldermen did not stick to their jobs; they frequently traded them. This was forbidden, on the theory that each employee ought to do his own work because he was more skilled in that work. There was also much informal helping of one man by others. In fact, the observation of this practice was one means of determining the cliques into which the group was divided. A great many things, in short, were going on in the observation room which ought not to have been going on. For this reason it was important that no one should "squeal" on the men.

A group chief was in immediate charge of the employees. He had to see that they were supplied with parts and that they conformed to the rules and standards of the work. He could reprimand them for misbehavior or poor performance. He transmitted orders to the men and brought their requests before the proper authorities. He was also responsible for reporting to the foreman all facts which ought to come to his attention. The behavior of the employees put him in an awkward position. He was perfectly well aware of the devices by which they maintained their production at a constant level. But he was able to do very little to bring about a change. For instance, there was the matter of claims for daywork allowance. Such claims were supposed to be based on stoppages beyond the control of the workers, but there was no good definition of what constituted such stoppages. The men had a number of possible excuses for claiming daywork allowance: defective materials, poor and slow work on the part of other employees, and so forth. If the group chief checked up on one type of claim, the workers could shift to another. In order to decide whether or not a particular claim was justified, he would have to stand over the group all day with a stop watch. He did not have time to do that, and in any case refusal to honor employees' claims would imply doubt of their integrity and would arouse their hostility. The group chief was a representative of management and was supposed to look after its interests. He ought to have put a stop to these practices and reported them to the foreman. But if he did so he would, to use the words of a short account of the observation room by Roethlisberger and Dickson, "lose sympathetic control of his men, and his duties as supervisor would become much more difficult." [2] He had to associate with the employees from day to day and from hour to hour. His task would become impossible if he had to fight a running fight with them. Placed in this situation, he chose to side with the men and report unchanged their claims for daywork. In fact there was very little else he could do, even if he wished. Morever, he was in a position to protect himself in case of trouble. The employees always had to give him reasons for any daywork claims they might make, and he entered the claims in a private record book. If anyone ever asked why so much daywork was being claimed, he could throw the blame wherever he wished. He could assert that materials had been defective or he could blame the inspectors, who are members of an outside organization. In still another respect, then, the Bank Wiring Observation Room group was not behaving as the logic of management assumed that it would behave.

Restriction of output is a common phenomenon of industrial plants. It is usually explained as a highly logical reaction of the workers. They have increased their output, whereupon their wage rates for piecework have been reduced. They are doing more for the same pay. They restrict their output in order to avoid a repetition of this experience. Perhaps this explanation holds good in some cases, but the findings of the Bank Wiring Observation Room suggest that it is too simple. The workers in the room were obsessed with the idea that they ought to hold their production level "even" from week to week, but they were vague as to what would happen if they did not. They said that "someone" would "get them." If they turned out an unusually high output one week, that record would be taken thereafter as an example of what they could do if they tried, and they would be "bawled out" if they did not keep up to it. As a matter of fact, none of the men in the room had ever experienced a reduction of wage rates. What is more, as Roethlisberger and Dickson point out, "changes in piece rates occur most frequently where there is a change in manufacturing process, and changes in manufacturing process are made by engineers whose chief function is to reduce unit cost wherever the saving will justify the change. In some instances, changes occur irrespective of direct labor cost. Moreover, where labor is a substantial element, reduction of output tends to increase unit costs and instead of warding off a change in the piece rate many actually induce one."

What happened in the observation room could not be described as a logical reaction of the employees to the experience of rate reduction. They had in fact no such experience. On the other hand, the investigators found that it could be described as a conflict between the technical organization of the plant and its social organization. By technical organization the investigators meant the plan, written or unwritten, according to which the Hawthorne plant was supposed to operate, and the agencies which gave effect to that plan. The plan included explicit rules as to how the men were to be paid, how they were to do their work, what their relations with their supervisors ought to be. It included also implicit assumptions on which the rules were based, one of the assumptions being that men working in the plant would on the whole act so as to further their economic interests. It is worth while pointing out that this assumption was in fact implicit, that the experts who devised the technical organization acted upon the assumption without ever stating it in so many words.

There existed also an actual social situation within the plant: groups of men, who were associated with one another, held common sentiments and had certain relations with other groups and other men. To some extent this social organization was identical with the technical plan and to some extent it was not. For instance, the employees were paid according to group payment plans, but the groups concerned did not behave as the planners expected them to behave.

The investigators considered the relations between the technical organization and the social. A certain type of behavior is expected of the higher levels of management. Their success is dependent on their being able to devise and institute rapid changes. Roethlisberger and Dickson describe what happens in the following terms: "Management is constantly making mechanical improvements and instituting changes designed to reduce costs or improve the quality of the product. It is constantly seeking new ways and new combinations for increasing efficiency, whether in designing a new machine, instituting a new method of control, or logically organizing itself in a new way." The assumption has often been made that these changes are designed to force the employee to do more work for less money. As a matter of fact, many of them have just the opposite purpose: to improve the conditions of work and enable the employee to earn higher wages. The important point here, however, is not the purpose of the changes but the way in which they are carried out and accepted.

Once the responsible officer has decided that a certain change ought to be made, he gives an order, and this order is transmitted "down the line," appropriate action being taken at every level. The question in which the investigators were interested was this: what happens when the order reaches the men who are actually doing the manual work? Roethlisberger and Dickson make the following observations: "The worker occupies a unique position in the social organization. He is at the bottom of a highly stratified organization. He is always in the position of having to accommodate himself to changes which he does not originate. Although he participates least in the technical organization, he bears the brunt of most of its activities." It is he, more than anyone, who is affected by the decisions of management, yet in the nature of things he is unable to share management's preoccupations, and management does little to convince him that what he considers important is being treated as important at the top—a fact which is not surprising, since there is no adequate way of transmitting to management an understanding of the considerations which seem important at the work level. There is something like a failure of communication in both directions— upward and downward.

The worker is not only "asked to accommodate himself to changes which he does not initiate, but also many of the changes deprive him of those very things which give meaning and significance to his work." The modern industrial worker is not the handicraftsman of the medieval guild. Nevertheless, the two have much in common. The industrial worker develops his own ways of doing his job, his own traditions of skill, his own satisfactions in living up to his standards. The spirit in which he adopts his own innovations is quite different from that in which he adopts those of management. Furthermore, he does not do this work as an isolated human being, but always as a member of a group, united either through actual cooperation on the job or through association in friendship. One of the most important general findings of the Western Electric researches is the fact that such groups are continually being formed among industrial workers, and that the groups develop codes and loyalties which govern the relations of the members to one another. Though these codes can be quickly destroyed, they are not formed in a moment. They are the product of continued, routine interaction between men. "Constant interference with such codes is bound to lead to feelings of frustration, to an irrational exasperation with technical change in any form, and ultimately to the formation of a type of employee organization such as we have described—a system of practices and beliefs in opposition to the technical organization."

The Bank Wiring Observation Room seemed to show that action taken in accordance with the technical organization tended to break up, through continual change, the routines and human associations which gave work its value. The behavior of the the employees could be described as an effort to protect themselves against such changes, to give management the least possible opportunity of interfering with them. When they said that if they increased their output, "something" was likely to happen, a process of this sort was going on in their minds. But the process was not a conscious one. It is important to point out that the protective function of informal organization was not a product of deliberate planning. It was more in the nature of an automatic response. The curious thing is that as Professor Mayo pointed out to the Committee, these informal organizations much resemble formally organized labor unions, although the employees would not have recognized the fact.

Roethlisberger and Dickson summarize as follows the results of the intensive study of small groups of employees: "According to our analysis the uniformity of behavior manifested by these groups was the outcome of a disparity in the rates of change possible in the technical organization, on the one hand, and in the social organization, on the other. The social sentiments and customs of work of the employees were unable to accommodate themselves to the rapid technical innovations introduced. The result was to incite a blind resistance to all innovations and to provoke the formation of a social organization at a lower level in opposition to the technical organization."

It is curious how, at all points, the Relay Assembly Test Room and the Bank Wiring Observation Room form a contrast. In the former, the girls said that they felt free from the pressure of supervision, although as a matter of fact they were far more thoroughly supervised than they ever had been in their regular department. In the latter, the men were afraid of supervision and acted so as to nullify it. The Bank Wiremen were in the position of having to respond to technical changes which they did not originate. The Relay Assemblers had periodic conferences with the superintendent. They were told what experimental changes were contemplated; their views were canvassed; and in some instances they were allowed to vote on what had been proposed. They were part of an experiment which they felt was interesting and important. Both groups developed an informal social organization, but while the Bank Wiremen were organized in opposition to management, the Relay Assemblers were organized in cooperation with management in the pursuit of a common purpose. Finally, the responses of the two groups to their industrial situation were, on the one hand, restriction of output and, on the other, steady and welcome increase of output. These contrasts carry their own lesson.

Notes

1. This research has been described in detail in a number of papers and in at least three books. The books are: Elton Mayo, *The Human Problems*

of an *Industrial Civilization* (New York: The Macmillan Company, 1933); T. N. Whitehead, *The Industrial Worker*, 2 vols. (Cambridge: Harvard University Press, 1938); F. J. Roethlisberger and W. J. Dickson, *Management and the Worker* (Cambridge: Harvard University Press, 1939).

2. F. J. Roethlisberger and W. J. Dickson, *Management and the Worker* (Boston: Harvard Business School, Division of Research, Business Research Studies No. 9). (All quotations relating to the Western Electric researches are from this study as well as from the book of the same title by the same authors).

ERVING GOFFMAN

On The Characteristics
of Total Institutions

◆

Erving Goffman, 1922–   , is Professor of Sociology at the University of California. In The Presentation of Self in Everyday Life, Asylums, *and other works, he has explored the structure of the normal personality, with particular attention to the ways in which the self preserves its identity and integrity. In his essay, "On the Characteristics of Total Institutions," Goffman, like Durkheim, studies an abnormal or borderline social phenomenon, namely the total institution, in order to understand the normal personality. His account of the material and social prerequisites of ordinary self-esteem and self-identity should be read with Schaar's psychological analysis of loyalty. Both essays show us how deeply the influences of our material culture and society reach into the inner recesses of even the most independent personality.*

I.

Social establishments—institutions in the everyday sense of that term—are places such as rooms, suites of rooms, buildings, or plants in which activity of a particular kind regularly goes on. In sociology we do not have a very apt way of classifying them. Some establishments, like Grand Central Station, are open to

Reprinted by permission of the publisher from *The Prison, Studies in Institutional Organization and Change,* ed. Donald R. Cressey (New York: Holt, Rinehart and Winston, Inc., 1961). Copyright © 1961 by Holt, Rinehart and Winston, Inc.

anyone who is decently behaved; others, like the Union League Club of New York or the laboratories at Los Alamos, are felt to be somewhat snippy about who is let in. Some, like shops and post offices, have a few fixed members who provide a service and a continuous flow of members who receive it. Others, like homes and factories, involve a less changing set of participants. Some institutions provide the place for activities from which the individual is felt to draw his social status, however enjoyable or lax these pursuits may be; other institutions, in contrast, provide a place for associations felt to be elective and unserious, calling for a contribution of time left over from more serious demands. In this book another category of institutions is singled out and claimed as a natural and fruitful one because its members appear to have so much in common—so much, in fact, that to learn about one of these institutions we would be well advised to look at the others.

II.

Every institution captures something of the time and interest of its members and provides something of a world for them; in brief, every institution has encompassing tendencies. When we review the different institutions in our Western society, we find some that are encompassing to a degree discontinuously greater than the ones next in line. Their encompassing or total character is symbolized by the barrier to social intercourse with the outside and to departure that is often built right into the physical plant, such as locked doors, high walls, barbed wire, cliffs, water, forests, or moors. These establishments I am calling *total institutions,* and it is their general characteristics I want to explore.[1]

The total institutions of our society can be listed in five rough groupings. First, there are institutions established to care for persons felt to be both incapable and harmless; these are the homes for the blind, the aged, the orphaned, and the indigent. Second, there are places established to care for persons felt to be both incapable of looking after themselves and a threat to the community, albeit an unintended one: TB sanitaria, mental hospitals, and leprosaria. A third type of total institution is organized to protect the community against what are felt to be intentional dangers to it, with the welfare of the persons thus sequestered not the immediate issue: jails, penitentiaries, P.O.W. camps, and concentration camps. Fourth, there are institutions purportedly established the better to pursue some worklike task and justifying themselves only on these instrumental grounds: army barracks, ships, boarding schools, work camps, colonial compounds, and large mansions from the point of view of those who live in the servants' quarters. Finally, there are those establishments designed as retreats from the world even while often serving also as training stations for the religious; examples are abbeys, monasteries, convents, and other cloisters. This classification of total institutions is not neat, exhaustive, nor of immediate analytical use, but it does provide a purely denotative definition of the category as a concrete starting point. By anchoring the initial definition of total institutions in this way, I hope to be able to discuss the general characteristics of the type without becoming tautological.

Before I attempt to extract a general profile from this list of establishments, I would like to mention one conceptual problem: none of the elements I will describe seems peculiar to total institutions, and none seems to be shared by every one of them; what is distinctive about total institutions is that each exhibits to an intense degree many items in this family of attributes. In speaking of "common characteristics," I will be using this phrase in a way that is restricted but I think logically defensible. At the same time this permits using the method of ideal types, establishing common features with the hope of highlighting significant differences later.

III.

A basic social arrangement in modern society is that the individual tends to sleep, play, and work in different places, with different co-participants, under different authorities, and without an over-all rational plan. The central feature of total institutions can be described as a breakdown of the barriers ordinarily separating these three spheres of life. First, all aspects of life are conducted in the same place and under the same single authority. Second, each phase of the member's daily activity is carried on in the immediate company of a large batch of others, all of whom are treated alike and required to do the same thing together. Third, all phases of the day's activities are tightly scheduled, with one activity leading at a prearranged time into the next, the whole sequence of activities being imposed from above by a system of explicit formal rulings and a body of officials. Finally, the various enforced activities are brought together into a single rational plan purportedly designed to fulfill the official aims of the institution.

Individually, these features are found in places other than total institutions. For example, our large commercial, industrial, and educational establishments are increasingly providing cafeterias and free-time recreation for their members; use of these extended facilities remains voluntary in many particulars, however, and special care is taken to see that the ordinary line of authority does not extend to them. Similarly, housewives or farm families may have all their major spheres of life within the same fenced-in area, but these persons are not collectively regimented and do not march through the day's activities in the immediate company of a batch of similar others.

The handling of many human needs by the bureaucratic organization of whole blocks of people—whether or not this is a necessary or effective means of social organization in the circumstances—is the key fact of total institutions. From this follow certain important implications.

When persons are moved in blocks, they can be supervised by personnel whose chief activity is not guidance or periodic inspection (as in many employer-employee relations) but rather surveillance—a seeing to it that everyone does what he has been clearly told is required of him, under conditions where one person's infraction is likely to stand out in relief against the visible, constantly examined compliance of the others. Which comes first, the large blocks of managed people, or the small supervisory staff, is not here at issue; the point is that each is made for the other.

In total institutions there is a basic split between a large managed group, conveniently called inmates, and a small supervisory staff. Inmates typically live in the institution and have restricted contact with the world outside the walls; staff often operate on an eight-hour day and are socially integrated into the outside world.[2] Each grouping tends to conceive of the other in terms of narrow hostile stereotypes, staff often seeing inmates as bitter, secretive, and untrustworthy, while inmates often see staff as condescending, highhanded, and mean. Staff tends to feel superior and righteous; inmates tend, in some way at least, to feel inferior, weak, blameworthy, and guilty.[3]

Social mobility between the two strata is grossly restricted;

social distance is typically great and often formally prescribed. Even talk across the boundaries may be conducted in a special tone of voice, as illustrated in a fictionalized record of an actual sojourn in a mental hospital:

> "I tell you what," said Miss Hart when they were crossing the day-room. "You do everything Miss Davis says. Don't think about it, just do it. You'll get along all right."
>
> As soon as she heard the name Virginia knew what was terrible about Ward One. Miss Davis. "Is she the head nurse?"
>
> "And how," muttered Miss Hart. And then she raised her voice. The nurses had a way of acting as if the patients were unable to hear anything that was not shouted. Frequently they said things in normal voices that the ladies were not supposed to hear; if they had not been nurses you would have said they frequently talked to themselves. "A most competent and efficient person, Miss Davis," announced Miss Hart.[4]

Although some communication between inmates and the staff guarding them is necessary, one of the guard's functions is the control of communication from inmates to higher staff levels. A student of mental hospitals provides an illustration:

> Since many of the patients are anxious to see the doctor on his rounds, the attendants must act as mediators between the patients and the physician if the latter is not to be swamped. On Ward 30, it seemed to be generally true that patients without physical symptoms who fell into the two lower privilege groups were almost never permitted to talk to the physician unless Dr. Baker himself asked for them. The persevering, nagging delusional group—who were termed "worry warts," "nuisances," "bird dogs," in the attendants' slang—often tried to break through the attendant-mediator but were always quite summarily dealt with when they tried.[5]

Just as talk across the boundary is restricted, so, too, is the passage of information, especially information about the staff's plans for inmates. Characteristically, the inmate is excluded from knowledge of the decisions taken regarding his fate. Whether the official grounds are military, as in concealing travel destination from enlisted men, or medical, as in concealing diagnosis, plan of treatment, and approximate length of stay from tuberculosis patients,[6] such exclusion gives staff a special basis of distance from and control over inmates.

All these restrictions of contact presumably help to maintain the antagonistic stereotypes.[7] Two different social and cultural worlds develop, jogging alongside each other with points of official contact but little mutual penetration. Significantly, the institutional plant and name come to be identified by both staff and inmates as somehow belonging to staff, so that when either grouping refers to the views or interests of "the institution," by implication they are referring (as I shall also) to the views and concerns of the staff.

The staff-inmate split is one major implication of the bureaucratic management of large blocks of persons. . . .

THE INMATE WORLD

The recruit comes into the establishment with a conception of himself made possible by certain stable social arrangements in his home world. Upon entrance, he is immediately stripped of the support provided by these arrangements. In the accurate language of some of our oldest total institutions, he begins a series of abasements, degradations, humiliations, and profanations of self. His self is systematically, if often unintentionally, mortified. He begins some radical shifts in his *moral career,* a career composed of the progressive changes that occur in the beliefs that he has concerning himself and significant others.

The processes by which a person's self is mortified are fairly standard in total institutions;[8] analysis of these processes can help us to see the arrangements that ordinary establishments must guarantee if members are to preserve their civilian selves.

The barrier that total institutions place between the inmate and the wider world marks the first curtailment of self. In civil life, the sequential scheduling of the individual's roles, both in the life cycle and in the repeated daily round, ensures that no one role he plays will block his performance and ties in another. In total institutions, in contrast, membership automatically disrupts role scheduling, since the inmate's separation from the wider world lasts around the clock and may continue for years. Role dispossession therefore occurs. In many total institutions the privilege of having visitors or of visiting away from the establishment is completely withheld at first, ensuring a deep initial break with past roles and an appreciation of role dispossession. A report on cadet life in a military academy provides an illustration:

This clean break with the past must be achieved in a relatively short period. For two months, therefore, the swab is not allowed to leave the base or to engage in social intercourse with non-cadets. This complete isolation helps to produce a unified group of swabs, rather than a heterogenous collection of persons of high and low status. Uniforms are issued on the first day, and discussions of wealth and family background are taboo. Although the pay of the cadet is very low, he is not permitted to receive money from home. The role of the cadet must supersede other roles the individual has been accustomed to play. There are few clues left which will reveal social status in the outside world.[9]

I might add that when entrance is voluntary, the recruit has already partially withdrawn from his home world; what is cleanly severed by the institution is something that had already started to decay.

Although some roles can be re-established by the inmate if and when he returns to the world, it is plain that other losses are irrevocable and may be painfully experienced as such. It may not be possible to make up, at a later phase of the cycle, the time not now spent in educational or job advancement, in courting, or in rearing one's children. A legal aspect of this permanent dispossession is found in the concept of "civil death": prison inmates may face not only a temporary loss of the rights to will money and write checks, to contest divorce or adoption proceedings, and to vote but may have some of these rights permanently abrogated.[10]

The inmate, then, finds certain roles are lost to him by virtue of the barrier that separates him from the outside world. The process of entrance typically brings other kinds of loss and mortification as well. We very generally find staff employing what are called admission procedures, such as taking a life history, photographing, weighing, fingerprinting, assigning numbers, searching, listing personal possessions for storage, undressing, bathing, disinfecting, haircutting, issuing institutional clothing, instructing as to rules, and assigning to quarters.[11] Admission procedures might better be called "trimming" or "programming" because in thus being squared away the new arrival allows himself to be shaped and coded into an object that can be fed into the administrative machinery of the establishment, to be worked on smoothly by routine operations. Many of these procedures depend upon attributes such as weight or fingerprints that the individual possesses merely because he is a member of the largest and most abstract of social categories, that of human being. Action taken on the basis of such attributes necessarily ignores most of his previous bases of self-identification.

Because a total institution deals with so many aspects of its inmates' lives, with the consequent complex squaring away at admission, there is a special need to obtain initial co-operativeness from the recruit. Staff often feel that a recruit's readiness to be appropriately deferential in his initial face-to-face encounters with them is a sign that he will take the role of the routinely pliant inmate. The occasion on which staff members first tell the inmate of his deference obligations may be structured to challenge the inmate to balk or to hold his peace forever. Thus these initial moments of socialization may involve an "obedience test" and even a will-breaking contest: an inmate who shows defiance receives immediate visible punishment, which increases until he openly "cries uncle" and humbles himself.

An engaging illustration is provided by Brendan Behan in reviewing his contest with two warders upon his admission to Walton prison:

"And 'old up your 'ead, when I speak to you."

" 'Old up your 'ead, when Mr. Whitbread speaks to you," said Mr. Holmes.

I looked round at Charlie. His eyes met mine and he quickly lowered them to the ground.

"What are you looking round at, Behan? Look at me."

*   *   *

I looked at Mr. Whitbread. "I am looking at you," I said.

"You are looking at Mr. Whitbread—what?" said Mr. Holmes.

"I am looking at Mr. Whitbread."

Mr. Holmes looked gravely at Mr. Whitbread, drew back his open hand, and struck me on the face, held me with his other hand and struck me again.

My head spun and burned and pained and I wondered would it happen again. I forgot and felt another smack, and forgot, and another, and moved, and was held by a steadying, almost kindly hand, and another, and my sight was a vision of red and white and pity-coloured flashes.

"You are looking at Mr. Whitbread—what, Behan?"

I gulped and got together my voice and tried again till I got it out. "I, sir, please, sir, I am looking at you, I mean, I am looking at Mr. Whitbread, sir." [12]

Admission procedures and obedience tests may be elaborated into a form of initiation that has been called "the welcome," where staff or inmates, or both, go out of their way to give the recruit a clear notion of his plight.[13] As part of this rite of passage he may be called by a term such as "fish" or "swab," which tells him that he is merely an inmate, and, what is more, that he has a special low status even in this low group.

The admission procedure can be characterized as a leaving off and a taking on, with the midpoint marked by physical nakedness. Leaving off of course entails a dispossession of property, important because persons invest self feelings in their possessions. Perhaps the most significant of these possessions is not physical at all, one's full name; whatever one is thereafter called, loss of one's name can be a great curtailment of the self.[14]

Once the inmate is stripped of his possessions, at least some replacements must be made by the establishment, but these take the form of standard issue, uniform in character and uniformly distributed. These substitute possessions are clearly marked as really belonging to the institution and in some cases are recalled at regular intervals to be, as it were, disinfected of identifications. With objects that can be used up—for example, pencils—the inmate may be required to return the remnants before obtaining a reissue.[15] Failure to provide inmates with individual lockers and periodic searches and confiscations of accumulated personal property [16] reinforce property dispossession. Religious orders have appreciated the implications for self of such separation from belongings. Inmates may be required to change their cells once a year so as not to become attached to them. The Benedictine Rule is explicit:

For their bedding let a mattress, a blanket, a coverlet, and a pillow suffice. These beds must be frequently inspected by the Abbot, because of private property which may be found therein. If anyone be discovered to have what he has not received from the Abbot, let him be most severely punished. And in order that this vice of private ownership may be completely rooted out, let all things that are necessary be supplied by the Abbot: that is, cowl, tunic, stockings, shoes, girdle, knife, pen, needle, handkerchief, and tablets; so that all plea of necessity may be taken away. And let the Abbot always consider that passage in the Acts of the Apostles: "Distribution was made to each according as anyone had need." [17]

One set of the individual's possessions has a special relation to self. The individual ordinarily expects to exert some control over the guise in which he appears before others. For this he needs cosmetic and clothing supplies, tools for applying, arranging, and repairing them, and an accessible, secure place to store these supplies and tools—in short, the individual will need an "identity kit" for the management of his personal front. He will also need access to decoration specialists such as barbers and clothiers.

On admission to a total institution, however, the individual is likely to be stripped of his usual appearance and of the equipment and services by which he maintains it, thus suffering a personal defacement. Clothing, combs, needle and thread, cosmetics, towels, soap, shaving sets, bathing facilities—all these may be taken away or denied him, although some may be kept in inaccessible storage, to be returned if and when he leaves. In the words of St. Benedict's Holy Rule:

Then forthwith he shall, there in the oratory, be divested of his own garments with which he is clothed and be clad in those of the monastery. Those garments of which he is divested shall be placed in the wardrobe, there to be kept, so that if, perchance, he should ever be persuaded by the devil to leave the monastery (which God forbid), he may be stripped of the monastic habit and cast forth.[18]

As suggested, the institutional issue provided as a substitute for what has been taken away is typically of a "coarse" variety, ill-suited, often old, and the same for large categories of inmates. The impact of this substitution is described in a report on imprisoned prostitutes:

First, there is the shower officer who forces them to undress, takes their own clothes away, sees to it that they take showers and get their prison clothes—one pair of black oxfords with cuban heels, two pairs of much-mended ankle socks, three cotton dresses, two cotton slips, two pairs of panties, and a couple of bras. Practically all the bras are flat and useless. No corsets or girdles are issued.

There is not a sadder sight than some of the obese prisoners who, if nothing else, have been managing to keep themselves looking decent on the outside, confronted by the first sight of themselves in prison issue.[19]

In addition to personal defacement that comes from being stripped of one's identity kit, there is personal disfigurement that comes from direct and permanent mutilations of the body such as brands or loss of limbs. Although this mortification of the self by way of the body is found in few total institutions, still, loss of a sense of personal safety is common and provides a basis for anxieties about disfigurement. Beatings, shock therapy, or, in mental hospitals, surgery—whatever the intent of staff in providing these services for some inmates—may lead many inmates to feel that they are in an environment that does not guarantee their physical integrity.

At admission, loss of identity equipment can prevent the individual from presenting his usual image of himself to others. After admission, the image of himself he presents is attacked in another way. Given the expressive idiom of a particular civil society, certain movements, postures, and stances will convey lowly images of the individual and be avoided as demeaning. Any regulation, command, or task that forces the individual to adopt these movements or postures may mortify his self. In total institutions, such physical indignities abound. In mental hospitals, for example, patients may be forced to eat all food with a spoon.[20] In military prisons, inmates may be required to stand at attention whenever an officer enters the compound.[21] In religious institutions, there are such classic gestures of penance as the kissing of feet,[22] and the posture recommended to an erring monk that he

. . . lie prostrate at the door of the oratory in silence; and thus, with his face to the ground and his body prone, let him cast himself at the feet of all as they go forth from the oratory.[23]

In some penal institutions we find the humiliation of bending over to receive a birching.[24]

Just as the individual can be required to hold his body in a humiliating pose, so he may have to provide humiliating verbal responses. An important instance of this is the forced deference pattern of total institutions; inmates are often required to punctuate their social interaction with staff by verbal acts of deference, such as saying "sir." Another instance is the necessity to beg, importune, or humbly ask for little things such as a light for a cigarette, a drink of water, or permission to use the telephone.

Corresponding to the indignities of speech and action required of the inmate are the indignities of treatment others accord him. The standard examples here are verbal or gestural profanations: staff or fellow inmates call the individual names, curse him, point out his negative attributes, tease him, or talk about him or his fellow inmates as if he were not present.

Whatever the form or the source of these various indignities, the individual has to engage in activity whose symbolic implications are incompatible with his conception of self. A more diffuse example of this kind of mortification occurs when the individual is required to undertake a daily round of life that he considers alien to him—to take on a disidentifying role. In prisons, denial of heterosexual opportunities can induce a fear of losing one's masculinity.[25] In military establishments, the patently useless make-work forced on fatigue details can make men feel their time and effort are worthless.[26] In religious institutions there are special arrangements to ensure that all inmates take a turn performing the more menial aspects of the servant role.[27] An extreme is the concentration-camp practice requiring prisoners to administer whippings to other prisoners.[28]

There is another form of mortification in total institutions; beginning with admission a kind of contaminative exposure occurs. On the outside, the individual can hold objects of self-feeling—such as his body, his immediate actions, his thoughts, and some of his possessions—clear of contact with alien and contamination things. But in total institutions these territories of the self are violated; the boundary that the individual places between his being and the environment is invaded and the embodiments of self profaned.

There is, first, a violation of one's informational preserve regarding self. During admission, facts about the inmate's social statuses and past behavior—especially discreditable facts—are collected and recorded in a dossier available to staff. Later, in so far as the establishment officially expects to alter the self-regulating inner tendencies of the inmate, there may be group or individual confession—psychiatric, political, military, or religious, according to the type of institution. On these occasions the inmate has to expose facts and feelings about self to new kinds of audiences. The most spectacular examples of such exposure come to us from Communist confession camps and from *culpa* sessions that form part of the routine of Catholic religious institutions.[29] The dynamics of the process have been explicitly considered by those engaged in so-called milieu therapy.

New audiences not only learn discreditable facts about oneself that are ordinarily concealed but are also in a position to perceive some of these facts directly. Prisoners and mental patients cannot prevent their visitors from seeing them in humiliating circumstances.[30] Another example is the shoulder patch of ethnic identification worn by concentration-camp inmates.[31] Medical and security examinations often expose the inmate physically, sometimes to persons of both sexes; a similar exposure follows from collective sleeping arrangements and doorless toilets.[32] An extreme here, perhaps, is the situation of a self-destructive mental patient who is stripped naked for what is felt to be his own protection and placed in a constantly lit seclusion room, into whose Judas window any person passing on the ward can peer. In general, of course, the inmate is never fully alone; he is always within sight and often earshot of someone, if only his fellow inmates.[33] Prison cages with bars for walls fully realize such exposure.

*   *   *

I have considered some of the more elementary and direct assaults upon the self—various forms of disfigurement and defilement through which the symbolic meaning of events in the inmate's immediate presence dramatically fails to corroborate his prior conception of self. I would now like to consider a source of mortification that is less direct in its effect, with a significance for the individual that is less easy to assess: a disruption of the usual relationship between the individual actor and his acts.

The first disruption to consider here is "looping": an agency that creates a defensive response on the part of the inmate takes this very response as the target of its next attack. The individual finds that his protective response to an assault upon self is collapsed into the situation; he cannot defend himself in the usual way by establishing distance between the mortifying situation and himself.

Deference patterns in total institutions provide one illustration of the looping effect. In civil society, when an individual must accept circumstances and commands that affront his conception of self, he is allowed a margin of face-saving reactive expression —sullenness, failure to offer usual signs of deference, *sotto voce* profaning asides, or fugitive expressions of contempt, irony, and derision. Compliance, then, is likely to be associated with an expressed attitude to it that is not itself subject to the same degree of pressure for compliance. Although such self-protective expressive response to humiliating demands does occur in total institutions, the staff may directly penalize inmates for such activity, citing sullenness or insolence explicitly as grounds for further punishment. Thus, in describing the contamination of self resulting from having to drink soup from the beggar's bowl, Kathryn Hulme says of her subject that she

. . . blanked out from her facial expression the revolt that rose up in her fastidious soul as she drank her dregs. One look of rebellion, she knew, would be enough to invite a repetition of the awful abasement which she was sure she could never go through again, not even for the sake of the Blessed Lord Himself.[34]

The desegregating process in total institutions creates other instances of looping. In the normal course of affairs in civil society, audience and role segregation keep one's avowals and implicit claims regarding self made in one physical scene of activity from being tested against conduct in other settings.* In total institutions spheres of life are desegregated, so that an inmate's conduct in one scene of activity is thrown up to him by staff as a comment and check upon his conduct in another context. A mental patient's effort to present himself in a well-oriented, unantagonistic manner during a diagnostic or treatment conference may be directly embarrassed by evidence introduced concerning his apathy during recreation or the bitter comments he made in a letter to a sibling—a letter which the recipient has forwarded to the hospital administrator, to be added to the patient's dossier and brought along to the conference.

Psychiatric establishments of the advanced type provide excellent illustrations of the looping process, since in them didactic feedback may be erected into a basic therapeutic doctrine. A "permissive" atmosphere is felt to encourage the inmate to "project" or "act out" his typical difficulties in living, which can then be brought to his attention during group-therapy sessions.[35]

Through the process of looping, then, the inmate's reaction to his own situation is collapsed back into this situation itself, and he is not allowed to retain the usual segregation of these phases of action. A second assault upon the inmate's status as an actor may now be cited, one that has been loosely described under the categories of regimentation and tyrannization.

---

* In civil society, crimes and certain other forms of deviance affect the way in which the offender is received in all areas of life, but this breakdown of spheres applies mainly to offenders, not to the bulk of the population that does not offend in these ways or offends without being caught.

In civil society, by the time the individual is an adult he has incorporated socially acceptable standards for the performance of most of his activity, so that the issue of the correctness of his action arises only at certain points, as when his productivity is judged. Beyond this, he is allowed to go at his own pace.[36] He need not constantly look over his shoulder to see if criticism or other sanctions are coming. In addition, many actions will be defined as matters of personal taste, with choice from a range of possibilities specifically allowed. For much activity the judgment and action of authority are held off and one is on one's own. Under such circumstances, one can with over-all profit schedule one's activities to fit into one another—a kind of "personal economy of action," as when an individual postpones eating for a few minutes in order to finish a task, or lays aside a task a little early in order to join a friend for dinner. In a total institution, however, minute segments of a person's line of activity may be subjected to regulations and judgments by staff; the inmate's life is penetrated by constant sanctioning interaction from above, especially during the initial period of stay before the inmate accepts the regulations unthinkingly. Each specification robs the individual of an opportunity to balance his needs and objectives in a personally efficient way and opens up his line of action to sanctions. The autonomy of the act itself is violated.

Although this process of social control is in effect in all organized society, we tend to forget how detailed and closely restrictive it can become in total institutions. The routine reported for one jail for youthful offenders provides a striking example:

At 5:30 we were wakened and had to jump out of bed and stand at attention. When the guard shouted "One!" you removed your night shirt; at "Two!" you folded it; at "Three!" you made your bed. (Only two minutes to make the bed in a difficult and complicated manner.) All the while three monitors would shout at us: "Hurry it up!" and "Make it snappy!"

We also dressed by numbers: shirts on at "One!"; pants at "Two!"; socks at "Three!"; shoes at "Four!" Any noise, like dropping a shoe or even scraping it along the floor, was enough to send you to the line. . . . Once downstairs everyone faced the wall at strict attention, hands at side, thumbs even with trouser seams, head up, shoulders back, stomach in, heels together, eyes straight ahead, no scratching or putting hands to face or head, no moving even the fingers.[37]

A jail for adults provides another example:

The silence system was enforced. No talking outside the cell, at meals or at work.

No pictures were allowed in the cell. No gazing about at meals. Bread crusts were allowed to be left only on the left side of the plate. Inmates were required to stand at attention, cap in hand, until any official, visitor or guard moved beyond sight.[38]

And a concentration camp:

In the barracks a wealth of new and confusing impressions overwhelmed the prisoners. Making up beds was a particular source of SS chicanery. Shapeless and matted straw pallets had to be made as even as a board, the pattern of the sheets parallel to the edges, head bolsters set up at right angles. . . .[39]

. . . the SS seized on the most trifling offenses as occasions for punishment: keeping hands in pockets in cold weather; turning up the coat collar in rain or wind; missing buttons; the tiniest tear or speck of dirt on the clothing; unshined shoes . . . ; shoes that were too well shined—indicating that the wearer was shirking work; failure to salute, including so-called "sloppy posture"; . . . The slightest deviation in dressing ranks and files, or arranging the prisoners in the order of size, or any swaying, coughing, sneezing—any of these might provoke a savage outburst from the SS.[40]

From the military comes an example of the specifications possible in kit laying.

Now the tunic, so folded that the belt made it a straight edge. Covering it, the breeches, squared to the exact area of the tunic, with four concertinafolds facing forward. Towels were doubled once, twice, thrice, and flanked the blue tower. In front of the blue sat a rectangular cardigan. To each side a rolled puttee. Shirts were packed and laid in pairs like flannel bricks. Before them, pants. Between them, neat balls of socks, wedged in. Our holdalls were stretched wide, with knife, fork, spoon, razor, comb, toothbrush, lather brush, buttonstick, in that order, ranged across them.[41]

Similarly, an ex-nun is reported as having to learn to keep her hands still [42] and hidden and to accept the fact that only six specified items were permitted in one's pockets.[43] An ex-mental patient speaks of the humiliation of being doled out limited toilet paper at each request.[44] As suggested earlier, one of the most telling ways in which one's economy of action can be disrupted is the obligation to request permission or supplies for minor activities that one can execute on one's own on the outside, such as smoking, shaving, going to the toilet, telephoning, spending money, or mailing letters. This obligation not only puts the individual in a sub-missive or suppliant role "unnatural" for the adult but also opens up his line of action to interceptions by staff. Instead of having his request immediately and automatically granted, the inmate may be teased, denied, questioned at length, not noticed, or, as an ex-mental patient suggests, merely put off:

> Probably anyone who has never been in a similarly helpless posi-tion cannot realize the humiliation to anyone able bodied yet lacking authority to do the simplest offices for herself of having to beg re-peatedly for even such small necessities as clean linen or a light for her cigarette from nurses who constantly brush her aside with, "I'll give it to you in a minute, dear," and go off leaving her unsupplied. Even the canteen staff seemed to share the opinion that civility was wasted upon lunatics, and would keep a patient waiting indefinitely, while they gossiped with their friends.[45]

I have suggested that authority in total institutions is directed to a multitude of items of conduct—dress, deportment, manners —that constantly occur and constantly come up for judgment. The inmate cannot easily escape from the press of judgmental officials and from the enveloping tissue of constraint. A total institution is like a finishing school, but one that has many refine-ments and is little refined. I would like to comment on two aspects of this tendency toward a multiplication of actively enforced rulings.

First, these rulings are often geared in with an obligation to perform the regulated activity in unison with blocks of fellow inmates. This is what is sometimes called regimentation.

Second, these diffuse rulings occur in an authority system of the *echelon* kind: *any* member of the staff class has certain rights to discipline *any* member of the inmate class, thereby markedly increasing the probability of sanction. (This arrangement, it may be noted, is similar to the one that gives any adult in some small American towns certain rights to correct any child not in the immediate presence of his parents and to demand small services from him.) On the outside, the adult in our society is typically under the authority of a *single* immediate superior in connection with his work, or the authority of one spouse in con-nection with domestic duties; the only echelon authority he must face—the police—is typically not constantly or relevantly present, except perhaps in the case of traffic-law enforcement.

Given echelon authority and regulations that are diffuse, novel, and strictly enforced, we may expect inmates, especially new ones, to live with chronic anxiety about breaking the rules and the consequence of breaking them—physical injury or death in a concentration camp, being "washed out" in an officer's training school, or demotion in a mental hospital:

Yet, even in the apparent liberty and friendliness of an "open" ward, I still found a background of threats that made me feel something between a prisoner and a pauper. The smallest offence, from a nervous symptom to displeasing a sister personally, was met by the suggestion of removing the offender to a closed ward. The idea of a return to "J" ward, if I did not eat my food, was brandished at me so constantly that it became an obsession and even such meals as I was able to swallow disagreed with me physically, while other patients were impelled to do unnecessary or uncongenial work by a similar fear.[46]

In total institutions staying out of trouble is likely to require persistent conscious effort. The inmate may forego certain levels of sociability with his fellows to avoid possible incidents.

In concluding this description of the processes of mortification, three general issues must be raised.

First, total institutions disrupt or defile precisely those actions that in civil society have the role of attesting to the actor and those in his presence that he has some command over his world—that he is a person with "adult" self-determination, autonomy, and freedom of action. A failure to retain this kind of adult executive competency, or at least the symbols of it, can produce in the inmate the terror of feeling radically demoted in the age-grading system.[47]

A margin of self-expressive behavior—whether of antagonism, affection, or unconcern—is one symbol of self-determination. This evidence of one's autonomy is weakened by such specific obligations as having to write one letter home a week, or having to refrain from expressing sullenness. It is further weakened when this margin of behavior is used as evidence concerning the state of one's psychiatric, religious, or political conscience.

There are certain bodily comforts significant to the individual that tend to be lost upon entrance into a total institution—for example, a soft bed[48] or quietness at night.[49] Loss of this set of comforts is apt to reflect a loss of self-determination, too, for the individual tends to ensure these comforts the moment he has resources to expend.[50]

Loss of self-determination seems to have been ceremonialized in concentration camps; thus we have atrocity tales of prisoners being forced to roll in the mud,[51] stand on their heads in the snow, work at ludicrously useless tasks, swear at themselves,[52] or, in the case of Jewish prisoners, sing anti-Semitic songs.[53] A milder version is found in mental hospitals where attendants have been reported forcing a patient who wanted a cigarette to say "pretty please" or jump up for it. In all such cases the inmate is made to display a giving up of his will. Less ceremonialized, but just as extreme, is the embarrassment to one's autonomy that comes from being locked in a ward, placed in a tight wet pack, or tied in a camisole, and thereby denied the liberty of making small adjustive movements.

Another clear-cut expression of personal inefficacy in total institutions is found in inmates' use of speech. One implication of using words to convey decisions about action is that the recipient of an order is seen as capable of receiving a message and acting under his own power to complete the suggestion or command. Executing the act himself, he can sustain some vestige of the notion that he is self-determining. Responding to the question in his own words, he can sustain the notion that he is somebody to be considered, however slightly. And since it is only words that pass between himself and the others, he succeeds in retaining at least physical distance from them, however unpalatable the command or statement.

The inmate in a total institution can find himself denied even this kind of protective distance and self-action. Especially in mental hospitals and political training prisons, the statements he makes may be discounted as mere symptoms, with staff giving attention to non-verbal aspects of his reply.[54] Often he is considered to be of insufficient ritual status to be given even minor greetings, let alone listened to.[55] Or the inmate may find that a kind of rhetorical use of language occurs: questions such as, "Have you washed yet?" or, "Have you got both socks on?" may be accompanied by simultaneous searching by the staff which physically discloses the facts, making these verbal questions superfluous. And instead of being told to move in a particular direction at a particular rate, he may find himself pushed along by the guard, or pulled (in the case of overalled mental patients), or frog-marched. And finally, as will be discussed later, the inmate may find that a dual language exists, with the disciplinary facts of his life given a translated ideal phrasing by the staff that mocks the normal use of language.

The second general consideration is the rationale that is employed for assaults upon the self. The issue tends to place total institutions and their inmates into three different groupings.

In religious institutions the implications environmental arrangements have for the self are explicitly recognized:

> That is the meaning of the contemplative life, and the sense of all the apparently meaningless little rules and observances and fasts and obediences and penances and humiliations and labors that go to make up the routine of existence in a contemplative monastery: they all serve to remind us of what we are and Who God is—that we may get sick of the sight of ourselves and turn to Him: and in the end, we will find Him in ourselves, in our own purified natures which have become the mirror of His tremendous Goodness and of His endless love. . . .[56]

The inmates, as well as the staff, actively seek out these curtailments of the self, so that mortification is complemented by self-mortification, restrictions by renunciations, beatings by self-flagellations, inquisition by confession. Because religious establishments are explicitly concerned with the processes of mortification, they have a special value for the student.

In concentration camps and, to a lesser extent, prisons, some mortifications seem to be arranged solely or mainly for their mortifying power, as when a prisoner is urinated on, but here the inmate does not embrace and facilitate his own destruction of self.

In many of the remaining total institutions, mortifications are officially rationalized on other grounds, such as sanitation (in connection with latrine duty), responsibility for life (in connection with forced feeding), combat capacity (in connection with Army rules for personal appearance), "security" (in connection with restrictive prison regulations).

In total institutions of all three varieties, however, the various rationales for mortifying the self are very often merely rationalizations, generated by efforts to manage the daily activity of a large number of persons in a restricted space with a small expenditure of resources. Further, curtailments of the self occur in all three, even where the inmate is willing and the management has ideal concerns for his well-being.

Two issues have been considered: the inmate's sense of personal inefficacy and the relation of his own desires to the ideal interests of the establishment. The connection between these two issues is variable. Persons can voluntarily elect to enter a total institution and cease thereafter, to their regret, to be able to make such important decisions. In other cases, notably the religious, inmates may begin with and sustain a willful desire to be stripped and cleansed of personal will. Total institutions are fateful for the inmate's civilian self, although the attachment of the inmate to this civilian self can vary considerably.

The processes of mortification I have been considering have to do with the implications for self that persons oriented to a particular expressive idiom might draw from an individual's appearance, conduct, and general situation. In this context I want to consider a third and final issue: the relation between this symbolic-interaction framework for considering the fate of the self and the conventional psycho-physiological one centered around the concept of stress.

The basic facts about self in this report are phrased in a sociological perspective, always leading back to a description of the institutional arrangements which delineate the personal prerogatives of a member. Of course, a psychological assumption is also implied; cognitive processes are invariably involved, for the social arrangements must be "read" by the individual and others for the image of himself that they imply. But, as I have argued, the relation of this cognitive process to other psychological processes is quite variable; according to the general expressive idiom of our society, having one's head shaved is easily perceived as a curtailment of the self, but while this mortification may enrage a mental patient, it may please a monk.

Mortification or curtailment of the self is very likely to involve acute psychological stress for the individual, but for an individual sick with his world or guilt-ridden in it mortification may bring psychological relief. Further, the psychological stress often created by assaults on the self can also be produced by matters not perceived as related to the territories of the self—such as loss of sleep, insufficient food, or protracted decision-making. So, too, a high level of anxiety, or the unavailability of fantasy materials such as movies and books, may greatly increase the

psychological effect of a violation of the self's boundaries, but
in themselves these facilitating factors have nothing to do with
the mortification of the self. Empirically, then, the study of stress
and of encroachments on the self will often be tied together, but,
analytically, two different frameworks are involved.

*   *   *

Notes

1. The category of total institutions has been pointed out from time to
time in the sociological literature under a variety of names, and some
of the characteristics of the class have been suggested, most notably
perhaps in Howard Rowland's neglected paper, "Segregated Communities and Mental Health," in *Mental Health Publication of the
American Association for the Advancement of Science,* No. 9, edited
by F. R. Moulton, 1939. A preliminary statement of the present paper
is reported in *Group Processes,* Transactions of the Third (1956) Conference, edited by Bertram Schaffner (New York: Josiah Macy, Jr.
Foundation, 1957). The term "total" has also been used in its present
context in Amitai Etzioni, "The Organizational Structure of 'Closed'
Educational Institutions in Israel," *Harvard Educational Review,*
XXVII (1957), p. 115.
2. The binary character of total institutions was pointed out to me by
Gregory Bateson, and has been noted in the literature. See, for example, Lloyd E. Ohlin, *Sociology and the Field of Corrections* (New
York: Russell Sage Foundation, 1956), pp. 14, 20. In those situations
where staff are also required to live in, we may expect staff to feel
they are suffering special hardships and to have brought home to
them a status dependency on life on the inside which they did not
expect. See Jane Cassels Record, "The Marine Radioman's Struggle
for Status," *American Journal of Sociology,* LXII (1957), p. 359.
3. For the prison version, see S. Kirson Weinberg, "Aspects of the
Prison's Social Structure," *American Journal of Sociology,* XLVII
(1942), pp. 717–26.
4. Mary Jane Ward, *The Snake Pit* (New York: New American Library,
1955), p. 72.
5. Ivan Belknap, *Human Problems of a State Mental Hospital* (New
York: McGraw-Hill, 1956), p. 177.
6. A very full case report on this matter is provided in a chapter titled
"Information and the Control of Treatment," in Julius A. Roth's
forthcoming monograph on the tuberculosis hospital. His work promises to be a model study of a total institution. Preliminary statements
may be found in his articles, "What is an Activity?" *Etc.,* XIV (Autumn 1956), pp. 54–56, and "Ritual and Magic in the Control of
Contagion," *American Sociological Review,* XXII (1957), pp. 310–
14.
7. Suggested in Ohlin, *op. cit.,* p. 20.
8. An example of the description of these processes may be found in
Gresham M. Sykes, *The Society of Captives* (Princeton: Princeton

University Press, 1958), ch. iv, "The Pains of Imprisonment," pp. 63–83.

9. Sanford M. Dornbusch, "The Military Academy as an Assimilating Institution," *Social Forces*, XXXIII (1955), p. 317. For an example of initial visiting restrictions in a mental hospital, see D. McI. Johnson and N. Dodds, eds., *The Plea for the Silent* (London: Christopher Johnson, 1957), p. 16. Compare the rule against having visitors which has often bound domestic servants to their total institution. See J. Jean Hecht, *The Domestic Servant Class in Eighteenth-Century England* (London: Routledge and Kegan Paul, 1956), pp. 127–28.

10. A useful review in the case of American prisons may be found in Paul W. Tappen, "The Legal Rights of Prisoners," *The Annals*, CCXCIII (May 1954), pp. 99–111.

11. See, for example, J. Kerkhoff, *How Thin the Veil: A Newspaperman's Story of His Own Mental Crack-up and Recovery* (New York: Greenberg, 1952), p. 110; Elie A. Cohen, *Human Behaviour in the Concentration Camp* (London: Jonathan Cape, 1954), pp. 118–122; Eugen Kogon, *The Theory and Practice of Hell* (New York: Berkley Publishing Corp., n.d.), pp. 63–68.

12. Brendan Behan, *Borstal Boy* (London: Hutchinson, 1958), p. 40. See also Anthony Heckstall-Smith, *Eighteen Months* (London: Allan Wingate, 1954), p. 26.

13. For a version of this process in concentration camps, see Cohen, *op. cit.*, p. 120, and Kogon, *op. cit.*, pp. 64–65. For a fictionalized treatment of the welcome in a girls' reformatory see Sara Harris, *The Wayward Ones* (New York: New American Library, 1952), pp. 31–34. A prison version, less explicit, is found in George Dendrickson and Frederick Thomas, *The Truth About Dartmoor* (London: Gollancz, 1954), pp. 42–57.

14. For example, Thomas Merton, *The Seven Storey Mountain* (New York: Harcourt, Brace and Company, 1948), pp. 290–91; Cohen, *op. cit.*, pp. 145–47.

15. Dendrickson and Thomas, *op. cit.*, pp. 83–84, also *The Holy Rule of Saint Benedict*, Ch. 55.

16. Kogon, *op. cit.*, p. 69.

17. *The Holy Rule of Saint Benedict*, Ch. 55.

18. *The Holy Rule of Saint Benedict*, Ch. 58.

19. John M. Murtagh and Sara Harris, *Cast the First Stone* (New York: Pocket Books, 1958), pp. 239–40. On mental hospitals see, for example, Kerkhoff, *op. cit.*, p. 10. Ward, *op. cit.*, p. 60, makes the reasonable suggestion that men in our society suffer less defacement in total institutions than do women.

20. Johnson and Dodds, *op. cit.*, p. 15; for a prison version see Alfred Hassler, *Diary of a Self-Made Convict* (Chicago: Regnery, 1954), p. 33.

21. L. D. Hankoff, "Interaction Patterns Among Military Prison Personnel," *U.S. Armed Forces Medical Journal*, X (1959), p. 1419.

22. Kathryn Hulme, *The Nun's Story* (London: Muller, 1957), p. 52.

23. *The Holy Rule of Saint Benedict*, Ch. 44.

24. Dendrickson and Thomas, *op. cit.*, p. 76.

25. Sykes, *op. cit.*, pp. 70–72.

26. For example, T. E. Lawrence, *The Mint* (London: Jonathan Cape, 1955), pp. 34–35.

27. *The Holy Rule of Saint Benedict*, Ch. 35.

28. Kogon, *op. cit.*, p. 102.

29. Hulme, *op. cit.*, pp. 48–51.

30. Wider communities in Western society, of course, have employed this technique too, in the form of public floggings and public hangings, the pillory and stocks. Functionally correlated with the public emphasis on mortifications in total institutions is the commonly found strict ruling that staff is not to be humiliated by staff in the presence of inmates.

31. Kogon, *op. cit.*, pp. 41–42.

32. Behan, *op. cit.*, p. 23.

33. For example, Kogon, *op. cit.*, p. 128; Hassler, *op. cit.*, p. 16. For the situation in a religious institution, see Hulme, *op. cit.*, p. 48. She also describes a lack of aural privacy since thin cotton hangings are used as the only door closing off the individual sleeping cells (p. 20).

34. Hulme, *op. cit.*, p. 53.

35. A clear statement may be found in R. Rapoport and E. Skellern, "Some Therapeutic Functions of Administrative Disturbance," *Administrative Science Quarterly*, II (1957), pp. 84–85.

36. The span of time over which an employee works at his own discretion without supervision can in fact be taken as a measure of his pay and status in an organization. See Elliott Jaques, *The Measurement of Responsibility: A Study of Work, Payment, and Individual Capacity* (Cambridge: Harvard University Press, 1956). And just as "time-span of responsibility" is an index of position, so a long span of freedom from inspection is a reward of position.

37. Hassler, *op. cit.*, p. 155, quoting Robert McCreery.

38. T. E. Gaddis, *Birdman of Alcatraz* (New York: New American Library, 1958), p. 25. For a similar rule of silence in a British prison, see Frank Norman, *Bang to Rights* (London: Secker and Warburg, 1958), p. 27.

39. Kogon, *op. cit.*, p. 68.

40. *Ibid.*, pp. 99–100.

41. Lawrence, *op. cit.*, p. 83. In this connection see the comments by M. Brewster Smith on the concept of "chicken," in Samuel Stouffer *et al.*, *The American Soldier* (4 vols.; Princeton: Princeton University Press, 1949), Vol. I, p. 390.

42. Hulme, *op. cit.*, p. 3.

43. *Ibid.*, p. 39.

44. Ward, *op. cit.*, p. 23.

45. Johnson and Dodds, *op. cit.*, p. 39.

46. Johnson and Dodds, *op. cit.*, p. 36.

47. Cf. Sykes, *op. cit.*, pp. 73–76, "The Deprivation of Autonomy."

48. Hulme, *op. cit.*, p. 18; George Orwell, "Such, Such Were the Joys," *Partisan Review*, XIX (September-October, 1952), p. 521.

49. Hassler, *op. cit.*, p. 78; Johnson and Dodds, *op. cit.*, p. 17.

50. This is one source of mortification that civilians practice on themselves during camping vacations, perhaps on the assumption that a new sense of self can be obtained by voluntarily foregoing some of one's previous self-impregnated comforts.

51. Kogon, *op. cit.*, p. 66.

52. *Ibid.*, p. 61.

53. *Ibid.*, p. 78.

54. See Alfred H. Stanton and Morris S. Schwartz, *The Mental Hospital* (New York: Basic Books, 1954), pp. 200, 203, 205–6.

55. For an example of this non-person treatment, see Johnson and Dodds, *op. cit.*, p. 122.

56. Merton, *op. cit.*, p. 372.

Of the Limits to the Authority of Society Over the Individual

◆

John Stuart Mill, 1806–1873, was the godson of Jeremy Bentham. Raised by his father as a defender of the philosophy of utilitarianism, Mill moved beyond the simple hedonistic psychology of Bentham after coming under the influence of Alexis de Tocqueville and other Continental thinkers. His writings reflect a growing awareness of the new social problems created by industrialism and mass politics. In the famous essay, On Liberty, *Mill defends the rights of the individual, however eccentric he may be, against the attacks and pressures of social opinion and the power of the state. Mill asserts that society has no right to interfere with an individual's private life against his will, even in an attempt to help him. It is worth reflecting that much of modern social welfare legislation directly violates this fundamental "liberal" principle.*

*   *   *

What, then, is the rightful limit to the sovereignty of the individual over himself? Where does the authority of society begin? How much of human life should be assigned to individuality, and how much to society?

Each will receive its proper share, if each has that which more particularly concerns it. To individuality should belong the part of life in which it is chiefly the individual that is interested; to society, the part which chiefly interests society.

Though society is not founded on a contract, and though no good purpose is answered by inventing a contract in order to deduce social obligations from it, every one who receives the protection of society owes a return for the benefit, and the fact of living in society renders it indispensable that each should be bound to observe a certain line of conduct towards the rest. This conduct consists, first, in not injuring the interests of one another; or rather certain interests, which, either by express legal pro-

From John Stuart Mill, *On Liberty*, 1859.

vision or by tacit understanding, ought to be considered as
rights; and secondly, in each person's bearing his share (to be
fixed on some equitable principle) of the labors and sacrifices
incurred for defending the society or its members from injury
and molestation. These conditions society is justified in enforcing,
at all costs to those who endeavor to withhold fulfilment. Nor is
this all that society may do. The acts of an individual may be
hurtful to others, or wanting in due consideration for their welfare, without going the length of violating any of their constituted rights. The offender may then be justly punished by
opinion, though not by law. As soon as any part of a person's
conduct affects prejudicially the interests of others, society has
jurisdiction over it, and the question whether the general welfare
will or will not be promoted by interfering with it, becomes open
to discussion. But there is no room for entertaining any such
question when a person's conduct affects the interests of no
persons besides himself, or needs not affect them unless they like
(all the persons concerned being of full age, and the ordinary
amount of understanding). In all such cases there should be perfect freedom, legal and social, to do the action and stand the
consequences.

It would be a great misunderstanding of this doctrine, to
suppose that it is one of selfish indifference, which pretends that
human beings have no business with each other's conduct in
life, and that they should not concern themselves about the
well-doing or well-being of one another, unless their own interest
is involved. Instead of any diminution, there is need of a great
increase of disinterested exertion to promote the good of others.
But disinterested benevolence can find other instruments to
persuade people to their good, than whips and scourges, either
of the literal or the metaphorical sort. I am the last person to
undervalue the self-regarding virtues; they are only second in
importance, if even second, to the social. It is equally the business of education to cultivate both. But even education works by
conviction and persuasion as well as by compulsion, and it is by
the former only that, when the period of education is past, the
self-regarding virtues should be inculcated. Human beings owe to
each other help to distinguish the better from the worse, and
encouragement to choose the former and avoid the latter. They
should be forever stimulating each other to increased exercise of
their higher faculties, and increased direction of their feelings

and aims towards wise instead of foolish, elevating instead of degrading, objects and contemplations. But neither one person, nor any number of persons, is warranted in saying to another human creature of ripe years, that he shall not do with his life for his own benefit what he chooses to do with it. He is the person most interested in his own well-being: the interest which any other person, except in cases of strong personal attachment, offered to him, even obtruded on him, by others; but he, himself, has; the interest which society has in him individually (except as to his conduct to others) is fractional, and altogether indirect: while, with respect to his own feelings and circumstances, the most ordinary man or woman has means of knowledge immeasurably surpassing those that can be possessed by anyone else. The interference of society to overrule his judgment and purposes in what only regards himself, must be grounded on general presumptions; which may be altogether wrong, and even if right, are as likely as not to be misapplied to individual cases, by persons no better acquainted with the circumstances of such cases than those are who look at them merely from without. In this department, therefore, of human affairs, Individuality has its proper field of action. In the conduct of human beings towards one another, it is necessary that general rules should for the most part be observed, in order that people may know what they have to expect; but in each person's own concerns, his individual spontaneity is entitled to free exercise. Considerations to aid his judgment, exhortations to strengthen his will, may be offered to him, even obtruded on him, by others; but he, himself, is the final judge. All errors which he is likely to commit against advice and warning, are far outweighed by the evil of allowing others to constrain him to what they deem his good.

I do not mean that the feeling with which a person is regarded by others, ought not to be in any way affected by his self-regarding qualities or deficiencies. This is neither possible nor desirable. If he is eminent in any of the qualities which conduce to his own good, he is, so far, a proper object of admiration. He is so much the nearer to the ideal perfection of human nature. If he is grossly deficient in those qualities, a sentiment the opposite of admiration will follow. There is a degree of folly, and a degree of what may be called (though the phrase is not unobjectionable) lowness or depravation of taste, which, though it cannot justify doing harm to the person who manifests it, renders him necessarily and properly a subject of distaste, or, in extreme cases, even of contempt: a person could not have the opposite qualities in due strength without entertaining these feelings. Though doing no wrong to anyone, a person may so act as to compel us to judge him, and feel to him, as a fool, or as a being of an inferior order: and since this judgment and feeling are a fact which he would prefer to avoid, it is doing him a service to warn him of it beforehand, as of any other disagreeable consequence to which he exposes himself. It would be well, indeed, if this good office were much more freely rendered than the common notions of politeness at present permit, and if one person could honestly point out to another that he thinks him in fault, without being considered unmannerly or presuming. We have a right, also, in various ways, to act upon our unfavorable opinion of any one, not to the oppression of his individuality, but in the exercise of ours. We are not bound, for example, to seek his society; we have a right to avoid it (though not to parade the avoidance), for we have a right to choose the society most acceptable to us. We have a right, and it may be our duty to caution others against him, if we think his example or conversation likely to have a pernicious effect on those with whom he associates. We may give others a preference over him in optional good offices, except those which tend to his improvement. In these various modes a person may suffer very severe penalties at the hands of others, for faults which directly concern only himself; but he suffers these penalties only in so far as they are the natural, and, as it were, the spontaneous consequences of the faults themselves, not because they are purposely inflicted on him for the sake of punishment. A person who shows rashness, obstinacy, self-conceit—who cannot live within moderate means—who cannot restrain himself from hurtful indulgences—who pursues animal pleasures at the expense of those of feeling and intellect—must expect to be lowered in the opinion of others, and to have a less share of their favorable sentiments, but of this he has no right to complain, unless he has merited their favor by special excellence in his social relations, and has thus established a title to their good offices, which is not affected by his demerits towards himself.

What I contend for is, that the inconveniences which are strictly inseparable from the unfavorable judgment of others, are the only ones to which a person should ever be subjected for that portion of his conduct and character which concerns his own good, but which does not affect the interests of others in their relations with him. Acts injurious to others require a totally different treatment. Encroachment on their rights; infliction on them of any loss or damage not justified by his own rights; falsehood or duplicity in dealing with them; unfair or ungenerous use of advantages over them; even selfish abstinence from defending them against injury—these are fit objects of moral reprobation, and, in grave cases, of moral retribution and punishment. And not only these acts, but the dispositions which lead to them, are properly immoral, and fit subjects of disapprobation which may rise to abhorrence. Cruelty of disposition; malice and ill-nature; that most anti-social and odious of all passions, envy; dissimulation and insincerity; irascibility on insufficient cause, and resentment disproportioned to the provocation; the love of domineering over others; the desire to engross more than one's share of advantages (the πλεονεξία of the Greeks); the pride which derives gratification from the abasement of others; the egotism which thinks self and its concerns more important than everything else, and decides all doubtful questions in his own favor—these are moral vices, and constitute a bad and odious moral character: unlike the self-regarding faults previously mentioned, which are not properly immoralities, and to whatever pitch they may be carried, do not constitute wickedness. They may be proofs of any amount of folly, or want of personal dignity and self-respect; but they are only a subject of moral reprobation when they involve a breach of duty to others, for whose sake the individual is bound to have care for himself. What are called duties to ourselves are not socially obligatory, unless circumstances render them at the same time duties to others. The term duty to oneself, when it means anything more than prudence, means self-respect or self-development; and for none of these is any one accountable to his fellow-creatures, because for none of them is it for the good of mankind that he be held accountable to them.

The distinction between the loss of consideration which a person may rightly incur by defect of prudence or of personal dignity, and the reprobation which is due to him for an offence against the rights of others, is not a merely nominal distinction. It makes a vast difference both in our feelings and in our conduct towards him, whether he displeases us in things in which we think we have a right to control him, or in things in which we know that we have not. If he displeases us, we may express our distaste, and we may stand aloof from a person as well as from a thing that displeases us; but we shall not therefore feel called on to make his life uncomfortable. We shall reflect that he already bears, or will bear, the whole penalty of his error; if he spoils his life by mismanagement, we shall not, for that reason, desire to spoil it still further: instead of wishing to punish him, we shall rather endeavor to alleviate his punishment, by showing him how he may avoid or cure the evils his conduct tends to bring upon him. He may be to us an object of pity, perhaps of dislike, but not of anger or resentment; we shall not treat him like an enemy of society: the worst we shall think ourselves justified in doing is leaving him to himself, if we do not interfere benevolently by showing interest or concern for him. It is far otherwise if he has infringed the rules necessary for the protection of his fellow-creatures, individually or collectively. The evil consequences of his acts do not then fall on himself, but on others; and society, as the protector of all its members, must retaliate on him; must inflict pain on him for the express purpose of punishment, and must take care that it be sufficiently severe. In the one case, he is an offender at our bar, and we are called on not only to sit in judgment on him, but, in one shape or another, to execute our own sentence: in the other case, it is not our part to inflict any suffering on him, except what may incidentally follow from our using the same liberty in the regulation of our own affairs, which we allow to him in his.

The distinction here pointed out between the part of a person's life which concerns only himself, and that which concerns others, many persons will refuse to admit. How (it may be asked) can any part of the conduct of a member of society be a matter of indifference to the other members? No person is an entirely isolated being; it is impossible for a person to do anything seriously or permanently hurtful to himself, without mischief reaching at least to his near connections, and often far beyond them. If he injures his property, he does harm to those who directly or indirectly derived support from it, and usually diminishes, by a greater or less amount, the general resources of the community. If he deteriorates his bodily or mental faculties, he not only brings evil upon all who depended on him for any portion of their happiness, but disqualifies himself for rendering the services which he owes to his fellow-creatures generally; perhaps becomes a burden on their affection or benevolence; and if such conduct were very frequent, hardly any offence that is committed would detract more from the general sum of good. Finally, if by his vices or follies a person does no direct harm to others, he is nevertheless (it may be said) injurious by his example; and ought to be compelled to control himself, for the sake of those whom the sight or knowledge of his conduct might corrupt or mislead.

And even (it will be added) if the consequences of misconduct could be confined to the vicious or thoughtless individual, ought society to abandon to their own guidance those who are manifestly unfit for it? If protection against themselves is confessedly due to children and persons under age, is not society equally bound to afford it to persons of mature years who are equally incapable of self-government? If gambling, or drunkenness, or incontinence, or idleness, or uncleanliness, are as injurious to happiness, and as great a hindrance to improvement, as many or most of the acts prohibited by law, why (it may be asked) should not law, so far as is consistent with practicability and social convenience, endeavor to repress these also? And as a supplement to the unavoidable imperfections of law, ought not opinion at least to organize a powerful police against these vices, and visit rigidly with social penalties those who are known to practise them? There is no question here (it may be said) about restricting individuality, or impeding the trial of new and original experiments in living. The only things it is sought to prevent are things which have been tried and condemned from the beginning of the world until now; things which experience has shown not to be useful or suitable to any person's individuality. There must be some length of time and amount of experience, after which a moral or prudential truth may be regarded as established: and it is merely desired to prevent generation after generation from falling over the same precipice which has been fatal to their predecessors.

I fully admit that the mischief which a person does to himself, may seriously affect, both through their sympathies and their interests, those nearly connected with him, and in a minor degree, society at large. When, by conduct of this sort, a person is led to violate a distinct and assignable obligation to any other person or persons, the case is taken out of the self-regarding class, and becomes amenable to moral disapprobation in the proper sense of the term. If, for example, a man, through intemperance or extravagance, becomes unable to pay his debts, or, having undertaken the moral responsibility of a family, becomes from the same cause incapable of supporting or educating them, he is deservedly reprobated, and might be justly punished; but it is for the breach of duty to his family or creditors, not for the extravagance. If the resources which ought to have been devoted to them, had been diverted from them for the most prudent investment, the moral culpability would have been the same. George Barnwell murdered his uncle to get money for his mistress, but if he had done it to set himself up in business, he would equally have been hanged. Again, in the frequent case of a man who causes grief to his family by addiction to bad habits, he deserves reproach for his unkindness or ingratitude; but so he may for cultivating habits not in themselves vicious, if they are painful to those with whom he passes his life, or who from personal ties are dependent on him for their comfort. Whoever fails in the consideration generally due to the interests and feelings of others, not being compelled by some more imperative duty, or justified by allowable self-preference, is a subject of moral disapprobation for that failure, but not for the cause of it, nor for the errors, merely personal to himself, which may have remotely led to it. In like manner, when a person disables himself, by conduct purely self-regarding, from the performance of some definite duty incumbent on him to the public, he is guilty of a social offence. No person ought to be punished simply for being drunk; but a soldier or a policeman should be punished for being drunk on duty. Whenever, in short, there is a definite damage, or a definite risk of damage, either to an individual or to the public, the case is taken out of the province of liberty, and placed in that of morality or law.

But with regard to the merely contingent, or, as it may be called, constructive injury which a person causes to society, by conduct which neither violates any specific duty of the public, nor occasions perceptible hurt to any assignable individual except himself; the inconvenience is one which society can afford to bear, for the sake of the greater good of human freedom. If grown persons are to be punished for not taking proper care of themselves, I would rather it were for their own sake, than under pretence of preventing them from impairing their capacity of rendering to society benefits which society does not pretend it has a right to exact. But I cannot consent to argue the point as if society had no means of bringing its weaker members up to its ordinary standard of rational conduct, except waiting till they do something irrational, and then punishing them, legally or morally, for it. Society has had absolute power over them during all the early portion of their existence: it has had the whole period of childhood and nonage in which to try whether it could make them capable of rational conduct in life. The existing generation is master both of the training and the entire circumstances of the generation to come; it cannot indeed make them perfectly wise and good, because it is itself so lamentably deficient in goodness and wisdom; and its best efforts are not always, in individual cases, its most successful ones; but it is perfectly well able to make the rising generation, as a whole, as good as, and a little better than, itself. If society lets any considerable number of its members grow up mere children, incapable of being acted on by rational consideration of distant motives, society has itself to blame for the consequences. Armed not only with all the powers of education, but with the ascendency which the authority of a received opinion always exercises over the minds who are least fitted to judge for themselves; and aided by the *natural* penalties which cannot be prevented from falling on those who incur the distaste or the contempt of those who know them; let not society pretend that it needs, besides all this, the power to issue commands and enforce obedience in the personal concerns of individuals, in which, on all principles of justice and policy, the decision ought to rest with those who are to abide the consequences. Nor is there anything which tends more to discredit and frustrate the better means of influencing conduct, than a resort to the worse. If there be among those whom it is attempted to coerce into prudence or temperance, any of the material of which vigorous and independent characters are made, they will infallibly rebel against the yoke. No such person will ever feel that others have a right to control him in his concerns, such as they have to prevent him from injuring them in theirs; and it easily comes to be considered a mark of spirit and courage to fly in the face of such usurped authority, and do with ostentation the exact opposite of what it enjoins; as in the fashion of grossness which succeeded, in the time of Charles II, to the fanatical moral intolerance of the Puritans. With respect to what is said of the necessity of protecting society from the bad example set to others by the vicious or the self-indulgent; it is true that bad example may have a pernicious effect, especially the example of doing wrong to others with impunity to the wrongdoer. But we are now speaking of conduct which, while it does no wrong to others, is supposed to do great harm to the agent himself: and I do not see how those who believe this, can think otherwise than that the example, on the whole, must be more salutary than hurtful, since, if it displays the misconduct, it displays also the painful or degrading consequences which, if the conduct is justly censured, must be supposed to be in all or most cases attendant on it.

But the strongest of all the arguments against the interference of the public with purely personal conduct, is that when it does interfere, the odds are that it interferes wrongly, and in the wrong place. On questions of social morality, of duty to others, the opinion of the public, that is, of an overruling majority, though often wrong, is likely to be still oftener right; because on such questions they are only required to judge of their own interests; of the manner in which some mode of conduct, if allowed to be practised, would affect themselves. But the opinion of a similar majority, imposed as a law on the minority, on questions of self-regarding conduct, is quite as likely to be wrong as right; for in these cases public opinion means, at the best, some people's opinion of what is good or bad for other people; while very often it does not even mean that; the public, with the most perfect indifference, passing over the pleasure or convenience of those whose conduct they censure, and considering only their own preference. There are many who consider as an injury to themselves any conduct which they have a distaste for, and resent it as an outrage to their feelings; as a religious bigot, when charged with disregarding the religious feelings of others, has been known to retort that they disregard his feelings, by persisting in their abominable worship or creed. But there is no parity between the feeling of a person for his own opinion, and the feeling of another who is offended at his holding it; no more than between the desire of a thief to take a purse, and the desire of the right owner to keep it. And a person's taste is as much his own peculiar concern as his opinion or his purse. It is easy for any one to imagine an ideal public, which leaves the freedom and choice of individuals in all uncertain matters undisturbed, and only requires them to abstain from modes of conduct which universal experience has condemned. But where has there been seen a public which set any such limit to its censorship? or when does the public trouble itself about universal experience? In its interferences with personal conduct it is seldom thinking of anything but the enormity of acting or feeling differently from itself; and this standard of judgment, thinly disguised, is held up to mankind as the dictate of religion and philosophy, by nine tenths of all moralists and speculative writers. These teach that things are right because they are right; because we feel them to be so. They tell us to search in our own minds and hearts for laws of conduct binding on ourselves and on all others. What can the poor public do but apply these instructions, and make their own personal feelings of good and evil, if they are tolerably unanimous in them, obligatory on all the world?

*   *   *

FYODOR DOSTOYEVSKY

The Grand Inquisitor

Fyodor Dostoyevsky, 1821–1881, was a Russian novelist of enormous power and intensity. His major works include the immortal Crime and Punishment *and* The Brothers Karamazov, *the last of which contains the chapter reprinted here. Dostoyevsky explores in psychological and philosophical depth the conflict between humanitarian liberalism and traditional Christianity, an issue which dominated much of nineteenth century thought. Like all great artists however he transcends the particular limitations of his time and engages his art with the universal questions of good and evil. The parable of the* Grand Inquisitor *in* The Brothers Karamazov *is told by Ivan Karamazov, a liberated, westernized agnostic, to his saintly brother Alyosha, a primitive Christian imbued with a love for his mother Russia and Christ. Dostoyevsky himself was for many years a proponent of the new ideas imported into Russia from Western*

Reprinted from F. Dostoyevsky, *The Brothers Karamazov*, translated by Constance Garnett (New York: Modern Library, 1929).

*Europe, and this fact is revealed in the power of the Grand In-
quisitor's argument. The end of the parable is deliberately ambiguous,
for Dostoyevsky obviously feels that Ivan cannot be answered by
arguments, if he can be asnwered at all.*

*   *   *

"Rebellion? I am sorry you call it that," said Ivan earnestly. "One
can hardly live in rebellion, and I want to live. Tell me yourself, I challenge you—answer. Imagine that you are creating a
fabric of human destiny with the object of making men happy in
the end, giving them peace and rest at last, but that it was
essential and inevitable to torture to death only one tiny creature
—that baby beating its breast with its fist, for instance—and to
found that edifice on its unavenged tears, would you consent to
be the architect on those conditions? Tell me, and tell the truth."

"No, I wouldn't consent," said Alyosha softly.

"And can you admit the idea that men for whom you are
building it would agree to accept their happiness on the foundation of the unexpiated blood of a little victim? And accepting
it would remain happy for ever?"

"No, I can't admit it. Brother," said Alyosha suddenly, with
flashing eyes, "you said just now, is there a being in the whole
world who would have the right to forgive and could forgive?
But there is a Being and He can forgive everything, all and
for all, because He gave His innocent blood for all and everything. You have forgotten Him, and on Him is built the edifice,
and it is to Him they cry aloud: 'Thou are just, O Lord, for
Thy ways are revealed!' "

"Ah! the One without sin and His blood! No, I have not forgotten Him; on the contrary I've been wondering all the time
how it was you did not bring Him in before, for usually all
arguments on your side put Him in the foreground. Do you
know, Alyosha—don't laugh! I made a poem about a year ago.
If you can waste another ten minutes on me, I'll tell it to you."

"You wrote a poem?"

"Oh, no, I didn't write it," laughed Ivan, "and I've never
written two lines of poetry in my life. But I made up this poem
in prose and I remembered it. I was carried away when I made
it up. You will be my first reader—that is, listener. Why should
an author forgo even one listener?" smiled Ivan. "Shall I tell it
to you?"

"I am all attention," said Alyosha.

"My poem is called 'The Grand Inquisitor'; it's a ridiculous thing, but I want to tell it to you."

The Grand Inquisitor

"Even this must have a preface—that is, a literary preface," laughed Ivan, "and I am a poor hand at making one. You see, my action takes place in the sixteenth century, and at that time, as you probably learnt at school, it was customary in poetry to bring down heavenly powers on earth. Not to speak of Dante, in France, clerks, as well as the monks in the monasteries, used to give regular performances in which the Madonna, the saints, the angels, Christ, and God Himself were brought on the stage. In those days it was done in all simplicity. In Victor Hugo's 'Notre Dame de Paris' an edifying and gratuitous spectacle was provided for the people in the Hôtel de Ville of Paris in the reign of Louis XI in honour of the birth of the dauphin. It was called *Le bon jugement de la très sainte et gracieuse Vierge Marie,* and she appears herself on the stage and pronounces her *bon jugement.* Similar plays, chiefly from the Old Testament, were occasionally performed in Moscow too, up to the times of Peter the Great. But besides plays there were all sorts of legends and ballads scattered about the world, in which the saints and angels and all the powers of Heaven took part when required. In our monasteries the monks busied themselves in translating, copying, and even composing such poems—and even under the Tatars. There is, for instance, one such poem (of course, from the Greek), 'The Wanderings of Our Lady through Hell,' with descriptions as bold as Dante's. Our Lady visits Hell, and the Archangel Michael leads her through the torments. She sees the sinners and their punishments. There she sees among others one noteworthy set of sinners in a burning lake; some of them sink to the bottom of the lake so that they can't swim out, and 'these God forgets'—an expression of extraordinary depth and force. And so Our Lady, shocked and weeping, falls before the throne of God and begs for mercy for all in Hell—for all she has seen there, indiscriminately. Her conversation with God is immensely interesting. She beseeches Him, she will not desist, and when God points to the hands and feet of her Son, nailed to the Cross, and asks: 'How can I forgive His tormentors?'

she bids all the saints, all the martyrs, all the angels and archangels to fall down with her and pray for mercy on all without distinction. It ends by her winning from God a respite of suffering every year from Good Friday till Trinity day, and the sinners at once raise a cry of thankfulness from Hell, chanting: 'Thou art just, O Lord, in this judgment.' Well, my poem would have been of that kind if it had appeared at that time. He comes on the scene in my poem, but He says nothing, only appears and passes on. Fifteen centuries have passed since He promised to come in His glory, fifteen centuries since His prophet wrote, 'Behold, I come quickly'; 'Of that day and that hour knoweth no man, neither the Son, but the Father,' as He Himself predicted on earth. But humanity awaits him with the same faith and with the same love. Oh, with greater faith, for it is fifteen centuries since man has ceased to see signs from Heaven.

> No signs from Heaven come to-day
> To add to what the heart doth say.

There was nothing left but faith in what the heart doth say. It is true there were many miracles in those days. There were saints who performed miraculous cures; some holy people, according to their biographies, were visited by the Queen of Heaven herself. But the devil did not slumber, and doubts were already arising among men of the truth of these miracles. And just then there appeared in the north of Germany a terrible new heresy. 'A huge star like to a torch' (that is, to a church) 'fell on the sources of the waters and they became bitter.' These heretics began blasphemously denying miracles. But those who remained faithful were all the more ardent in their faith. The tears of humanity rose up to Him as before, awaited His coming, loved Him, hoped for Him, yearned to suffer and die for Him as before. And so many ages mankind had prayed with faith and fervour: 'O Lord our God, hasten Thy coming,' so many ages called upon Him, that in His infinite mercy He deigned to come down to His servants. Before that day He had come down, He had visited some holy men, martyrs and hermits as is written in their 'Lives.' Among us, Tyutchev, with absolute faith in the truth of his words, bore witness that:

> Bearing the Cross, in slavish dress
> Weary and worn, the Heavenly King

Our mother, Russia, came to bless,
And through our land went wandering.

And that certainly was so, I assure you.

"And behold, He deigned to appear for a moment to the people, to the tortured, suffering people, sunk in iniquity but loving Him like children. My story is laid in Spain, in Seville, in the most terrible time of the Inquisition, when fires were lighted every day to the glory of God, and 'in the splendid *auto da fé* the wicked heretics were burnt.' Oh, of course, this was not the coming in which He will appear according to His promise at the end of time in all His heavenly glory, and which will be sudden 'as lightning flashing from east to west.' No, He visited His children only for a moment, and there where the flames were crackling round the heretics. In His infinite mercy He came once more among men in that human shape in which He walked among men for three years fifteen centuries ago. He came down to the 'hot pavements' of the southern town in which on the day before almost a hundred heretics had, *ad majorem gloriam Dei,* been burnt by the cardinal, the Grand Inquisitor, in a magnificent *auto da fé,* in the presence of the king, the court, the knights, the cardinals, the most charming ladies of the court, and the whole population of Seville.

"He came softly, unobserved, and yet, strange to say, everyone recognized Him. That might be one of the best passages in the poem. I mean, why they recognized Him. The people are irresistibly drawn to Him, they surround Him, they flock about Him, follow Him. He moves silently in their midst with a gentle smile of infinite compassion. The sun of love burns in His heart, light and power shine from His eyes, and their radiance, shed on the people, stirs their hearts with responsive love. He holds out His hands to them, blesses them, and a healing virtue comes from contact with Him, even with His garments. An old man in the crowd, blind from childhood, cries out, 'O Lord, heal me and I shall see Thee!' and, as it were, scales fall from his eyes and the blind man sees Him. The crowd weeps and kisses the earth under His feet. Children throw flowers before Him, sing, and cry hosannah. 'It is He—it is He!' all repeat. 'It must be He, it can be no one but Him!' He stops at the steps of the Seville cathedral at the moment when the weeping mourners are bringing in a little open white coffin. In it lies a child of seven, the only daughter of a prominent citizen. The dead child lies hidden in flowers. 'He will raise your child,' the crowd shouts to the weeping mother. The priest, coming to meet the coffin, looks perplexed, and frowns, but the mother of the dead child throws herself at His feet with a wail. 'If it is Thou, raise my child!' she cries holding out her hands to Him. The procession halts, the coffin is laid on the steps at His feet. He looks with compassion, and His lips once more softly pronounce, 'Maiden, arise!' and the maiden arises. The little girl sits up in the coffin and looks round, smiling with wide-open wondering eyes, holding a bunch of white roses they had put in her hand.

"There are cries, sobs, confusion among the people, and at that moment the cardinal himself, the Grand Inquisitor, passes by the cathedral. He is an old man, almost ninety, tall and erect, with a withered face and sunken eyes, in which there is still a gleam of light. He is not dressed in his gorgeous cardinal's robes, as he was the day before, when he was burning the enemies of the Roman Church—at that moment he was wearing his coarse, old, monk's cassock. At a distance behind him come his gloomy assistants and slaves and the 'holy guard.' He stops at the sight of the crowd and watches it from a distance. He sees everything; he sees them set the coffin down at His feet, sees the child rise up, and his face darkens. He knits his thick grey brows and his eyes gleam with a sinister fire. He holds out his finger and bids the guards take Him. And such is his power, so completely are the people cowed into submission and trembling obedience to him, that the crowd immediately make way for the guards, and in the midst of deathlike silence they lay hands on Him and lead Him away. The crowd instantly bows down to the earth, like one man, before the old inquisitor. He blesses the people in silence and passes on. The guards lead their prisoner to the close, gloomy vaulted prison in the ancient palace of the Holy Inquisition and shut Him in it. The day passes and is followed by the dark, burning 'breathless' night of Seville. The air is 'fragrant with laurel and lemon.' In the pitch darkness the iron door of the prison is suddenly opened and the Grand Inquisitor himself comes in with a light in his hand. He is alone; the door is closed at once behind him. He stands in the doorway and for a minute or two gazes into His face. At last he goes up slowly, sets the light on the table and speaks.

"'Is it Thou? Thou?' but receiving no answer, he adds at

once: 'Don't answer, be silent. What canst Thou say, indeed? I know too well what Thou wouldst say. And Thou hast no right to add anything to what Thou hadst said of old. Why, then, art Thou come to hinder us? For Thou hast come to hinder us, and Thou knowest that. But dost Thou know what will be to-morrow? I know not who Thou art and care not to know whether it is Thou or only a semblance of Him, but to-morrow I shall condemn Thee and burn Thee at the stake as the worst of heretics. And the very people who have to-day kissed Thy feet, to-morrow at the faintest sign from me will rush to heap up the embers of Thy fire. Knowest Thou that? Yes, maybe Thou knowest it,' he added with thoughtful penetration, never for a moment taking his eyes off the Prisoner."

"I don't quite understand, Ivan. What does it mean?" Alyosha, who had been listening in silence, said with a smile. "Is it simply a wild fantasy, or a mistake on the part of the old man—some impossible *quid pro quo?*"

"Take it as the last," said Ivan, laughing, "if you are so corrupted by modern realism and can't stand anything fantastic. If you like it to be a case of mistaken identity, let it be so. It is true," he went on, laughing, "the old man was ninety, and he might well be crazy over his set idea. He might have been struck by the appearance of the Prisoner. It might, in fact, be simply his ravings, the delusion of an old man of ninety, over-excited by the *auto da fé* of a hundred heretics the day before. But does it matter to us, after all, whether it was a mistake of identity or a wild fantasy? All that matters is that the old man should speak out, should speak openly of what he has thought in silence for ninety years."

"And the Prisoner too is silent? Does He look at him and not say a word?"

"That's inevitable in any case," Ivan laughed again. "The old man has told Him He hasn't the right to add anything to what He has said of old. One may say it is the most fundamental feature of Roman Catholicism, in my opinion at least. 'All has been given by Thee to the Pope,' they say, 'and all, therefore, is still in the Pope's hands, and there is no need for Thee to come now at all. Thou must not meddle for the time, at least.' That's how they speak and write too—the Jesuits, at any rate. I have read it myself in the works of their theologians. 'Hast Thou the right to reveal to us one of the mysteries of that world from which Thou hast come?' my old man asks Him, and answers the question for Him. 'No, Thou hast not; that Thou mayest not add to what has been said of old, and mayest not take from men the freedom which Thou didst exalt when Thou wast on earth. Whatsoever Thou revealest anew will encroach on men's freedom of faith; for it will be manifest as a miracle, and the freedom of their faith was dearer to Thee than anything in those days fifteen hundred years ago. Didst Thou not often say then, "I will make you free"? But now Thou hast seen these "free" men,' the old man adds suddenly, with a pensive smile. 'Yes, we've paid dearly for it,' he goes on, looking sternly at Him, 'but at last we have completed that work in Thy name. For fifteen centuries we have been wrestling with Thy freedom, but now it is ended and over for good. Dost Thou not believe that it's over for good? Thou lookest meekly at men and deignest not even to be wroth with me. But let me tell Thee that now, to-day, people are more persuaded than ever that they have perfect freedom, yet they have brought their freedom to us and laid it humbly at our feet. But that has been our doing. Was this what Thou didst? Was this Thy freedom?' "

"I don't understand again," Alyosha broke in. "Is he ironical, is he jesting?"

"Not a bit of it! He claims it as a merit for himself and his Church that at last they have vanquished freedom and have done so to make men happy. 'For now' (he is speaking of the Inquisition, of course) 'for the first time it has become possible to think of the happiness of men. Man was created a rebel; and how can rebels be happy? Thou wast warned,' he says to Him. 'Thou hast had no lack of admonitions and warnings, but Thou didst not listen to those warnings; Thou didst reject the only way by which men might be made happy. But, fortunately, departing Thou didst hand on the work to us. Thou hast promised, Thou hast established by Thy word, Thou hast given to us the right to bind and to unbind, and now, of course, Thou canst not think of taking it away. Why, then, hast Thou come to hinder us?' "

"And what's the meaning of 'no lack of admonitions and warnings'?" asked Alyosha.

"Why, that's the chief part of what the old man must say."

" 'The wise and dread Spirit, the spirit of self-destruction and non-existence,' the old man goes on, 'the great spirit talked with

Thee in the wilderness, and we are told in the books that he "tempted" Thee. Is that so? And could anything truer be said than what he revealed to Thee in three questions and what Thou didst reject, and what in the books is called "the temptation"? And yet if there has ever been on earth a real stupendous miracle, it took place on that day, on the day of the three temptations. The statement of those three questions was itself the miracle. If it were possible to imagine simply for the sake of argument that those three questions of the dread spirit had perished utterly from the books, and that we had to restore them and to invent them anew, and to do so had gathered together all the wise men of the earth—rulers, chief priests, learned men, philosophers, poets—and had set them the task to invent three questions, such as would not only fit the occasion but express in three words, three human phrases, the whole future history of the world and of humanity—dost Thou believe that all the wisdom of the earth united could have invented anything in depth and force equal to the three questions which were actually put to Thee then by the wise and mighty spirit in the wilderness? From those questions alone, from the miracle of their statement, we can see that we have here to do not with the fleeting human intelligence but with the absolute and eternal. For in those three questions the whole subsequent history of mankind is, as it were, brought together into one whole, and foretold, and in them are united all the unsolved historical contradictions of human nature. At the time it could not be so clear, since the future was unknown; but now that fifteen hundred years have passed, we see that everything in those three questions was so justly divined and foretold, and has been so truly fulfilled, that nothing can be added to them or taken from them.

"'Judge Thyself who was right—Thou or he who questioned Thee then? Remember the first question; its meaning, in other words, was this: "Thou wouldst go into the world, and art going with empty hands, with some promise of freedom which men in their simplicity and their natural unruliness cannot even understand, which they fear and dread—for nothing has ever been more insupportable for a man and a human society than freedom. But seest Thou these stones in this parched and barren wilderness? Turn them into bread, and mankind will run after Thee like a flock of sheep, grateful and obedient, though for ever trembling, lest Thou withdraw Thy hand and deny them Thy bread." But Thou wouldst not deprive man of freedom and didst reject the offer, thinking, what is that freedom worth, if obedience is bought with bread? Thou didst reply that man lives not by bread alone. But dost Thou know that for the sake of that earthly bread the spirit of the earth will rise up against Thee and will strive with Thee and overcome Thee, and all will follow him, crying, "Who can compare with this beast? He has given us fire from heaven!" Dost Thou know that the ages will pass, and humanity will proclaim by the lips of their sages that there is no crime, and therefore no sin; there is only hunger? "Feed men, and then ask of them virtue!" that's what they'll write on the banner, which they will raise against Thee, and with which they will destroy Thy temple. Where Thy temple stood will rise a new building; the terrible tower of Babel will be built again, and though, like the one of old, it will not be finished, yet Thou mightest have prevented that new tower and have cut short the sufferings of men for a thousand years; for they will come back to us after a thousand years of agony with their tower. They will seek us again, hidden underground in the catacombs, for we shall be again persecuted and tortured. They will find us and cry to us, "Feed us, for those who have promised us fire from heaven haven't given it!" And then we shall finish building their tower, for he finishes the building who feeds them. And we alone shall feed them in Thy name, declaring falsely that it is Thy name. Oh, never, never can they feel themselves without us! No science will give them bread so long as they remain free. In the end they will lay their freedom at our feet, and say to us, "Make us your slaves, but feed us." They will understand themselves, at last, that freedom and bread enough for all are inconceivable together, for never, never will they be able to share between them! They will be convinced, too, that they can never be free, for they are weak, vicious, worthless and rebellious. Thou didst promise them the bread of Heaven, but, I repeat again, can it compare with earthly bread in the eyes of the weak, ever-sinful and ignoble race of man? And if for the sake of the bread of Heaven thousands and tens of thousands shall follow Thee, what is to become of the millions and tens of thousands of millions of creatures who will not have the strength to forgo the earthly bread for the sake of the heavenly? Or dost Thou care only for the tens of thousands of the great and strong, while the millions, numerous as the sands of the sea, who are weak but love Thee, must exist only for the sake of the great and strong? No, we care for the weak too. They are sinful and rebellious, but in the end they too will become obedient. They will marvel at us and look on us as gods, because we are ready to endure the freedom which they have found so dreadful and to rule over them—so awful it will seem to them to be free. But we shall tell them that we are Thy servants and rule them in Thy name. We shall deceive them again, for we will not let Thee come to us again. That deception will be our suffering, for we shall be forced to lie.

" 'This is the significance of the first question in the wilderness, and this is what Thou hast rejected for the sake of that freedom which Thou hast exalted above everything. Yet in this question lies hid the great secret of this world. Choosing "bread," Thou wouldst have satisfied the universal and everlasting craving of humanity—to find someone to worship. So long as man remains free he strives for nothing so incessantly and so painfully as to find someone to worship. But man seeks to worship what is established beyond dispute, so that all men would agree at once to worship it. For these pitiful creatures are concerned not only to find what one or the other can worship, but to find something that all would believe in and worship; what is essential is that all may be *together* in it. This craving for *community* of worship is the chief misery of every man individually and of all humanity from the beginning of time. For the sake of common worship they've slain each other with the sword. They have set up gods and challenged one another, "Put away your gods and come and worship ours, or we will kill you and your gods!" And so it will be to the end of the world, even when gods disappear from the earth; they will fall down before idols just the same. Thou didst know, Thou couldst not but have known, this fundamental secret of human nature, but Thou didst reject the one infallible banner which was offered Thee to make all men bow down to Thee alone—the banner of earthly bread; and Thou hast rejected it for the sake of freedom and the bread of Heaven. Behold what Thou didst further. And all again in the name of freedom! I tell Thee that man is tormented by no greater anxiety than to find someone quickly to whom he can hand over that gift of freedom with which the ill-fated creature is born. But only one who can appease their conscience can take over their freedom. In bread there was offered Thee an invincible banner; give bread, and man will worship Thee, for nothing is more certain than bread. But if someone else gains possession of his conscience—oh! then he will cast away Thy bread and follow after him who has ensnared his conscience. In that Thou wast right. For the secret of man's being is not only to live but to have something to live for. Without a stable conception of the object of life, man would not consent to go on living, and would rather destroy himself than remain on earth, though he had bread in abundance. That is true. But what happened? Instead of taking men's freedom from them, Thou didst make it greater than ever! Didst Thou forget that man prefers peace, and even death, to freedom of choice in the knowledge of good and evil? Nothing is more seductive for man than his freedom of conscience, but nothing is a greater cause of suffering. And behold, instead of giving a firm foundation for setting the conscience of man at rest for ever, Thou didst choose all that is exceptional, vague and enigmatic; Thou didst choose what was utterly beyond the strength of men, acting as though Thou didst not love them at all—Thou who didst come to give Thy life for them! Instead of taking possession of men's freedom, Thou didst increase it, and burdened the spiritual kingdom of mankind with its sufferings for ever. Thou didst desire man's free love, that he should follow Thee freely, enticed and taken captive by Thee. In place of the rigid ancient law, man must hereafter with free heart decide for himself what is good and what is evil, having only Thy image before him as his guide. But didst Thou not know that he would at last reject even Thy image and Thy truth, if he is weighed down with the fearful burden of free choice? They will cry aloud at last that the truth is not in Thee, for they could not have been left in greater confusion and suffering than Thou hast caused, laying upon them so many cares and unanswerable problems.

" 'So that, in truth, Thou didst Thyself lay the foundation for the destruction of Thy kingdom, and no one is more to blame for it. Yet what was offered Thee? There are three powers, three powers alone, able to conquer and to hold captive for ever the conscience of these impotent rebels for their happiness—those forces are miracle, mystery and authority. Thou hast rejected all three and hast set the example for doing so. When the wise and dread spirit set Thee on the pinnacle of the temple and said to Thee, "If Thou wouldst know whether Thou art the Son of God then cast Thyself down, for it is written: the angels shall hold him up lest he fall and bruise himself, and Thou shalt know then whether Thou art the Son of God and shalt prove then how great is Thy faith in Thy Father." But Thou didst refuse and wouldst not cast Thyself down. Oh! of course, Thou didst proudly and well, like God; but the weak, unruly race of men, are they gods? Oh, Thou didst know then that in taking one step, in making one movement to cast Thyself down, Thou wouldst be tempting God and have lost all Thy faith in Him, and wouldst have been dashed to pieces against that earth which Thou didst come to save. And the wise spirit that tempted Thee would have rejoiced. But I ask again, are there many like Thee? And couldst Thou believe for one moment that men, too, could face such a temptation? Is the nature of men such, that they can reject miracle, and at the great moments of their life, the moments of their deepest, most agonising spiritual difficulties, cling only to the free verdict of the heart? Oh, Thou didst know that Thy deed would be recorded in books, would be handed down to remote times and the utmost ends of the earth, and Thou didst hope that man, following Thee, would cling to God and not ask for a miracle. But Thou didst not know that when man rejects miracle he rejects God too; for man seeks not so much God as the miraculous. And as man cannot bear to be without the miraculous, he will create new miracles of his own for himself, and will worship deeds of sorcery and witchcraft, though he might be a hundred times over a rebel, heretic and infidel. Thou didst not come down from the Cross when they shouted to Thee, mocking and reviling Thee, "Come down from the Cross and we will believe that Thou art He." Thou didst not come down, for again Thou wouldst not enslave man by a miracle, and didst crave faith given freely, not based on miracle. Thou didst crave for free love and not the base raptures of the slave before the might that has overawed him for ever. But Thou didst think too highly of men therein, for they are slaves, of course, though rebellious by nature. Look around and judge; fifteen centuries have passed, look upon them. Whom hast Thou raised up to Thyself? I swear, man is weaker and baser by nature than Thou hast believed him! Can he, can he do what Thou didst? By showing him so much respect, Thou didst, as it were, cease to feel for him, for Thou didst ask far too much from him—

Thou who hast loved him more than Thyself! Respecting him less, Thou wouldst have asked less of him. That would have been more like love, for his burden would have been lighter. He is weak and vile. What though he is everywhere now rebelling against our power, and proud of his rebellion? It is the pride of a child and a schoolboy. They are little children rioting and barring out the teacher at school. But their childish delight will end; it will cost them dear. They will cast down temples and drench the earth with blood. But they will see at last, the foolish children, that, though they are rebels, they are impotent rebels, unable to keep up their own rebellion. Bathed in their foolish tears, they will recognise at last that He who created them rebels must have meant to mock at them. They will say this in despair, and their utterance will be a blasphemy which will make them more unhappy still, for man's nature cannot bear blasphemy, and in the end always avenges it on itself. And so unrest, confusion and unhappiness—that is the present lot of man after Thou didst bear so much for their freedom! Thy great prophet tells, in vision and in image, that he saw all those who took part in the first resurrection and that there were of each tribe twelve thousand. But if there were so many of them, they must have been not men but gods. They had borne Thy cross, they had endured scores of years in the barren, hungry wilderness, living upon locusts and roots—and Thou mayest indeed point with pride at those children of freedom, of free love, of free and splendid sacrifice for Thy name. But remember that they were only some thousands; and what of the rest? And how are the other weak ones to blame, because they could not endure what the strong have endured? How is the weak soul to blame that it is unable to receive such terrible gifts? Canst Thou have simply come to the elect and for the elect? But if so, it is a mystery and we cannot understand it. And if it is a mystery, we too have a right to preach a mystery, and to teach them that it's not the free judgment of their hearts, not love that matters, but a mystery which they must follow blindly, even against their conscience. So we have done. We have corrected Thy work and have founded it upon *miracle, mystery* and *authority*. And men rejoiced that they were again led like sheep, and that the terrible gift that had brought them such suffering was, at last, lifted from their hearts. Were we right teaching them this? Speak! Did we not love mankind, so meekly acknowledging their feebleness, lovingly lightening their burden, and permitting their weak nature even sin with our sanction? Why hast Thou come now to hinder us? And why dost Thou look silently and searchingly at me with Thy mild eyes? Be angry. I don't want Thy love, for I love Thee not. And what use is it for me to hide anything from Thee? Don't I know to Whom I am speaking? All that I can say is known to Thee already. And is it for me to conceal from Thee our mystery? Perhaps it is Thy will to hear it from my lips. Listen, then. We are not working with Thee but with *him*—that is our mystery. It's long—eight centuries—since we have been on *his* side and not on Thine. Just eight centuries ago we took from him what Thou didst reject with scorn, that last gift he offered Thee, showing Thee all the kingdoms of the earth. We took from him Rome and the sword of Cæsar, and proclaimed ourselves sole rulers of the earth, though hitherto we have not been able to complete our work. But whose fault is that? Oh, the work is only beginning, but it has begun. It has long to await completion and the earth has yet much to suffer, but we shall triumph and shall be Cæsars, and then we shall plan the universal happiness of man. But Thou mightest have taken even the sword of Cæsar. Why didst Thou reject that last gift? Hadst Thou accepted that last counsel of the mighty spirit, Thou wouldst have accomplished all that man seeks on earth— that is, someone to worship, someone to keep his conscience, and some means of uniting all in one unanimous and harmonious ant-heap, for the craving for universal unity is the third and last anguish of men. Mankind as a whole has always striven to organise a universal state. There have been many great nations with great histories, but the more highly they were developed the more unhappy they were, for they felt more acutely than other people the craving for world-wide union. The great conquerors, Timours and Genghis Khans, whirled like hurricanes over the face of the earth striving to subdue its people, and they too were but the unconscious expression of the same craving for universal unity. Hadst Thou taken the world and Cæsar's purple, Thou wouldst have founded the universal state and have given universal peace. For who can rule men if not he who holds their conscience and their bread in his hands? We have taken the sword of Cæsar, and in taking it, of course have rejected Thee and followed *him*. Oh, ages are yet to come of the confusion of free thought, of their science and cannibalism. For having begun to build their tower of Babel without us, they will end, of course, with cannibalism. But then the beast will crawl to us and lick our feet and spatter them with tears of blood. And we shall sit upon the beast and raise the cup, and on it will be written, "Mystery." But then, and only then, the reign of peace and happiness will come for men. Thou art proud of Thine elect, but Thou hast only the elect, while we give rest to all. And besides, how many of those elect, those mighty ones who could become elect, have grown weary waiting for Thee, and have transferred and will transfer the powers of their spirit and the warmth of their heart to the other camp, and end by raising their *free* banner against Thee! Thou didst Thyself lift up that banner. But with us all will be happy and will no more rebel nor destroy one another as under Thy freedom. Oh, we shall persuade them that they will only become free when they renounce their freedom to us and submit to us. And shall we be right or shall we be lying? They will be convinced that we are right, for they will remember the horrors of slavery and confusion to which Thy freedom brought them. Freedom, free thought and science will lead them into such straits and will bring them face to face with such marvels and insoluble mysteries, that some of them, the fierce and rebellious, will destroy themselves; others, rebellious but weak, will destroy one another, while the rest, weak and unhappy, will crawl fawning to our feet and whine to us: "Yes, you were right, you alone possess His mystery, and we come back to you, save us from ourselves!"

" 'Receiving bread from us, they will see clearly that we take the bread made by their hands from them, to give it to them, without any miracle. They will see that we do not change the stones to bread, but in truth they will be more thankful for taking it from our hands than for the bread itself! For they will remember only too well that in old days, without our help, even the bread they made turned to stones in their hands, while since they have come back to us, the very stones have turned to bread in their hands. Too, too well will they know the value of complete submission! And until men know that, they will be unhappy. Who is most to blame for their not knowing it, speak? Who scattered the flock and sent it astray on unknown paths? But the flock will come together again and will submit once more, and then it will be once for all. Then we shall give them the quiet humble happiness of weak creatures such as they are by nature. Oh, we shall persuade them at last not to be proud, for Thou didst lift them up and thereby taught them to be proud. We shall show them that they are weak, that they are only pitiful children, but that childlike happiness is the sweetest of all. They will become timid and will look to us and huddle close to us in fear, as chicks to the hen. They will marvel at us and will be awe-stricken before us, and will be proud at our being so powerful and clever, that we have been able to subdue such a turbulent flock of thousands of millions. They will tremble impotently before our wrath, their minds will grow fearful, they will be quick to shed tears like women and children, but they will be just as ready at a sign from us to pass to laughter and rejoicing, to happy mirth and childish song. Yes, we shall set them to work, but in their leisure hours we shall make their life like a child's game, with children's songs and innocent dance. Oh, we shall allow them even sin, they are weak and helpless, and they will love us like children because we allow them to sin. We shall tell them that every sin will be expiated, if it is done with our permission, that we allow them to sin because we love them, and the punishment for these sins we take upon ourselves. And we shall take it upon ourselves, and they will adore us as their saviours who have taken on themselves their sins before God. And they will have no secrets from us. We shall allow or forbid them to live with their wives and mistresses, to have or not to have children—according to whether they have been obedient or disobedient—and they will submit to us gladly and cheerfully. The most painful secrets of their conscience, all, all they will bring to us, and we shall have an answer for all. And they will be glad to believe our answer, for it will save them from the great anxiety and terrible agony they endure at present in making a free decision for themselves. And all will be happy, all the millions of creatures except the hundred thousand who rule over them. For only we, we who guard the mystery, shall be unhappy. There will be thousands of millions of happy babes, and a hundred thousand sufferers who have taken upon themselves the curse of the knowledge of good and evil. Peacefully they will die, peacefully they will expire in Thy name, and beyond the grave they will find nothing but death. But we shall keep the secret, and for their happiness we shall allure them with the reward of heaven and eternity. Though if there were anything in the other world, it certainly would not be for such as they. It is prophesied that Thou wilt come again in victory, Thou will come with Thy chosen, the proud and strong, but we will say that they have only saved themselves, but we have saved all. We are told that the harlot who sits upon the beast, and holds in her hands the *mystery*, shall be put to shame, that the weak will rise up again, and will rend her royal purple and will strip naked her loathsome body. But then I will stand up and point out to Thee the thousand millions of happy children who have known no sin. And we who have taken their sins upon us for their happiness will stand up before Thee and say: "Judge us if Thou canst and darest." Know that I fear Thee not. Know that I too have been in the wilderness, I too have lived on roots and locusts, I too prized the freedom with which Thou hast blessed men, and I too was striving to stand among Thy elect, among the strong and powerful, thirsting "to make up the number." But I awakened and would not serve madness. I turned back and joined the ranks of those *who have corrected Thy work.* I left the proud and went back to the humble, for the happiness of the humble. What I say to Thee will come to pass, and our dominion will be built up. I repeat, to-morrow Thou shalt see that obedient flock who at a sign from me will hasten to heap up the hot cinders about the pile on which I shall burn Thee for coming to hinder us. For if anyone has ever deserved our fires, it is Thou. To-morrow I shall burn Thee. Dixi.'"

Ivan stopped. He was carried away as he talked and spoke with excitement; when he had finished, he suddenly smiled.

Alyosha had listened in silence; towards the end he was greatly moved and seemed several times on the point of interrupting, but restrained himself. Now his words came with a rush.

"But . . . that's absurd!" he cried, flushing. "Your poem is in praise of Jesus, not in blame of Him—as you meant it to be. And who will believe you about freedom? Is that the way to understand it? That's not the idea of it in the Orthodox Church . . . That's Rome, and not even the whole of Rome, it's false— those are the worst of the Catholics, the Inquisitors, the Jesuits! . . . And there could not be such a fantastic creature as your Inquisitor. What are these sins of mankind they take on themselves? Who are these keepers of the mystery who have taken some curse upon themselves for the happiness of mankind? When have they been seen? We know the Jesuits, they are spoken ill of, but surely they are not what you describe? They are not that at all, not at all. . . . They are simply the Romish army for the earthly sovereignty of the world in the future, with the Pontiff of Rome for Emperor . . . that's their ideal, but there's no sort of mystery or lofty melancholy about it. . . . It's simple lust of power, or filthy earthly gain, of domination—something like a universal serfdom with them as masters—that's all they stand for. They don't even believe in God, perhaps. Your suffering inquisitor is a mere fantasy."

"Stay, stay," laughed Ivan, "how hot you are! A fantasy, you say, let it be so! Of course it's a fantasy. But allow me to say: do you really think that the Roman Catholic movement of the last centuries is actually nothing but the lust of power, of filthy earthly gain? Is that Father Païssy's teaching?"

"No, no, on the contrary, Father Païssy did once say something rather the same as you . . . but of course it's not the same, not a bit the same," Alyosha hastily corrected himself.

"A precious admission, in spite of your 'not a bit the same.' I ask you why your Jesuits and Inquisitors have united simply for vile material gain? Why can there not be among them one martyr oppressed by great sorrow and loving humanity? You see, only suppose that there was one such man among all those who desire nothing but filthy material gain—if there's only one like my old inquisitor, who had himself eaten roots in the desert and made frenzied efforts to subdue his flesh to make himself free and perfect. But yet all his life he loved humanity, and suddenly his eyes were opened, and he saw that it is no great moral blessedness to attain perfection and freedom, if at the same time one gains the conviction that millions of God's creatures have been created as a mockery, that they will never be capable of using their freedom, that these poor rebels can never turn into giants to complete the tower, that it was not for such geese that the great idealist dreamt his dream of harmony. Seeing all that he turned back and joined—the clever people. Surely that could have happened?"

"Joined whom, what clever people?" cried Alyosha, completely carried away. "They have no such great cleverness and no mysteries and secrets. . . . Perhaps nothing but Atheism, that's all their secret. Your inquisitor does not believe in God, that's his secret!"

"What if it is so? At last you have guessed it. It's perfectly true, it's true that that's the whole secret, but isn't that suffering,

at least for a man like that, who has wasted his whole life in
the desert and yet could not shake off his incurable love of humanity? In his old age he reached the clear conviction that
nothing but the advice of the great dread spirit could build up
any tolerable sort of life for the feeble, unruly, 'incomplete, empirical creatures created in jest.' And so, convinced of this, he sees
that he must follow the council of the wise spirit, the dread
spirit of death and destruction, and therefore accept lying and
deception, and lead men consciously to death and destruction,
and yet deceive them all the way so that they may not notice
where they are being led, that the poor blind creatures may at
least, on the way, think themselves happy. And note, the deception is in the name of Him in Whose ideal the old man had so
fervently believed all his life long. Is not that tragic? And if
only one such stood at the head of the whole army 'filled with
the lust of power only for the sake of filthy gain'—would not one
such be enough to make a tragedy? More than that, one such
standing at the head is enough to create the actual leading idea
of the Roman Church, with all its armies and Jesuits, its highest
idea. I tell you frankly that I firmly believe that there has always
been such a man among those who stood at the head of the
movement. Who knows, there may have been some such even
among the Roman Popes. Who knows, perhaps the spirit of that
accursed old man who loves mankind so obstinately in his own
way, is to be found even now in a whole multitude of such old
men, existing not by chance but by agreement, as a secret league
formed long ago for the guarding of the mystery, to guard it
from the weak and the unhappy, so as to make them happy. No
doubt it is so, and so it must be indeed. I fancy that even
among the Masons there's something of the same mystery at the
bottom, and that that's why the Catholics so detest the Masons
as their rivals breaking up the unity of the idea, while it is so
essential that there should be one flock and one shepherd. . . .
But from the way I defend my idea I might be an author impatient of your criticism. Enough of it."

"You are perhaps a Mason yourself!" broke suddenly from
Alyosha. "You don't believe in God," he added, speaking this
time very sorrowfully. He fancied besides that his brother was
looking at him ironically. "How does your poem end?" he asked,
suddenly looking down. "Or was it the end?"

"I meant to end it like this. When the Inquisitor ceased speaking he waited some time for his Prisoner to answer him. His

silence weighed down upon him. He saw that the Prisoner had listened intently all the time, looking gently in his face and evidently not wishing to reply. The old man longed for Him to say something, however bitter and terrible. But He suddenly approached the old man in silence and softly kissed him on his bloodless aged lips. That was all his answer. The old man shuddered. His lips moved. He went to the door, opened it, and said to Him: 'Go, and come no more . . . come not at all, never, never!' And he let Him out into the dark alleys of the town. The Prisoner went away."

"And the old man?"

"The kiss glows in his heart, but the old man adheres to his idea."

"And you with him, you too?" cried Alyosha, mournfully. Ivan laughed.

"Why, it's all nonsense, Alyosha. It's only a senseless poem of a senseless student, who could never write two lines of verse. Why do you take it seriously? Surely you don't suppose I am going straight off to the Jesuits, to join the men who are correcting His work? Good Lord, it's no business of mine. I told you, all I want is to live on to thirty, and then . . . dash the cup to the ground!"

"But the little sticky leaves, and the precious tombs, and the blue sky, and the woman you love! How will you live, how will you love them?" Ayosha cried sorrowfully. "With such a hell in your heart and your head, how can you? No, that's just what you are going away for, to join them . . . if not, you will kill yourself, you can't endure it!"

"There is a strength to endure everything," Ivan said, with a cold smile.

"What strength?"

"The strength of the Karamazovs—the strength of the Karamazov baseness."

"To sink into debauchery, to stifle your soul with corruption—yes?"

"Possibly even that . . . only perhaps till I am thirty I shall escape it, and then."

"How will you escape it? By what will you escape it? That's impossible with your ideas."

"In the Karamazov way, again."

"'Everything is lawful,' you mean? Everything is lawful, is that it?"

Ivan scowled, and all at once turned strangely pale.

"Ah, you've caught up yesterday's phrase, which so offended Miüsov—and which Dmitri pounced upon so naïvely and paraphrased!" he smiled queerly. "Yes, if you like, 'everything is lawful,' since the word has been said. I won't deny it. And Mitya's version isn't bad."

Alyosha looked at him in silence.

"I thought that going away from here I have you at least," Ivan said suddenly, with unexpected feeling; "but now I see that there is no place for me even in your heart, my dear hermit. The formula, 'all is lawful,' I won't renounce—will you renounce me for that—yes?"

Alyosha got up, went to him and softly kissed him on the lips.

"That's plagiarism," cried Ivan, highly delighted. "You stole that from my poem. Thank you, though. Get up, Alyosha, it's time we were going, both of us."

They went out, but stopped when they reached the entrance of the restaurant.

"Listen, Alyosha," Ivan began in a resolute voice. "If I am really able to care for the sticky little leaves I shall only love them, remembering you. It's enough for me that you are somewhere here, and I shan't lose my desire for life yet. Is that enough for you? Take it as a declaration of love if you like. And now you go to the right and I to the left. And it's enough, do you hear? enough. I mean even if I don't go away to-morrow (I think I certainly shall go) and we meet again, don't say a word more on these subjects. I beg that particularly. And about Dmitri too, I ask you specially never speak to me again," he added, with sudden irritation; "it's all exhausted, it has all been said over and over again, hasn't it? And I'll make you one promise in return for it. When at thirty I want to 'dash the cup to the ground,' wherever I may be, I'll come to have one more talk with you, even though it were from America, you may be sure of that. I'll come on purpose. It will be very interesting to have a look at you, to see what you'll be by that time. It's rather a solemn promise, you see. And we really may be parting for seven years or ten. Come, go now to your Pater Seraphicus, he is dying. If he dies without you, you will be angry with me for having kept you. Good-bye, kiss me once more; that's right, now go."

Ivan turned suddenly and went his way without looking back.

It was just as Dmitri had left Alyosha the day before, though the parting had been very different. The strange resemblance flashed like an arrow through Alyosha's mind in the distress and dejection of that moment. He waited a little, looking after his brother. He suddenly noticed that Ivan swayed as he walked and that his right shoulder looked lower than his left. He had never noticed it before. But all at once he turned too, and almost ran to the monastery. It was nearly dark, and he felt almost frightened; something new was growing up in him for which he could not account. The wind had risen again as on the previous evening, and the ancient pines murmured gloomily about him when he entered the hermitage copse. He almost ran. "Pater Seraphicus—he got that name from somewhere—wherefrom?" Alyosha wondered. "Ivan, poor Ivan, and when shall I see you again? . . . Here is the hermitage. Yes, yes, that he is, Pater Seraphicus, he will save me—from him and for ever!"

Several times afterwards he wondered how he could on leaving Ivan so completely forget his brother Dmitri, though he had that morning, only a few hours before, so firmly resolved to find him and not to give up doing so, even should he be unable to return to the monastery that night.

Suggestions for Further Reading

(*Books marked with* * *are available in paperback editions.*)

For additional insight into the social dimension of personality, George Herbert Mead's *Mind, Self and Society* (Chicago, 1934) is the best single work available. Students interested in the work of Erving Goffman can turn as well to his *The Presentation of Self in Everyday Life* (New York, 1959),* where they will find a systematic treatment of the concept of "role." An excellent antidote to George Homans on the work process is Daniel Bell's suggestive essay, "Work and its Discontents," found in his *The End of Ideology* (New York, 1961). Paul Goodman's collection of essays on the problems of youth and young adulthood, *Growing Up Absurd* (New York, 1960),* also deals with myths and realities of work in modern industrial society. David Riesman's account of the "autonomous personality" in *The Lonely Crowd* offers an ideal of the non-controlled individual.

The nature of interpersonal control in situations of conflict has been explored brilliantly in a technical work on bargaining theory by Thomas Schelling, *The Strategy of Conflict* (Cambridge, Mass., 1960). A related work which is easier for the non-specialist is Anatol Rapoport's *Fights, Games, and Debates* (Ann Arbor, 1960). Solomon Asch's famous experiment on the ability of social pressure to alter belief is reported in *Scientific American* for November, 1955, under the title "Opinions and Social Pressure." More general discussion of the morality of "social engineering" can be found in Roscoe Pound's *Social Control Through Law* (New Haven, 1942) and in a group of essays entitled *Social Control in a Free Society* (Philadelphia, 1960) ed. by R. E. Spiller. William H. Whyte, Jr., in *The Organization Man* (New York, 1957),* has explored the effects of pressure for conformity on the executive middle class of modern America.

Philosophical discussions of the legitimacy of social control can be traced back as far as Plato's *The Republic*, where an affirmative answer seems to be given, and to the same author's *Gorgias*, which takes a considerably less sanguine view of "rhetoric." A modern psychological defense based upon the so-called behaviorist approach is B. F. Skinner's utopia (or some might say, anti-utopia) *Walden Two* (New York, 1962).*

Mill's doctrine of individual liberty is explored in C. L. Street, *Individualism and Individuality in the Philosophy of John Stuart Mill* (Milwaukee, 1926). A contrary view, which treats Mill's position as an ideological cover for the interests of the bourgeoisie, is brilliantly set forth in Karl Marx's essay on Bruno Bauer's *The Jewish Question*, misleadingly titled *World Without Jews* in the translation by Dagobert Runes (New York, 1959).* Dostoyevsky's philosophy is discussed in *Dostoyevsky: A Collection of Critical Essays* (New York, 1962),* edited by Rene Wellek, and in Avrahm Yarmolinsky's *Dostoevsky, His Life and Art* (New York, 1957).

The topic of social control has been a dominant theme in twentieth century literature. Among the best known treatments are George Orwell's *1984*, Arthur Koestler's *Darkness at Noon* (London, 1940),* and Franz Kafka's *The Trial* (New York, 1957).*